RESTITUTION IN PRIVATE INTERNATIONAL LAW

Restitution in Private International Law

GEORGE PANAGOPOULOS
B. A., LL.B (hons.) (Mon.) B.C.L., D.Phil. (Oxon)

Barrister and Solicitor of Victoria, Australia
Solicitor, England and Wales

• HART •
PUBLISHING
OXFORD – PORTLAND OREGON
2000

Hart Publishing
Oxford and Portland, Oregon

Published in North America (US and Canada) by
Hart Publishing c/o
International Specialized Book Services
5804 NE Hassalo Street
Portland, Oregon
97213-3644
USA

Distributed in the Netherlands, Belgium and Luxembourg by
Intersentia, Churchillaan 108
B2900 Schoten
Antwerpen
Belgium

Hart Publishing Ltd is a specialist legal publisher based in Oxford, England.
To order further copies of this book or to request a list of other
publications please write to:

Hart Publishing Ltd, Salter's Boatyard, Oxford OX1 4LB
Telephone: +44 (0)1865 245533 or Fax: +44 (0)1865 794882
e-mail: mail@hartpub.co.uk
www.hartpub.co.uk

British Library Cataloguing in Publication Data
Data Available
ISBN 1 84113–142–3 (cloth)

Typeset by Hope Services (Abingdon) Ltd.
Printed in Great Britain on acid-free paper
by Biddles Ltd, Guildford and King's Lynn.

"ἀλλὰ πειρᾶται τῇ ζημίᾳ ἰσάζειν, ἀφαιρῶν τὸ κέρδος . . . ὥστε τὸ ἐπανορθωτικὸν δίκαιον ἂν εἴη τὸ μέσον ζημίας καὶ κέρδους"

Ἀριστοτέλης, Ἠθικὰ Νικομάχεια, V 4 1132α 9–10, 18–19

"but (the judge) tries to equalize things by the penalty he imposes, taking away the gain . . . therefore the restitutionary justice is the mean between loss and gain"

Aristotle, *Nicomachean Ethics* V 4 1132a 9–10, 18–19

Preface

This book is based on my doctoral thesis, which was submitted at the University of Oxford in July 1999. It has since been revised and updated.

The subject matter of this book involves the marriage of two areas of law, restitution and private international law. These are areas which first attracted my attention as an undergraduate at Monash University. This interest became more intense, something more like a passion, whilst studying for the B.C.L. at Oxford.

My greatest thank you and debt is to Adrian Briggs (of St Edmund Hall, Oxford) and Lionel Smith (of St Hugh's College, Oxford). I was in the very fortunate position of having two supervisors, each one a leading light in his respective field: private international law and restitution respectively. Their supervision and generous assistance can not be overstated. Having two supervisors always kept me on my toes, as each one had a different perspective. Their different perspectives greatly assisted my ability to synthesise these two difficult areas of law. Their influence can be seen throughout the book.

Many thanks must also go to my doctoral examiners, Professors Peter Birks and Jonathan Hill. Their comments and views during the examination process were of particular assistance in converting the thesis into a book.

During my years of graduate study at Oxford I had the benefit of the views and assistance of a number of people to whom I am also indebted. Directly, or indirectly, they helped me with this work. They include Professor Martin Davies, Professor Francis Reynolds, Edwin Peel, Professor Francis Rose, William Swadling, Dirk Verse, Simone Degeling, Robert Stevens, Francesco Giglio, Søren Schonberg, James Edelman, Alexandros Stratakis and Dionysios Flambouras. A warm thank you to Virginia Mavrika for her assistance and support, both whilst working on the thesis and whilst writing this book.

Finally, I wish to also thank my parents, Konstantinos and Maria Panagopoulos, for their continued love and support.

London G.C.P.
St George's Day, 2000

Table of Contents

PART II CHARACTERISATION OF RESTITUTIONARY CLAIMS

PART III CHOICE OF LAW RULES FOR RESTITUTIONARY ISSUES

PART IV JURISDICTION IN RESTITITUTIONARY CLAIMS

Table of Cases

Table of Legislation

EUROPEAN

NATIONAL

Australia

United States

Works Frequently Cited

Birks	P.B. Birks, *An Introduction to the Law of Restitution* (revised edition, Oxford, 1989)
Birks, *Laundering and Tracing*	P.B. Birks, "Overview: Tracing, Claiming and Defences", in P.B. Birks, *Laundering and Tracing* (Oxford, 1995)
Briggs and Rees	A. Briggs & P. Rees, *Civil Jurisdiction and Judgments*, 2nd ed. (London, 1997)
Burrows	The Law of Restitution (Oxford, 1993)
Chambers	R. Chambers, *Resulting Trusts* (Clarendon Press, Oxford, 1997)
Cheshire and North	Cheshire and North's, *Private International Law* (13th ed. by P.M. North and J.J. Fawcett, Oxford, 1999)
Dicey and Morris	Dicey and Morris, *The Conflict of Laws* (13th ed. by L. Collins, London, 2000)
Fawcett and Torremans	J.J. Fawcett and P. Torremans, *Intellectual Property and Private International Law* (Oxford, 1998)
Goff and Jones	Lord Goff of Chieveley and G.H. Jones, *The Law of Restitution*, 5th ed. (London, 1997)
Jaffey	C.M. Clarkson and J. Hill, *Jaffey on the Conflict of Laws* (London, 1997)
Markesinis	B.S. Markesinis, W. Lorenz and G. Danneman, *The German Law of Obligations, Volume I, The Law of Contracts and Restitution: A Comparative Introduction* (Oxford, 1997)
Mason and Carter	K. Mason, Q.C. and J. Carter, *Restitution Law in Australia* (Sydney, 1996)
Meagher, Gummow and Lehane	R.P. Meagher, W.M.C. Gummow and J.R.F. Lehane, *Equity: Doctrines and Remedies*, 3rd ed. (Sydney, 1992)
Morris	J.D. McClean, *Morris: The Conflict of Laws*, 4th ed. (London, 1993)
Smith	L. Smith, *The Law of Tracing* (Oxford, 1997)
Stathopoulos	*Μ. Π. Σταθόπουλου, Γενικό Ενοχικό Δίκαιο, γ' έκδ* (*Αθήνα*, 1998). M.P. Stathopoulos, *Law of Obligations—General Part*, 3rd ed. (Athens, 1998)

Zimmerman	R. Zimmerman, *The Law of Obligations: Roman Foundations of the Civilian Tradition* (Oxford, 1996)
Zweigert and Kötz	K. Zweigert and H. Kötz, *An Introduction to Comparative Law*, 3rd ed. (Oxford, 1988)

Introduction

THE TOPIC OF restitution in private international law is one of the most significant current issues facing private international law. It requires significant analysis through mainly unchartered areas. The recognition of the law of restitution as a separate area of law, based on the unified principle of unjust enrichment, occurred in relatively recent times. The treatment of restitution claims in private international law remains largely uncertain. This is understandable given the recent development of this area as a matter of domestic law. The examination of it to date has been anything but comprehensive. The handful of authorities and academic writings do not provide a consistent and thorough approach.

Given that the law of restitution is still a recent newcomer in the common law world, it has been considered appropriate to provide a brief examination of the English domestic law of restitution and highlight some of the issues which arise, particularly those which may be of significance in private international law. We must have an adequate understanding of our subject matter as a matter of domestic law, before projecting it onto the private international law screen. The first Part therefore provides a "map" of the domestic law of restitution. The topic of subrogation is not examined in this work and is therefore not included within the map of the law of restitution. Where appropriate, comparisons have been made with certain other legal systems.

The question of characterisation is essential in private international law, particularly when dealing with a new area, such as restitution, for which there are few authorities. Characterisation is examined in the second Part. The relevant choice of law rule and thus, the potentially applicable law, depend on the way a matter is characterised. Characterisation also has ramifications for jurisdictional purposes, namely whether a particular matter falls within one jurisdictional provision or another. Yet, the great significance of characterisation here arises from the fact that the law of restitution cuts across several areas of law. Restitutionary claims arise in the context of contracts and wrongs; they may be at law or in equity; they may give rise to personal or proprietary remedies, while they may be contingent on tracing. All these different situations are analysed separately so that we may identify the boundaries between matters of restitution and other connected matters. In doing so, we come to a closer understanding of what constitutes a restitutionary issue for characterisation purposes.

The third Part examines the choice of law rule or rules for matters of restitution. Various choice of law rules have been proposed in academic writings, the

U.S. Restatement or referred to in the cases. Such choice of law rules include the law of the "place of enrichment", the "proper law of the obligation", or alternatively, the law of a related issue such as the law of a connected contract. None of these proposed choice of law rules are binding. Therefore a rare opportunity exists to consider the question of the choice of law rule for restitutionary issues from first principles. It has been considered useful to examine all the relevant authorities and the possible choice of law rules. A new choice of law rule is put forward which, it is submitted, is better suited to finding the *lex causae* for restitutionary matters, while also accommodating the criticisms of the other proposed choice of law rules. It focuses on the variety of circumstances giving rise to a claim in unjust enrichment.

As a pre-requisite to commencing an international restitutionary claim, the courts must have jurisdiction to hear the claim. This is a particularly important consideration where the defendant is located outside the jurisdiction. It may seem odd that the questions of jurisdiction are dealt with in the fourth and final Part. However, the question of whether a matter falls within one jurisdictional provision or another pre-supposes a degree of characterisation, albeit for jurisdictional purposes. Moreover, the issue of applicable law may enter the examination of a jurisdictional question. It was therefore considered preferable that the topic of jurisdiction for restitutionary claims be subsequent to the examination of characterisation and choice of law. Jurisdiction requires a separate examination of the jurisdictional rules under the Brussels and related Conventions, as well as the traditional rules as contained in the Civil Procedure Rules. The former potentially apply to cases where a restitutionary claim is brought and the defendant is domiciled in one of the European Union or EFTA Member States, or where the courts of one of those states have jurisdiction by virtue of land situated within such state, or by virtue of a choice of court agreement. In other cases, the traditional rules will apply.

PART I

A MAP THROUGH THE LAW OF RESTITUTION

1

A Map Through the Law of Restitution

I THE EXISTENCE OF A SEPARATE LAW OF RESTITUTION

> It is clear that any civilized system of law is bound to provide remedies for cases of what has been called unjust enrichment or unjust benefit, that is to prevent a man from retaining the money of or some benefit derived from another which it is against conscience that he should keep. Such remedies in English law are generically different from remedies in contract or in tort, and are now recognized to fall within a third category of the common law which has been called quasi-contract or restitution.[1]

IT IS WIDELY accepted now that a separate English law of restitution exists. This area of law is concerned with reversing a defendant's unjust enrichment at the plaintiff's expense. Unlike the established areas of contract and tort, the recognition of a discrete law of restitution is relatively new in the common law world.

The law of restitution finds its basis in the principle against unjust enrichment. The basic premise is that a person has a right to have restored to him a benefit gained at his expense by another, if the receipt of the benefit by the other would be unjust. Restitution is in fact the legal response.[2] The causative event is unjust enrichment and is a more appropriate term to describe this area of law, as one refers to contract and tort, rather than, for example, compensation.[3] Moreover, restitution may be available in circumstances other than those generated by unjust enrichment. Nevertheless, the term restitution is more prevalent in the literature dealing with this topic. As such, both terms are used in this work and, unless otherwise indicated, no significance is attached to the use of either.

An action for restitution of an unjust enrichment is essentially based on what was often referred to as the common law action for quasi-contract. This covered the common law actions for money had and received, money paid, *quantum meruit* and *quantum valebat*. In addition, it is also based on various equitable actions which can be explained in accordance with the principle against unjust enrichment, as well as rescission, resulting in restitution of money and services.

[1] *Fibrosa Spolka Akcyjna* v. *Fairbairn Lawson Combe Barbour Ltd.*[1943] A.C. 32, 62–3, *per* Lord Wright.

[2] The word remedy will be used in addition to and synonymous with the phrase legal response in this book.

[3] See P. Birks, "Misnomer" in W. Cornish, *et.al.* (ed.), *Restitution: Past, Present and Future* (Oxford, 1998) ch. 1.

It is also concerned with issues of tracing and subrogation.[4] These sporadic situations and claims all share a common unity and are subject to the unitary principle of unjust enrichment.

Traditionally, English law, as well as many other common law systems, did not recognise a law of restitution based on the unifying principle of unjust enrichment. The various areas cited above, which form part of the law of restitution, were treated as having no relationship to each other, while the relevant common law actions were explained in terms of implied contract, or "quasi-contract".[5] That is, the obligation, for example, of a defendant to repay a mistaken payment was said to be based on the defendant's implied promise to pay it back upon receipt.

The implied contract theory provided an inadequate explanation as to when and why a promise should be implied and thus as to when a defendant might be liable. It received great academic attack.[6] A separate law of restitution based on the principle of unjust enrichment was advocated for a significant period, both judicially[7] and academically,[8] before judicial recognition was finally given to such a body of law in *Lipkin Gorman* v. *Karpnale Ltd.*,[9] while the implied contract theory of restitution was categorically rejected in *Westdeutsche Landesbank Girozentrale* v. *Islington London BC.*[10] The unifying principle of unjust enrichment has now been accepted in all main common law jurisdictions as a separate body of law.[11] Such restitutionary claims could more accurately now be described as actions for restitution of an unjust enrichment, *or of value received*.

[4] The topic of subrogation will not be examined in this book.

[5] *Sinclair* v. *Brougham* [1914] A.C. 398 (H.L.); see also H. Hanbury, "The Recovery of Money" (1924) 40 L.Q.R. 31; A. Denning, "Quantum Meruit and the Statute of Frauds" (1925) 41 L.Q.R. 79; W. Holdsworth, "Unjustifiable Enrichment" (1939) 55 L.Q.R. 37; A. Denning, "Quantum Meruit: The case of *Craven-Ellis* v. *Canons Ltd.* (1939) 55 L.Q.R. 54; A. Simpson, *A History of the Common Law of Contract: The Rise of the Action of Assumpsit* (Oxford, 1975), pp.489–505.

[6] P. Winfield, *Province of the Law of Tort* (Cambridge, 1931), pp.119, 131–41; Jackson, *The History of Quasi-Contract in English Law* (Cambridge, 1936), p.123; P. Winfield (1937) 53 L.Q.R. 447, 448; W. Friedman (1937) 53 L.Q.R. 449, 451; Lord Wright of Durley, "*Sinclair* v. *Brougham*" (1938) 6 C.L.J. 305; Goff and Jones, *The Law of Restitution* (London, 1966), pp.5–11; Birks, pp.29–39; A. Burrows, "*Contract, Tort and Restitution*" (1983) 99 L.Q.R. 217, 233–4.

[7] *Craven-Ellis* v. *Canons Ltd.* [1936] 2 K.B. 403, 412 *per* Greer L.J.; *Brook's Wharf & Bull Wharf Ltd.* v. *Goodman Bros.* [1937] 1 K.B. 534, 545, *per* Lord Wright M.R.; *Fibrosa Spolka Akcyjna* v. *Fairbairn Lawson Combe Barbour Ltd.*[1943] A.C. 32, 62–3, *per* Lord Wright; *Nelson* v. *Larholt* [1948] 1 K.B. 339; *Government of India* v. *Taylor* [1955] A.C. 491, 513, *per* Lord Keith; *Kirri Cotton Co.* v. *Dewani* [1960] A.C. 192, 204–5, *per* Lord Denning; *Nissan* v. *A.G.* [1968] 1 Q.B. 286, 352, *per* Winn L.J.; *Greenwood* v. *Bennett* [1973] 1 Q.B. 195, 202 *per* Lord Denning; *Barclays Bank* v. *W.J. Simms Son & Cooke (Southern) Ltd.* [1980] Q.B. 677.

[8] See Restatement of the Law of Restitution (1937, American Law Institute); W. Seavey and A. Scott, "Restitution" (1938) 54 L.Q.R. 29; D. Logan, "Restatement on Restitution" (1938) 2 M.L.R. 153; R. Goff and G.Jones, *The Law of Restitution* (London, 1966), pp.11–33; P. Birks, *Introduction to the Law of Restitution* (Oxford, 1985), pp.16–25; A. Burrows, "*Contract, Tort and Restitution*" (1983) 99 L.Q.R. 217.

[9] [1991] 2 A.C. 548.

[10] [1996] A.C. 669.

[11] Restatement of the Law of Restitution (1937, American Law Institute); *Deglman* v. *Guaranty Trust Co of Canada* [1954] 3 D.L.R. 785 (S.C.C.); *Pettkus* v. *Becker* (1981) 117 D.L.R. (3d) 257; *Pavey & Mathews Pty Ltd.* v. *Paul* (1987) 162 C.L.R. 221 (H.C.A.); *A.N.Z. Banking Group Ltd.* v.

Much of the recent academic work on the law of restitution has focused on explaining the existing authorities in accordance with the principle of unjust enrichment. The approach has been not to treat this area as a "new" doctrine, but rather as a re-classification, or re-organisation, of an already existing body of law.[12] As such, the various cases, which were previously classified as quasi-contractual, equitable, or as raising issues of rescission, tracing or subrogation, are rationalised in accordance with the unified principle of unjust enrichment. The cases and authorities are re-classified accordingly, while an explanation is sought for those cases which do not fit within the framework of the principle of unjust enrichment. It should be noted that while the most significant weight of academic opinion accepts the principle of unjust enrichment, there nevertheless remain certain sceptics.[13]

2 THE ELEMENTS OF A RESTITUTIONARY CLAIM

The plaintiff[14] must satisfy three essential steps so as to succeed in a claim for restitution.[15] First, it must be shown that the defendant was enriched by the receipt of a benefit. Secondly, that enrichment must have been gained at the plaintiff's expense. Thirdly, the receipt of the enrichment must in the circumstances be unjust. Finally, the plaintiff's restitutionary claim may nevertheless be defeated by the defence of change of position, or other possible defences.

2.1 Enrichment

The first essential element is to show that the defendant was enriched through the receipt of a benefit. We may draw a distinction between money and benefits in kind. There is generally no particular problem where the enrichment consists of money; "[b]y its receipt, the recipient is inevitably benefited".[16] The issue of enrichment becomes more problematic where the defendant has received a non-money benefit.

Westpac Banking Corp. (1988) 164 C.L.R. 662 (H.C.A.); *National Bank of New Zealand Ltd* v. *Waitaki International Processing (NI) Ltd* [1999] 2 N.Z.L.R. 211 (N.Z.C.A.).

[12] See for example Birks, pp.18–22, 26–7; Goff and Jones, pp.4–5, 14–16; A. Burrows and E. McKendrick, *Cases and Materials on the Law of Restitution* (Oxford, 1997), p.2.

[13] S. Hedley, "Unjust Enrichment as the Basis of Restitution—An Overworked Concept" (1985) 5 *Legal Studies* 56; S. Stoljar, *The Law of Quasi-Contract*, 2nd. ed. (Canberra, 1989); S. Hedley, "Unjust Enrichment" [1995] C.L.J. 578.

[14] Under the new Civil Procedure Rules, which came into force on 26 April 1999, the term "claimant" has replaced "plaintiff". However, as nearly all the cases dealt with in this book pre-date the new rules, whilst the term plaintiff is still used in other common law jurisdictions, it was considered more convenient to use the traditional term.

[15] Goff and Jones, p.15; Birks, pp.20–2; Burrows, pp.6–7.

[16] *B.P. Exploration Co. Ltd.* v. *Hunt (No.2)* [1979] 1 W.L.R. 783, 799, *per* Robert Goff J. See also Goff and Jones, p.16; Birks, p.110.

Unlike certain civilian systems, the common law has not adopted an objective evaluation of enrichment.[17] Instead, the issue of enrichment is determined in relation to the particular defendant. The common law position is one of subjective enrichment, or enrichment susceptible to the argument of "subjective devaluation".[18] Although there may exist a market in relation to the benefit received, which may be able to apply an objective value, the emphasis is on the defendant's choice. The defendant may not have desired the particular benefit, or may nevertheless not have been prepared to pay the objective market value for it.[19]

Nevertheless, situations exist where the common law overcomes subjective devaluation, such that a benefit in kind will constitute an enrichment. According to Goff and Jones, and Birks, non-money benefits are recoverable in two main categories of cases.[20] First, where the non-money benefit constitutes an incontrovertible benefit.[21] That is, where the benefit is a realised, or realisable benefit, or where the benefit results in the saving of an inevitable or necessary expenditure.[22] Secondly, where the recipient has freely accepted the enrichment.[23] That is where a recipient knows that a benefit is being offered to him non-gratuitously and where he, having the opportunity to reject it, elects to accept it. A significant number of authorities and judicial statements may be cited in support of free acceptance as a basis of establishing enrichment.[24]

[17] See D. Verse, "Improvements and Enrichment: A Comparative Analysis" [1998] R.L.R. 85. An objective approach to the issue of enrichment is adopted under French and Italian law: see G. Bonet, "Quasi-contrats, Enrichissement sans cause" in *Juris Classeur, Droit Civil* (Paris, 1988), app. art. 1370–81, n.67; P. Trimarchi, *L'arricchimento Senza Causa* (Milano, 1962), pp.8–17. The preferred view under German law is that the issue of enrichment is a subjective test, determined in relation to the particular defendant: see Verse, *op.cit.*, 89; D. Verse, *Verwendungen im Eigentümer-Besitzer-Verhältnis* (Tübingen, 1999) pp. 129–37; D. Lieb, *Münchener Kommentar: Kommentar zum Bügerlichen Gesetzbuch*, 3rd ed. (Munich, 1997), BGB 812, n.262–4; P. Bassage, *Palandt: Bürgerliches Gesetzbuch, Kommentar*, 59th ed. (Munich, 2000), BGB 951, n.21. Greek law also adopts a subjective test, with the focus on a notion akin to an incontrovertible benefit, described as benefits with a direct and tangible possibility of economic realisation: Stathopoulos, p.328.

[18] Birks, pp.109–14; Burrows, p.9; Goff and Jones, p.18.

[19] See also *Ministry of Defence* v. *Ashman* [1993] 2 E.G.L.R 102, 105, *per* Hoffmann L.J.

[20] Goff and Jones, pp.18–26, 166–72, 179–80, 404–5, 409–12, 478–82; Birks, pp.114–24. It should be noted that in Beatson's view, except in very limited circumstances, a service can never be an enrichment, as it rarely satisfies the "exchange-value" test: J. Beatson, *The Use and Abuse of Unjust Enrichment* (Oxford, 1991), pp.21–44.

[21] See also Burrows, pp.9–11.

[22] *Proctor & Gamble Phillipine Manufacturing Corporation* v. *Peter Cremer GmbH (The Manila)* [1988] 3 All E.R. 843. Also *Monks* v. *Poynice Pty. Ltd.* (1987) 11 A.C.L.R. 637 (N.S.W.S.C.); *Regional Municipality of Peel* v. *The Queen* (1993) 98 D.L.R. (4th) 140 (S.C.C.).

[23] See also P. Birks, "In Defence of Free Acceptance" in A. Burrows, *Essays on the Law of Restitution* (Oxford, 1991), pp.105, 127–32. Burrows argues that free acceptance is not a basis for establishing enrichment: A. Burrows, "Free Acceptance and the Law of Restitution" (1988) 104 L.Q.R. 576, 578–80; Burrows, pp.12–13. See also M. Garner, "The Role of Subjective Benefit in the Law of Unjust Enrichment" (1990) 10 O.J.L.S. 42.

[24] *Lamb* v. *Bunce* (1815) 4 M & S 275; *Weatherby* v. *Banham* (1832) 5 C. & P. 288; *Paynter* v. *Williams* (1833) 1 Cr & M 810; *Alexander* v. *Vane* (1836) 1 M. & W. 511; *Leigh* v. *Dickeson* (1884) 15 Q.B.D. 60, 64–5; *Falcke* v. *Scottish Imperial Insurance Co.* (1886) 34 Ch. D. 234, 249; *Re Cleadon Trust* [1939] Ch. 286; *Steele* v. *Tardiani* (1946) 72 C.L.R. 386 (H.C.A.); *Pavey & Mathews Pty Ltd.* v. *Paul* (1987) 162 C.L.R. 221 (H.C.A.); *Monks* v. *Poynice Pty. Ltd.* (1987) 11 A.C.L.R. 637 (N.S.W.S.C.).

2.2 At the Plaintiff's Expense

So as to be entitled to restitution, the plaintiff must be able to show that the defendant's enrichment was at his expense.[25] This element is significant for a number of reasons. First, it is only by showing that the defendant's enrichment was at *his* expense, and not at someone else's, that the plaintiff will be able to claim restitution. In this sense, the "at the expense of" element gives the plaintiff standing for an action in restitution.

Secondly, the "at the expense of" element conceals two different concepts in the law of restitution. On the one hand, it applies to those situations where the defendant's gain represents a corresponding loss to the defendant. Birks has identified this as "subtractive unjust enrichment". On the other hand, the "at the expense of" phrase can also apply to situations where the defendant's gain has been acquired by committing a wrong against the plaintiff. In such a situation the defendant's gain will not necessarily correspond with a loss to the plaintiff.

According to Birks, the two meanings of the "at the expense of" element, mark an important division in the law of restitution between unjust enrichment by subtraction (or autonomous unjust enrichment), and unjust enrichment by wrongdoing.[26] In the former, no wrong need be established, whereas in the latter a wrong committed by the defendant must be established and restitution is merely one of several possible remedial responses, together with, for example, compensation or injunctive relief. This division drawn by Birks has generally won widespread support both judicially[27] and academically.[28] It is a division of paramount importance and its significance will be discussed further in the context of restitution for wrongs.

2.3 Unjust Receipt of the Value of the Benefit

Restitution will not automatically follow where the defendant has been enriched at the plaintiff's expense. The defendant's receipt of the benefit, or the value of the benefit, must, in the circumstances, be unjust. That is, there must be a reason why the defendant must make restitution of the enrichment at the plaintiff's expense. In asking this question, the law of restitution could follow one of two basic models. It could award restitution where the defendant's enrichment at the plaintiff's expense was unjustified, or without legal cause.

[25] Goff and Jones, pp.37–41; Birks, pp.132–9; Burrows, pp.16–21.

[26] Birks, pp.22–7; 40–4.

[27] *Macmillan Inc.* v. *Bishopsgate Investment Trust Plc.* (*No.3*) [1995] 1 W.L.R. 978, 988–99, *per* Millett J., *affd* without reference to this point [1996] 1 W.L.R. 387 (C.A.); *Halifax* v. *Thomas* [1995] 4 All E.R. 673, 677, *per* Peter Gibson L.J., with whom Simon Brown and Glidewell L.JJ. agreed; *Beloit Canada Ltd.* v. *Valmet-Dominion Inc.* [1997] 3 F.C. 497.

[28] Goff and Jones, pp.40–1; L. Smith, "The Province of the Law of Restitution" (1992) 71 Can. Bar Rev. 672; Mason and Carter, pp.600–1. *Cf.* J. Beatson, *The Use and Abuse of Unjust Enrichment* (Oxford, 1991), pp.208–43.

This is the basic model adopted by most civilian systems.[29] Alternatively, the law could award restitution in specific situations, thereby seeking to ascertain particular unjust factors or categories. The common law has adopted the latter model. In the tradition of the common law, like cases are treated alike, and thus, cases must fall within the specific unjust categories, or pigeon-holes, which give rise to restitution. In this way, abstract concepts of "unjustified" or "unjust" are avoided. As noted by Deane J., in *Pavey & Mathews Pty Ltd.* v. *Paul*,[30] the adoption of the principle of unjust enrichment "is not to assert a judicial discretion to do whatever idiosyncratic notions of what is fair and just might indicate". Rather, the principle:

> constitutes a unifying concept which explains why the law recognizes, *in a variety of distinct categories of case*, an obligation on the part of a defendant to make fair and just restitution for a benefit derived at the expense of a plaintiff and which assists in the determination, by the ordinary processes of legal reasoning, of the question whether the law should, in justice recognize such an obligation in a new developing category of case . . .[31] (*emphasis added*)

The exact number of unjust factors is by no means settled.[32] Restitution may be awarded in cases of mistake of fact,[33] mistake of law,[34] failure of consideration,[35] duress or illegitimate pressure,[36] and *ultra vires* demands by public authorities.[37] Restitution is also awarded in cases of unauthorised transfers, or

[29] See Art. 812, German Civil Code; Art. 904, Greek Civil Code; Art. 62, Swiss Code of Obligations; s.1, Israel Unjust Enrichment Law, 1979. Systems in the French legal tradition have a middle situation. Traditionally, these systems had a *condictio indebiti*, which was a limited right of restitution, requiring both that a debt was not due and that there had been a mistake. Thus, Art. 1376, French *Code Civil* contains a general provision for the restoration of payments made pursuant to a debt which was not due—"*reçoit par erreur ou sciemment ce qui ne lui est pas dû s'oblige à le restituer à celui de qui il l'a indûment reçu*"; also Arts. 1491–2, Québec Civil Code. Although generalised rights of restitution have been created, they are subsiduary to the more specific *condictio*, or claims for payments which are not due. (Art. 1493, Civil Code of Québec provides for restitution "if there is no justification for the enrichment or the impoverishment"). See also Italian Civil Code, Arts. 2033ff, *esp*. Art. 2041.

[30] (1987) 162 C.L.R. 221, 256

[31] *Id.*, 256–7.

[32] *CTN Cash and Carry Ltd.* v. *Gallaher Ltd.* [1994] 4 All E.R. 714, 720, *per* Sir Donald Nicholls V.-C.

[33] *Kerrison* v. *Glynn, Mills, Currie & Co.* (1911) 81 LJKB 465 (H.L.); *R.E. Jones Ltd.* v. *Waring & Gillow Ltd.* [1926] A.C. 670 (H.L.); *Craven-Ellis* v. *Canons Ltd.* [1936] 2 K.B. 403 (C.A.); *Barclays Bank* v. *W.J. Simms Son & Cooke (Southern) Ltd.* [1980] Q.B. 677; *A.N.Z. Banking Group Ltd.* v. *Westpac Banking Corporation* (1988) 164 C.L.R. 353 (H.C.A.) *Lloyds Bank Plc.* v. *Independent Insurance Co. Ltd.* [1999] 2 W.L.R. 986.

[34] *Kleinwort Benson* v. *Lincoln City Council* [1999] 2 A.C. 349.

[35] *P.* v. *P.* [1916] 2 I.R. 400; *Rowland* v. *Divall* [1923] 2 K.B. 500; *Chillingworth* v. *Esche* [1924] 1 Ch. 97; *Fibrosa Spolka Akcyjna* v. *Fairbairn Lawson Combe Barbour Ltd.*[1943] A.C. 32; *Re Ame's Settlement* [1946] Ch. 217; *Goss* v. *Chilcott* [1996] A.C. 788 (P.C.).

[36] Also referred to as "compulsion". *Astley* v. *Reynolds* (1731) 2 Str. 915; *Maskell* v. *Horner* [1915] 3 K. B. 106 (C.A.); *Mason* v. *N.S.W.* (1959) 102 C.L.R. 108 (H.C.A.); *Universe Tankships* v. *I.T.W.F. The Universe Sentinel* [1983] A.C. 366 (H.L.); *Dimskal Shipping Co. S.A.* v. *ITWF* (*The Evia Luck* (No.2)) [1992] 2 A.C. 152.

[37] *Woolwich Equitable Building Society* v. *I.R.C* [1993] 1 A.C. 70; *British Steel Plc* v. *C & E Commissioners* [1997] 2 All E.R. 366 (C.A.).

what is also described as ignorance,[38] as well as in cases of a compulsory discharge of another's liability.[39] Furthermore, there are several other unjust factors which are put forward as explanations of various cases. These include free acceptance,[40] unconscientious receipt, illegality,[41] incapacity[42] and certain other forms of policy motivated restitution. There is some debate as to the existence of some of the more controversial unjust factors.

Finally, it should be noted that issues may arise as to the exact ambit of the particular unjust factors. For example, there is debate as to whether a failure of consideration must be total. Likewise, the issue of what sort of pressure might be considered illegitimate might also be debated. Thus, over and above the existence of a particular unjust factor, there may be a further question of what the exact boundaries of that unjust factor might be. While most legal systems of the common law world may agree on the existence of specific unjust factors which give rise to restitution, there may be differences as to the existence and the scope of these unjust factors.

3 PERSONAL AND PROPRIETARY REMEDIES—PROPRIETARY RESTITUTION[43]

The English law of restitution grants both personal and proprietary remedies so as to reverse an unjust enrichment. It may either hold that the defendant owes the amount of enrichment, or alternatively, that the plaintiff owns the enrichment. The availability of proprietary remedies, or proprietary restitution, is somewhat unique to the common law and alien to civilian systems.[44] The

[38] The chief proponent of ignorance as an unjust factor is Birks. He cites cases such as *Clarke* v. *Shee and Johnson* (1774) 1 Cowp. 197, 98 E.R. 1041; *Holiday* v. *Sigil* (1826) 2 C. & P. 176; *Banque Belge* v. *Hambrouck* [1921] 1 K.B. 321; *Nelson* v. *Larholt* [1948] 1 K.B. 339; *Re Diplock* [1948] Ch. 465; *Lipkin Gorman* v. *Karpnale Ltd.* [1991] 2 A.C. 548; as well as cases of knowing receipt such as *Agip (Africa) Ltd.* v. *Jackson* [1990] 1 Ch. 265 (Millet J.) [1991] Ch. 547 (C.A.); *Polly Peck International plc* v. *Nadir (No.2)* [1992] 4 All E.R. 769. See Birks, pp.140–6; P. Birks, "The English Recognition of Unjust Enrichment" [1991] L.M.C.L.Q. 473.

[39] *Exall* v. *Partridge* (1799) 8 T.R. 308; *Johnson* v. *Rail Mail Steam Packet Co.* (1867) L.R. 3 C.P. 38; *Moule* v. *Garrett* (1872) L.R. 7 Ex. 101; *Edmunds* v. *Walingford* (1885) 14 Q.B.D. 811; *Gebhardt* v. *Saunders* [1892] 2 Q.B. 452; *Brook's Wharf & Bull Wharf Ltd.* v. *Goodman Bros* [1937] 1 K.B. 534. See also Goff and Jones, ch. 15.

[40] The chief proponents of free acceptance as an unjust factor are Goff and Jones, pp.18–22, and Birks, pp.265–93; also P. Birks, "In Defence of Free Acceptance" in A. Burrows, *Essays on the Law of Restitution* (Oxford, 1991), pp.105, 109–27.

[41] Goff and Jones, pp.498–519; Birks, pp.299–303; Burrows, pp.333–44.

[42] Goff and Jones, pp.523–38; Burrows, pp.322–32.

[43] See generally Goff and Jones, ch. 2; Birks, pp.83–98 and 358–94; P. Birks, *Restitution—the Future* (Sydney,1992), ch. 5 (hereafter Birks, *Restitution—the Future*); Burrows, pp.28–9; Parker and Mellows, *The Modern Law of Trusts* (7th ed. by A.J. Oakley, London, 1998), pp.710–43 (hereafter Parker and Mellows); M.J. Tilbury, *Civil Remedies: Volume One, Principles of Civil Remedies* (Sydney, 1990), pp.199–200, 243–57 (hereafter Tilbury); Mason and Carter, pp.93–101; Smith, pp.292–6.

[44] See Zimmerman, ch. 26; Zweigert and Kötz, pp.559–61; R. Zimmerman and J. Du Plessis, "Basic Features of the German Law of Unjustified Enrichment" [1994] R.L.R. 14; Markesinis, pp.755–9; Stathopoulos, pp.344–5.

personal restitutionary claim, or *in personam* claim, seeks to impose a personal obligation on the defendant to make restitution of the value of such enrichment.[45] Such liability is imposed on the defendant in relation to the value received irrespective of whether the defendant retains such value.[46] The obligation to make restitution therefore is simply in the form of a money judgment for the payment of an equivalent sum.[47] Thus, the *in personam* liability is similar to damages for breach of contract, or for torts.

In a claim for proprietary restitution a proprietary remedy is sought. Claims for proprietary restitution proceed against specific property and are therefore commonly also known as *in rem* claims. The court may declare that the defendant holds property on a constructive[48] or resulting trust[49] for the plaintiff's benefit, or it may grant a lien over a particular fund,[50] in circumstances where it would be unjust for the defendant to retain such assets against the plaintiff. Cases of proprietary restitution are invariably equitable proprietary claims.[51] These cases can be rationalised in accordance with existing understanding of the law of restitution based on the principle of unjust enrichment.[52] Thus, claims of proprietary restitution are directed against a specified asset of the defendant, in order to prevent the latter's unjust enrichment at the plaintiff's expense.

[45] Goff and Jones, p.68; Birks, pp.49–50 and 396–401; A.S. Burrows, pp.28–9; Mason and Carter, pp.90–2.

[46] *Trustee of the property of F.C. Jones & Sons* v. *Jones* [1997] Ch. 159, 168, *per* Millett L.J. The plaintiff's liability is of course subject to a possible defence of change of position: see below §6.1.

[47] See for example *Re Goldcorp Exchange Ltd.* (in receivership) [1995] 1 A.C. 74, 102–3; *Trustee of the property of F.C. Jones & Sons* v. *Jones* [1997] Ch. 159, 168, *per* Millett L.J.

[48] *Chase Manhattan Bank N.A.* v. *Israel-British Bank (London) Ltd.* [1981] Ch. 105; *LAC Minerals Ltd.* v. *International Corona Resources Ltd.* (1989) 61 D.L.R. (4th) 14; *A.G. for Hong Kong* v. *Reid* [1994] 1 AC 324.

[49] See generally Chambers, *Resulting Trusts*; see also Birks, pp.54–64; Smith, pp.294–5; P. Millett, "Tracing the Proceeds of Fraud" (1991) 107 L.Q.R. 71, 76, 80; P. Birks, "Restitution and Resulting Trusts" in Goldstein (ed.), *Equity and Contemporary Legal Developments* (1992), p.335; P. Birks, "Proprietary Rights as Remedies" in P. Birks (ed.), *The Frontiers of Liability*, vol. 2 (1994) 222–3; H. Norman, "Tracing the Proceeds of Crime" in P. Birks (ed.), *Laundering and Tracing* (Clarendon Press, Oxford 1995), pp.95, 102; S. Worthington, "Proprietary Restitution—Void, Voidable and Uncomplete Contracts" (1995) 9 T.L.Int. 113; P. Millett, "Restitution and Constructive Trusts" (1998) 114 L.Q.R. 399, 401. *Cf.* W. Swadling, "A New Role for Resulting Trusts?" (1996) 16 Leg. St. 110, approved in *Westdeutsche Landesbank Girozentrale* v. *Islington LBC* [1996] A.C. 669.

[50] *Re Hallett's Estate* (1880) 13 Ch. D. 696; *Re Oatway* [1903] 2 Ch. 356; *Roscoe Ltd.* v. *Winder* [1915] 1 Ch. 62; *Re Diplock* [1948] Ch. 465; *Foskett* v. *Mckeown* [1998] Ch. 265. *Re Hallet's Estate* suggests that where a trustee or other fiduciary uses trust money to purchase property for himself, the beneficiary will have a choice between a beneficial interest, or a lien on the relevant asset as security for the trust money used to purchase it: (1880) 13 Ch. D. 696, 708–9.

[51] Goff and Jones, p.75; Mason and Carter, p.93; R. Millett, "Restitution and Constructive Trusts" (1998) 114. L.Q.R. 399, 409–10.

[52] *Nelson* v. *Larholt* [1947] 1 K.B. 339, 343, *per* Denning J.; *Carl Zeiss Stiftung* v. *Herbert Smith & Co. (No.2)* [1969] 2 Ch. 276, 300–1, *per* Edmund Davies L.J.; *Pettkus* v. *Becker* (1981) 117 D.L.R. (3d) 257; *Chase Manhattan Bank N.A.* v. *Israel-British Bank (London) Ltd.* [1981] Ch. 105; *Trustee of the property of F.C. Jones & Sons* v. *Jones* [1997] Ch. 159, 168, *per* Millett L.J. See also *Hussey* v. *Palmer* [1972] 1 W.L.R. 1286, 1290A, *per* Lord Denning M.R.

3.1 The Nature of Proprietary Restitution

Whereas most restitutionary claims generally impose an *in personam* obligation so as to reverse an unjust enrichment, the availability of such a claim will not automatically give rise to proprietary restitution.[53] Unlike *in personam* claims for restitution, claims for proprietary restitution are dependant on the defendant retaining the value of the enrichment received. Thus, the plaintiff must not only show that the defendant was unjustly enriched at his expense. He must also show that enrichment has survived in the defendant's hands and that in the circumstances he is able to assert a proprietary claim over such enrichment. Claims for proprietary restitution will however be defeated by a successful defence of *bona fide* purchaser for value without notice.[54]

The fact that proprietary restitution proceeds against specific assets is the great attraction and the main explanation for bringing a claim for proprietary restitution. First, the plaintiff may rely on a right *in rem* so as to assert priority in an insolvency over unsecured creditors.[55] Secondly, the *in personam claim* may be statute barred, or otherwise unenforceable,[56] whereas the proprietary claim might not. Thirdly, it may be that the *res* surviving in the defendant's hands is more valuable than the original enrichment received by the defendant.[57] Fourthly, a proprietary claim may attract a higher form of interest, not available in the case of a personal claim, for example, compound interest.[58] Finally, there is the added tactical advantage of security when proceeding against a particular piece of property, as well as relief from the difficulties of valuation involved in calculating damages, compensation or account of profits.[59]

3.2 Proprietary Claims and Proprietary Restitution

A distinction is drawn between proprietary claims generated by an event other than unjust enrichment, or what are sometimes referred to as "pure proprietary claims", and restitutionary proprietary claims.[60] The restitutionary proprietary

[53] *Muschinski* v. *Dodds* (1988) 160 C.L.R. 583, 615, *per* Deane J.; *LAC Minerals Ltd.* v. *International Corona Resources Ltd.* (1989) 61 D.L.R. (4th) 14, 48, *per* La Forest J.; *Re Goldcorp Exchange Ltd.* (*in receivership*) [1995] 1 A.C. 74.

[54] See §6.2.

[55] See for example *Chase Manhattan Bank N.A.* v. *Israel-British Bank* (*London*) *Ltd.* [1981] Ch. 105.

[56] See for example *Sinclair* v. *Brougham* [1914] A.C. 398; *Kartika Ratna Thahir* v. *P.T. Pertambangan Minyak dan Gas Bumi Negara* (*Pertamina*) [1994] 3 S.L.R. 257, 264–5 (C.A. of Singapore) (hereafter *Thahir* v. *Pertamina*).

[57] *Re Tilley's Will Trusts* [1967] Ch. 1179; *Australian Postal Corp.* v. *Lutak* (1991) 21 N.S.W.L.R. 584, 590, *per* Bryson J; *Foskett* v. *Mckeown* [2000] 2 W.L.R. 1299 (H.L.).

[58] *Westdeutsche Landesbank Girozentrale* v. *Islington LBC* [1996] A.C. 669.

[59] *L.A.C. Minerals Ltd.* v. *International Corona Resources Ltd.* (1989) 61 D.L.R. (4th) 14, 48–9 (S.C.C.).

[60] See Goff and Jones, pp.73–4; Birks, pp.14–16, 25, 49–73, 87–93; P. Birks, "The Burden on the Bank" in F. Rose (ed.), *Restitution and Banking Law* (Oxford: 1998) 189, pp.192–4; Tilbury, 200;

claim is a claim to reverse an unjust enrichment. It covers those situations where the plaintiff claims to be entitled to an interest in an asset in the defendant's hands, without claiming that the particular asset was at all times his. Often, he will be claiming an interest in an asset, which represents the traceable value of his original money or property. In the case of proprietary restitution, the law grants a proprietary remedy so as to effect restitution of an unjust enrichment. The taxonomic division between proprietary restitution and proprietary claims generated by some other event has a significant consequence. A claim of proprietary restitution will be subject to a defence of change of position whereas other proprietary claims will not. The latter "are not infected by that weakness of all rights which do not arise from unjust enrichment, namely vulnerability to change in position".[61]

3.3 Circumstances giving rise to Proprietary Restitution

The issue of the availability of restitution through proprietary remedies is beyond the scope of this work. Nevertheless, it is desirable to give a brief description of the circumstances giving rise to proprietary restitution. In general, there are two basic elements which need to be satisfied for a successful claim of proprietary restitution. First, despite having parted with an asset, the plaintiff has retained, or obtained, a legal or equitable interest[62] in such property.[63] Secondly, it must also be shown that the value of the plaintiff's original property has traceably survived into the defendant's hands. The plaintiff must trace the value of his initial property, into the property which is the subject of his claim.[64]

Claims of proprietary restitution are invariably in equity.[65] Some of the situations in which proprietary restitution has been awarded include the following:

(1) Where the plaintiff has been deprived of his equitable property. Thus, if trust property is transferred in breach of trust, the beneficiary will have a claim for proprietary restitution in the form of an equitable proprietary claim, in relation to the traceable product of such trust property.[66]

Mason and Carter, p.94; see also R. Grantham, "Doctrinal Bases for the Recognition of Proprietary Rights" (1996) 16 O.J.L.S. 561; K. Barker, "After Change of Position: Good Faith Exchange in the Modern Law of Restitution" in Birks (ed.), *Laundering and Tracing* (1995) 191, pp.211–14. *Cf.* Burrows, pp.369–75.

61 P. Birks, "The Burden on the Bank" in F. Rose (ed.), *Restitution and Banking Law* (Oxford: 1998) 189, p.193.

62 Also referred to as a "proprietary base".

63 See *Cave* v. *Cave* (1880) 15 Ch. D. 639; *Chase Manhattan Bank N.A.* v. *Israel-British Bank (London) Ltd.* [1981] Ch. 105; *Re Goldcorp Exchange Ltd.* (*in receivership*) [1995] 1 A.C. 74; P. Birks, *Establishing a Proprietary Base* [1995] R.L.R. 83; Birks, *Laundering and Tracing*, pp.289, 311–15.

64 See below §5.1 and 5.2.

65 *Cf. Trustee of the property of F.C. Jones & Sons* v. *Jones* [1997] Ch. 159, 168, *per* Millett L.J., 171, *per* Beldam L.J.

66 *Re Diplock* [1948] Ch. 465; *Cave* v. *Cave* (1880) 15 Ch. D. 639.

(2) Where the plaintiff's property has been stolen. The plaintiff may obtain an equitable interest in the traceable proceeds of such property.[67]
(3) Where the plaintiff has parted with property, but due to an unjust factor, he retains, or obtains, an equitable interest. Thus, it has been held that a person who mistakenly pays another, retains an equitable interest in such money and that the recipient holds the traceable proceeds of such money as constructive trustee.[68] Similarly, where the plaintiff's property is obtained by fraud, the plaintiff may have a proprietary interest in the traceable proceeds.[69] More simply, where the plaintiff has forwarded money or property upon a certain basis which has failed, the defendant may hold such property or money, or its traceable proceeds, upon trust where it would be against good conscience for him to retain such property or money.[70] Recently however, the House of Lords has held that the plaintiff does not obtain an equitable interest, where property or money is transferred under a void contract.[71]

4 RESTITUTION FOR WRONGS

4.1 Availability of Restitution for Wrongs

In certain situations, the law allows the plaintiff restitution in relation to a wrong. Smith has more accurately described this as "disgorgement" for a wrong,[72] as unlike cases of restitution of an unjust enrichment, or subtractive unjust enrichment, the defendant is not restoring the value of the plaintiff's wealth. Instead the defendant is required to disgorge his wrongfully acquired gains. Nevertheless, owing to its widespread use among much of the literature, the phrase restitution for wrongs will be used in addition to the preferred expression of disgorgement for wrongs.

The relevant wrong may be a tort, a breach of contract[73] or an equitable wrong. Restitutionary remedies are not allowed in relation to all wrongs. Much controversy surrounds the issue of when restitution, or disgorgement, is

[67] *Black* v. *Freedman* (1910) 12 C.L.R. 105; *Stocks* v. *Wilson* [1913] 2 K.B. 235; *R. Leslie Ltd.* v. *Sheill* [1914] 3 K.B. 607; *Westdeutsche Landesbank Girozentrale* v. *Islington LBC* [1996] A.C. 669, 716, *per* Lord Browne-Wilkinson. It may however be argued that this category falls within (3) below, in that where money or property is stolen, the relevant unjust factor is ignorance.

[68] *Chase Manhattan Bank N.A.* v. *Israel-British Bank (London) Ltd.* [1981] Ch. 105.

[69] *Car & Universal Finance Co. Ltd.* v. *Caldwell* [1965] 1 Q.B. 525; *Agip(Africa) Ltd.* v. Jackson [1990] 1 Ch. 265 (Millett J.) [1991] Ch. 547 (C.A.); *Lipkin Gorman* v. *Karpnale Ltd.* [1991] 2 A.C. 548, 572F, *per* Lord Goff.

[70] *Hussey* v. *Palmer* [1972] 1 W.L.R. 1286; *Pettkus* v. *Becker* (1981) 117 D.L.R. (3d) 257; *Muschinski* v. *Dodds* (1988) 160 C.L.R. 583; *Kais* v. *Turvey* (1994) 17 Family Law Reports (Aus) 498; *Castle Phillips Finance* v. *Piddington* [1995] 1 F.L.R. 783.

[71] *Westdeutsche Landesbank Girozentrale* v. *Islington LBC* [1996] A.C. 669.

[72] L. Smith, "The Province of the Law of Restitution" (1992) 71 C.B.R. 672, 694–9. See also Smith, pp.19–21, 297–9; J. Edelman, "Gain-based Remedies for Wrongdoing" [2000] 74 A.L.J. 231.

[73] On the availability of damages for breach of contract see *A. G.* v. *Blake*, 27 July 2000 (unreported) (HL). See also Law Commission, *Aggravated, Exemplary and Restitutionary Damages* (L.C.C.P. No.132) (1993); L. Smith, "Disgorgement of the Profits of Breach of Contract: Property, Contract and Efficient Breach" (1994) 24 Can. Bus. L.J. 121.

available for wrongs. In *A.G.* v. *Guardian Newspapers Ltd. (No.2)*,[74] Lord Goff recognised specific categories of cases where a defendant is required to make restitution in respect of benefits acquired through his own wrongful act. His Lordship stated:

> An important section of the law of restitution is concerned with cases in which a defendant is required to make restitution in respect of benefits acquired through his own wrongful act—notably cases of waiver of tort; of benefits acquired by certain criminal acts; of benefits acquired in breach of a fiduciary relationship; and of course, of benefits acquired in breach of confidence. The plaintiff's claim to restitution is usually enforced by an account of profits made by the defendant through his wrong at the plaintiff's expense.[75]

4.2 Taxonomic Location of Restitution for Wrongs

There is some debate as to the taxonomic location of "restitution for wrongs". Much of this is due to the fact that the common law claims which allowed restitution were classified under the old implied contract theory. However, restitution for wrongs claims do not easily fit within the principle of unjust enrichment. The defendant's gain will not necessarily represent a corresponding loss to the plaintiff.[76] The relevant connection between the plaintiff and the gain to the defendant is, that the gain has been made in breach of a duty to the plaintiff-victim. A division may therefore be drawn between unjust enrichment by subtraction, or autonomous unjust enrichment, and restitution for wrongs.[77] In the first category, no wrong has to be established, the defendant's gain will correspond with the plaintiff's loss and an independent cause of action arises. In the second category, the cause of action depends on the commission of a wrong, while the plaintiff may have suffered no or little loss. Restitution may be one of several possible remedial responses to that wrong.[78] Thus, unlike cases of autonomous unjust enrichment, in cases of restitution for wrongs, it is said that the defendant is made to "give up" rather than to "give back".

There are two main theories as to the taxonomical position of restitution for wrongs. First, it can be viewed as a cause of action in unjust enrichment, which is separate from the wrong. The same facts may give rise to two separate causes of action.[79] Alternatively, the cause of action is in relation to the particular

74 [1990] 1 A.C. 109.

75 *Id.*, 286.

76 Goff and Jones, pp.40, 709; Birks, pp.40–1; Burrows, p.376.

77 See Birks, pp.23–4, 40–4, 313–18; Birks, *Restitution—the Future*, ch. 1; Burrows, pp.16–21, 376–80; Goff and Jones, pp.40–1, 709–12; Mason and Carter, p.598.

78 Other possible remedies might include compensation or injunctive relief.

79 J. Beatson, *The Use and Abuse of Unjust Enrichment* (Oxford, 1991), pp.25–8, 206–43; P.D. Maddaugh and J. McCamus, *The Law of Restitution* (Aurora, 1990), p.507; I. Jackman, "Restitution and Wrongs" [1989] C.L.J. 302. *Chesworth* v. *Farrar* [1967] 1 Q.B. 407 may be cited as supporting this theory. See also *Arab Monetary Fund* v. *Hashim* [1996] 1 Lloyd's Rep. 589.

wrong. There is no cause of action in unjust enrichment. The restitutionary remedy is merely a remedial response for the particular wrong.[80] Thus, restitution for wrongs may be seen either as being an action *qua* wrong or an action in unjust enrichment. The preferred view is that restitution, or disgorgement, for wrongs should not be viewed as lying in unjust enrichment, but rather as an alternative remedial response to a wrong. It will therefore be assumed in this work that as a matter of English domestic law, restitution for wrongs does not form part of the law of unjust enrichment. Moreover, the words restitutionary, restitution and unjust enrichment are used in this work to describe matters which are part of the law of unjust enrichment. Therefore, the phenomenon of restitution, or disgorgement, for wrongdoing, will be spelt out so as to not to confuse it with restitution of an unjust enrichment. The phrases "restitution for wrongs" or "disgorgement for wrongs" will therefore be employed to describe those circumstances where restitution is a remedial response to a wrong and not an independent action.

5 TRACING

Many unjust enrichment claims involve an element of tracing. At the same time, not all claims involving tracing will necessarily be generated by unjust enrichment. An example of a claim involving tracing which is generated by unjust enrichment is where a mistaken payer brings a claim in relation to the identifiable proceeds of a mistaken payment.[81] At the other end of the spectrum, a seller might claim proprietary rights in the proceeds of a buyer's sale of goods, where the relevant sales contract provides that the seller retains legal or equitable ownership of the goods.[82]

5.1 What is Tracing?

Tracing may be employed whenever a party has an interest in showing that the value received in one form at one moment is held in another form at another

[80] *United Australia Ltd.* v. *Barclay's Bank Ltd.* [1941] A.C. 1; *Macmillan Inc.* v. *Bishopsgate Investment Trust Plc.* (*No.3*) [1995] 1 W.L.R. 978, 988–99, *per* Millett J.; *Halifax* v. *Thomas* [1995] 4 All E.R. 673, 677, *per* Peter Gibson L.J., with whom Simon Brown and Glidwell L.JJ. agreed; *Beloit Canada Ltd.* v. *Valmet-Dominion Inc.* [1997] 3 F.C. 497. Goff and Jones, pp.40–1; Birks, p.316; Birks, *Restitution the Future*, ch. 1; P. Birks, "The Concept of a Civil Wrong" in D. Owen (ed.), *Philosophical Foundations of Tort Law* (Oxford, 1995), p.31; L. Smith, "The Province of the Law of Restitution" (1992) 71 Can. Bar Rev. 672; Mason and Carter, pp.600–1.

[81] See for example *Chase Manhattan Bank N.A.* v. *Israel-British Bank* (*London*) *Ltd.* [1981] Ch. 105.

[82] See for example *Aluminium Industrie Vaasen BV* v. *Romalpa Aluminium Ltd.* [1976] 1 W.L.R. 676 (C.A.); N. Palmer, "Reservation of Title" (1992) 5 J. of Contract Law 175; B. Collier, *Romalpa Clauses: Reservation of Title in Sale of Goods Transactions* (Sydney, 1989); G. McCormack, *Reservation of Title*, 2nd ed. (London, 1995).

moment. That is, although property or money are no longer held in their original form, their value has survived. Tracing was characteristically described by Millett L.J. in *Boscawen* v. *Bajwa* as "neither a claim nor a remedy but a process".[83] As noted by Birks, tracing is never a hunt for the original asset. It is a process which is distinct and separate from that of claiming.[84]

The nature of tracing is further illustrated by the distinction drawn between "tracing" and "following".[85] "Following", is the process of identifying property in its original form. On the other hand, "tracing" is the process of identifying any new asset acquired in exchange for the original property. Thus, where a plaintiff's car is stolen, the plaintiff may try to locate, through the various transactions, where the car has ended up. This is following. Where however the plaintiff's car is stolen and then substituted for money, the plaintiff may assert a claim in relation to the money. It is the process of tracing which determines that the money represents the value of the car. Tracing is therefore the law's way of determining when one asset stands in the place of another. However, unlike the process of following, tracing is not an exclusively factual situation. It will inevitably involve the application of legal rules, namely the rules of tracing, to the particular facts.

5.2 Why do we Trace?

We often trace so as to claim. The purpose of tracing is to bring a claim in relation to a new asset, which would have been available in relation to an original asset. Upon a successful tracing exercise, the plaintiff may, for example, establish either a proprietary or personal claim against the defendant.[86] The process of tracing is therefore distinct from the actual claim.[87] The conventional reasons why someone may wish to trace are as follows:

(i) The plaintiff may wish to bring a proprietary claim. Such a claim may be on the basis of unjust enrichment,[88] an equitable wrong,[89] or on the basis of a reservation of title clause in a sales contract.[90]

[83] [1995] 4 All E.R. 769, 776. Similar distinctions have been previously drawn between the claim and the means of identification or ascertainment in other cases; see for example *Taylor* v. *Plumer* (1815) 3 M. & S. 562; *Sinclair* v. *Brougham* [1914] A.C. 398, 419, *per* Viscount Haldane; *Re Diplock* [1948] Ch. 465, 536–7; *Chase Manhattan Bank N.A.* v. *Israel-British Bank (London) Ltd.* [1981] Ch. 105, 122D.

[84] Birks, *Laundering and Tracing*, pp.291–5; see also Smith, pp.11–14.

[85] See Smith, pp.6–10; Birks, *Laundering and* Tracing, pp.291–2. See also *Foskett* v. *McKeown* [2000] 2 W.L.R. 1299, 1322 *per* Lord Millett.

[86] Birks, *Laundering and* Tracing, pp.300–2, 305–7; Smith, p.24–33; Mason and Carter, p.95.

[87] Birks, *Laundering and* Tracing, pp.290–2, 300–2; Smith, pp.10–14, 130–2.

[88] *Chase Manhattan Bank N.A.* v. *Israel-British Bank (London) Ltd.* [1981] Ch. 105.

[89] *A.G. for Hong Kong* v. *Reid* [1994] 1 A.C. 324. See also *L.A.C. Minerals Ltd.* v. *International Corona Resources Ltd.* (1989) 61 D.L.R. (4th) 14 (S.C.C.); *Thahir* v. *Pertamina* [1994] 3 S.L.R. 257 (C.A. of Singapore).

[90] *Aluminiumm Industrie Vaasen BV* v. *Romalpa Aluminium Ltd.* [1976] 1 W.L.R. 676 (C.A.)

(ii) The plaintiff may seek a personal claim. This may be a claim for an order that there be an account on the ground of knowing receipt,[91] or it may be a claim for money had and received.[92]

(iii) Finally, tracing may be employed outside the field of personal and proprietary claims. For example, it may be employed in the context of the Theft Act.[93] Alternatively, it may be used to show that an asset is exempt from a statutory scheme for the division of matrimonial property,[94] or property of a bankrupt,[95] on the ground that it is the traceable proceeds of an exempt asset.

In addition to the above, tracing may be employed in a restitutionary claim so as to show that the defendant was enriched at the plaintiff's expense and not at someone else's.[96] This will be particularly the case in three-party situations where the defendant was not enriched directly at the expense of the plaintiff. In such circumstances, a successful tracing exercise will show the necessary causal connection, namely that the value of the plaintiff's impoverishment can be traced into the defendant's hands.

5.3 Tracing at Law and in Equity

The tracing rules differ as between law and equity.[97] The existence of such separate rules may potentially add another problem when an issue of tracing arises in private international law. Although it is not the purpose here to examine the law of tracing from a domestic law point of view, it nevertheless will be useful to note the different rules.

The common law recognises the tracing of property into substitute products.[98] In tracing the plaintiff's property into substitutes, no distinction is drawn between a chose in action, such as the debt of a bank to its customer, and any other asset. Tracing may therefore follow a cheque or its proceeds.[99] Tracing is

[91] *Agip (Africa) Ltd.* v. *Jackson* [1990] 1 Ch. 265; *Eagle Trust plc* v. *S.B.C. Securities Ltd.* [1992] 4 All E.R. 488, 500, *per* Vinelott J.; *El Ajou* v. *Dollar Land Holdings Plc* [1993] 3 All E.R. 717, 739, *per* Millett J. (reversed on different grounds) [1994] 2 All E.R. 685.

[92] *Banque Belge pour l'Etranger* v. *Hambrouck* [1921] 1 K.B. 321; *Lipkin Gorman* v. *Karpnale Ltd.* [1991] 2 A.C. 548.

[93] See ss.24(2) and 28(1)(b) of the Theft Act 1968.

[94] See *Gasparetto* v. *Gasparetto* (1988) 15 R.F.L. (3d) 401 (Ont. H.C.); *Mitller* v. *Mitller* (1988) 17 R.F.L. (3d) 113 (Ont. H.C.); *Deyell* v. *Deyell* (1991) 90 Sask R 81 (C.A.).

[95] See s.67(1)(b) *Bankruptcy and Insolvency Act* 1985 c.B-3 (Canada); ss.116(2), 116 (2D)–(4) *Bankruptcy Act* 1966 (Cth).

[96] *Lipkin Gorman* v. *Karpnale Ltd.* [1991] 2 A.C. 548, 559H-560A, *per* Lord Templeman, 572E, *per* Lord Goff; see also Burrows, pp.28–9; Mason and Carter, p.95.

[97] It should be noted that although there are some strong arguments in favour of not distinguishing between tracing at law and in equity, see Smith, pp.120–30, 165–74; Birks, *Laundering and* Tracing, pp.295–300, the division is alive and well according to recent authority: see for example *Trustee of the property of F.C. Jones & Sons* v. *Jones* [1997] Ch. 159.

[98] *Taylor* v. *Plumer* (1815) 3 M. & S. 562; *Banque Belge pour l'Etranger* v. *Hambrouk* [1921] 1 K.B. 321; *Lipkin Gorman* v. *Karpnale Ltd.* [1991] 2 A.C. 548; *Trustee of the property of F.C. Jones & Sons* v. *Jones* [1996] 3 W.L.R. 703.

[99] *Cf.* P. Millett, "Tracing the Proceeds of Fraud" (1991) 107 L.Q.R. 71, 73–4.

also possible when the property, or its substitute, is money going in and out of bank accounts.[100] However, the main limitation of common law tracing is that money cannot be traced once it has been mixed with other money.[101] The justification for this is that in such circumstances the money ceases to be identifiable. The common law therefore takes a strict approach to tracing, being limited to cases of clean substitutions. Thus, due to these limitations there is little resort to common law tracing.

Equity has been more flexible than the common law in relation to tracing. The significant difference between tracing at common law and equity is that equity allows the plaintiff to trace into, and out of, a mixed fund.[102] In tracing into a mixed fund, equity draws a distinction between the situation where the plaintiff's money is mixed with that of a trustee and with that of an innocent volunteer. Where the plaintiff's money is mixed with that of an innocent volunteer, the moneys in the fund belong *pro tanto* to the parties' contributions.[103] However, where a mixed fund is held in a current bank account, the anomalous "first in first out" rule applies.[104] Thus, the beneficiary's money that first goes in is presumed to go out first. Where the plaintiff's money is mixed with that of a trustee, equity makes a presumption in favour of the plaintiff beneficiary in respect of any identifiable part of the fund remaining.[105] Equity's flexibility in allowing a plaintiff to trace into a mixed fund, does not allow tracing into property that has been dissipated and subsequently restored.[106]

It is said, that as a prerequisite to tracing in equity, a fiduciary relationship must be established which calls the equitable jurisdiction into being.[107] The

[100] *Banque Belge pour l'Etranger* v. *Hambrouk* [1921] 1 K.B. 321; Scrutton L.J. in *Banque Belge* held that money could not be traced into and out of a bank account at common law, on the basis that it is not the plaintiff's money that is drawn out.

[101] *Re Diplock* [1948] Ch. 465, 518; *Agip (Africa) Ltd.* v. *Jackson* [1990] 1 Ch. 265, 285. *Lipkin Gorman* v. *Karpnale Ltd.* [1991] 2 A.C. 548, 573, per Lord Goff.

[102] *Re Hallett's Estate* (1880) 13 Ch. D. 696; *Brady* v. *Stapleton* (1952) 88 C.L.R. 322; *Agip (Africa) Ltd.* v. *Jackson* [1991] Ch. 547; *affg* [1990] Ch. 265.

[103] *Sinclair* v. *Brougham* [1914] A.C. 398.

[104] *Clayton's Case* (1815) 1 Mer 572. In *Barlow Clowes International Ltd.* v. *Vaughan* [1992] 4 All E.R. 22, it was held not to extend to a fund intended to be held as a common investment fund. Smith argues that the rule in *Clayton's Case* is a presumption of intention and has in fact nothing to do with tracing: Smith, pp.185–94. This was the position adopted by the Supreme Court of Canada in *Re OSC and Greymac Credit Corp.* [1988] 52 D.L.R. (4th) 767. Furthermore, in *Barlow Clowes International Ltd.* v. *Vaughan* [1992] 4 All E.R. 22, Leggatt L.J. also considered that the rule in *Clayton's Case* was irrelevant to tracing: *id.*, 44.

[105] *Re Hallet's Estate* (1879) 13 Ch. D. 696; *Re Oatway* [1903] 2 Ch. 356.

[106] *James Roscoe (Bolton)* v. *Winder* [1915] 1 Ch. 62; *Lofts* v. *Macdonald* (1974) 3 A.L.R. 404; *Re Dover* (1981) 6 A.C.L.R. 307; *Bishopsgate Inv. Management* v. *Homan* [1995] Ch. 211.

[107] *Re Diplock* [1948] Ch. 465; *Chase Manhattan Bank N.A.* v. *Israel-British Bank (London) Ltd.* [1981] Ch. 105; *Agip (Africa) Ltd.* v. *Jackson* [1990] 1 Ch. 265; *Boscawen* v. *Bajwa* [1995] 4 All E.R. 769. The Court of Appeal in *Re Diplock* [1948] Ch. 465, 532, 540, interpreted *Sinclair v. Brougham* [1914] A.C. 398, as standing for the proposition that a fiduciary relationship is a prerequisite to tracing in equity. There is doubt as to whether *Sinclair* v. *Brougham* does in fact stand for this proposition: see Goff and Jones, p.104; Parker and Mellows, p.719; Smith, 125–6, 128. Moreover, Smith argues that the Court of Appeal in *Re Diplock* did not say anything about any fiduciary pre-requisite for conducting tracing in equity: pp.127–8.

correctness of the rule requiring the existence of a fiduciary relationship so as to trace in equity has been questioned.[108] In *Westdeutsche*,[109] Lord Browne-Wilkinson stated that an owner may trace in equity as against a thief.[110] It therefore can be argued that this does away with the need for a fiduciary relationship, as a thief cannot be a fiduciary. At any rate, the rule has been eroded, in that the courts have often little difficulty in finding a fiduciary relationship.[111]

6 DEFENCES

Claims in unjust enrichment will be subject to a variety of defences. Two in particular need to be examined for present purposes: the defence of change of position and that of *bona fide* purchaser for value without notice. Other possible defences include ministerial receipt,[112] counter-restitution,[113] illegality[114] and incapacity.[115]

6.1 Change of Position

An integral component of the House of Lords recognition of the principle of unjust enrichment in *Lipkin Gorman* v. *Karpnale Ltd.*[116] was the defence of change of position.[117] A defendant will not be liable for restitution to the extent that he has changed his position in good faith. Many issues concerning the defence remain unresolved. In formulating the defence, Lord Goff was "anxious that, . . . nothing should be said at this stage to inhibit the development of the defence on a case by case basis".[118] Nevertheless, certain matters should be observed for present purposes. First, the defence is an integral part of a claim in

[108] Goff and Jones, pp.103–5; P. Birks, *Laundering and* Tracing, p.297; Smith, pp.120–30; Parker and Mellows, pp.719–21; P. Millett, "Tracing the Proceeds of Fraud" (1991) 107 L.Q.R. 71, 75. See also Meagher, Gummow and Lehane, p.134.

[109] *Westdeutsche Landesbank Girozentrale* v. *Islington LBC* [1996] A.C. 669.

[110] *Id.*, 716.

[111] See for example *Chase Manhattan Bank N.A.* v. *Israel-British Bank (London) Ltd.* [1981] Ch. 105; *Agip (Africa) Ltd.* v. *Jackson* [1990] 1 Ch. 265, 290, *per* Millett J.; Parker and Mellows, p.720. See also *Aluminium Industrie Vaasen BV* v. *Romalpa Aluminium Ltd.* [1976] 1 W.L.R. 676, 687–90, *per* Roskill L.J., 693, *per* Goff L.J., where the Court of Appeal inferred a fiduciary relationship from the provisions of the relevant sales contract.

[112] See W. Swadling, "The Nature of Ministerial Receipt" in P. Birks (ed.), *Laundering and Tracing* (Oxford, 1995), pp.243–60.

[113] See E. McKendrick, "Total Failure of Consideration and Counter-Restitution: Two Issues or One?" in P. Birks (ed.), *Laundering and Tracing* (Oxford, 1995) pp.217–43; P. Birks, "Total Failure of Consideration" in F.D. Rose (ed.), *Consensus ad Idem* (London, 1996), pp.179–202.

[114] See F. Rose, "Restitutionary and Proprietary Consequences of Illegality" in F.D. Rose (ed.), *Consensus ad Idem* (London, 1996), pp.203–34; Goff and Jones, pp.607–12.

[115] See Goff and Jones, ch. 25.

[116] [1991] 2 A.C. 548.

[117] *Id.*, 578–81.

[118] *Id.*, 580.

unjust enrichment. The defence encompasses the "competition between the demand of restitution and the general interest of security of receipts".[119] As such, it may be viewed as an almost inseparable component to a claim in restitution. Secondly, the defence as formulated by Lord Goff is not limited to situations where a defendant has altered his position in reliance of the validity of the payment. Thus, the defence would be available to an innocent recipient of a payment which was later stolen from him.[120] Finally, the defence has been held not to be available where a defendant changes his position prior to receipt.[121]

6.2 Defence of *Bona Fide* Purchaser

A claim for restitution may be subject to the defence of *bona fide* purchase for value without notice.[122] The defence of *bona fide* purchaser is of particular significance in relation to claims for proprietary restitution. It will generally only be open to a third party, or indirect recipient.[123] The preferred view is that the *bona fide* purchase rule exists as a separate defence rather than a component of the plaintiff's cause of action.[124]

The defence of *bona fide* purchaser for value operates at two different levels; namely at law and in equity. It is said that the effect of the defence is to protect transactional security[125] and the sanctity of contracts,[126] thereby facilitating economic activity and the free transfer of wealth.[127] The issue however of whether the defence should or should not be available is ultimately a means for

[119] P. Birks, "Change of Position: The Nature of the Defence and its Relationship to Other Restitutionary Defences" in M. McInnnes (ed.), *Restitution: Developments in Unjust Enrichment* (Melbourne, 1996), p.49.

[120] See Goff and Jones, p.822; P. Birks, "Change of Position: The Nature of the Defence and its Relationship to Other Restitutionary Defences" in M. McInnnes (ed.), *Restitution: Developments in Unjust Enrichment,* p.49, 62–3; R. Nolan, "Change of Position" in P. Birks (ed.), *Laundering and Tracing* (Oxford, 1995), pp.145–8, 149–50.

[121] *South Tyneside Metropolitan B.C.* v. *Svenska International plc* [1995] 1 All E.R. 545.

[122] Goff and Jones, pp.842–5; K. Barker, "After Change of Position: Good Faith Exchange in the Modern Law of Restitution" in P. Birks (ed.), *Laundering and Tracing* (Oxford, 1995), p.194 (hereafter Barker); Birks, p.440; Burrows, p.473; Birks, *Laundering and Tracing*, pp.319–20. See also *Lipkin Gorman* v. *Karpnale Ltd.* [1991] 2 A.C. 548; *El Ajou* v. *Dollar Land Holdings Plc* [1993] 3 All E.R. 717, 739, *per* Millett J. (reversed on different grounds) [1994] 2 All E.R. 685. *Cf.* W. Swadling, "Restitution and *Bona Fide* Purchase" in Swadling (ed.), *The Limits of Restitutionary Claims: A Comparative Analysis*, (London, 1997), ch. 4 (hereafter Swadling).

[123] Burrows, p.472; K. Barker, pp.199–202; Birks, p.439; Swadling, pp.80–3; Smith, pp.386–91.

[124] *Pilcher* v. *Rawlins* (1872) 7 Ch. App. 259; *A.G.* v. *Biphosphated Guano Co.* (1879) 11 Ch. D. 327; *Re Nisbet and Potts' Contract* [1906] 1 Ch. 391; *Black* v. *Freedman* (1910) 12 C.L.R. 105, 110, *per* O'Connor J; *Nelson* v. *Larholt* [1947] 1 K.B. 339; *G.L. Baker Ltd.* v. *Medway Building and Supplies Ltd.* [1958] 1 W.L.R. 1216; *Lipkin Gorman* v. *Karpnale Ltd.* [1991] 2 A.C. 548. See also Barker, pp.205–11; Meagher Gummow and Lehane, pp.257–9.

[125] *Bishopsgate Motor Finance Co. Ltd.* v. *Transport Brakes Ltd.* [1949] 1 K.B. 322, 336–7, *per* Denning L.J.; also G.K. Scott, "Restitution from an Innocent Transferee Who is not a Purchaser for Value" (1949) 62 Harv.L.R. 1002, 1008.

[126] Burrows, pp.472–3.

[127] Barker, pp.192–3.

determining which of two innocent persons should bear the loss. At both levels, it is a means for determining the circumstances under which an otherwise defective title may be perfected.[128]

At common law, the maxim *nemo dat quod non habet*, expresses the general principle in relation to the transfer of property. A transferor can only pass title to that which he has. Money is an exception to the common law rule, so thus a person who receives money as a *bona fide* purchaser for value takes legal title to it, irrespective of any weaknesses in the transferor's title.[129] This exception also applies equally to negotiable instruments.[130] In equity, a person who acquires legal title to property as a *bona fide* purchaser for value takes such property free of any equitable interests affecting it.[131] The defence will not apply where the defendant merely acquires an equitable interest. It should be noted that in equity, the defence of *bona fide* purchaser is applicable to all forms of property.

[128] Swadling, pp.69, 80.

[129] *Miller* v. *Race* (1758) 1 Burr 452, 457–8, *per* Lord Mansfield; *Clarke* v. *Shee and Johnson* (1774) 1 Cowp. 197, 199–201, *per* Lord Mansfield; *Nelson* v. *Larholt* [1947] 1 K.B. 339; *Lipkin Gorman* v. *Karpnale* [1991] 2 A.C. 548, 572 *per* Lord Goff.

[130] The rule in relation to negotiable instruments is covered by s.29(1) Bills of Exchange Act 1882. Traditionally, the defence was also available to purchasers of goods in market overt. This however was recently abolished in the Sale of Goods (Amendment) Act 1994.

[131] *Bassett* v. *Nosworthy* (1673) Rep temp Finch 102; 23 ER 55; *Phillips* v. *Phillips* (1862) 4 De G.F. & J. 201; 45 E.R. 1015; *Pilcher* v. *Rawlins* (1872) 7 Ch. App. 259; *Cave* v. *Cave* (1880) 15 Ch. D. 639; *Taylor* v. *Russell* [1892] A.C. 244.

PART II

CHARACTERISATION OF RESTITUTIONARY CLAIMS

2

Characterisation in General

I THE NEED FOR CHARACTERISATION

WHERE A CAUSE of action has an international element added to it, the first natural question is to ask what law governs such a claim or claims. To answer this question, one must find the relevant choice of law rule, whose connecting factor will point to a particular system of law. For example, a claim relating to a contract is generally governed by the law chosen by the parties.[1] This general proposition is the choice of law rule, while "the law chosen by the parties" is the connecting factor. To arrive at the relevant conflicts rule, and thus to the relevant connecting factor, presupposes that one has already characterised the matter into a particular judicial category. In the example cited, this would be as a contractual matter.

In *Macmillan Inc.* v. *Bishopsgate Investment Trust Plc* (*No.3*)[2] Staughton L.J. recognised the ascertainment of the proper law, or *lex causae*, as a three-step process:

> First, it is necessary to characterise the issue that is before the court. Is it, for example, about the formal validity of marriage? Or intestate succession to movable property? Or interpretation of a contract? The second stage is to select the rule of conflict of laws which lays down a connecting factor for the issue in question. Thus, the formal validity of marriage is to be determined, for the most part, by the law of the place where it is celebrated . . . Thirdly, it is necessary to identify a system of law which is tied by the connecting factor found in stage two to the issue characterised in stage one.[3]

Thus, the first step is the process of characterisation or classification. It determines which matters or issues are of such a nature, namely that they have a sufficient theoretical unity, as to warrant a single legal system applying to the determination of such an issue or matter. Thus, when faced with a restitutionary claim, the court must characterise the relevant matter or issue so as to be directed to the relevant choice of law rule or rules. The process of characterisation is therefore an essential threshold question, separate to the actual choice of law stage.[4]

[1] This is the basic position both at common law, *Amin Rasheed Shipping Corp.* v. *Kuwait Insurance Co.* [1984] A.C. 50, and under statute, Article 3(1) of the Rome Convention on the Law Applicable to Contractual Obligations, contained in Schedule 1 of the Contracts (Applicable Law) Act 1990; see also Dicey and Morris, Rule 173.

[2] [1996] 1 W.L.R. 387.

[3] *Id.*, 391–2.

[4] See A. Briggs, "Restitution Meets the Conflict of Laws" [1995] R.L.R. 94, 96.

There is a general difficulty encountered when characterising restitutionary claims.[5] This is due to two main factors. First of all, there are the general problems associated with characterisation.[6] Secondly, the law of restitution is still in a developing, if not embryonic, stage. Given the law of restitution's history,[7] it is inevitable that a degree of uncertainty will exist, at the domestic level, as to the exact location of its borders. It is also therefore inevitable that there will be difficulty in dealing with such claims in private international law, especially at the point of characterisation. Moreover, the law of restitution cuts across several areas of law, each of which could justify a separate characterisation and, thus, attract a different choice of law rule. Restitutionary claims may arise in the context of contracts, wrongs or independently. They may be at law or in equity and they may give rise to personal or proprietary remedies. Thus, despite the existence of restitutionary elements, certain recent cases have been characterised as raising contractual[8] or title[9] issues and therefore attracted the respective choice of law rules.

The two difficulties mentioned above meet head-on and are further compounded by the fact that the English conflict of laws has adopted a Romanistic-civilian model of the law. The divisions within the English conflict of laws do not necessarily square up with those present in English domestic law. In the former, matters of contract, tort and unjust enrichment are treated as being part of the law of obligations, whereas there is a clear division between the choice of law rules for property and those for obligations. Yet, the English law of restitution grants both personal and proprietary remedies,[10] while proprietary remedies may also be available for certain wrongs.[11] A particular matter must fall within one or another choice of law rule and thus there is a particular difficulty where, for example, a proprietary right is generated by unjust enrichment. Moreover, categorising choice of law rules as obligations pre-supposes we know the answer to our quest. There is no reason to assume that a particular causative event will, under the *lex causae*, necessarily give rise to an obligation. Furthermore, certain areas of English domestic law have an uncertain location in the English conflict of laws. Although there are rules dealing with torts, there are no rules for equitable wrongs, while both the position of equitable matters in general and tracing in private international law are also unclear.

[5] See for example *Dimskal Shipping Co. S.A.* v. *ITWF* (*The Evia Luck* (*No.2*)) [1992] 2 A.C. 152; *Macmillan Inc.* v. *Bishopsgate Investment Trust Plc* (*No.3*) [1996] 1 W.L.R. 387; *Kleinwort Benson Ltd.* v. *Glasgow City Council* [1999] 1 A.C. 153.

[6] See below A, §2.1 and 2.2.

[7] See above ch. 1.1.

[8] *Dimskal Shipping Co. S.A.* v. *ITWF* (*The Evia Luck* (*No.2*)) [1992] 2 A.C. 152.

[9] *Macmillan Inc.* v. *Bishopsgate Investment Trust Plc* (*No.3*) [1996] 1 W.L.R. 387.

[10] See above ch. 1.3.

[11] See *A.G. for Hong Kong* v. *Reid* [1994] 1 A.C. 324; *Kartika Ratna Thahir* v. *P.T. Pertambangan Minyak dan Gas Bumi Negara* (*Pertamina*)[1994] 3 S.L.R. 257 (C.A. of Singapore) (hereafter *Thahir* v. *Pertamina*); *L.A.C. Minerals Ltd.* v. *International Corona Resources Ltd.* (1989) 61 D.L.R. (4th) 14 (S.C.C.). See also *Boardman* v. *Phipps* [1967] 2 A.C. 46.

Finally, there is little judicial authority on restitutionary claims in private international law. It should be noted that it was not until the sixth edition of Dicey's *The Conflict of Laws*,[12] that a separate choice of law rule for restitutionary matters appeared. An insufficient number of cases have come before the courts so as to provide a clearer picture as to what constitutes a restitutionary claim for the purposes of private international law.

2 THE PROCESS OF CHARACTERISATION

2.1 Problems Associated with Characterisation

The process of characterisation, or classification, is probably the most nebulous in the conflict of laws. To date, there has been little express judicial recognition of characterisation,[13] while many of the civilian systems have no specific provision in relation to characterisation.[14] Yet, despite its elusiveness, the significance of characterisation is paramount.[15] The particular way a matter is characterised can result in the consequential application of different sets of rules. Thus, a plaintiff may wish to characterise a matter in a particular way so as to attract the application of a more advantageous choice of law rule.[16]

Although, the process of characterisation is a separate step from the possible choice of law rule, it has been suggested that one should keep in mind the potential choice of law rule consequential to a particular characterisation.[17] For example, if the relevant choice of law rule were succession to moveables is governed by the *lex domicilii* of the deceased, characterisation involves deciding precisely which issues should be governed by the *lex domicilii*. One difficulty with this methodology is that the choice of law rule for restitution has not been definitively settled. Moreover, it undermines the autonomy of the characterisation stage. It effectively amounts to proceeding directly from the facts to the appropriate law and applying it, not as a matter of legal principle, but as a matter of judicial discretion.

[12] *Dicey's Conflict of Laws*, 6th ed. by J.H.C. Morris (Sweet and Maxwell, London, 1949), Rule 167. Such matters were previously dealt with in private international law in accordance with the implied contract theory, where they were largely treated as contracts: see Ch. 10, §§2.2.1 and 2.2.2.

[13] *Macmillan Inc.* v. *Bishopsgate Investment Trust Plc* (*No.3*) [1996] 1 W.L.R. 387, is probably one of the first English cases expressly referring to this issue.

[14] For example the relevant provisions of Private International Law in both the Greek and German Civil Codes do not contain provisions dealing with characterisation: see Book 1, Chapter 2, *Private International Law*, Arts. 4–33, Greek Civil Code; Art. 3–46 of the Introductory Law of the German Civil Code. Contrast this with §12 (1), Spanish Civil Code.

[15] *Macmillan Inc.* v. *Bishopsgate Investment Trust Plc* (*No.3*) [1996] 1 W.L.R. 387, 417, *per* Aldous L.J. Dicey and Morris describe the process as "unavoidable": Dicey and Morris, p.35. See also C. Forsyth, "Characterisation Revisited" (1998) 114 L.Q.R. 141. *Cf.* Morris, pp.422–3.

[16] See for example *Ogden* v. *Ogden* [1908] P.46; *Re Cohn* [1945] Ch. 5; *Re Maldonado* [1954] P.223; *Re Bonacina* [1912] 2 Ch. 394; *Macmillan Inc.* v. *Bishopsgate Investment Trust Plc* (*No.3*) [1996] 1 W.L.R. 387.

[17] See Dicey and Morris, pp.42–3.

Cheshire and North recognise two basic problems that arise in the process of characterisation or classification.[18] First, in some cases, there is the difficulty in determining whether a question falls naturally within one judicial category or another. These are the borderline cases where a question could be characterised in more than one way. Secondly, it may be that the *lex fori* and some other potentially relevant law hold diametrically opposed views on the correct classification of a matter.[19]

According to Cheshire and North, there are two basic approaches to characterisation. The first approach is to give the question, or the issue, the meaning that it bears under English internal law; that is, that of the *lex fori*. We may for convenience call this the *lex fori* approach to characterisation. As the relevant choice of law rules arise under the *lex fori*, it should determine the issues which will fall within such rules. To do otherwise, would result in the *lex fori* losing control over the application of its own conflicts rules. Furthermore, it is inevitable that a judge cannot help but characterise a matter in accordance with the legal ideas of the *lex fori*. The second approach is to approach the matter through the application of general principles of universal application.[20] One argument in favour of this approach is that, since classification is required for a case containing a foreign element, it should not necessarily be identical with that which would be appropriate in a purely domestic case. This approach sounds good in theory but is difficult to put into practice. The authors of Cheshire and North dismiss this approach as being "scarcely practicable to do so whilst there are no commonly agreed general jurisprudential principles".[21]

In practice, characterisation is effected on the basis of the law of the forum. This is the accepted position under the common law[22] and in most civilian systems.[23] However, the court must not rigidly confine itself to concepts or

[18] Cheshire and North, pp.36–7.

[19] See also O. Kahn-Freund, *General Problems of Private International Law* (Sijthoff, 1976), p.223 (hereafter, Kahn-Freund).

[20] See Beckett, "The Question of Classification ("Qualification") in Private International Law" (1934) 15 B.Y.I.L. 46.

[21] Cheshire and North, p.37.

[22] See *Bathyanay* v. *Walford* (1887) 36 Ch. D. 269; *Ogden* v. *Ogden* [1908] P.46; *Apt* v. *Apt* [1948] P.83; *National Bank of Greece and Athens S.A.* v. *Metliss* [1957] A.C. 509; *Adams* v. *National Bank of Greece S.A.* [1961] A.C. 255; *G & H Montage GmbH* v. *Irvani* [1990] 1 W.L.R. 667, 678 *per* Mustill L.J. (C.A.); *Macmillan Inc.* v. *Bishopsgate Investment Trust Plc (No.3)* [1996] 1 W.L.R. 387, 407, *per* Auld L.J. See also Cheshire and North, p.38; Dicey and Morris, p.1487; Jaffey, p.493. *Cf. Re Maldonado* [1954] P. 223.

[23] See Art. 12(1) of the Spanish Civil Code; Kegel, *Internationales Privatrecht*, 7th ed. (München, 1995), pp.246–7; J. Kropholler, *Internationales Privatrecht*, 3rd. ed. (Tübingen, 1997), pp.106–11; R. van Rooij and M.V. Polak, *Private International Law in the Netherlands* (The Hague, 1987), p.241; M. Reimann, *Conflict of Laws in Western Europe* (New York, 1995) p.26; *Κρίσπης*, *Ιδιωτικό Διεθνές Δίκαιο*, *Γενικόν Μέρος* (*Αθήνα*, 1979) *σ*. 219–41 [Krispes, *Private International Law*, *General Part* (Athens, 1970) pp.219–28]; *Γραμματικάκη-Αλεξίου κ.α.*, *Ιδιωτικό Διεθνές Δίκαιο* (*Θεσσαλονίκη*, 1997) *σσ*. 55–6 [Grammatikaki-Alexiou *et. al.*, Private International Law (Thessalonike, 1997) pp.55–6]; P. Mayer, *Droit International Privé*, 6th ed. (Paris, 1998), pp.108–16.

categories of the *lex fori*.[24] The *lex fori* will characterise in accordance with its rules in a liberal manner, not insisting that all its technical requirements are complied with. This method of characterisation could be referred to as the "liberal" or "enlightened" *lex fori*. Therefore, under private international law, concepts such as "contract", "tort", "corporation" and "unjust enrichment" are to be given a liberal interpretation. For example, in *Re Bonacina*[25] the Court of Appeal characterised the matter before it as contractual even though the relevant foreign agreement was not supported by consideration.[26] Likewise, in *Batthyanay* v. *Walford*,[27] an action akin to waste, in relation to land situated in Austria and Hungary and subject to a *fidei commiss*, was characterised by the Court of Appeal as being in implied contract.[28] There was no indication that an Austrian court would have characterised it as such; something which at any rate would have been highly unlikely. Nor could it be confidently said that this foreign claim was on all fours with an English claim in implied contract. What is significant for present purposes, is that the Court of Appeal was not deterred by the fact that the particular foreign claim was not recognised under English law. It characterised it in accordance with what it considered to be the closest equivalent under the *lex fori*. Characterisation therefore is ultimately a question of substance and not of form. Although the selection of such issues or matters is determined by the *lex fori*, it is done so in a liberal manner.

2.2 The "Thing" to be Characterised?

It is submitted that there is also a third problem, which arises in relation to characterisation, possibly more fundamental than the two recognised by Cheshire and North. There is the inherent problem of determining the "thing" to be characterised. It is all very well to say that the *lex fori* is not to be applied strictly; however, a significant inquiry is isolating the thing to be characterised. This problem is particularly prevalent in relation to international restitutionary claims. It is not clear in fact whether it is the claim,[29] the rule,[30] the question,[31]

[24] *Macmillan Inc.* v. *Bishopsgate Investment Trust Plc (No.3)* [1996] 1 W.L.R. 387, 407, *per* Auld L.J. See also Cheshire and North, pp.38–9; Dicey and Morris, pp.38–43, 45–8, 1472; Kahn-Freund, pp.227–36.

[25] [1912] 2 Ch. 394.

[26] The same approach will presumably be adopted in relation to torts under s.9(2) of the Private International Law (Miscellaneous Provisions) Act 1995.

[27] (1887) 36 Ch.D. 269.

[28] There are strong arguments for doubting the correctness of the Court of Appeal's characterisation in *Batthyanay* v. *Walford*: see below ch. 7.3.3.

[29] Which can also be equated with the "cause of action": Cheshire and North, p.36; J. Bird, "Choice of Law" in F.Rose (ed.), *Restitution and the Conflict of Laws* (Oxford, 1995), p.75. In *Sayers* v. *International Drilling Co. NV* [1971] 1 W.L.R. 1176, 1181, Denning M.R. considered that one system of law must be applied to all the issues, including claim and defence.

[30] See *Re Cohn* [1945] Ch. 5, 7–8; *Re Maldonado* [1954] P. 223, 245, *per* Evershed M.R.

[31] *Ogden* v. *Ogden* [1908] P. 46, 57, 65, 74; *Beaudoin* v. *Trudel* [1937] 1 D.L.R. 216, 222, *per* Macdonnell J.A. (Ont.C.A.) ; *Re Maldonado* [1954] P. 223, 239, 244, *per* Evershed M.R. See also

the subject,[32] the issues[33] or the issue[34] that has to be characterised.[35] These words have often been used loosely and interchangeably.[36] Part of the solution to the problem of characterising restitution may lie within the area of characterisation itself.

Recently, in *Macmillan Inc.* v. *Bishopsgate Investment Trust Plc* (*No. 3*),[37] the Court of Appeal indicated that it is in fact the "issue", or "the issue in dispute", which has to be properly characterised.[38] However, the exact meaning of the word "issue" received little clarification. The plaintiff, Macmillan, was a publicly listed company in which the late Robert Maxwell and his family held an interest. Macmillan had a majority shareholding of 10.6m shares in Berlitz, which were registered in Macmillan's name in New York. These shares were transferred to Bishopsgate Investment Trust plc ("Bishopsgate"), a company owned and controlled by Robert Maxwell. They were to be held by Bishopsgate as nominee for the account and benefit of Macmillan. Bishopsgate was not to take any action in relation to the shares without the express consent of Macmillan. Fraudulently, the shares were then used to secure debts of companies privately owned by Maxwell and his family. After default, following the collapse of the Maxwell empire, the shares ended up in the names of three banks, namely the second to fourth defendants.

Macmillan brought proceedings claiming, *inter alia*, recovery of the shares or their proceeds of sale. Specifically it argued that the shares had been pledged in breach of trust and that accordingly the receivers of such shares held them on constructive trust. As Berlitz was a New York company and the shares were transferred in New York, a natural choice of law issue arose. The defendant argued by way of defence, that it was a *bona fide* purchaser for value without notice. The Court of Appeal held that the process of characterisation was to be directed at the particular issue or issues which arise and not the cause of action. Accordingly the issue was no longer whether the plaintiff had a cause of action for restitution. The issue was whether the defendants had a defence of *bona fide* purchase for value without notice, or put in another way, whether they had priority of title.

What will constitute an "issue"? A particular claim may have several issues, each potentially governed by its own choice of law rule.[39] However, this is not

Cheshire and North, p.36; J.Collier, *Conflict of Laws*, 2nd ed. (1994), p.16, states that it is the "legal question".

[32] J.D. Falconbridge, *Characterisation in the Conflict of Laws* (1937) 53 L.Q.R. 235, 236.

[33] *Sayers* v. *International Drilling Co. NV* [1971] 1 W.L.R. 1176, 1181, per Denning M.R.

[34] *Macmillan Inc.* v. *Bishopsgate Investment Trust Plc.* (*No.3*) [1996] 1 W.L.R. 387, 399, *per* Staughton L.J., 406, *per* Auld L.J., 418, *per* Aldous L.J.

[35] It has also been suggested that it is the "dispositive rule or rules alleged to be applicable to the situation before the court" that has to be classified: Nygh, *Conflict of Laws in Australia*, 6th ed. (Sydney, 1995), 220 *et. seq*. See also C. Forsyth, "Characterisation Revisited" (1998) 114 L.Q.R. 141.

[36] See for example, Sykes and Pryles, *Australian Private International Law*, 3rd ed. (Melbourne, 1991), p.206; Cheshire and North, p.36; *Re Maldonado* [1954] P. 223, 247, *per* Jenkins L.J.

[37] [1996] 1 W.L.R. 387.

[38] *Id.*, 399, *per* Staughton L.J., 406, *per* Auld L.J., 418, *per* Aldous L.J.

[39] *Id.*, 399, *per* Staughton L.J., 418, *per* Aldous L.J.

to say that every possible issue which will arise is to be characterised separately. Thus, in the *Evia Luck (No.2)*,[40] the issue of whether there was "duress" was not characterised separately. It was governed by the applicable law, namely the law of the contract. Where however a plaintiff sues in tort, it is possible that a separate issue, say a contractual defence, may arise.[41] Likewise there may exist a separate procedural issue.[42] In *Macmillan*, the proprietary issue, that of whether the defendant was a *bona fide* purchaser, was a separate issue to be governed by its own choice of law rule.[43] The word "issue" must mean those types of matters which are capable of falling within a recognisable choice of law rule; [44] or, where no such choice of law rule exists, warrant the creation of a new choice of law rule.

It has been submitted by Forsyth that the object of characterisation is in fact rules of law and that it was essentially rules of law which were characterised by the Court of Appeal in *Macmillan*.[45] He argues that behind every cause of action or "issue" lie legal rules. Therefore, the characterisation of either effectively amounts to a characterisation of legal rules. According to Forsyth, if it is legal rules which are to be characterised then it follows that the *lex fori* approach cannot be used in a straightforward or mechanical way to characterise. Forsyth acknowledges that the opposing alternative, of characterising in accordance with the *lex causae*, must be rejected. Consequently, he suggests that a *via media* be adopted, that is an "enlightened *lex fori*" approach to characterisation.

While one can only agree with Forsyth's support for the enlightened or liberal *lex fori*, his observations in relation to rules of law being the subject matter of characterisation do not reflect the current, nor an ideal, state of the conflict of laws. The approach of characterising rules of law unnecessarily complicates the process of characterisation. It is true that the issues characterised are of a legal nature and have legal consequences. It is not mere facts which are characterised.

[40] *Dimskal Shipping Co. S.A.* v. *ITWF* (*The Evia Luck* (*No.2*)) [1992] 2 A.C. 152 (H.L.).

[41] Where a claim in tort is met by a defence that, a contract between the alleged tortfeasor and victim exempts or limits liability, the solution submitted by various writers and pursuant to authority is to separately characterise the two issues (see L. Collins, "Interaction between Contract and Tort" (1967) 16 I.C.L.Q. 103; O. Kahn-Freund, "Contractual Defences to Delictual Claims" (1968) II Hague Recueil 129–57; P. North, "Contractual Defences to Torts" (1977) 26 I.C.L.Q. 914; P. Carter (1983) 54 BYIL 301; see also A. Briggs, "From Complexity to Anticlimax: Restitution and Choice of Law" [1996] R.L.R. 88, 90. See also: *Coupland* v. *Arabian Gulf Oil Co.* [1983] 1 W.L.R. 1136). First, it must be determined whether the exemption clause in the contract is "admissible" as a defence to liability in tort. This is to be characterised as an issue of tort to be determined by the *lex delicti*. Secondly, the validity of the exemption clause in the contract and its consequential effect is characterised as a contractual issue, which is governed by the proper law of the contract.

[42] *Macmillan Inc.* v. *Bishopsgate Investment Trust Plc.* (*No.3*) [1996] 1 W.L.R. 387, 399, *per* Staughton L.J.

[43] Article 15 of the Hague Convention on Trusts, contained in the Recognition of Trusts Act 1987, recognises the existence of separate issues to those governing the validity of the trust, from its construction, its effects and administration, as set out in Article 8. Such separate issues include the transfer of title to property (Art. 15(d)) and are to be governed by their existing choice of law rules, notwithstanding that a different law may apply to the issues relating to the trust.

[44] *Id.*, 391, *per* Staughton L.J.

[45] C. Forsyth, "Characterisation Revisited" (1998) 114 L.Q.R 141.

However, characterisation is not directed towards legal rules *per se*. The matters characterised are neutral as to a particular system of law. As will be demonstrated, they are generic legal issues or judicial categories which relate to particular choice of law rules. They help identify a particular system of law but are not strictly defined by a particular legal system. To talk in terms of characterising "rules of law" merely adds further confusion to the process of characterisation.

The rationale of the Forsyth approach is that a characterisation issue arises by virtue of the fact that the parties in a particular case seek the application of alternative rules.[46] That is, the plaintiff may claim that a particular issue is governed by the rule from country A, while the defendant may claim that the same issue is to be governed by the relevant rule from country B. Thus he argues, in *Macmillan*, the defendant banks claimed that they were *bona fide* purchasers for value and that this was governed by the relevant New York rule, whereas Macmillan argued that this was governed by the relevant rule of English law. Thus, the matter was characterised as relating to legal title to shares. There are a number of problems with this methodology. First, it presupposes that there are only two alternative competing legal systems, or rules, namely the ones whose application is pleaded by the parties, and that the conflict of laws is all about selecting the right one. It may be that neither of the pleaded legal systems is applicable. The choice of law rule may point to a third legal system, in which case characterising the two legal rules put forward may be a pointless exercise given that neither of the two might apply.[47] Secondly, it may be that the relevant rules pleaded by each party differ to such an extent that they warrant different characterisations. Thus, in *Macmillan*, the defendant banks argued in favour of the *bona fide* purchaser for value rule of New York. The plaintiff on the other hand argued in favour of an English receipt-based, restitutionary liability. The two rules were fundamentally different. Yet, the Court of Appeal avoided this entanglement by characterising the relevant "issue", namely that of whether the defendants had acquired a good title.

Thirdly, characterising rules of law may lose sight of the actual issue. For example, in *Ogden* v. *Ogden*,[48] the relevant French rule required parental con-

[46] C. Forsyth, "Characterisation Revisited" (1998) 114 L.Q.R 143, 154–7.

[47] The court will not establish foreign law *ex officio*, as this is an issue of fact to be pleaded and proved by the parties. Moreover, unless otherwise proved, or proved satisfactorily, foreign law and the *lex fori* are presumed to be the same, in which case the latter will apply: see Fentiman, *Foreign Law in English Courts* (Oxford, 1998), pp.62, 183, 70–4; Dicey and Morris, Rule 18. Where a party does not plead and prove the applicable foreign law, his claim or defence may fail: see *Waterford Wedgewood plc.* v. *David Nagli Ltd.* [1998] F.S.R. 92; Fentiman, pp.68–70. Nevertheless, the law of a state not pleaded by the parties may potentially apply and therefore the process of characterisation goes beyond classifying merely the rules put forward by the parties. The choice of law rules apply automatically by operation of domestic law. Thus, the governing law must be applied, or at least identified. In a tort claim, for example, the court might conceivably hold, pursuant to ss.11 and 12 of the Private International Law (Miscellaneous Provisions) Act 1995, that the applicable law is neither of those put forward by the parties.

[48] [1908] P. 46.

sent for a son under the age of twenty-five to marry. No such equivalent rule existed under English law. The Court of Appeal correctly, it is submitted, characterised the matter as raising an issue of formal validity of marriage,[49] which was governed by the *lex loci celebrationis*; this was the real issue. As the marriage had taken place in England, the marriage was valid. Had the Court of Appeal characterised the relevant rule of law, namely that a son under the age of twenty-five required parental consent to marry, it probably would have characterised the matter as raising an issue of capacity. As capacity to marry is governed by the law of the party's antenuptial domicile,[50] namely France in the case of the son, such a marriage would have been held invalid. Such a result would have meant that an English domicile who enters into a marriage in England, which is valid under English law, with a foreigner, would discover the marriage to be invalidated by an incapacity which though existing under foreign law, did not exist under English law.

Finally, characterising a "rule of law" is tantamount to characterising in accordance with the *lex causae*.[51] Proceeding from a rule of law suggests that the we already know the applicable law. The exercise in characterisation becomes pointless. It seems absurd to characterise a potentially applicable rule of law, when the applicable law is yet to be determined. It should be the *lex causae* which points us to the rule of law and not the rule of law which points us to the *lex causae*. Although Forsyth specifically rejects the *lex causae* approach to characterisation, it is submitted that the distinction between characterising a rule of law, that is with reference to a specific legal system, and characterising in accordance with the *lex causae* is a semantic one. Problems with characterising rules of law are illustrated in *Re Cohn*.[52] A mother and a daughter, still domiciled in Germany, were killed in a London air raid in circumstances where it was impossible to say which of them had died first. The distribution of the mother's estate was governed by German law as the *lex ultimi domicilii*.[53] If the daughter had survived the mother, her estate would participate in the distribution. If however they had died simultaneously, her estate would not participate. According to the relevant German rule, they would be presumed to have died simultaneously, whereas under the relevant English rule[54] they were presumed to have died in order of age. Uthwatt J. rightly characterised the matter as

[49] *Id.*, 57. The Court of Appeal considered that, had this been characterised as a matter of capacity, on the authority of *Sottomayor* v. *De Barros* (*No.2*) (1879) 5 P.D. 94, the same result would have been reached, on the basis that the question of the husband's capacity would have been governed by English law: *id.*, 75–7. Nevertheless, even this alternative analysis still supports the assertion that it is the issue and not the rule which is characterised.

[50] Dicey and Morris, Rule 68.

[51] The great supporter of this view was Wolff: see Wolff, *Private International Law*, 2nd ed. (Oxford, 1950), ss.138–57; also Despagnet, "Des conflits de lois relatifs à la qualification des rapports juridiques" 25 *Clunet* 253, 261. This view has been much criticised and few writers have adopted it: see Dicey and Morris, p.36; Collier, p.18; Cheshire and North, pp.38–9; Morris, p.419; Kahn-Freund, pp.223–36.

[52] [1945] Ch. 5.

[53] The law of the domicile at the time of death.

[54] Namely s.184 of the Law of Property Act 1925.

raising an issue of succession to moveables.[55] This was governed by German law, as the domicile of the deceased, which included the subsidiary issue of whether it was "necessary for the efficacy of the disposition in her favour that [the daughter] should survive [the mother]". Had the judge merely characterised the relevant rules, this would not have led to the relevant choice of law rule. It may have been found that the German rule was substantive and the English rule procedural, in which case both would have applied; or vice versa, in which case neither would have applied. None of this would have helped locate the relevant "issue" and thus the relevant choice of law rule.

If, as Forsyth admits, the "issue" is essentially a synonym for the "rule of law",[56] then it is of little assistance to use the latter phrase as it merely clouds the issue of what it is to be characterised. Moreover, to suggest that *Macmillan* really stands for the proposition that it is rules of law which are to be characterised is a rather creative reading of the case. All of their Lordships were quite clear that it was in fact the "issue" or "issue in dispute" which was to be characterised.[57] Although, admittedly, Auld L.J. remarks that characterisation of the issue or issues thrown up by the claim and the defence "requires a parallel exercise in classification of the relevant rule of law", this is merely a recognition of the fact that the relevant issues are in the form of rules of law. This is not to say that the court is to characterise a rule of law as part of the particular legal system. This is confirmed by the fact that Auld L.J. goes on to say that although characterisation is governed by the *lex fori*, it "should not be constrained by particular notions or distinctions of the domestic law of the *lex fori*, *or of that of the competing system of law*" (*emphasis added*). Likewise, most of the commentary on *Macmillan* has interpreted the case as representing the principle that it is "issues" which are to be characterised.[58]

Characterisation is directed at the particular issue or issues which may arise. A particular claim may have several issues, each capable of attracting its own choice of law rule. Although it is not facts which are characterised, an issue is not a specific legal rule. The term "issue" ultimately refers to those matters which fall within a recognisable choice of law rule, or are of such a nature as to warrant the creation of a new choice of law rule.

[55] *Re Cohn* [1945] ch. 5, 7. See also the discussion of this case in Kahn-Freund, pp.223–5.

[56] C. Forsyth, "Characterisation Revisited" (1998) 114 L.Q.R 141, 149.

[57] *Macmillan Inc.* v. *Bishopsgate Investment Trust Plc.* (*No.3*) [1996] 1 W.L.R. 387, 399, *per* Staughton L.J., 406–7, *per* Auld L.J., 418, *per* Aldous L.J.

[58] See A. Briggs, "From Complexity to Anticlimax: Restitution and Choice of Law" [1996] R.L.R. 88, 90; A. Briggs [1996] B.Y.I.L. 577, 605–6; R. Stevens (1996) 112 L.Q.R. 198, 199; J. Bird, "Choice of Law Rule for Priority Disputes in Relation to Shares" [1996] L.M.C.L.Q. 57, 58; J. Stevens, "Restitution or Property? Priority and Title to Shares in the Conflict of Laws" [1996] 59 M.L.R. 741, 743–4.

3

Characterisation of Restitutionary Claims

I ONE ISSUE OR SEVERAL?

ONE OF THE preliminary questions, which needs to be addressed in characterising restitutionary claims, is determining whether one or several issues arise. When a restitutionary matter arises, does this give rise to a single characterisation, or does a restitutionary claim potentially give rise to one of several characterisations, depending on the particular issue which arises? In the former situation, the single characterisation would attract a single choice of law rule. In the latter, each issue in dispute would give rise to a possibly different choice of law rule.

As discussed in the first chapter, there are several elements to a restitutionary claim. First, it must be shown that the defendant was enriched. Secondly, the enrichment must be at the defendant's expense, and thirdly, it must be unjust in the circumstances for the defendant to have received such enrichment. Finally, the restitutionary claim will be subject to defences and in particular that of change of position. It therefore could be argued that when a restitutionary claim arises, the approach should be to separately characterise the various issues.[1] As part of the main restitutionary claim, three distinct issues of enrichment, of whether such enrichment was at the plaintiff's expense, and of whether such retention is unjust, could therefore arise. A distinct issue may also arise as to whether the defendant is able to rely on defences, particularly that of change of position. Finally, certain other issues, such as that of tracing, or whether a proprietary or personal remedy is available may also warrant a distinct characterisation.

The approach suggested above is both contrary to authority and against common sense. Such an approach would lead to a myriad of choice of law rules, as many as there are potential issues in any restitutionary claim. It would make dealing with restitution unnecessarily complex in private international law and would be in stark contrast to the treatment of contractual or tortious claims. The correct approach, it will be argued, is to treat restitutionary claims as essentially giving rise to a single issue for the purposes of characterisation. Is there a

[1] This is the general approach adopted by R. Stevens, "The Choice of Law Rules of Restitutionary Obligations", in F. Rose (ed.), *Restitution and the Conflict of Laws* (Oxford, 1995), *esp.* p.186. See also Cheshire and North, p.690.

duty to make restitution on the basis that the defendant has been unjustly enriched at the plaintiff's expense? Such an issue must point to a single choice of law rule, which in turn will direct us to the most appropriate law to govern this issue.[2]

2 THE ARGUMENTS IN FAVOUR OF A SINGLE CHARACTERISATION ISSUE

2.1 Consistent with the Approach in Relation to Contract and Tort

The characterisation of a single restitutionary issue is consistent with the general approach adopted in relation to contracts and torts. If unjust enrichment is the third main form of civil liability, standing next to contract and tort, it would make sense to characterise unjust enrichment in a similar way for the purposes of private international law. Both in matters concerning contract and tort, the general approach is to characterise issues as contractual or tortious, and not to separately characterise every possible issue which may arise in establishing a contractual or a tortious claim. There must be compelling arguments for adopting a different approach in relation to unjust enrichment.

In the case of contracts, the Rome Convention[3] applies to "contractual obligations".[4] Its scope extends to[5] issues of performance, interpretation, rights under the contract, termination, damages and other related matters, such as the material validity of a contract.[6] These matters fall within the contractual characterisation and are not treated as independent issues. Besides certain specific issues,[7] most issues relating to contracts are characterised as contractual issues and determined in accordance with the contractual choice of law rule.[8] Insofar as the process of characterisation is concerned, the position under the common law was in all material respects identical.

[2] It may be that such a choice of law rule has several limbs to it, so as to deal with a variety of situations: see for example Rule 200 of Dicey and Morris.

[3] Convention on the Law Applicable to Contractual Obligations, to be found in the Contracts (Applicable Law) Act 1990 (hereafter the "Rome Convention").

[4] Art. 1(1).

[5] See Art. 10.

[6] See Art. 8.

[7] The issue of capacity is specifically excluded from the scope of the Convention, Art. 1(2)(a). It could therefore be seen as liable to raise a separate issue. Likewise, the issue of "formal validity" of the contract is dealt with by Art. 9 which has a validating effect by alternative reference to both the law of the contract and the *lex loci contractus*. Matters of illegality are dealt with as questions of public policy, or *ordre public*, under Art. 16.

[8] It should also be noted that there are certain types of contracts and contractual obligations to which the Convention does not apply. These include contractual obligations relating to wills and succession (Art. 1(2)(b)); negotiable instruments (Art. 1(2)(c)); arbitration agreements and agreements on the choice of court (Art. 1(2)(d)); in a company law context (Art. 1(2)(e)); question of whether an agent is able to bind a principal (Art. 1(2)(f)); trusts (Art. 1(2)(g)); and insurance (Art. 1(3)). These exceptions are either not contractual matters and have been spelled out for the sake of clarity, or they are exceptions for which it was felt the Convention should not apply. Despite these exceptions, the general unitary characterisation in relation to contractual matters applies.

In the case of torts, the analogy is more striking. A tort usually requires several steps before it can be established. It generally needs to be shown that there was some sort of duty which was breached. An analogy here may be drawn with establishing that the enrichment was unjust. A separate issue may arise as to what the standard of such duty was, so as to determine whether a breach did in fact occur. In relation to many torts, it must also be shown that there was damage caused by the tort. A causation issue may therefore also arise, that is, it must be the defendant's breach which caused the plaintiff's loss. A parallel here may be drawn with showing that the enrichment was "at the plaintiff's expense". Finally, an issue may also arise as to the plaintiff's loss. As this goes to the measure of recovery, a parallel may be drawn with establishing enrichment. Issues such as remoteness of damage, or other such matters which might limit recovery, could find their parallel in the defence of change of position.

In private international law, torts are not treated as being made up of several issues for the purposes of characterisation. A unitary approach is adopted. Under the Private International Law (Miscellaneous Provisions) Act 1995 (the "Act"), the rules under the Act are "to be used for determining issues relating to tort".[9] Characterisation is directed towards "torts" and not to the specific elements constituting torts.[10] The choice of applicable law provisions in ss. 11 and 12 are directed at finding the law applicable to the tort and not at a law which might apply in relation to each specific issue.[11] Thus, torts are given a unitary characterisation.[12]

The above analysis illustrates the approach adopted in characterising matters of contract and tort. Contract and tort are considered to be causative events of such a nature, as to generally warrant the application of a single legal system to determine the various component elements arising under these respective issues. The various component elements are not isolated for characterisation purposes as contract and tort have a sufficient theoretical unity. A unitary approach should also be adopted in relation to unjust enrichment which also shares the same theoretical unity. This theoretical unity includes the defence of change of position which is an integral part of a claim in unjust enrichment.[13] The defence

[9] s.9(1).

[10] Traditionally, under the common law double actionability rule, the courts did not have to face the task of characterising torts. The choice of law rule at common law required that the claim amount to a tort according to English domestic law: see *Phillips* v. *Eyre* (1870) L.R. 6 Q.B. 1; *Boys* v. *Chaplin* [1971] A.C. 356. There was no need to characterise a claim as tortious, in situations where it may not have been a tort in English domestic law.

[11] See also Cheshire and North, pp.626–7, 632.

[12] s.12 of the Act allows for a law other than the law applicable under the general rule to determine one of the issues arising in the case, where it appears "substantially more appropriate" that it be determined by that other law. This provision is part of the general exception to the general choice of law rule. It does not suggest that particular issues are to be separately characterised and thereby attract their own choice of law rule. Instead, it allows the court a degree of flexibility to not apply the law which would otherwise have been applicable, *inter alia*, "any of the issues arising in the case" where it considers it "substantially more appropriate to do so". Such situations are, at any rate, unlikely to be common.

[13] See above, 1.6.1.

of change of position is an issue going to enrichment and to the general question of whether restitution should be available.[14] It therefore must also be determined by the same system of law as that which governs the general issue of restitution. As unjust enrichment comprises separate rights and obligations which stand beside contract and tort, there must be compelling arguments for adopting a different approach. In fact, as will be further illustrated, there are compelling arguments for adopting the same approach in relation to matters of unjust enrichment.

2.2 Permutations of Legal Systems

There is a compelling argument for adopting a unitary approach to the characterisation of unjust enrichment. If one were to characterise each and every element or component of the claim, international restitutionary claims would become akin to a lottery. One would be able to recover in circumstances where recovery may not be possible under any one system of law. Moreover, a potentially different system of law may apply to each and every element making up the claim. The more "issues" there are, the greater the number of characterisations, the greater the number of choice of law rules and the greater the number of possibly different legal systems applying so as to establish a right of restitution. Restitution in private international law would become an extremely complex and arbitrary process. Recovery would no longer depend on whether the restitutionary claim has been established under the *lex causae*, but rather, it would depend on whether the right permutation of legal systems arose.

For example, as a result of a mistake, the plaintiff's sub-contractor may have performed services to the defendant's car in jurisdiction β. The plaintiff resides in jurisdiction α, where he also suffered from the mistake. The defendant resides and has the benefit of the car in jurisdiction γ. It may be said that there are three issues here for the purposes of characterisation. First, there is the issue of whether the defendant was enriched, which for argument's sake is governed by the law of γ, as the law of the place where the defendant had the benefit of the enrichment. Secondly, there is the issue of whether the enrichment was unjust, which might be governed by the law of α, as the place where the unjust factor arose, namely the place where the plaintiff suffered from the mistake. Finally, there is also an issue of whether the enrichment was in fact at the plaintiff's expense, which again for argument's sake is governed by the law of β, as the law of the place where the services were performed and thus where the plaintiff was impoverished. It may be that the plaintiff is able to establish that a restitutionary obligation is owed, by establishing that each element is satisfied under its respective law. However, it

[14] In describing the defence of change of position in *Lipkin Gorman* v. *Karpnale Ltd.* [1991] 2 A.C. 548, 579, Lord Goff stated that "where an innocent defendant's position is so changed that he will suffer an injustice if called upon to repay or to repay in full, the injustice of requiring him so to repay outweighs the injustice of denying the plaintiff restitution".

may also be the case that no one single legal system recognises the existence of a restitutionary obligation on the particular facts. Under the law of α, there may be no enrichment, as the defendant is able to subjectively devalue a non-money benefit and it cannot be shown that the defendant either freely accepted, or saved a necessary expenditure. Under the law of β, the mistake was not of a sort giving rise to restitution, as the mistake must be a liability mistake. While finally, under the law of γ, the enrichment was not at the plaintiff's expense, but rather at the sub-contractor's, as the law of γ would award restitution on the basis of the relevant performance.[15] In such a case, it would be inappropriate to allow the plaintiff to recover based on this permutation of legal systems, where in fact there would be no recovery under any one of the legal systems. It is mere coincidence that the requisite elements have been satisfied by the respective legal systems applicable to them and recovery should not be based on such a fortuity. Moreover, it might also be considered inappropriate to disallow recovery in circumstances where an obligation exists under the law of α and β and the particular element is not successful under the law of γ (see Table 1).

TABLE 1: Example of the disadvantage of separately characterising the component elements of an unjust enrichment claim

Jurisdiction:	α	β	γ
Event:	Plaintiff resides in jurisdiction	Plaintiff performs services to defendant's car	Place where defendant resides and enjoys benefit of improvement
Component of Claim/Issue	Unjust factor	Impoverishment/at the expense of factor	Place of enrichment
Completion of action under relevant legal system	1. Enrichment: ☒ 2. At the expense of: ☑ 3. Unjust: ☑	1. Enrichment: ☑ 2. At the expense of: ☑ 3. Unjust: ☒	1. Enrichment: ☑ 2. At the expense of: ☒ 3. Unjust: ☑

* The plaintiff's claim will not succeed under any of the potentially applicable legal systems. However, if each component of the claim is separately characterised and governed by a different legal system, his claim will be successful if the component is satisfied under the relevant legal system.

The above analysis illustrates the fundamental danger in treating each and every element as a potential issue for the purposes of characterisation. First, it makes the conflict of laws unnecessarily complex. If each element which may arise is treated as an issue, it may lead to a multitude of legal systems applying to any one matter. Secondly, besides becoming unpredictable, the success of an

[15] An issue of change of position could also have been added to the above example, whereby such issue was governed by the law of a fourth legal system, under which, although all three elements to the claim were present, the defence had been established and thereby prevented restitution.

international claim depends on a fortuitous permutation of legal systems. If the right legal systems apply to the right issues, a claim may be successful. Yet, this may be in spite of the fact that the remaining elements to a claim might not be satisfied under that particular law, and in fact it may even be that the claim would not have succeeded under any relevant legal system.

2.3 Consistent with Authority

There is no authority to suggest that restitutionary matters are to be characterised as anything other than a single issue. There is no suggestion in the cases that each and every issue which arises under a restitutionary claim is to be characterised separately. The few cases that deal in any way with a restitutionary claim as a matter of private international law all characterise it as a single restitutionary issue.[16] Thus, in *Arab Monetary Fund* v. *Hashim*,[17] Saville L.J.[18] characterised the relevant issue as the obligation to restore the benefit of an enrichment obtained at another's expense. The characterisation process did not focus on issues of whether there was an enrichment, on whether it was unjust, or whether such enrichment was at the plaintiff's expense. Rather, it focused on the unifying issue of whether there was a "right in the third party [the AMF] to recover the unjust enrichment and thus the correlative obligation on the bribe giver and receiver to disgorge the ill-gotten gains".[19] Likewise, in *Chase Manhattan Bank N.A.* v. *Israel-British Bank (London) Ltd.*,[20] Goulding J. saw the issue as "whether the equitable right of a person who pays money by mistake to trace and claim such money under the law of New York is conferred by substantive law or is of a merely procedural character".[21] What is significant is that the right to restitution, albeit in an equitable proprietary form, was characterised as a single issue, encompassing both the ability to trace and the availability of a proprietary remedy.

There is no suggestion in Dicey and Morris that restitution is to be characterised as anything but a single issue.[22] Rule 200 characterises in terms of "[t]he obligation to restore the benefit of an enrichment obtained at another person's expense". Although paragraph (2) of the rule refers to different ways of deter-

[16] See *Chase Manhattan Bank N.A.* v. *Israel-British Bank (London) Ltd.* [1981] Ch. 105; *Pettkus* v. *Becker* (1981) 117 D.L.R. (3d) 257, 278; *Re Jogia* [1988] 1 W.L.R. 484; *Thahir* v. *Pertamina* [1994] 3 S.L.R. 257 (C.A. of Singapore); *Arab Monetary Fund* v. *Hashim* [1996] 1 Lloyd's Rep. 589; *Macmillan Inc.* v. *Bishopsgate Investment Trust Plc. (No.3)* [1996] 1 W.L.R. 387.

[17] [1996] 1 Lloyd's Rep. 589, 597.

[18] With whom Nourse L.J. expressly agreed, *id.* 593.

[19] *Id.*, 597.

[20] [1981] Ch. 105.

[21] *Id.*, 122D. It should be noted that the parties had agreed that the law of New York applied as the *lex causae*. The real issue in dispute was whether the trust arose as a matter of substantive law, thereby giving priority to the winding up proceedings, or as a matter of procedural law.

[22] See also R. Leslie, "Unjustified Enrichment in the Conflict of Laws" (1998) 2 Edinburgh Law Review 233, 235.

mining the proper law of the obligation,[23] nevertheless there is a single restitutionary characterisation. The issue is simply whether there is a right of restitution and not several component issues. On the other hand, while recognising the argument that matters of unjust enrichment may be characterised as several component issues, Cheshire and North provide no final view on this.[24] Moreover Cheshire and North's discussion of restitution in private international law is generally premised around a single restitutionary issue.[25]

2.4 Macmillan v. Bishopsgate: Which is the Issue?

Part of the problem in characterising restitutionary claims lies in the case of *Macmillan Inc.* v. *Bishopsgate Investment Trust Plc.*[26] Much can be resolved by properly understanding this case. As already discussed, the Court of Appeal stated that the process of characterisation is to be directed at the issue or issues which arise and not the entire claim. This could be seen as ammunition for the argument that one is to characterise the particular elements which are required in establishing a right of restitution. An "issue" may arise in relation to any one of these elements and the restitutionary claim may succeed or fail depending on whether this element can be established.

The Court of Appeal did not seek to rewrite the conflict of laws in relation to characterisation. Instead, they were giving judicial expression to a position which has always been obvious. The term "claim" is very ambiguous and imprecise. A "claim" can comprise of many matters, some of them not even in dispute. The process of characterisation is directed at certain judicial categories, or issues, for the purposes of the conflict of laws.[27] In certain situations it may appear to the court to be clearly inappropriate that a particular issue should fall within any of the existing conflict rules. Such exceptional circumstances may warrant a separate characterisation and therefore having a new choice of law rule developed.[28] That is not to say that each and every issue which may arise is to be separately characterised and thereby have a choice of law rule developed.

Thus, for example, in a claim for tort, there may arise an issue of damage, the quantum of damages or of whether the defendant was negligent. It would be wrong to characterise each and every one of these issues. The essential issue is whether a tort has been committed thereby making the defendant liable. There is, in such a case, one "issue" for the purposes of private international law.

[23] The proper law of the obligation, according to Dicey and Morris, is determined in accordance with whether the obligation arises in connection with a contract, a transaction concerning an immovable, or in other circumstances: see below ch. 6.2.

[24] Cheshire and North, p.690.

[25] See generally Cheshire and North, ch. 20.

[26] *Macmillan Inc.* v. *Bishopsgate Investment Trust Plc.* (*No.3*) [1996] 1 W.L.R. 387.

[27] See also J. Bird, "Choice of Law Rule for Priority Disputes in Relation to Shares: *Macmillan* v. *Bishopsgate* (*No.3*)" [1996] L.M.C.L.Q. 57, 59.

[28] Dicey and Morris, p.42.

However, where for example a contractual defence is brought in relation to a claim in tort, a separate issue arises, warranting a separate characterisation, which is to be determined in accordance with its own choice of law rule.[29] So too in a restitutionary claim, the various issues which may arise should not be characterised separately. There may arise issues of whether there was enrichment, of whether it was unjust or whether the defendant may rely on the defence of change of position. Yet, there is essentially one issue, that of whether there exists a right of restitution so as to reverse an unjust enrichment. This is the issue which must be characterised. However, just as in the case of contractual defences to torts, separate ancillary issues[30] may arise which warrant an independent characterisation. For example, there may arise an issue of whether the defendant can rely on a defence of *bona fide* purchaser for value.[31] Alternatively, a preliminary contractual issue may arise, that is whether the relevant contract was in fact ineffective.[32] The process of characterisation should be directed to those sorts of issues which are capable of attracting their own choice of law rule or are of such a nature as to warrant the creation of a new choice of law rule.[33] Such issues are ones which are of such a nature so as to warrant the application of a particular legal system for their determination.

This is exactly the situation which arose in *Macmillan Inc.* v. *Bishopsgate Investment Trust Plc.* A majority of the Court of Appeal recognised that the plaintiff's claim was restitutionary.[34] However, an ancillary proprietary issue[35] arose and the defence of *bona fide* purchaser was characterised as a separate, self-contained issue, attracting its own choice of law rule. The analogy here must be drawn with where a contractual defence is brought to a claim in tort. On a preferable view, the plaintiff's claim in *Macmillan* was the equivalent of a *vindicatio* in equity: a direct assertion of a proprietary right not generated by unjust enrichment.[36] Thus, no issue of unjust enrichment arose. As the benefi-

[29] *Coupland* v. *Arabian Gulf Oil Co.* [1983] 1 W.L.R. 1136. See also L. Collins, "Interaction between Contract and Tort" (1967) 16 I.C.L.Q. 103; O. Kahn-Freund, "Contractual Defences to Delictual Claims" (1968) II Hague Recueil 129–57; P. North, "Contractual Defences to Torts" (1977) 26 I.C.L.Q. 914; P. Carter (1983) 54 B.Y.I.L. 301; see also A. Briggs, "From Complexity to Anticlimax: Restitution and Choice of Law" [1996] R.L.R. 88, 90.

[30] An ancillary issue is one that is distinct from the main issue identified in the claim and is capable of attracting its own choice of law rule. Its distinctiveness as an issue and hence its capability to attract a separate choice of law rule, is based on the fact that it falls within a recognisable choice of law rule, or, on the ancilliary issue being of such a distinct nature, in that it does not share the same theoretical unity as the main issue, as to warrant the creation of a new choice of law rule.

[31] See below, ch. 4, §§3.4 and 5.3.1.

[32] See below ch. 4, §§1.1, 1.2.

[33] See also above ch. 2.2.2.

[34] [1996] 1 W.L.R. 387, 398, *per* Staughton L.J., 417, *per* Aldous L.J. This was also recognised by Millett J. at first instance: *Macmillan Inc.* v. *Bishopsgate Investment Trust Plc.* (*No.3*) [1995] 1 W.L.R. 978, 988F–G, 990D.

[35] See above n.30. See also below ch. 4, §§3.4 and 5.3.1.

[36] W. Swadling, "A Claim in Restitution?" [1996] L.M.C.L.Q. 63; P. Birks, "The Burden on the Bank" in F.Rose (ed.), *Restitution and Banking Law* (Oxford, 1998), pp.189, 191–3. See also J. Stevens, "Restitution or Property? Priority and Title to Shares in the Conflict of Laws" [1996] 59 M.L.R. 741.

ciary of shares, the plaintiff was merely asserting its pre-existing equitable interest in the shares.[37] As such, there never was an issue of unjust enrichment in the first place. On either view, the term "issue" is clearly directed at those recognised judicial categories which are capable of attracting their own choice of law rule. It is not directed at constituent elements or components to a claim which may be disputed or in issue.

[37] As noted by Birks, "A right which persists through a transfer, where 'persists' really means what it says, that it existed before the event and survived after it, is not generated by unjust enrichment": Birks, *Laudering and Tracing*, p.318.

4

Specific Restitutionary Characterisations

I RESTITUTION AND CONTRACT

UNJUST ENRICHMENT CLAIMS often arise in the context of contracts. A contract may be invalid, void, frustrated, rescinded, or terminated, and a consequential restitutionary claim may follow. To use the language of Mason and Carter, the actual or purported contract is for whatever reason "ineffective".[1] As a result of the ineffectiveness of the contract, a consequential claim for restitution may lie. As a matter of domestic law, the exact boundary between the law of contract and restitution is debated and not as yet settled.[2] This difficulty is compounded by the fact that, at least in this particular context, the restitutionary claim is consequential to a contract, or at least a purported contract. That is to say, there is a contract, or purported contract, looming in the background. Both the law of contract and the law of restitution could potentially have something to say on the matter, as the restitutionary and contractual issues meet head on.

As a matter of private international law, the fact that the claim arises with a contractual factual background, raises the question of whether the matter is best viewed as contractual, restitutionary, or possibly both at different times. The process of characterisation must sort out the restitutionary from the contractual issues when a contract becomes ineffective. Depending on whether an issue is considered to be restitutionary or contractual may give rise to a different choice of law rule or rules, or may even invoke different jurisdictional rules.

It is important to identify what we mean by a restitutionary claim brought consequential to an ineffective contract. Dicey and Morris speak in terms of a restitutionary claim arising "in connection with a contract".[3] This last phrase is particularly broad and vague. This could refer to restitutionary claims, where the enrichment, in relation to which restitution is claimed, was provided pursuant to an actual or purported contract which is ineffective. Alternatively, it may refer to situations where there is, or was, an underlying contractual relationship between the parties. Furthermore, the word "contract" in this context

[1] Mason and Carter, ch. 9.

[2] Chitty on Contracts (28th ed. by H. Beale, London, 1999) Vol. I, p.81 (hereafter Chitty on Contracts).

[3] Rule 200(2)(a).

could mean a wide variety of things. It could refer to an existing contract, a previously valid contract which has been discharged or avoided, or it could even include purported contracts which were never effective. The commentary gives the example of "where a party seeks to recover money paid pursuant to an ineffective contract".[4] For present purposes, in examining characterisation of restitutionary matters in the context of contracts, we are concerned with those situations where a benefit is conferred, in relation to which restitution is claimed, pursuant to a contract, whether actual or purported, which was or later becomes ineffective.

1.1 Independent Restitutionary Issue

Under English domestic law, the restitutionary claim which follows an ineffective contract is independent of the contract. It arises independently of the contract through the law of restitution or unjust enrichment. Viscount Simon L.C. stated in *Fibrosa Spolka Akcyjna* v. *Fairbairn Lawson Combe Barbour Ltd*:

> The claim of a party, who has paid money under a contract, to get the money back, on the ground that the consideration for which he paid it has totally failed, is not based on any provision contained in the contract, but arises because, in the circumstances that have happened, the law gives a remedy in quasi-contract to the party who has not got that for which he bargained. It is a claim to recover money to which the defendant has no further right because, in the circumstances that have happened, the money must be regarded as received to the plaintiff's use.[5]

Similarly, Lord Wright observed in relation to the restitutionary basis of recovery of failure of consideration:

> The payment [under the contract] was originally conditional. The condition of retaining it is eventual performance. Accordingly, when that condition fails, the right to retain the money must simultaneously fail. It is not like a claim for damages for breach of the contract which would generally differ in measure and amount, nor is it a claim under a contract. It is in theory and is expressed to be a claim to recover money, received to the use of the plaintiff.[6]

The separateness of the consequential restitutionary claim was also recently emphasised by the House of Lords in *Kleinwort Benson Ltd.* v. *Glasgow City Council*,[7] where it was held by a majority that a claim for restitution under a void contract did not fall within Article 5(1) of the Brussels Convention, as the relevant obligation under such a claim is not a contractual obligation but rather one that lies in unjust enrichment. It should also be noted that the minority did

[4] Dicey and Morris p.1493.

[5] [1943] A.C. 32, 46.

[6] *Id.*, 65. See also *Pavey & Mathews Pty Ltd.* v. *Paul* (1987) 162 C.L.R. 221; *Deglman* v. *Guaranty Trust Co. of Canada* [1954] 3 D.L.R. 785.

[7] [1999] 1 A.C. 153.

not disagree as to the basis of the consequential restitutionary obligation[8] but rather, on the particular interpretation to be given to Article 5(1).[9]

It would therefore follow that, if the restitutionary right of recovery under an ineffective contract is independent of the contract, the contractual choice of law rule need not apply. As it is the law of restitution which gives rise to these independent claims, the restitutionary counterpart in private international law should determine the choice of law questions.[10] The restitutionary issues are therefore separate from the contractual ones for the purposes of characterisation.

However, it could be argued that the cases cited are merely authority for the proposition that the consequential restitutionary claim arises independently as a matter of domestic law. This is not to say that the same necessarily follows as a matter of private international law. Moreover, there are even arguments supporting the proposition that all restitutionary claims arising in the context of contracts should be characterised as contractual or at least governed by the law of the contract.[11] As it is the law of the contract which determines the contract's ineffectiveness, it should also determine the consequential restitutionary claims. What needs to be addressed here is whether, for the purposes of characterisation, separate restitutionary issues arise in cases of ineffective contracts.

There are compelling reasons for separately characterising a restitutionary issue arising under an ineffective contract, both as a matter of principle and as a matter of authority. First, as a general rule, it makes good sense for the rules of private international law to take note of the general structure of domestic law. Although not strictly bound by the rules of domestic law, private international law must, at the end of the day, respect the fundamental divisions within domestic law. This, after all, is the essential tenet of characterising in accordance with the "liberal" *lex fori*.[12] Thus, where as a matter of domestic law, a claim consequential to an ineffective contract is classified as a separate obligation lying in restitution and not contract, there must be compelling arguments before this is to be characterised as anything other than restitutionary.[13]

Secondly, unless one assumes that connected restitutionary matters will always be governed by the law of the real or supposed contract, then it logically follows that consequential restitutionary issues must be characterised

[8] *Id.*, 176F.

[9] Namely, the minority held that the connecting factor of the "obligation in question" in Art. 5(1), should be interpreted as including the supposed obligation under the contract whose existence is in dispute and therefore extend to consequential restitutionary claims in such situations: *ibid.*

[10] Such a view is even more compelling, if one accepts argument put forward by Smith, that the same set of facts should potentially allow for concurrent liability in contract and unjust enrichment: S. Smith, "Concurrent Liability in Contract and Unjust Enrichment: The Fundamental Breach Requirement" (1999) 115 L.Q.R. 245.

[11] See P. Brereton, "Restitution and Contract", in F. Rose (ed.), *Restitution and the Conflict of Laws* (Oxford, 1995), pp.143–8 (hereafter Brereton). See also R. Stevens, "The Choice of Law Rules of Restitutionary Obligations" in F. Rose (ed.), *Restitution and the Conflict of Laws* (Oxford, 1995) pp.160–76 (hereafter Stevens); Dicey and Morris, pp.1493–4. See also *Etler* v. *Kertesz* (1961) 26 D.L.R. (2d) 209.

[12] See generally above ch. 2.2.1.

[13] See also Dicey and Morris, p.1487.

separately. Dicey and Morris do not provide a clear guide as to whether consequential restitutionary issues are to be separately characterised. Proceeding from the premise that the law which governed the real or supposed contract will govern the restitutionary consequences, it is stated that:

> [i]t will . . . be generally unecessary to decide whether the claim for an order to settle the rights of the parties in the aftermath of a failed contract is to be characterised for choice of law purposes as a contractual or a restitutionary matter".[14]

This statement is inconsistent with a later statement, where the editors of Dicey and Morris reject the conclusion that: "the law which governed the contract should invariably govern the claim for restitution".[15] Logically, if the law of the ineffective contract will not invariably apply to the consequential restitutionary issue, then it makes good sense to separately characterise such issue.[16] Accordingly, the earlier comment by the editors of Dicey and Morris is not particularly helpful. Restitution, to reverse an unjust enrichment, is imposed independently by operation of law and not through the volition of the parties. Presumably, the respective choice of law rule will reflect the nature of such an issue. The contractual choice of law rule has been moulded to accommodate contractual issues. There must be convincing reasons for applying the law of the contract to consequential restitutionary issues.[17] Given the independence of restitution, it is preferable to develop a choice of law rule that is sensitive to restitutionary matters.

Thirdly, the decision of the House of Lords in *The Evia Luck* (*No.2*),[18] supports the proposition that consequential restitutionary issues are to be separately characterised, as a matter of private international law. In this case, a Panamanian flagged vessel berthed in a Swedish port. It was informed by the International Transport Workers Federation (the "ITWF") that the vessel would be "blacked" unless the plaintiff owners entered into ITWF employment contracts with the crew, paying crew wages in accordance with ITWF scales, backdated to the commencement of the employment contracts. The plaintiffs submitted to the demands. Subsequently the plaintiffs sought a declaration that they had lawfully avoided the contracts on the ground of duress. They also claimed restitution of the payments made under the contracts avoided for duress.

[14] Dicey and Morris, pp.1493–4. This is a surprising departure from the commentary in the previous edition of Dicey and Morris, where it was stated that: "since the obligation to make restitution is imposed by law, it should not depend on the law chosen (expressly or impliedly) by the parties to govern a contract, if that is the underlying transaction out of which the claim arises, because the relation out of which the restitutionary obligation arises does not depend on the volition of the parties. Furthermore, restitutionary obligations are distinct from contractual obligations and it is well established that the former obligations arise even if there is no underlying contractual obligation between the parties". See Dicey and Morris, *The Conflict of Laws* (12th ed. by L. Collins, London, 1993), pp.1473–4.

[15] *Id.*, p.1495.

[16] See Cheshire and North, pp.673, 686–7.

[17] See Burrows, pp.492–3.

[18] *Dimskal Shipping Co.* v. *International Transport Workers Federation* [1992] 2 A.C. 152.

The parties had agreed that the relevant contracts were governed by English law as their proper law. Under English law, the actions of the ITWF were unlawful, whereas under Swedish law they were lawful. Therefore the specific issue before the House of Lords was whether the actions by the ITWF were legitimate or not. Lord Goff, who gave the leading speech, considered that the issue of whether the contract could be avoided for duress was to be determined by the proper law of the contract. This was a separate issue to the question of restitution. Lord Goff relevantly stated that "before the owners could establish any right to recover the money, they had first to avoid the relevant contract", while "once the contract was avoided, the money paid under it was recoverable in restitution".[19] No separate issue as to what law governed the restitutionary claim arose, as the parties had agreed that question of entitlement to restitution was to be governed by English law.[20] In fact, as the parties had agreed that the contract would be governed by English law, the only real issue was whether the contract could be avoided on the basis of duress. This much was recognised by Lord Goff, who stated that "[t]he present case is, however, concerned with the anterior question whether the pressure exerted by the ITWF constituted duress enabling the owners to avoid the contract . . .".[21]

It is submitted that the two issues were separate. The avoidance of the contract on the basis of duress was a contractual issue, determinable by the law applicable to the contract. The subsequent restitutionary claim was a restitutionary issue, which, as agreed by the parties, was governed by English law. In the particular case, no consequential restitutionary issue arose for decision. The real issue was whether industrial conduct, which was legitimate in Sweden, could nevertheless constitute duress and avoid an English contract. Thus, Lord Goff relevantly summed up:

> Accordingly in the present case we look to English law, as the proper law, to discover whether the contract may, as a matter of principle, be affected by duress and, if so, what constitutes duress for this purpose; what impact such duress must have exercised upon the formation of the contract; and what remedial action is available to the innocent party. We know, of course, that by English law a contract induced by duress is voidable by the innocent party; . . . It follows therefore that, prima facie at least, whether or not economic pressure amounts to duress sufficient to justify avoidance of the relevant contract by the innocent party is a matter for the proper law of the contract, wherever that pressure has been exerted.[22]

Thus, the law of the contract will determine the subsequent remedial action available to the innocent party. This envisages matters such as the avoidance of the contract. It does not however extend to the consequential restitutionary claim. The former is a contractual issue while the latter is not. Lord Goff's omission to refer to consequential restitutionary claims in the above passage

[19] *Id.*, 165D.
[20] *Id.*, 163.
[21] *Id.*, 165E.
[22] *Id.*, 168.

cannot be considered coincidental. The *Evia Luck* was a case where the restitutionary claim was fundamental to the action and the remedial action available to the innocent party under the law of the contract was carefully described. Lord Goff further observed:

> "If a person enters into . . . a contract, he has for most purposes to accept the regime of the proper law of the contract; and if under that regime a particular form of conduct constitutes duress, or for that matter undue influence, rendering the contract voidable wherever the relevant conduct occurs, he has in my opinion to accept the consequences of his conduct under that system of law.[23]

Brereton suggests that it is unclear whether the reference to consequences includes restitution.[24] It is submitted that the consequences referred to are intended to apply to those issues affecting the contract as such. Again, there is no indication that such consequences are intended to apply to consequential restitutionary claims. Thus, in the immediately following sentence, Lord Goff continues:

> [h]e should not assume that, simply because his conduct is lawful in the place overseas where it is performed, it cannot for that reason render an English contract voidable for duress.

This further omission of reference to possible restitutionary claims cannot be considered coincidental. Thus, it is submitted that the case supports the proposition that restitutionary claims arising in connection with a contract are to be separately characterised.

In *Baring Bros. & Co. Ltd.* v. *Cunninghame District Council*,[25] Lord Penrose held that the consequential restitutionary issues arising under a void contract are to be separately characterised and governed by a separate choice of law rule. Restitution was available only because there was no contract. It was therefore not attractive to proceed to give effect to a term of a purported contract when it had no validity as between the parties. It was held that the restitutionary issues are to be determined by a restitutionary choice of law rule, namely the proper law with which the critical facts have their closest and most real connection.

That restitutionary issues arising in the context of contracts are to be separately characterised is further supported by the Contracts (Applicable Law) Act 1990, implementing the Rome Convention. According to Article 10(1)(e), *inter alia*, its scope extends to the consequences of nullity of the contract. The United Kingdom has reserved the right not to apply Article 10(1)(e) under s.2(2) of the Act; the reason being that under English and Scots law, the right to recover the consequences of nullity of the contract forms part of the law of restitution, not

23 *Dimskal Shipping Co.* v. *International Transport Workers Federation* [1992] 2 A.C. 152, 169.
24 See Brereton, p.170.
25 *The Times*, 30 September, 1996.

of contract.[26] As such, the relevant choice of law rules are those applicable to restitutionary rather than those applicable to contractual issues.

Thus, in conclusion, insofar as the process of characterisation is concerned, the consequential restitutionary claims to an ineffective contract must be characterised as separate restitutionary issues. This, it should be noted, is independent of the inquiry as to the possible choice of law rule for such restitutionary issues. However, irrespective of the nature of such a choice of law rule, the restitutionary issues which arise in the context of ineffective contracts are sufficiently distinct to warrant an independent characterisation.

1.2 The Scope of the Restitutionary Issue

Having established that, for the purposes of characterisation, independent restitutionary issues arise in the context of ineffective contracts, our next concern is to determine the exact scope of such restitutionary issues. That is, which are the restitutionary and which are the non-restitutionary issues in such circumstances? We must be able to draw some sort of line between these two types of issues. This inquiry concerns two alternative arguments, located at the two opposite ends of the spectrum. One results in broadening the category of restitutionary issues, while the other limits it. These alternative arguments will assist in determining the exact scope of the restitutionary issue in the context of ineffective contracts.

At one end of the spectrum, there is a strong argument for saying that not all issues which seem to fall into the broad category of restitution should be characterised as restitutionary issues. Whether the relevant matter is characterised as contractual or restitutionary should turn on the type of ineffectiveness in issue. Thus, a consequential restitutionary claim which arises under a void contract may be viewed differently from one which arises under a valid contract which is discharged as a result of a breach. In the former case, as the contract was void, there never was a contract. There is a strong argument for not characterising the consequential restitutionary issue as contractual. As there never was a contract, under the law applicable to the purported contract, there is no reason for giving effect to a term of the non-contract which was never valid, namely the law expressly or impliedly chosen by the parties, to the consequential restitutionary issue. Such a term was never valid. Neither party could rely on the terms of the non-contract to impose restrictions upon the restitutionary claim as a matter of domestic law.[27] The same should follow as a matter of private international law.[28]

[26] See the Lord Advocate, Hansard (H.L.) 12 Dec 1989 col 1271; Cheshire and North, pp.600, 673; Chitty on Contracts, pp.1589, 1637, 1647; Dicey and Morris, pp.1496–7. See also Giuliano-Lagarde Report, p.33. *Cf.* Brereton, pp.166–7, 172–4.

[27] *Rover International Ltd.* v. *Cannon Film Sales Ltd.* [1989] 1 W.L.R. 912, 927–8, *per* Kerr L.J.; also P. Birks, "Restitution and Ineffective Contracts" (1990) 2 J.C.L. 227, 231–3.

[28] *Baring Bros. & Co. Ltd.* v. *Cunninghame District Council*, *The Times*, 30 September, 1996. See also *Kleinwort Benson Ltd.* v. *Glasgow City Council* [1999] 1 A.C. 153.

However, in the case of a valid contract which is, for example, subsequently discharged or frustrated, there is greater scope for arguing that the law of the contract should have a say in the regulation of the parties' rights and obligations. Up until a certain point in time there was a valid contract, a term of which was the chosen law. There is a strong argument for giving full effect to the parties' intention and that therefore, the law of the contract should also cover the consequential restitutionary issues. That is, it should not only determine whether the once valid contract has become ineffective but also the subsequent mopping up. A key inquiry therefore is determining whether and to what extent the law of, for example, a discharged or frustrated contract should regulate consequential restitutionary claims. Will the input of the law of the contract depend on the manner in which the contract became, or was, ineffective? Two points need to be emphasised in answering these questions. First, as in the case of void contracts, so too in the case of contracts which are avoided or discharged, the consequential restitutionary claims do not arise *ex contractu*. They are independent obligations imposed by law and are no less so because of the fact that the contract was valid, at least for some period of time. Thus, although a frustrated contract is valid up until the time of frustration,[29] and although a contract entered into under duress is merely voidable and not void,[30] the restitutionary obligation is no less independent. This was recently highlighted by Lord Goff in *Kleinwort Benson Ltd.* v. *Glasgow City Council.*[31] It was noted that unlike in some other systems of law, a claim to recover, on the ground of failure of consideration, money paid under a valid contract is, as a matter of English law, classified as a claim in restitution based on unjust enrichment.[32] Thus, characterising in accordance with the liberal *lex fori* should still take account of these divisions under domestic law.

It will be recalled that the United Kingdom reservation in relation to Article 10(1)(e) of the Rome Convention is a clear indication that the "consequences of nullity" are not to be characterised as contractual. Nevertheless, it may be argued that the restitutionary consequences of breach and frustration fall within Article 10(1)(c) and (d) respectively.[33] Therefore, a restitutionary claim arising after the termination of a contract, or its frustration, is to be characterised as a

[29] *Fibrosa Spolka Akcyjna* v. *Fairbairn Lawson Combe Barbour Ltd.*[1943] A.C. 32.

[30] The accepted view is that a contract entered into under duress is voidable: *Lynch* v. *D.P.P. of Northern Ireland* [1975] A.C. 653, 695; *North Ocean Shipping Co. Ltd.* v. *Hyundai Construction Co. Ltd.* [1979] Q.B. 705; *Pao On* v. *Lau Yiu Long* [1980] A.C. 614, 634; *Universe Tankships* v. *I.T.W.F.* (*The Universe Sentinel*) [1983] 1 A.C. 366, 383, 400; *Dimskal Shipping Co.* v. *International Transport Workers Federation* [1992] 2 A.C. 152, 168. It should be noted that in *Barton* v. *Armstrong* [1976] A.C. 104, 120, certain deeds were declared void for duress. The authors of *Chitty on Contracts* state that despite the comments expressed by the majority of the Privy Council in *Barton* v. *Armstrong*, this was not a point in issue, while the fact that the majority drew an analogy with fraud, as well as the reference to "setting aside a disposition for duress", *id.*, 118, supports the view that contracts under duress are voidable: *Chitty on Contracts*, pp.413–14, 431.

[31] [1999] 1 A.C. 153.

[32] *Id.*, 171.

[33] See Dicey and Morris, p.1487, n.16; Brereton, pp.166–7; Stevens, pp.194–5.

contractual issue. Yet, as the Rome Convention only applies to "contractual obligations",[34] Article 10(1)(c) and (d) should not apply to the consequential restitutionary matters. Nonetheless, it is conceivable that the phrase "contractual obligations" may receive a Convention interpretation, extending its scope to claims to recover consideration paid under a valid contract which is subsequently discharged.[35]

Secondly, in seeking to distinguish between the different shades of ineffectiveness in issue, the process of characterisation would be engaging in an unnecessarily complex and arbitrary exercise. Essentially, whether an issue were to be considered restitutionary or contractual would depend on an analysis of the manner in which the particular contract became ineffective. Was the contract initially effective or was it ineffective *ab initio* under the applicable law? Different legal systems may provide different answers to the same circumstances. The way an issue would be characterised, and thus the applicable choice of law rule, would depend on the way in which the applicable law rendered a contract ineffective in any given set of circumstances. This it is submitted would be a complex and arbitrary process whose detailed focus would result in losing sight of the fundamental question, namely, whether the relevant issue is essentially contractual or restitutionary. A right to restitution which arises by operation of law should still attract a separate characterisation, irrespective of the way in which the contract became ineffective.

At the other end of the spectrum, there is an argument which could potentially enlarge the scope of restitutionary issues in the context of ineffective contracts. It could be argued that not only should the consequential restitutionary claim be considered a restitutionary issue, but in many circumstances, the actual event which renders the contract ineffective. Where, for example, a contract is avoided as a result of duress, the ability to pull back the contract arises by operation of law and not through the agreement. It is not a right which arises through the consent of the parties and thus, it would be inappropriate for the law of the contract to regulate such an issue. Where for example a defendant forces a plaintiff to enter a contract, holding a gun to the latter's head, why should the law of the contract determine the effect of the duress? As the contract was procured under duress, so too was the chosen law. A plaintiff who has coerced a defendant to enter into a contract, may have also procured a choice of law suitable to his means. The plaintiff may have specifically chosen a law which would not render the contract ineffective. These considerations highlight a potential problem in treating the issue of a contract's ineffectiveness solely as a contractual issue, determinable by the law of the contract.

[34] Art. 1(1). See also Cheshire and North, p.673.

[35] See for example *Kleinwort Benson Ltd.* v. *Glasgow City Council* [1999] 1 A.C. 153, 171, *per* Lord Goff, in the context of the Brussels Convention. Similarly, in *Agnew* v. *Länsförsäkringsbølagens AB*, [2000] 2 W.L.R. 497, a majority of the House of Lords (Lords Nicholls, Woolf and Cooke) held that a pre-contractual obligation, to avoid misrepresentation and non-disclosure, was a "contractual obligation" for the purposes of Art. 5(1) of the Lugano Convention.

As a matter of authority, it is clear that the ineffectiveness of a contract is determined by the law of the contract. This is notwithstanding the fact that such ineffectiveness does not arise through the actual agreement but by operation of law. The *Evia Luck (No.2)*[36] makes this clear. Lord Goff relevantly stated:

> If a person enters into . . . a contract, he has for most purposes to accept the regime of the proper law of the contract; and if under that regime a particular form of conduct constitutes duress, or for that matter undue influence, rendering the contract voidable wherever the relevant conduct occurs, he has in my opinion to accept the consequences of his conduct under that system of law.[37]

This of course pre-supposes that an actual "agreement" has been entered into. The courts however will not apply a foreign rule of law where it is incompatible with the public policy of the forum. This principle applies both as a matter of common law[38] and under Article 16 of the Rome Convention and deals with the argument raised above. Despite a contract's validity under its applicable law, such a contract may nevertheless be held ineffective if it is manifestly incompatible with the public policy of the forum.[39] Thus, in *Kaufman* v. *Gerson*,[40] a contract entered into under coercion was held not to be enforceable, even though it was enforceable under the law governing the contract. In *Royal Boskalis Westminster NV* v. *Mountain*,[41] the principle in *Kaufman* v. *Gerson* was reconciled with that in the *Evia Luck*. It was recognised that there are essentially two classes of duress—"duress that is so shocking that the English court will not enforce the contract irrespective of whether it is valid under its governing law, and a lesser form of duress, whose legitimacy and effect falls to be determined by the proper law of the contract".[42] Phillips L.J. further added:

> Mr Aikens conceded implicitly that this must be so in that he submitted that the *Dimskal* case had not overruled *Kaufman* v. *Gerson* . . ., though it might have narrowed its effect. I think that he was right to make that concession. The duress in the *Dimskal Shipping Co.* case was not of such a type as to "violate some moral principle, which if it is not, ought to be universally respected": see [1904] 1 K.B. 591, 598. It would be strange if duress of that type were to be rendered acceptable to the English court by virtue of the effect of a choice of law clause induced by the same duress, or because the law of the country with which the contract induced by duress had the closest connection regarded the duress as acceptable.[43]

36 *Dimskal Shipping Co.* v. *International Transport Workers Federation* [1992] 2 A.C. 152.
37 *Id.*, 169.
38 See *Rousillon* v. *Rousillon* (1880) 14 Ch.D. 351; *Kaufman* v. *Gerson* [1904] 1 K.B. 591; *Trendtex Trading Corp.* v. *Crédit Suisse* [1982] A.C. 679. Also *Hope* v. *Hope* (1857) 8 De G.M. & G. 731.
39 *Kaufman* v. *Gerson* [1904] 1 K.B. 591; *Dimskal Shipping Co.* v. *International Transport Workers Federation* [1992] 2 A.C. 152, 168, *per* Lord Goff; *Royal Boskalis Westminster NV* v. *Mountain* [1999] Q.B. 674 (C.A.). See also Dicey and Morris, p.1279.
40 [1904] 1 K.B. 591.
41 [1999] Q.B. 674 (C.A.).
42 *Id.*, 724, *per* Phillips L.J. Also *id.*, 689, *per* Stuart-Smith L.J.
43 *Id.*, 724.

It therefore follows that, although, as a general rule, the question of whether a contract is ineffective depends on the law governing the contract, nevertheless, there may be acts of coercion, duress or fraud, which may be considered so severe, or manifestly incompatible with the public policy of the forum, that the court will not enforce the contract, irrespective of whether it is valid under its applicable law. What is significant here is that the question of the contract's effectiveness is a contractual issue which is subject to the public policy of the forum. It is not a restitutionary issue despite the non-contractual, or non-consensual, origin of the factor rendering the contract ineffective.

1.3 Restitution for Breach of Contract

It has been submitted that the question of whether a contract is ineffective is essentially a contractual issue to be determined by the law of the contract. On the other hand, the consequential restitutionary claim which may follow is to be considered a restitutionary issue. This will include the situation where restitution is claimed upon a contract being terminated as a result of a breach.[44] There will however exist situations where restitutionary claims in the context of contracts should be considered contractual issues. In the case where a plaintiff seeks to recover restitutionary damages under a valid contract, such a question should be viewed as a contractual issue, to be determined by the law applicable to the contract.[45] Restitution for breach of contract does not form part of the law of unjust enrichment but is rather a particular remedial response.[46] Although it is uncertain when restitutionary damages for breach of contract are available under English law,[47] other systems of law have taken a broad view.[48] Accordingly the courts may be faced with the task of characterising such claims.

2 CHARACTERISATION OF EQUITABLE RIGHTS AND OBLIGATIONS

As already noted in the first chapter, many restitutionary claims are in equity. The role of equity adds a further complication to the characterisation process. There is a degree of uncertainty and difficulty in relation to claims in equity in private international law. This therefore needs to be addressed as a self-contained issue. There is some doubt as to whether equitable rights and obligations, are generated by the *lex causae* namely the law applicable to the relevant

[44] *Kleinwort Benson Ltd.* v. *Glasgow City Council* [1999] 1 A.C. 153, 171.

[45] Burrows, p.494; Dicey and Morris, p.1495, n. 63.

[46] See ch 1.4; also below §4.1.

[47] See *Surrey County Council* v. *Bredero Homes Ltd.* [1993] 1 W.L.R. 1361; *Cf. A.G.* v. *Blake* [1998]1 All E.R. 833.

[48] See for example *Adras Ltd.* v. *Harlow & Jones GmbH* (1988) 42(1) PD; [1995] R.L.R. 235 (Israel S.C.).

issue, or whether they are simply created by the *lex fori*.[49] If it is the latter, then there is arguably no role for the conflict of laws in relation to equitable matters, subject to an initial jurisdictional question.

There is a view that equitable rights and remedies are administered by the court in accordance with the *lex fori*.[50] As long as there is jurisdiction, the court can require the parties to act in accordance with the court's equitable principles, because equity acts on the conscience of the parties and *in personam*.[51] Thus, English law has been applied as the *lex fori*, to grant specific performance in relation to foreign land, without any inquiry as to whether it was the proper law of the contract.[52] However, this is to be contrasted with cases where the application of equitable rights, in relation to land overseas, has been governed by the law of the contract under which those equitable rights arose.[53] It is submitted, that equitable issues should be characterised in the same way as their counterparts at law, namely in accordance with the causative event giving rise to the equitable response. The phrase "causative event" refers to the particular event which gives rise to the response. It refers to generic issues such as contract, tort or unjust enrichment. It is a phrase which is helpful in identifying the particular legal counterpart to an equitable suit or issue.[54] Accordingly, equitable issues should be placed in the same categories as non-equitable issues for the purposes of characterisation. This is the prevalent view among writers.[55] Therefore, when faced with an equitable claim for restitution of an unjust enrichment containing international elements, the court should characterise this issue in accordance with the event giving rise to the equitable remedy, namely the unjust

[49] See R.W. White, "Equitable Obligations in Private International Law: The Choice of Law" [1986] Syd.L.R. 92, 106–9; L. Barnard, "Choice of Law in Equitable Wrongs" [1992] C.L.J. 474, 475–8; G. Panagopoulos, "Cross-Border Tracing" [1998] R.L.R. 73, 82–3. See also Dicey and Morris, p.1499.

[50] *Re The Anchor Line (Henderson Brothers) Limited* [1937] Ch. 483, 488; *National Commercial Bank* v. *Wimborne* (1978) 5 B.P.R. 11, 598 (N.S.W.S.C.); *United States Surgical Corp.* v. *Hospital Products International Pty Ltd.*[1982] 2 N.S.W.L.R. 766 (the case was appealed to the N.S.W. Court of Appeal and to the High Court of Australia, where both confirmed the trial court's finding that no conflict of laws issue arose as there was no material difference between the relevant systems of law). See also *Lightning* v. *Lightning Electrical Contractors Limited & ors.*, 23 April 1998 (unreported) (C.A.); *A.G. for the U.K.* v. *Heinemann Publishers Australia Pty Ltd.* (1987) 10 N.S.W.L.R. 86, 151, *per* Kirby P. (N.S.W.C.A.): *Arab Monetary Fund* v. *Hashim*, 15 June 1994 (unreported); *Kuwait Oil Tanker Company* v. *Al Bader*, The Independent, January 11, 1999.

[51] See also §3.3 below.

[52] *Re The Anchor Line (Henderson Brothers) Limited* [1937] Ch. 483.

[53] *Ex parte Holthausen*; *re Schiebler* [1874] L.R. 9 Ch. 722; *British South Africa Co.* v. *De Beers Consolidated Mines Limited* [1910] 2 Ch. 502, 510, *per* Farwell L.J., 520, *per* Kennedy L.J. (reversed by the House of Lords on different grounds); *Re Smith*; *Lawrence* v. *Kitson* [1916] 2 Ch. 206.

[54] See generally §3 below in relation to the characterisation of equitable proprietary interests and in particular §§3.3 to 3.4.

[55] R.W. White, "Equitable Obligations in Private International Law: The Choice of Law" [1986] Syd.L.R. 92, 108; J. Bird, "Choice of Law" in F. Rose (ed.), *Restitution and the Conflict of Laws* (Oxford, 1995), p.78 (hereafter Bird); Halsbury's Laws of England (4th ed. (reissue)), Vol. 8(1) par. 890, p.662; Stevens, pp.188–9; G. Panagopoulos, "Cross-Border Tracing" [1998] R.L.R. 73, 82–3; S. Lee, "Restitution, Public Policy and the Conflict of Laws" (1998) 20 U.Q.L.J. 1, 6–7. See also Dicey and Morris, p.1499; E. Peel, "Jurisdiction under the Brussels Convention", in F.Rose, *Restitution and the Conflict of Laws* (Oxford, 1995), p.37.

enrichment. As such, a claim for knowing receipt may be characterised as a matter of unjust enrichment,[56] while a claim for knowing assistance may be characterised as a wrong.[57] Similarly, when examining a claim for breach of a fiduciary duty, it may be said that the fiduciary relationship is contractual in nature and that therefore the breach raises a contractual issue.[58]

Recent authorities support the proposition that equitable matters do attract a choice of law rule reflecting that of the relevant issue,[59] particularly in the field of unjust enrichment. In *Pettkus* v. *Becker*,[60] a *de facto* spouse brought proceedings in Ontario seeking a constructive trust over immovable property. Although the question of the applicable law was not pleaded, the Supreme Court of Canada considered that it was the law of Quebec and not of Ontario which arguably applied, on the basis that the unjust enrichment[61] arose under the law of Quebec.[62] What is significant here, is that although the relevant claim was in equity, there was no suggestion that the law of Ontario should automatically apply as the law of the forum. In *Chase Manhattan Bank N.A.* v. *Israel-British Bank (London) Ltd.*[63] the plaintiff claimed a constructive trust in relation to a mistaken payment made into a New York bank account. Goulding J. held that the plaintiff's equitable interest arose under the substantive law of New York.[64] It was not suggested that the *lex fori* should generally apply owing to the plaintiff's claim being in equity. The issue was characterised as restitutionary. Likewise in *Thahir* v. *Pertamina*,[65] both the legal claim, in the form of a claim for money had and received, and the equitable proprietary claim, were characterised as restitutionary and governed by the relevant choice of law rule.[66] In *Arab Monetary Fund* v. *Hashim (No.9)*,[67] Chadwick J. characterised an

[56] See further §4.3.4 below.

[57] See further §4.3.3 below.

[58] See further §4.3.2 below.

[59] *Augustus* v. *Permanent Trustee Co. (Canberra) Ltd.* (1971) 124 C.L.R. 245 (H.C.A.); *Chase Manhattan Bank N.A.* v. *Israel-British Bank (London) Ltd.* [1981] Ch. 105; *Pettkus* v. *Becker* (1981) 117 D.L.R. (3d) 257, 278; *A.G. for the U.K.* v. *Heinemann Publishers Australia Pty Ltd.* (1987) 10 N.S.W.L.R 86, 192, *per* McHugh J.A. (N.S.W.C.A.) (1988) 165 C.L.R. 30, 49–53, *per* Brennan J.; *El Ajou* v. *Dollar Holdings Ltd.* [1993] 3 All E.R. 717, 736 (reversed on different grounds) [1994] 2 All E.R. 685; *Arab Monetary Fund* v. *Hashim (No.9)*, *The Times*, 11 October 1994; *Thahir* v. *Pertamina* [1994] 3 S.L.R. 257; *Macmillan Inc.* v. *Bishopsgate Investment Trust Plc. (No.3)* [1995] 1 W.L.R. 978, 989 *affd* without reference to this point [1996] 1 W.L.R. 387 (C.A.); *Arab Monetary Fund* v. *Hashim* [1996] 1 Lloyd's Rep. 589; *Paramasivam* v. *Flynn* (1998) 160 A.L.R. 203 (F.C.A). See also *Nissenberg* v. *Felleman* 162 N.E. 2d 304 (Mass. 1959) .

[60] (1981) 117 D.L.R. (3d) 257 (S.C.C.).

[61] There is an argument that cases such as *Pettkus* v. *Becker* are not really about unjust enrichment but about fulfilling expectation losses: See for example Smith, p.368; P. Birks, "Mixing and Tracing" (1992) 45(2) C.L.P. 69, 96 n.70; S. Gardner, "Rethinking Family Property" (1993) 109 L.Q.R 263; *Cf.* L. Smith [1994] R.L.R. 102, 103.

[62] *Id.*, 278 *per* Dickson J. who delivered judgment on behalf of the majority.

[63] [1981] Ch. 105.

[64] *Id.*, 127B.

[65] [1994] 3 S.L.R. 257.

[66] *Id.*, 276. It should be noted that Lai Kew Chai J., in the court at first instance, had held that the claim in equity was governed by the *lex fori*: [1993] 1 S.L.R. 735, 787–91.

[67] *The Times*, 11 October 1994. Also *Grupo Torras S.A.* v. *Al-Sabah* [1999] C.L.C. 1, 469 (Q.B.D.).

equitable claim for knowing assistance as a tort for choice of law purposes. More significantly, in *Arab Monetary Fund* v. *Hashim*,[68] a claim to recover a bribe, which under the *lex fori* constituted an equitable wrong, was characterised by the Court of Appeal as a restitutionary issue.[69] It is therefore submitted that, the authorities referred to support the proposition that matters in equity are to be characterised in the same way as their legal counterparts.

Moreover, there has been growing support in favour of bridging the gap between the rules at law and in equity. In particular, in *El Ajou* v. *Dollar Land Holdings plc*,[70] Millett J. recognised that the action for knowing receipt is equity's counterpart to the common law action for money had and received, for choice of law purposes, and therefore "both can be classified as receipt based restitutionary claims".[71] In *Royal Brunei Airlines Sdn. Bhd.* v. *Tan*,[72] the equitable liability for "knowing", or "dishonest",[73] assistance, was said by the Privy Council to be a close analogy of the tort of inducing a breach of contract at law.[74] Parallel views have been expressed by various academics.[75] It is therefore submitted that equitable rights and obligations should generally be viewed as counterparts to legal rights and obligations, having merely a different historical basis, and therefore should be characterised by reference to the causative event or issue.[76] That is to say, they are to be categorised by reference to the various choice of law rule categories. Thus, a claim that the defendant holds the traceable proceeds of fraudulently acquired cheques on constructive trust,[77] should be seen as the equitable counterpart of a common law claim for money had and received in relation to such proceeds.[78] Both can be viewed as restitutionary,

[68] [1996] 1 Lloyd's Rep. 589.

[69] It will be submitted further below that the issue was erroneously characterised as restitutionary and should have been characterised as contractual: see below, §§4.2 and 4.3.

[70] [1993] 3 All E.R. 717 (reversed on different grounds) [1994] 2 All E.R. 685.

[71] *Id.*, 736, also 739.

[72] [1995] 2 A.C. 378.

[73] The Privy Council stated that the word "dishonest" was to be preferred to the word "knowing" to describe the liability of an accessory to a trustee's breach of trust: *id.*, 391C.

[74] *Id.*, 387B–C. See also L. Smith, "Constructive Fiduciaries" in P. Birks (ed.), *Privacy and Loyalty* (Oxford, 1997) pp.249, 258–61; Meagher, Gummow and Lehane, p.881.

[75] See J. Beatson, *The Use and Abuse of Unjust Enrichment* (Oxford, 1991), ch. 9; P. Birks, "Equity in the Modern Law: An Exercise in Taxonomy" [1996] 26 U.W.A.L.R. 1. In *The Law of Tracing*, Smith argues that as a matter of principle and authority, there should be no distinction drawn between tracing at law and in equity: ch. 5, pp.161–218; also Goff and Jones, pp.93, 114, 745. See also M. Tugendhat, "Assisting a Breach of Duty by a Fiduciary, the Common Law and Money Laundering" in F. Rose (ed.), *Restitution and Banking Law* (Oxford, 1998) ch. 9; J. Martin, "Recipient Liability after Westdeutsche" [1998] Conv. 13.

[76] See *Banque Belge pour l'Etranger* v. *Hambrouk* [1921] 1 K.B. 321, 335, *per* Atkin L.J., 330, *per* Scrutton L.J.; *Nelson* v. *Larholt* [1948] 1 K.B. 339, 343, *per* Denning J.; *United Scientific Holdings Ltd.* v. *Burnley Borough Council* [1978] A.C. 904, 925–6; *Mahesan* v. *Malaysia Government Officers' Co-operative Housing Society Ltd.* [1979] A.C. 374, 380, *per* Lord Diplock; *Lord Napier and Ettrick* v. *Hunter* [1993] A.C. 713, 743D, *per* Lord Goff.

[77] See for example *Black* v. *Freedman* (1910) 12 C.L.R. 105; *G.L.Baker Ltd.* v. *Medway Building & Supplies Ltd.* [1958] 1 W.L.R. 1216; *Polly Peck International plc* v. *Nadir & others* (No.2) [1992] 4 All E.R. 769.

[78] See *Banque Belge pour l'Etranger* v. *Hambrouk* [1921] 1 K.B. 321; *Lipkin Gorman* v. *Karpnale Ltd.* [1991] 2 A.C. 548.

raising an issue of whether there exists a duty to make restitution, whether through a common law remedy, or through an equitable proprietary remedy.[79]

When classifying equitable issues, one should focus on the substance rather than the form, to find the appropriate characterisation. The relevant factor must be the causative event which creates the equitable response. The alternative would mean that issues would be characterised in accordance with whether they were in equity or at law. If characterised as being separate equitable issues, they would, on some authority, be governed by the *lex fori*. Potentially, different choice of law rules would then apply to similar matters, depending on whether they are in equity or at law. Thus, a claim for money had and received would be characterised as restitutionary, to be governed by the applicable law for restitutionary issues, whereas its equitable proprietary counterpart, a claim that the recipient of a mistaken payment holds the proceeds on constructive trust, would be viewed as a claim for an equitable remedy, to be administered by the court in accordance with the equitable principles of the *lex fori*. Moreover, there can be no justification for having a separate choice of law rule for matters in equity. It would be undesirable to import the law-equity distinction into the conflict of laws, more than one hundred and twenty-five years after the Judicature Act 1873.

3 PROPRIETARY RESTITUTION

As discussed in the first part, the English law of restitution grants both personal and proprietary remedies. Proprietary restitution describes those situations where a proprietary remedy is awarded so as to reverse an unjust enrichment. It is to be distinguished from where a proprietary interest is generated by some other event. One of the most difficult issues in dealing with restitutionary claims under private international law is that of proprietary restitution. Being unique to common law systems,[80] the characterisation of proprietary restitution is crucial. The success of a claim of proprietary restitution will largely depend on whether the *lex causae* recognises such claims.

As previously noted, the English conflict of laws has adopted a heavily Romanistic-civilian model of the law. Contract, tort and unjust enrichment choice of law rules are placed within what is described as the law of obligations and stand in contrast to property choice of law rules. Consequently, an English court is faced with the difficult decision of placing matters within one or the other side of this divide, despite the fact that a proprietary interest may be created by a causative event such as a wrong or an unjust enrichment. There are a variety of options that may confront a court in characterising a claim for proprietary restitution. Each one is supported by significant legal and policy

[79] *Nelson* v. *Larholt* [1948] 1 K.B. 339, 343, *per* Denning J.
[80] See ch. 1.3.

arguments in its favour. The four basic options available are a proprietary characterisation; a restitutionary characterisation; an equitable characterisation; and finally a characterisation which is to an extent a hybrid of the others. It is preferable to identify the various options available and examine the arguments in support of each one, before reaching a conclusion as to the preferred characterisation.

3.1 The Proprietary Approach

Where a claim for proprietary restitution raises choice of law issues, one approach would be to give it a proprietary characterisation. Since the matter affects proprietary interests, or has proprietary consequences, the essential issue is one of title, or an interest in property, and should therefore be characterised accordingly. The argument would follow that the *source* of the proprietary consequence is not the relevant issue for characterisation purposes. That is, the fact that proprietary rights are generated by events which form part of the law of unjust enrichment, does not dilute the proprietary nature of the issue.

Such an approach is based on one of two basic assumptions. First, it presupposes that the proprietary consequence of a claim should be the overriding focus. Alternatively, or concurrently, it presupposes that proprietary restitution really forms part of the law of property, in that it is concerned with rights in property. As such, two distinct arguments could be raised in favour of a proprietary characterisation of proprietary restitution. The first is based on a general principle of the conflict of laws to characterise issues relating to property as proprietary. The second is based on the domestic presumption that proprietary restitution forms part of the law of property.

3.1.1 Characterisation of Issues Affecting Property

There are strong reasons for arguing that issues affecting property should generally be characterised as proprietary, so that the *lex situs*, or a choice of law rule reflecting on the fact that the issue is proprietary, is applied.[81] It is thus argued that the choice of law rules applicable to property should not vary according to whether English domestic law views a claim as restitutionary.[82] By characterising an issue affecting property as anything but proprietary, a choice of law rule will apply which might not reflect that of the *lex situs*, or another choice of law rule consequential to a proprietary characterisation and therefore ignore the proprietary nature of the issue.

This is based on three main arguments. First, it is argued that a person who deals with property must know who has title to it for the purposes of certainty

[81] This argument would apply *a fortiori* in relation to immovables.
[82] See Stevens, p.182; Jaffey, p.275; *Cf.* Cheshire and North, pp.673–4.

and security of transactions. This certainty can best be achieved by the *lex situs*. The preference for the *lex situs* is based on its efficacy *vis-à-vis* third parties. So as to ensure certainty in relation to property rights, a third party intending to acquire an interest in property must be protected from the risk that such a thing might be subject to a foreign law.[83] Secondly, it is further argued that the *lex situs* must always have primacy over property situated within its jurisdiction.[84] It is not for a foreign law to dictate rights in relation to property situated in a foreign jurisdiction.

These two arguments are essentially based on practical policy considerations. The comity of nations dictates that courts should try and observe this principle strictly, so that in turn other courts will observe and respect this principle in relation to property within their jurisdiction. As such, to characterise proprietary restitution in a manner otherwise than proprietary would amount to both a degree of uncertainty in relation to third party rights, while it would also deny the *lex situs* power in relation to property within its jurisdiction.

Finally, practical considerations dictate that a court will not, or should not, make orders which at the end of the day cannot be enforced. Where property is situated overseas, an order affecting such property is pointless if there is no way of ensuring that it will be carried out. Thus, the common law courts will generally decline jurisdiction, if the issue affects title to immovables overseas.[85] The parallel to this is that common law courts will generally not enforce a foreign court's judgment in relation to land situated outside that country.[86] For practical reasons, such issues should be characterised as proprietary. Likewise, although not categorically declining jurisdiction, the courts will be reluctant to ignore the fact that property is situated abroad when dealing with issues concerning moveables. In most cases, issues will be characterised as proprietary, and thus attract a law which represents the interest of the *lex situs*. For example, irrespective of the fact that title may pass under a contract and that this issue could be determined under the contract, such issues are characterised as proprietary and are generally governed by the *lex situs* at the time of transfer and not by the *lex contractus*. A possible explanation may be that the foreign court is presumably more likely to enforce a foreign order made under its law, than one made pursuant to foreign law.[87] Although it is admittedly difficult to prove the

[83] *Re Anziani* [1930] 1 Ch. 407, 420; *Macmillan Inc.* v. *Bishopsgate Investment Trust Plc.* (*No.3*) [1996] 1 W.L.R. 387, 424–5, *per* Aldous L.J.; M. Wolff, *Private International Law*, 2d ed. (Oxford, 1950), pp.511–12; Cheshire and North, p.942.

[84] See Dicey and Morris, pp.964–5, 995–6.

[85] *British South Africa Co.* v. *Companhia de Moçambique* [1893] A.C. 602; s.30, Civil Jurisdiction and Judgments Act 1982; *Re Polly Peck International Plc* [1998] 3 All E.R. 812. In *Potter* v. *Broken Hill Co. Pty. Ltd.* (1906) 3 C.L.R. 479, the High Court of Australia applied this principle to a foreign patent.

[86] *Boyse* v. *Coclough* (1854) 1 K. & J. 124; *Re Hoyles* [1911] 1 Ch. 179, 185–6 (C.A.); *Re Trepca Mines Ltd.* [1960] 1 W.L.R. 1273, 1277 (C.A.); *Duke* v. *Andler* [1932] 4 D.L.R. 529 (S.C.C.); *Raeburn* v. *Raeburn*, 20 March 1997 (unreported) (H.C. of Antigua and Barbuda). See also Dicey and Morris, Rule 40(2); *Cf. Chapman Estate* v. *O'Hara* [1988] 2 W.W.R. 275 (Sask.C.A.).

[87] See for example *Simpson* v. *Fogo* (1863) 1 H. & M.195; *Cf. Luther* v. *Sagor* [1921] 3 K.B. 532, 558; *Carl Zeiss Stiftung* v. *Rayner & Keeler Ltd.* (*No.2*) [1967] 1 A.C. 853, 917–18, 922, 978.

above assertions, they nevertheless help illustrate further arguments as to why a proprietary characterisation may be viewed as the more appropriate.

Further to the above policy arguments, one could say that a general proprietary characterisation of issues affecting property, is consistent with the existing position. For example, the existing choice of law rule in relation to the transfer of tangible moveables is that of the *lex situs* at the time of transfer.[88] The choice of law rule is based on a characterisation of the issue as proprietary, or dealing with transfer of title. It is not characterised by reference to the transfer, so as to attract a choice of law rule reflecting such transfer, for example the law of the contract. In other words, it focuses on the proprietary interest itself rather than the mode by which such proprietary interest is created. As Diplock L.J. stated in *Hardwick Game Farm* v. *Suffolk Agricultural Poultry Producers Association*:[89]

> A contract made in England and governed by English law for the sale of specific goods situated in Germany, although it would be effective to pass the property in the goods at the moment the contract was made if the goods were situate in England, would not have that effect if under German law . . . delivery of the goods was required in order to transfer the property in them. This can only be because the property passes at the place where the goods themselves are.[90]

The argument would follow, that the characterisation focus is on the proprietary interest itself rather than on the mode by which such proprietary interest was created, namely the causative event which gave rise to the alleged transfer of title. A distinction is therefore drawn between issues affecting the title to the property and the actual transfer. Thus, where a plaintiff claims a proprietary interest, or remedy, resulting from the law of restitution, the issue should be characterised as proprietary and not in accordance with the unjust enrichment which gave rise to the proprietary result.

If this approach is correct in relation to moveables, it would be argued that it applies *a fortiori* in relation to immovables. The policy arguments cited above are even stronger in relation to land and other immovables. Thus, there is a general reluctance for the courts to even assume jurisdiction in matters relating to title to foreign land,[91] let alone characterise issues of title as anything other than proprietary.[92] It would therefore follow that this argument would apply *a fortiori* insofar as proprietary restitution arises in connection with immovables.

[88] Dicey and Morris, Rule 116; *Inglis* v. *Usherwood* (1801) 1 East 515; *Cammell* v. *Sewell* (1858) 5 H. & N. 728; 157 E.R. 1371; *Winkworth* v. *Christie, Manson & Woods Ltd.*[1980] Ch. 496; *Hardwick Game Farm* v. *Suffolk Agricultural Poultry Producers Association* [1966] 1 W.L.R. 287, 330, *affd* [1969] 2 A.C. 31 (H.L.).

[89] [1966] 1 W.L.R. 287 (C.A.), *affd* [1969] 2 A.C. 31 (H.L.)

[90] *Ibid.*, 330F–G.

[91] *British South Africa Co.* v. *Companhia de Moçambique* [1893] A.C. 602; *Hesperides Hotels Ltd.* v. *Aegean Turkish Holidays Ltd.* [1979] A.C. 508.

[92] *Norton* v. *Florence Land and Public Works Co.* (1877) 7 Ch.D. 332; *Re Ross* [1930] 1 Ch. 377. *Cf. Penn* v. *Lord Baltimore* (1750) 1 Ves. Sen. 444; 27 E.R. 1132; *Richard West* v. *Dick* [1969] 2 Ch. 424; *Re Piercy* [1895] 1 Ch. 83; see generally below §3.3.

Most issues affecting the transfer of intangible moveables, namely debts and other choses in action, are governed by what could be described as the proper law of the intangible. Thus, the assignability of an intangible moveable, the relationship between the assignee and the debtor, the conditions under which the assignment can be invoked against the debtor and questions as to the discharge of the debtor's obligations, are governed by the law of the right to which the assignment relates.[93] Although this choice of law rule is different from that applying to tangible moveables, in that it does not adopt a *lex situs* choice of law rule,[94] it is nevertheless essentially a proprietary characterisation. The question asked is what law governs the transfer of an intangible, and thus, the characterisation process focuses on the thing being transferred or assigned and not on the actual transfer or assignment. Given the difficulty in locating an intangible, the law which creates this thing is considered the most appropriate one to govern many issues concerning its transfer.[95]

Thus, it can be argued that as matters affecting property are generally characterised as proprietary, so too should proprietary restitution. The fact that the proprietary interest arises to effect restitution should not make any difference. A general distinction already exists under the existing choice of law rules between issues concerning the transfer of property and those concerning the validity of the transfer. This distinction should therefore be preserved and apply in relation to proprietary restitution. Proprietary rights may be created through various ways, one of which is through the law of unjust enrichment. The issue therefore, of whether the plaintiff will have a proprietary interest in the property in the defendant's hands, is a proprietary issue. A choice of law rule reflecting the proprietary nature of the issue should apply.

3.1.2 Proprietary Restitution as Part of the Law of Property

The second main argument in favour of a proprietary characterisation is based on the view that proprietary restitution is really about rights in property. It can be argued that, from a domestic point of view, proprietary restitution does not

[93] Art. 12(2) Rome Convention; Dicey and Morris, Rule 118(2); see also *Trendtex Trading Corporation* v. *Crédit Suisse* [1982] A.C. 679. There is a contrary view, which would refer this question to the *lex situs* of the intangible: see R. Goode, *Commercial Law*, 2d. ed (London, 1995), pp.1126, 1130; M. Moshinsky, "The Assignment of Debts in the Conflict of Laws" (1992) 108 L.Q.R. 591.

[94] The *situs* of a debt is generally considered to be the place where the debtor resides: *N.Y. Life Assurance* v. *Public Trustee* [1924] 2 Ch. 101, 119; *Kwok Chi Leung Karl* v. *Comm. of Estate Duty* [1988] 1 W.L.R. 1035, 1040; *Cf.* Dicey and Morris, p.923.

[95] The essential validity of the assignment of a chose is governed by the law which governs the contract between assignor and assignee: Dicey and Morris, Rule 118(1). Here, the focus is on the assignment and its validity rather than on the thing being assigned. This situation applies where the characterised issue is whether the assignment *per se* is binding. This is akin to the situation where for example the issue in dispute is whether a contract to sell goods overseas was formally valid. It is not concerned with situations where the issue is priority of title to a chose, which may be collateral to the effectiveness of an assignment: *Kelly* v. *Selwyn* [1905] 2 Ch. 117.

belong within the law of unjust enrichment.[96] Such an argument could be based on an understanding of the law of restitution as being limited to *in personam* claims. Moreover, as English law has not as yet adopted the remedial constructive trust,[97] it might be argued that all proprietary remedies are institutional and therefore arise *ex lege*. The existence of such interests should therefore be viewed as proprietary issues and not as issues of restitution.[98]

If one does accept that proprietary restitution is merely about the creation or identification of rights in property, then this argument may be accepted. However, as has been illustrated, there is significant authority supporting the existence of claims for proprietary restitution so as to reverse an unjust enrichment.[99] Although it may give rise to proprietary interests, the restitutionary proprietary claim is distinguishable from other proprietary claims.

Putting the strict domestic arguments aside, it may nevertheless be open to a court to take a broad approach to characterisation and therefore ignore the domestic distinctions between a proprietary claim generated by unjust enrichment and one generated by another event. Accordingly, as most non-common law systems do not recognise an equivalent of proprietary restitution, the flexible *lex fori* could adopt a proprietary characterisation for the purposes of private international law. Therefore, where a plaintiff claims a constructive trust on the basis of an unjust enrichment, in relation to property held by the defendant outside the jurisdiction, the issue could be characterised as proprietary. The question of whether the plaintiff is entitled to a beneficial interest would be determined by the *lex situs*, or if an intangible by the law of the intangible. Thus, where the property for example amounts to a tangible moveable and was transferred to the defendant in Germany, the plaintiff would be denied a proprietary remedy on the basis that German law does not recognise such an interest. This would be the case irrespective of the fact that a constructive trust arose under English law, which was the applicable law to the issue of unjust enrichment.

3.2 The Restitutionary Approach to Characterisation

The obvious alternative to a proprietary characterisation of proprietary restitution is a restitutionary characterisation. As it is the law of unjust enrichment which gives rise to the proprietary remedy, the issue in dispute is really about the

[96] See G. Virgo, "Reconstructing the law of restitution" [1996] 10 Trust Law Int., 20; see also J. Stevens, "Restitution or Property? Priority and Title to Shares in the Conflict of Laws" [1996] 59 M.L.R. 741; W. Swadling, "A Claim in Restitution?" [1996] L.M.C.L.Q. 63; G. Virgo, "What is the Law of Restitution About?" in W.R. Cornish & ors., *Restitution: Past, Present and Future* (Oxford, 1998), pp.312–18.

[97] *Westdeutsche Landesbank Girozentrale* v. *Islington LBC* [1996] A.C. 669, 716, *per* Lord Browne-Wilkinson; *Re Polly Peck International plc* (*No.2*) [1998] 3 All E.R. 812 (C.A.). See also Goff and Jones, pp.84–91.

[98] See L. Barnard, "Choice of Law in Equitable Wrongs" [1992] C.L.J. 474, 478–80.

[99] See above ch. 1.3.

existence of a right to restitution. The proprietary result is merely a remedy. The matter therefore ought to be characterised as restitutionary. There are two arguments which will be explored in support of a restitutionary characterisation. First, whereas a proprietary characterisation is appropriate in relation to issues concerning the voluntary transfer of property, it is not so appropriate in the case of proprietary restitution. In the latter case, the essential issue is whether there exists a restitutionary right of the type that might give the proprietary remedy sought; the question is not merely one of title. It is the restitutionary right which tells us whether a proprietary consequence will follow, and by focusing on the issue of property, we are divorcing ourselves from the restitutionary issue.

The second main argument is based on the fact that almost all claims for proprietary restitution are in equity. Proprietary restitution is mainly made possible by virtue of the fact that the courts of equity have traditionally awarded proprietary remedies rather than damages. The courts have viewed equitable proprietary claims as raising issues of obligation and not of title, for the purposes of private international law. Thus, those equitable proprietary remedies which are equity's way of reversing an unjust enrichment, should be characterised as restitutionary.

3.2.1 A Pure Restitutionary Characterisation

There is a strong argument for saying that the proprietary consequence of proprietary restitution should not influence the characterisation process. The choice of law rules which apply as a result of a proprietary characterisation are more appropriate in the context of voluntary transfers of property and issues of competing titles. They are wholly inappropriate in the case of proprietary restitution.[100] In the former, the essential issue is the transfer of title and the related issue of competing titles. Similar considerations would also apply in relation to cases of governmental seizure, where there also exists an issue of title and the *lex situs'* control over property. These should be given a proprietary characterisation so as to provide the necessary degree of certainty and to allow the *lex situs* paramount influence over property within its jurisdiction. In the case of proprietary restitution, these policy considerations are of little persuasion. The essential issue is one of whether there exists an unjust enrichment of the type that might give the proprietary remedy sought.

Moreover, a proprietary characterisation in relation to matters affecting property is not absolute. For example, where a person dies intestate, title to moveable property is determined by the law of the domicile of the deceased[101] and not by the *lex situs*. What is significant is that matters of succession are characterised as ones dealing with succession and not as ones of property.[102] The

[100] See also Bird, p.81.

[101] Dicey and Morris, Rule 132.

[102] Thus, although succession to immovables of an intestate is governed by the *lex situs*, the matter is characterised as one of succession and not title to property.

issue is characterised in accordance with what might propel title and not with the essence of title itself. It helps illustrate that a proprietary characterisation does not apply automatically wherever issues of property are concerned.

The main difference between *in personam* restitutionary claims and proprietary restitutionary claims is one of remedy. If one truly wanted to give effect to a law which governed a particular issue, then this should not be limited to the question of liability, but it should extend to the extent and the nature of such liability. The remedy in this sense is an inseparable component of the actual liability. It is well accepted that a matter should not be characterised in accordance with the particular remedy sought.[103] Thus, a contractual claim seeking a remedy of specific performance should not be placed into a different category from one seeking damages for breach, or alternatively a declaration.[104] Both are essentially disputes about a contract and thus, the question of what law governs such matters should be governed by the relevant choice of law rule for contracts. If one were of the view that the remedy should not be separated from the actual issue of liability to be enforced, in that the remedy is as much a part of the substance of the claim, it is inappropriate to characterise a proprietary remedy separately. It would therefore follow that, both the nature of a remedy, as well as the fact that it may not be recognised by a potentially applicable foreign law, should not affect the characterisation process.

Phrantzes v. *Argenti*[105] could be cited for the general proposition that, for the purposes of private international law, the remedy is an inseparable component of the right or obligation. Under Greek law, the defendant was obliged to constitute a dowry on behalf of his daughter upon her marriage. The plaintiff's claim was refused as there was no appropriate remedy available to the court which could, or could sufficiently, enforce the exact right vested in the plaintiff by Greek law. Lord Parker C.J. stated:

> "if the machinery by way of remedies here is so different from that in Greece as to make the right sought to be enforced a different right, that right would not . . . be enforced in this country".[106]

The court was therefore restricted because it could not apply the remedy sought. Had the court applied its own remedies, it would not have been truly giving effect to the Greek law, but rather it would be enforcing "a right which the plaintiff does not possess under Greek law".[107] Thus, *Phrantzes* v. *Argenti* could be said to stand for the proposition that a foreign legal claim includes its particular remedies, no matter how peculiar these may be. The particular remedy is an integral part which should not be segregated.

[103] *Chase Manhattan Bank N.A.* v. *Israel-British Bank (London) Ltd.* [1981] Ch. 105, 124; *Mckain* v. *R.W. Miller & Co. (SA)* (1991) 174 C.L.R. 1, 24–5, *per* Mason C.J., 48–9, *per* Deane J. (H.C.A.); Cheshire and North, pp.70, 84–5. See also *Phrantzes* v. *Argenti* [1960] 2 Q.B. 19.

[104] See *Richard West* v. *Dick* [1969] 2 Ch. 424.

[105] [1960] 2 Q.B. 19.

[106] *Id.*, 35–6.

[107] *Id.*, 36.

There are also authorities for the proposition that the remedy should not be characterised separately from the restitutionary issue, even where the remedy sought is a proprietary remedy. In *Chase-Manhattan Bank N.A.* v. *Israel-British Bank*,[108] a New York bank mistakenly paid US$2 million to a second bank in New York, for the account of the defendant bank which carried on business in London. The paying bank claimed that it was entitled to the mistaken payment in equity. Specifically, it argued that, where a person mistakenly pays another, equity will consider that the recipient holds that money as constructive trustee for the payer. It argued this because the defendant was being wound up, and it sought a priority over other creditors.

Although the plaintiff's contention that the claim was governed by the law of New York was conceded by the defendant, it denied that the imposition of the constructive trust formed part of the *lex causae*. The defendant argued that the constructive trust was a remedy imposed by the *lex fori*. Thus, as a constructive trust had not as yet arisen under the *lex causae*, the *lex fori* could not now impose one, as the defendant's property had already been impressed with a trust as a result of the winding up proceedings.

Goulding J. held that under New York law the defendant had become a constructive trustee of the moneys. The plaintiff's equitable interest in the property and thus, the imposition of the trust on the recipient, was a rule of substantive law and was not a mere result of a remedial or procedural rule.[109] It is also significant that the imposition of the constructive trust was not segregated from the substantial issue, nor was it characterised as something separate from the main claim. That is, the matter was not separately characterised as raising an issue of title to the money in the bank account and therefore governed by the law governing the chose. Nor was it characterised as raising issues of beneficial title to property and thereby decided according to the proper law governing the trust.[110]

[108] [1981] Ch. 105. See also *Trustor AB* v. *Smallbone*, 9 May 2000 (unreported) (C.A.).

[109] *Id.*, 127B. Burrows argues that, Goulding J.'s decision that the constructive trust arose under substantive law was *obiter*, as he found that the law of England and New York were the same on the central facts of the case, such that it did not matter which law governed: see Burrows, p.497. It is submitted that this interpretation of the case is incorrect. As the defendant's assets had already been impressed with a trust, as a result of the winding-up proceedings, the plaintiff needed to show that the constructive trust had arisen under the substantive law and not under a remedial rule governed by the *lex fori*. In this way the plaintiff's money would have remained unaffected by the winding-up proceedings. As it was agreed that the substantive law was that of New York, the plaintiff had to show that the constructive trust had arisen by the law of New York, prior to the winding up proceedings. The argument that it was New York that applied is also consistent with Lord Browne-Wilkinson's reinterpretation of *Chase-Manhattan* in *Westdeutsche Landesbank Girozentrale* v. *Islington LBC* [1996] A.C. 669, 714–15, where he concludes that the law of New York and England were in fact different; see also G. Panagopoulos, "Cross-Border Tracing" [1998] R.L.R. 73, 78–9.

[110] The proper law of a trust is determined under Art.7 of the Hague Convention on the Law applicable to Trusts and their Recognition. It should be noted that s.1(2) of the Recognition of Trusts Act 1987 provides that the Convention applies to both express trusts and those arising by law. This must however be read subject to Art. 3, which provides that the Convention "applies only to trusts created voluntarily and evidenced in writing".

In *Pettkus* v. *Becker*[111] a *de facto* spouse brought a claim for proprietary restitution over immovable property situated in Ontario. The Supreme Court of Canada allowed her claim for a constructive trust on the basis of unjust enrichment and noted that, although not specifically pleaded, such a claim was arguably governed by Quebec law and not by the law of Ontario, on the basis that the unjust enrichment was most closely connected with Quebec.[112] What is significant is that it was not considered that the law of Ontario should apply on the basis that the property was situated in Ontario. That is to say, the Supreme Court of Canada did not characterise the relevant issue as proprietary but rather as an issue of unjust enrichment.

A similar approach was taken by the Court of Appeal of Singapore in *Thahir* v. *Pertamina*.[113] Pertamina, an Indonesian state enterprise, sought to recover bribes received by its former agent, General Thahir. However, as the proceeds of such bribes were in bank accounts, and the bank had sought interpleader relief, it was held that Pertamina had to show a proprietary claim to the moneys as opposed to a personal claim against the other party. The claim to recover the bribes, both at law and in equity, was characterised as restitutionary, to be governed by the law of Singapore. Such law also determined the availability of a proprietary remedy. The issue of the proprietary remedy was not characterised as something separate from the main restitutionary issue. It was an inseparable component. Thus, in *Thahir* v. *Pertamina*, a claim for proprietary restitution was characterised as restitutionary and not as proprietary.[114]

English law, as the *lex fori*, must, on general principles, decide whether a claim is to be characterised as the assertion of a right to recover an unjust enrichment notwithstanding the particular remedy sought. As the English law of restitution allows both *in personam* and *in rem* claims to reverse an unjust enrichment, both should be characterised as restitutionary, irrespective of whether a proprietary or a personal remedy is asserted. In conclusion, it can therefore be argued that in cases of proprietary restitution, the characterisation should focus on the causative event giving rise to the proprietary remedy. As it is the unjust enrichment which gives rise to the proprietary response, it is its applicable law which should determine when and how a proprietary remedy should arise. A proprietary characterisation would distract the attention from the law of the restitutionary event, to that of where the property was arbitrarily situated.

3.3 The "Equity" Aspect of Proprietary Restitution

As a matter of English domestic law, claims for proprietary restitution are invariably in equity. This fact is particularly significant. When dealing with

[111] (1981) 117 D.L.R. (3d) 257.
[112] (1981) 117 D.L.R. (3d) 278.
[113] *Thahir* v. *Pertamina* [1994] 3 S.L.R. 257.
[114] See §4.3.2 below for a further discussion of the characterisation of cases such as *Pertamina*.

claims for international proprietary restitution, these will inevitably be in equity. In fact, one of the reasons why proprietary restitution is available in common law systems is due to the operation of equity and the way it can act in relation to property. Traditionally, equity awarded proprietary remedies rather than damages,[115] and thus restitution was effected through the creation of proprietary interests.[116] As already discussed, there is a degree of uncertainty and difficulty in relation to claims in equity in private international law.[117] It was concluded that equitable rights and obligations are to be characterised in accordance with the relevant causative event giving rise to the equitable response. However, it is also said that for the purposes of private international law, equity acts *in personam*. What *prima facie* may seem to amount to a proprietary issue may be an *in personam* issue, arising by virtue of an equity between the parties. Thus, there is a further argument, as well as a further explanation, for characterising proprietary restitution in accordance with the causative event arising between the parties and not by reference to the proprietary remedy.

3.3.1 *The in personam Nature of Equity*

There is significant authority for the proposition that for the purposes of private international law, equitable rights are treated as if they were nothing more than rights *in personam*.[118] The basis for this view is what could be called the rule in *Penn* v. *Lord Baltimore*.[119] Although this rule relates to the issue of jurisdiction, it arguably has significant ramifications for the purposes of characterisation. The courts of England can act *in personam* upon a person within the jurisdiction to enforce a personal obligation incumbent upon him when the subject matter is land abroad. The English courts cannot act upon the land directly but can act upon the conscience of the defendant. They do this by making a decree of specific performance against the defendant and treating him as being in contempt of court if he disobeys. As such, the relevant order does not actually impinge upon the title, which is an issue solely for the *lex situs*.[120] Issues concerning land abroad are therefore dealt with indirectly via equity's *in personam* jurisdiction.

[115] Meagher, Gummow and Lehane, pp.634–50.

[116] Smith, p.294.

[117] See above §2.

[118] *Penn* v. *Lord Baltimore* (1750) 1 Ves. Sen. 444; 27 E.R. 1132; *Re Courtney, ex parte Pollard* (1840) 4 Deac. 27; *British South Africa Co.* v. *De Beers Consolidated Mines Limited* [1910] 2 Ch. 502 (reversed by the House of Lords on different grounds); *Re Smith*; *Lawrence* v. *Kitson* [1916] 2 Ch. 206; *In re Anchor Line (Henderson Bros.) Ltd.* [1937] 1 Ch. 483, 488; *Richard West* v. *Dick* [1969] 2 Ch. 424; *El Ajou* v. *Dollar Land Holdings plc* [1993] 3 All E.R. 717, 736j-737a. See also *National Commercial Bank* v. *Wimborne* (1978) 5 B.P.R. 11, 598 (N.S.W.S.C.); *Lightning* v. *Lightning Electrical Contractors Limited & ors.*, 23 April 1998 (unreported) (C.A.); Meagher, Gummow and Lehane, p.98.

[119] (1750) 1 Ves. Sen. 444; 27 E.R. 1132.

[120] See *Lord Portalington* v. *Soulby* (1834) 3 My. & K. 104, 108; *Companhia de Moçambique* v. *British South Africa Co.* [1892] 2 Q.B. 358, 364.

Under the rule in *Penn* v. *Lord Baltimore* the courts have been able to order specific performance in relation to a contract to sell land *ex juris*,[121] make a company liable in relation to an equitable charge on foreign land,[122] and direct trustees to sell foreign land and hold the proceeds on trust, in accordance with a will.[123] Furthermore, the ability of the courts to make equitable orders in relation to land abroad applies *a fortiori* in relation to moveables, whether tangible or intangible.

More recently, in *El Ajou* v. *Dollar Land Holdings plc*,[124] Millett J. emphasised the *in personam* nature of equity in private international law.[125] Although equitable rights may give rise to both proprietary and personal consequences, "they are classified as personal rights for the purpose of private international law".[126] It was stated that:

> An English court of equity will compel a defendant who is within the jurisdiction to treat assets in his hands as trust assets if, having regard to their history and his state of knowledge, it would be unconscionable for him to treat them as his own.[127]

The assertion that equity acts *in personam* for the purposes of private international law may seem to be a convenient common law nicety to give its courts greater jurisdiction. However, this assertion has been accepted by the European Court of Justice (ECJ) in *Webb* v. *Webb*,[128] in the context of the Brussels Convention. A father purchased a flat in France, however the legal title was vested in his son. The father and son had a falling out, and the father sought to obtain the property. Proceedings were brought in England for a declaration that the son held the property as trustee and for an order requiring him to execute the necessary documents to vest legal title in the father. The son challenged the jurisdiction of the English court on the ground that the action related to a right *in rem* in immovable property and that, accordingly, the French courts had exclusive jurisdiction by virtue of Article 16(1) of the Brussels Convention.[129] The son argued that the ultimate purpose of the father's action was to establish proprietary rights over the flat. Therefore, the action came within the exclusive jurisdiction of the French courts. The father argued that his claim was based on a fiduciary relationship between himself and his son, and was not seeking a declaration that he was the legal owner, or an order for possession or rectification

121 *Richard West* v. *Dick* [1969] 2 Ch. 424.

122 *Mercantile Investment & General Trust Co.* v. *River Plate Trust Loan & Agency Co.* [1892] 2 Ch. 303.

123 *Re Piercy* [1895] 1 Ch. 83.

124 [1993] 3 All E.R. 717; (reversed on different grounds) [1994] 2 All E.R. 685 (C.A.).

125 *Id.*, 736–7.

126 *Ibid.*

127 *Id.*, 737.

128 (294/92) [1994] E.C.R. I–1717.

129 Art. 16(1)(a) gives the courts of the Contracting State in which land is situated exclusive jurisdiction "in proceedings which have as their object rights *in rem* in immovable property or tenancies of immovable property".

of any register. Thus, his claim did not relate to rights *in rem* in immovable property, within the meaning of Article 16(1).

The ECJ held that the matter did not come within the exclusive jurisdiction of the French courts. Exclusivity of jurisdiction on courts of the *lex situs* is justified where proceedings involve disputes in relation to the property. Here, the immovable nature of the property held in trust, and its location, were irrelevant to the issues to be determined.[130] The issue was whether the father could enforce a personal right against the defendant.[131] The father did not "claim that he already [enjoyed] rights directly relating to the property which were enforceable against the whole world, but [sought] only to assert rights as against the son".[132]

Although the case was concerned with the issue of exclusive jurisdiction under the Brussels Convention,[133] the case may be used as an illustration of the "*in personam*" nature of equity. In particular, it illustrates that matters of proprietary restitution are characterised as if they were obligations; that is, by reference to the causative event giving rise to the proprietary equitable interest. The above proposition finds support in two main considerations. First, the decision in *Webb* went beyond a mere requirement that Article 16(1) be interpreted strictly. As noted by Birks, if this was the case, the ECJ could have concentrated on the question of whether the claim in *Webb* was such an assertion of rights *in rem* as fell within the mischief for which exclusive jurisdiction was supposed to be the remedy.[134] It clearly went beyond this and distinguished the father's claim. Secondly, the particular trust claimed was a resulting trust and not an express trust. There is a respectable view that resulting trusts arise so as to reverse an unjust enrichment.[135] That is, they arise by operation of law and that they operate to return specific property to its provider because he or she (i) provided that property; and (ii) did not intend to benefit the recipient. The case does not describe the claim by the father for a resulting trust as being

[130] *Cf*. A. Briggs (1994) 110 L.Q.R. 527; *P. Birks*, "In rem or in personam?" (1994) 8 Trust.L.Int., 99.

[131] In *Re Hayward* [1997] Ch. 45, a claim by a trustee in bankruptcy to be entitled to the debtor's share of a villa in Spain, was held to fall within Art. 16 of the Brussels Convention and thus subject to the exclusive jurisdiction of the Spanish Courts. *Webb* v. *Webb* was distinguished on the basis that the relevant claim in that case was equitable and therefore personal: *id*., 57. As the trustee in bankruptcy's claim was to a legal right "it [was] difficult to contemplate any right more clearly a right in rem than a right to legal ownership such as is claimed by the trustee in the present case": *ibid*. See also *Ashurst* v. *Pollard* [2000] 2 All E.R. 772 (Ch.D).

[132] (294/92) [1994] E.C.R. I–1717, 1738 (para. 15).

[133] See Ch. 9, §4.3.3, for a discussion of the case from a jurisdictional perspective.

[134] P. Birks, "In rem or in personam?" (1994) 8 Trust.L.Int. 99, 101.

[135] See generally Chambers; see also Birks, pp.54–64; Smith, pp.294–5; P. Millett, "Tracing the Proceeds of Fraud" (1991) 107 L.Q.R. 71, 76, 80; P. Birks, "Restitution and Resulting Trusts" in Goldstein (ed.), *Equity and Contemporary Legal Developments* (1992), p.335; P. Birks, "Proprietary Rights as Remedies" in P. Birks (ed.), *The Frontiers of Liability*, vol. 2 (1994) 222–3; H. Norman, "Tracing the Proceeds of Crime", in P. Birks (ed.), *Laundering and Tracing* (Clarendon Press, Oxford 1995) 95, 102; S. Worthington, "Proprietary Restitution—Void, Voidable and Uncomplete Contracts" (1995) 9 T.L.Int. 113; R. Millett, "Restitution and Constructive Trusts" (1998) 114. L.Q.R. 399, 401–2. *Cf* W. Swadling, "A New Role for Resulting Trusts?" (1996) 16 Leg. St. 110, approved in *Westdeutsche Landesbank Girozentrale* v. *Islington LBC* [1996] A.C. 669.

restitutionary. However, if one accepts that resulting trusts arise by operation of law[136] and that they form part of the law of restitution, then *Webb* may further illustrate that such matters are to be characterised as if they were obligations; that is, by reference to the causative event which gives rise to the proprietary remedy. Likewise, as already discussed,[137] in *Pettkus* v. *Becker* the Supreme Court of Canada did not characterise a claim for a constructive trust over immovable property as a proprietary issue but rather as an issue of unjust enrichment.[138] Given the equitable nature of the claim, it could characterise it as if it were an obligation.

3.3.2 *In personam Characterisation of Proprietary Restitution*

Although the rule in *Penn* v. *Baltimore* primarily developed in connection with whether the English courts could exercise equitable jurisdiction in relation to foreign land, it can nevertheless be argued that these authorities are relevant to the characterisation of proprietary restitution. In these decisions, the fact that the remedy sought may affect land abroad is inconsequential. As the emphasis is on the court's *in personam* jurisdiction over the defendant, the issue is not to be characterised in relation to the particular property but by reference to the causative event arising between the parties. Moreover, the cases dealing with proprietary restitution and the conflict of laws clearly show that, for the purposes of characterisation, claims for proprietary restitution raise an issue of unjust enrichment and not of property.[139] Therefore, owing to the fact that they arise by operation of law, and the fact that they are in equity, matters of proprietary restitution are to be characterised as if they were obligations, or *in personam* rights, for choice of law purposes. Consequently, they are to be characterised by reference to the causative event which gives rise to the proprietary remedy and not by reference to the proprietary remedy. Thus, in those situations where the law gives rise to a proprietary remedy so as to reverse an unjust enrichment, this should be characterised as matter of unjust enrichment. Likewise, in those situations where a proprietary remedy is claimed in relation to wrongdoing,[140] this should be characterised as a wrong, namely either a tort, breach of trust or an equitable wrong.[141]

[136] See Chambers, p.3.

[137] See above pp.69–70.

[138] (1981) 117 D.L.R. (3d) 257; see also *Chase Manhattan Bank N.A.* v. *Israel-British Bank (London) Ltd.* [1981] Ch. 105.

[139] For example *Chase Manhattan Bank N.A.* v. *Israel-British Bank (London) Ltd.* [1981] Ch. 105; *Pettkus* v. *Becker* (1981) 117 D.L.R. (3d) 257; *Thahir* v. *Pertamina* [1994] 3 S.L.R. 257.

[140] See for example *A.G. for Hong Kong* v. *Reid* [1994] 1 A.C. 324.

[141] See below, §§4.1 and 4.3.

3.3.3 Equitable Interests Created via Consensual Transfers

The fact that equity acts *in personam* for the purposes of private international law, should not necessarily mean that all equitable proprietary interests should be characterised by reference to a causative event. It should only be in relation to those equitable proprietary remedies which are created by operation of law. Those equitable interests which are created through a consensual transfer should be seen as raising issues of title and therefore characterised as proprietary. It will be recalled that the significant policy arguments in favour of a proprietary characterisation are particularly applicable in the context of consensual transfers of property and the connected issue of competing titles.[142] The preference for a proprietary characterisation is based on its efficacy *vis-à-vis* third parties and its promotion of certainty in relation to the acquisition of property rights. For the purposes of the conflict of laws, equitable proprietary interests created via a consensual transfer are examples of equity's counterpart to a legal title. Thus, where a beneficiary under an express trust wishes to assert an equitable interest in trust property, this should be characterised as an assertion of title, albeit equitable, and therefore not characterised as an obligation or by reference to a causative event. It is akin to a *vindicatio* in equity, or what is also referred to as a "pure proprietary" claim. The preferred view is that the plaintiff's claim in *Macmillan*[143] was exactly this.[144] As the beneficiary of shares, the plaintiff was merely asserting its pre-existing equitable interest in shares which had been created through a consensual transfer.[145]

These are to be distinguished from cases where equity allows an equitable proprietary remedy.[146] For the purposes of characterisation these will not be questions of title but will be characterised by reference to the causative event. Thus, a proprietary remedy, claimed in relation to the proceeds of a wrong, does not arise through a consensual transfer. It arises by operation of law and the issue for characterisation purposes is the relevant causative event, namely the wrong.[147] Likewise, where a plaintiff claims that the defendant holds the traceable proceeds of stolen moneys on trust, he is asserting an equitable title, which arises by operation of law. It is not a title which arises by virtue of a voluntary

142 See above, pp.62–4, 67.

143 *Macmillan Inc.* v. *Bishopsgate Investment Trust Plc.* (*No.3*) [1996] 1 W.L.R. 387. For an account of the facts of the case see p.32.

144 For the alternative view see p.44 above and pp.77–78 below.

145 W. Swadling, "A Claim in Restitution?" [1996] L.M.C.L.Q. 63. P. Birks, "The Burden on the Bank" in F. Rose (ed.), *Restitution and Banking Law* (Oxford: 1998), 189, 191–3. See also J. Stevens, "Restitution or Property? Priority and Title to Shares in the Conflict of Laws" (1996) 59 M.L.R. 741.

146 Stevens argues, "[t]he essence of restitution is that the court orders one person to give up to another the amount of enrichment that he has received, whether by means of a personal or a proprietary remedy. However, when the court recognises that a person holds property subject to the pre-existing rights of another, there is no sense in which the court orders the reversal of an unjust enrichment" (1996) 59 M.L.R. 741, 745.

147 Whether such an issue should be characterised as an unjust enrichment or as a wrong is a further matter which will be dealt with below: §4.

transfer and therefore should be characterised as being an unjust enrichment. Therefore in *Macmillan*, had the defendant banks sold the shares and Macmillan then claimed that the banks held the proceeds on constructive trust, this should have been characterised as an issue of unjust enrichment. Macmillan would no longer be asserting its pre-existing equitable title to shares which arose through a consensual transfer. Instead, it would be claiming a beneficial title to the proceeds which arose by operation of law, namely through the causative event of unjust enrichment.[148]

It is therefore submitted that an assertion of title to property, in equity, should be characterised as proprietary, where such title arises by virtue of a voluntary transfer. Where however the equitable proprietary interest arises by operation of law, such an issue must be characterised by reference to the particular causative event. The next question is whether the relevant issue is restitutionary, or otherwise. Where an equitable proprietary remedy is asserted so as to reverse an unjust enrichment, it should be characterised as restitutionary. Proprietary restitution therefore will attract a restitutionary characterisation.

3.4 The Hybrid Approach to the Characterisation of Proprietary Restitution

Although it has been submitted that claims for proprietary restitution should *prima facie* be characterised as restitutionary, one must also accommodate the policy arguments in favour of a proprietary characterisation. As discussed earlier, the English approach is to characterise in accordance with the issue in dispute, while a particular matter may consist of more than one issue.[149] Having this in mind, it is submitted that a hybrid, or two-step, characterisation will be the most appropriate in certain circumstances. That is, as there will possibly exist both restitutionary and proprietary issues, both have a role to play. Although the roles of each one may be different, the result is that the serious arguments and considerations in support of either characterisation can be accommodated. As already examined,[150] the defence of *bona fide* purchaser is a separate defence, independent of the unjust enrichment which generated the proprietary interest, as a matter of domestic law. It is also appropriate that it be a separate issue as a matter of private international law.

In applying a dual, or hybrid, characterisation approach, an analogy may be drawn with the situation of contractual defences to tortious liability in private international law.[151] In such situations, a claim in tort is met by a defence that

[148] See also Ch. I, C, §2; also *Chase Manhattan Bank N.A.* v. *Israel-British Bank (London) Ltd.* [1981] Ch. 105.

[149] Above, ch. 2.2.2.

[150] See Ch. 1.6.2.

[151] See L. Collins, "Interaction between Contract and Tort" (1967) 16 I.C.L.Q. 103; O. Kahn-Freund, "Contractual Defences to Delictual Claims" (1968) II Hague Recueil 129–57; P. North, "Contractual Defences to Torts" (1977) 26 I.C.L.Q. 914; P. Carter (1983) 54 B.Y.I.L. 301; see also A. Briggs, "From Complexity to Anticlimax: Restitution and Choice of Law" [1996] R.L.R. 88, 90.

a contract between the alleged tortfeasor and victim exempts or limits liability. As with proprietary restitution, this situation raises at least two separate possible issues and therefore at least two potential characterisations.[152] The solution submitted by various writers and pursuant to authority,[153] is to apply a two-step test. First, it must be determined whether the exemption clause in the contract is "admissible" as a defence to liability in tort. This issue is characterised as an issue of tort to be determined by the *lex delicti.* Secondly, the validity of the exemption clause and its consequential effect is a contractual issue, which is to be governed by the proper law of the contract. Thus, where an employee sues his employer in negligence and the employer claims a limitation of liability pursuant to the contract, it must be for the law of the tort to determine whether a contractual defence is admissible.[154] Assuming that it is, it is then for the law of the contract to determine whether on its construction the particular exemption clause is valid and whether it applies in the particular case.[155]

The above analysis in relation to contractual defences to tort claims could be applied *mutatis mutandis* in relation to the characterisation of proprietary restitution. A claim for proprietary restitution raises at least two, distinct, possible issues; each one deserving its own characterisation and thus, an applicable choice of law rule. First, it must be determined under the law governing the restitutionary issue, whether it would allow a proprietary remedy. This is the first possible issue, whether there exists an unjust enrichment of the sort which gives rise to proprietary restitution. Secondly, there may be an ancillary issue relating to the property in question which should be characterised separately. For example, where a defence of *bona fide* purchaser for value is raised, this should be characterised as a proprietary issue, which will generally be governed by the *lex situs* or another appropriate law. Likewise, an issue of specification, or accession may also raise an ancillary proprietary question.[156] Thus, on one view[157] of *Macmillan*,[158] although a majority recognised that the plaintiff's claim was restitutionary,[159] the defence of *bona fide* purchaser was characterised as a separate self-contained issue, attracting its own choice of law rule.[160] This is supported by the fact that all of their Lordships indicated that it was the issue and

152 The Hague Convention of Trusts, contained in the Recognition of Trusts Act 1987, also provides for such an approach. Art. 15, recognises the existence of separate issues to be governed by their respective choice of law rule(s). Such separate issues include, for example, the transfer of title to property (Art.15(d)). They are independent from those issues, set out in Art. 8, which attract the choice of law rule for trusts, such as the validity of the trust, its construction, its effects and administration.

153 *Coupland* v. *Arabian Gulf Oil Co.* [1983] 1 W.L.R. 1136.

154 *Id.*, 1151 et seq.

155 *Coupland* v. *Arabian Gulf Oil Co.* [1983] 1 W.L.R. 1136, 1153, *per* Goff L.J.; P. Carter (1983) 54 B.Y.B.I.L. 301. See also *Sayers* v. *International Drilling Co. N/V* [1971] 1 W.L.R. 1176.

156 See *Zahnrad Fabrik Passau GmbH* v. *Terex Ltd.* 1986 S.L.T. 84.

157 The alternative view of *Macmillan* is discussed above: p.75.

158 *Macmillan Inc.* v. *Bishopsgate Investment Trust Plc.* (*No.3*) [1996] 1 W.L.R. 387.

159 *Id.*, 398, *per* Staughton L.J., 417, *per* Aldous L.J.

160 Such an approach was also put forward by Millett J. in *Macmillan Inc.* v. *Bishopsgate Investment Trust Plc.* (*No.3*) [1995] 1 W.L.R. 978, 989G–H, D–E.

not the claim which is to be characterised.[161] Moreover, such an approach was also suggested by the Court of Appeal in *Lightning* v. *Lightning Electrical Contractors Limited*.[162] Peter Gibson L.J. stated that a prior equitable interest may be defeated "where there has been a transfer of the property to a third party with notice of an equity but by the *lex situs* governing the transfer, the transfer extinguished the plaintiff's equity".[163] This statement recognises the existence of ancillary proprietary issues, which may defeat prior equitable interests, such as those created by proprietary restitution.

There is great sense in characterising ancillary proprietary issues separately. First, where a defendant purchases property for value, he may be quite removed from the original restitutionary issue. Inevitably, he will be a third party.[164] There is no reason why the issue of whether he has independently acquired an indefeasible title should be governed by the same choice of law rule as that governing the restitutionary issue. A subsequent purchase is sufficiently removed from the restitutionary issue as to attract its own characterisation and, therefore, choice of law rule.

Furthermore, a separate characterisation of ancillary proprietary matters takes into account many of the policy considerations in favour of a proprietary characterisation.[165] For example, suppose A steals his employer's money in England and uses the money to purchase a car in France. A then sells this car to C in France. The employer then brings an action in England against C, claiming that C holds the car on trust for his benefit, on the basis that the car represents the traceable proceeds of the employer's money. A separate characterisation of the question of whether C has acquired a good title to the car sufficiently protects security of transactions. It gives the recipient, C, a degree of certainty and, to an extent, preserves the *lex situs'* control over the property. If therefore under the *lex situs*, title will pass to a *bona fide* recipient without notice and there is no need to show that this was for value,[166] only a separate characterisation can

[161] See also A. Briggs, "From Complexity to Anticlimax: Restitution and Choice of Law" [1996] R.L.R. 88, 90–1.

[162] 23 April 1998 (unreported).

[163] It should be noted that it was assumed that the prior equity would be governed by the *lex fori*, on the basis that the parties were amenable to the court's jurisdiction. This is reflective of the traditional view that equitable right interests are *ipso facto* governed by the *lex fori*. As has been previously submitted equitable issues are to be characterised according to their legal counterparts and attract the appropriate choice of law rule (see above Ch. 2, §2). Nevertheless, this statement shows that prior equitable interests may be defeated by ancillary proprietary issues as a matter of private international law.

[164] See ch. 1.6.2.

[165] See above, pp.62–4.

[166] For example Art. 2779 of the French Civil Code provides that "En matiere de meuble la possesion vaut titre": "In matters of movables, possession is equivalent to title". This effectively means that *bona fide* possession amounts to title. The article goes on to provide the original owner with a right to reclaim his original property in cases of theft or loss within three years of the loss or theft. Nevertheless, title vests in the good faith recipient. Theft or loss has been interpreted narrowly, such that it is limited to its meaning under criminal law and not extended to other fraudulent situations: Civ. 19 juin 1928: *DP* 1929, 1, 45; see Code Civil, Dalloz ed. (Paris, 2000), p.1763. Similarly, Art. 1036 of the Greek Civil Code provides: "*Following the alienation of a movable pursuant to article*

properly protect the recipient's interest. If the law governing the restitutionary issue were to be applied, it may not adequately provide the same security. An innocent recipient who assumed he acquired good title under the *lex situs*, may be surprised if he were told by a foreign court that this belongs to a party of whom he has no knowledge. That is, that under the foreign court's law, he never did acquire title, and that the plaintiff has a proprietary claim.

At the same time, it is the law of the restitutionary issue which must determine whether the claimant acquired a proprietary interest in the relevant property. It is inappropriate that the law of where the property is situated should dictate whether the plaintiff is entitled to a proprietary remedy. This may lead to arbitrary results. For example, an employee steals his employer's money in England and specifically transfers it into another particular jurisdiction, specifically because it does not recognise proprietary rights generated by unjust enrichment. The plaintiff's proprietary remedy over the traceable proceeds should not be defeated merely because the *lex situs* does not recognise such remedies. This is especially so where an ancillary proprietary issue does not arise, thereby giving the defendant a legitimate defence, as was the case in *Macmillan*.

Thus, in conclusion, it is submitted that there should be separate characterisations of the restitutionary and proprietary issues as they arise. This two-step process accommodates the arguments in favour of both characterisations. Furthermore, it is consistent with existing authority in relation to what is to be characterised. If we are to characterise the "issue" and not the entire claim, it is an inevitable consequence that we can only adopt this two-step approach. Finally, the dual characterisation approach is the preferred view in relation to contractual defences in torts, and thus it is preferable that a similar approach be adopted whenever separate issues arise from the interaction of different areas of the law.

3.4.1 The Scope of the Ancillary Proprietary Issue

The question of whether an ancillary proprietary issue arises is one for the *lex fori*. In a claim for proprietary restitution, the *lex fori* will characterise the issue raised by the defence and determine whether this gives rise to an ancillary proprietary issue. In characterising such an issue it will determine whether it falls within one of the existing choice of law rules dealing with the acquisition of

1034 [dealing with the transfer of movables], *the acquirer shall become the owner thereof, even if ownership of the thing did not belong to the alienator, except if at the time of transmission of possession the acquirer acted in bad faith*". There is an exception where the owner is dispossessed of the thing transmitted as a result of theft or loss, however, this exception does not apply in relation to money or negotiable instruments: Kerameus and Kozyris, *An Introduction to Greek Law*, 2nd revised ed. (Deventer, 1993), p.128. In the situation where the moveable acquired by the recipient represents the traceable value of the plaintiff's original property, these defences are likely to be applicable, even in a situation of theft or loss as the moveable in the defendant's possession will not be the stolen or lost moveable.

property, or whether it is of such a nature as to warrant a new choice of law rule. Under the current conflict of laws, property can be acquired in a number of ways. It may be acquired by a voluntary transfer, by a governmental seizure or by succession under a will or intestacy. A proprietary interest may, *inter alia*, also be created under a specification or accession.

The exact scope of the ancillary proprietary issue involves a careful balance between the competing policy arguments in favour of both a restitutionary and proprietary characterisation. It may be considered desirable that the scope of the ancillary proprietary issue not be defined too widely. The mischief sought to be avoided here is preventing a fraudster, or an otherwise not *bona fide* party, from defeating an otherwise valid claim for proprietary restitution by moving assets into a jurisdiction and acquiring title under its laws.[167] For example, stolen money could be used to purchase shares in another jurisdiction. By virtue of the fact that the fraudster acquired title to the shares under the *lex situs*, the plaintiff's proprietary remedy will have been defeated. Thus, all that a fraudster or launderer would need to do is acquire a title to property in a foreign jurisdiction. As such, it may be seen as appropriate to somehow limit the acquisition of titles under foreign laws in such a way as to prevent this sort of situation.

A key problem therefore arises where a defendant claims to have acquired a good title under the *lex situs*, or some equivalent thereof, in circumstances where common sense might dictate against defeating a legitimate proprietary claim, as recognised by the law governing the restitutionary issue. For example, the defendant may claim that he has acquired title under the *lex situs* to a moveable, which constitutes the traceable proceeds of the plaintiff's money, by virtue of possession. The question is whether such issues should be characterised as ancillary proprietary issues. It may be considered preferable that an ancillary proprietary issue only arise in circumstances where there was a defence akin to that of a *bona fide* purchaser for value without notice.[168] Although the rule under the particular jurisdiction may differ from the *bona fide* purchaser rule under English law, nevertheless the liberal *lex fori* can examine the issue raised by the defence and determine whether it gives rise to a separate proprietary characterisation, by virtue of the fact that the defendant claims to be a *bona fide* purchaser or an equivalent thereof.

The delicate balance, between allowing a separate characterisation of ancillary proprietary issues (which may arise in claims for proprietary restitution) and the need to not allow too broad an ambit for such proprietary issues, may ultimately be achieved through the public policy of the forum. In *Winkworth* v.

167 In the case of intangible moveables, title could be acquired under the law governing the debt.

168 Such was recognised by Peter Gibson L.J. in *Lightning* v. *Lightning Electrical Contractors*, 23 April 1998 (unreported). It was relevantly stated that a prior equitable interest in foreign land may be defeated where "there has been a transfer of the property to a third party with notice of an equity but by the *lex situs* governing the transfer, the transfer extinguished the plaintiff's equity".

Christie, Manson & Woods Ltd.,[169] Slade J. recognised five exceptions to the *lex situs* rule in relation to the assignment of moveable tangibles.[170] For present purposes, these include where a purchaser had not acted *bona fide* and also where the particular law of the *situs* is contrary to English public policy.[171] Such a principle could be extended to deal with the concerns raised above in relation to ancillary proprietary issues. Where a defendant raises a defence to a claim for proprietary restitution, that he acquired good title to such property under a foreign law, such an ancillary proprietary issue will be unsuccessful if he was not *bona fide*, or where the particular foreign law on which he relies is considered to be contrary to the public policy of the *forum*. This principle could act as a screen and thereby prevent too broad a scope for the ancillary proprietary issue.

Thus, in conclusion, where a defendant raises a defence that he has acquired title to the property in question, this, *prima facie*, raises a separate proprietary issue to be determined by the appropriate choice of law rule for the acquisition of the particular type of property. The characterisation process will determine whether an ancillary proprietary issue arises, while the applicable law will tell us whether such a defence has been made out. Nevertheless, the *lex fori* will maintain a degree of control over such proprietary defences by limiting their scope where the defendant was not *bona fide* or where the recognition of such acquisition of title is contrary to public policy. In this way, not all alleged acquisitions of title under foreign law will defeat international claims for proprietary restitution, only those which satisfy the strong considerations in support of a proprietary characterisation.

4 CHARACTERISATION OF RESTITUTION FOR WRONGS

As already discussed, the law may allow restitution, or disgorgement,[172] in relation to a wrong.[173] As a matter of English domestic law, the exact taxonomical position of restitution for wrongs is debated. The preferred view is that restitution for wrongs is a cause of action in the wrong, giving rise to restitution as a remedial response.[174] However, there is also a view that it is a separate cause of action in unjust enrichment.[175] A separate question therefore arises as to the characterisation of restitution for wrongs as a matter of private international law.

[169] [1980] Ch. 496.

[170] *Id.*, 501, 514.

[171] The other exceptions are: where goods are in transit; where there is an overriding statute of the *lex fori*; and also where special rules might apply to determine the relevant law governing the effect of general assignments of moveables on bankruptcy or succession.

[172] See L. Smith, "The Province of the Law of Restitution" (1992) 71 C.B.R. 672, 694–9.

[173] See ch. 1.4.1.

[174] See ch. 1.4.2.

[175] Beatson, pp.25–8, 206–43; Maddaugh and McCamus, p.507; I. Jackman, "Restitution for Wrongs" (1989) 48 C.L.J. 302. See also *Chesworth* v. *Farrar* [1967] 1 Q.B. 407.

It has been submitted by writers that restitution for wrongs claims should be characterised by reference to the wrong; that is, as issues of tort, contract and also possibly equitable wrongs.[176] Moreover, the greater bulk of academic opinion supports a similar taxonomical characterisation as a matter of domestic law. However, the few cases dealing with restitution for wrongs in private international law have not necessarily adopted this approach.[177] Instead, they have adopted a restitutionary characterisation, particularly in relation to restitution for equitable wrongdoing. It is therefore appropriate to separately examine both the arguments in favour of a wrongs characterisation and the cases dealing with restitution for wrongs in private international law.

4.1 Characterisation as "Wrongs"

The main argument in favour of characterising restitution for wrongs as belonging to the category of "wrongs", stems from our understanding of this area as a matter of domestic law. As already noted, restitution for wrongs does not fit within the existing framework of autonomous unjust enrichment. The three basic elements to a claim in unjust enrichment are not all present. Although there is enrichment, the defendant's gain does not necessarily relate to a corresponding loss, or deprivation, to the plaintiff. The relevant connection between the plaintiff and the defendant's gain is that the gain has been made in breach of a duty to the plaintiff-victim. Restitution for wrongs cases award a restitutionary remedy in respect of a wrong. The relevant causative event is the wrong and not unjust enrichment. Taxonomically therefore, they form part of the law of wrongs, albeit with a restitutionary remedy.

Proceeding from such a proposition, while keeping in mind that characterisation is effected by the *lex fori* in a liberal manner, restitution for wrongdoing is to be characterised generally as a wrong and not as an issue of unjust enrichment. If the relevant causative event is the wrong and not unjust enrichment, then there must be compelling arguments to the contrary for characterising restitution for wrongs as anything other than a wrong, for the purposes of private international law. Both Bird and Stevens have concluded that such cases are to be characterised as wrongs.[178] In such an event, restitution for wrongs is really part of the area dealing with wrongs under private international law and strictly speaking falls beyond the scope of this book. Restitution for torts is to be characterised as a "tort", in accordance with the Private International Law

[176] Bird, p.76; Stevens, pp.187–91; Jaffey, p.278. Stevens considers that equitable wrongs should be characterised as torts. See also Dicey and Morris, pp.1487–8, 1499; Cheshire and North, pp.693–5.

[177] *Thahir* v. *Pertamina* [1994] 3 S.L.R. 257; *Arab Monetary Fund* v. *Hashim* [1996] 1 Lloyd's Rep. 589.

[178] Bird, p.76; Stevens, pp.187–91; see also Jaffey, p.278. McLeod has argued that "waiver of tort" cases should be characterised as restitutionary and not as tortious: J. McLeod, *The Conflict of Laws* (Calgary, 1983), p.573.

(Miscellaneous Provisions) Act 1995; where restitution is sought for breach of contract, this is to be characterised as a contractual matter, governed by the law applicable to the contract.

According to Dicey and Morris, restitution for torts cases are to be characterised as tortious.[179] However, it seems that all other restitution for wrongs claims are to be characterised as "restitution of an unjust enrichment".[180] This covers claims "in which a defendant is said to be in conscience obliged to compensate the claimant for breach of an obligation which arises neither from or in connection with a contract nor with tort".[181] It is said to include "claims such as for an account, or for equitable compensation, for breach of confidence" and extends to "the recovery of bribes accepted in breach of fiduciary duty". It is not particularly clear why this residual category of cases should be characterised as restitutionary. Some of the claims described are not even restitutionary in the remedial sense, while the causative event for all these claims is not unjust enrichment. What is particularly objectionable is that one is given the impression that these matters are to be characterised as restitutionary, if for no other reason, because they do not fit anywhere else. This approach is reminscent of the now outdated category of "quasi-contract", which comprised all those miscellaneous actions that did not fit within contract or tort. The question of whether restitution for wrongs cases are to be characterised as restitution, wrongs or otherwise must be answered through reasoning. They should not be placed into a category simply because they do not fit in anywhere else.

Assuming restitution for wrongs claims are to be characterised as wrongs, there are nevertheless certain further issues which need to be explored. Under certain civilian systems, what English domestic law refers to as restitution for wrongs forms part of the law of unjustified enrichment. This is, for example, the case as a matter of German[182] and Greek law.[183] Thus, a German or a Greek court is likely to characterise a claim for restitution for wrongdoing as lying in unjustified enrichment. For example, suppose the defendant allegedly infringes the plaintiff's intellectual property right in Germany by copying a particular product and selling it in England. In an action by the plaintiff seeking an account of profits, or restitution, a natural question of characterisation will arise. As a

[179] Dicey and Morris, pp.1487–8.

[180] *Id.*, p.1488.

[181] *Ibid.*

[182] This is where under German law the defendant is enriched other than by performance, as contained in the second limb of the general rule in §812(1). Restitution for wrongs is largely covered by the *Eingriffskondiktion* (interference with another's right): see Markesinis, pp.713, 740–1, 743–9.

[183] §904, Greek Civil Code, which is the general unjustified enrichment provision, provides that a person may be enriched, *inter alia*, from the property of, or, through causing damage to, another. The *Areios Pagos* (Supreme Court of Greece) has held that there does not need to be a correspondence between the plaintiff's impoverishment and the defendant's gain, while the word damage was also given a broad interpretation: (1959) *AΠ* 201/59, *No.B. T7*, *σ*.715. Stathopoulos argues that the infringement of a property, or similar right, will potentially attract the operation of Art. 904, even where actual loss has not been suffered by the plaintiff: Stathopoulos, pp.328–30.

matter of English law, the relevant issue would be characterised as a tort,[184] and thus the applicable law will be determined under ss. 11 and 12 of the Private International Law (Miscellaneous Provisions) Act 1995.[185] In contrast, the German court would be likely to characterise the relevant claim for restitution as a matter of unjustified enrichment.[186] This is a classic example of the type of problem envisaged by Cheshire and North in relation to characterisation.[187] That is where there is a clear difference in the way the *lex fori* and a potentially applicable foreign law may characterise the same matter. As discussed previously, characterisation is conducted by the *lex fori* and although a foreign court may characterise a matter differently, the *lex fori* should not be unduly influenced by this. Thus, in the example just cited, an English court should characterise the above issue as a matter of tort and not unjustified enrichment. It will do this in a liberal manner and therefore not insist that all the technical requirements of English law are met. This means that even if the alleged intellectual property infringement might not be recognised by English law, or does not constitute a tort as a matter of English domestic law, nevertheless the liberal *lex fori* will characterise this as a tort.[188]

4.2 Cases Dealing with International Restitution for Wrongs

The few cases dealing with international restitution for wrongs have not adopted a "wrongs" characterisation. Instead they have characterised the relevant matters as being in restitution. Notably, these cases have been instances of equitable wrongs. *Arab Monetary Fund* v. *Hashim*,[189] concerned a claim by the plaintiff to recover the proceeds of a bribe. The plaintiff brought alternative claims for breach of contract, tort and unjust enrichment. The Court of Appeal characterised the restitutionary claim to recover the bribe as being in unjust

[184] The infringement of intellectual property is characterised as tortious: see *House of Spring Gardens Ltd.* v. *Waite* [1991] 1 Q.B. 241, 253 (copyrights); *Mölnlycke AB* v. *Proctor & Gamble Ltd.* [1992] 1 W.L.R. 1112, 1117 (patents). See also Fawcett and Torremans, p.150.

[185] The general test which will be adopted to determine the applicable law will be the law of the country in which the most significant element or elements occurred: s.11(2)(c). Although the infringement may have occurred in Germany, it is arguable that the most significant element or elements occurred in England where the relevant product was sold, or alternatively that English law should apply under the exception in s.12.

[186] See for example BGH 9 March 1989, BGHZ 107, 117 (to be found in Markesinis, p.802, case 137).

[187] See above p.30.

[188] Section 9(2) of the Private International Law (Miscellaneous Provisions) Act 1995 provides that "characterisation is a matter for the courts of the forum". The preferred view is that this implies a liberal characterisation of "torts": See Dicey and Morris, pp.1517–18; Cheshire and North, pp.618–19; C. Morse, "Torts in Private International Law: A New Statutory Framework" (1996) 45 I.C.L.Q. 888, 893–4; A. Briggs, "Choice of law in tort and delict" [1995] L.M.C.L.Q. 519, 521–2; Fawcett and Torremans, p.150. *Cf.* however A. Briggs, "Choice of law in tort and delict" [1995] L.M.C.L.Q. 519, 521–2; P. Carter (1996) 112 L.Q.R. 190, 193.

[189] [1996] 1 Lloyd's Rep. 589. This case was decided after the publication of Barnard's article.

enrichment, thereby attracting the relevant choice of law rule.[190] It is noteworthy that the claim in tort was separately characterised and the double actionability rule was applied.[191] A similar approach was taken by the Court of Appeal of Singapore in *Thahir* v. *Pertamina*.[192] Pertamina, an Indonesian state enterprise, sought to recover bribes received by its former agent. The claims to recover such bribes, both at law and in equity, were characterised as restitutionary, falling within the corresponding choice of law rule in Dicey and Morris.

There is however a view that the restitutionary claim in *Arab Monetary Fund* v. *Hashim*, was characterised as being in unjust enrichment because it was not a restitution for wrongs case.[193] The plaintiff's claim for restitution can be explained in terms of subtractive unjust enrichment, in that there was a corresponding overpayment, and therefore impoverishment, by the plaintiff, which corresponded to the amount of the bribe.[194] Thus, the restitutionary characterisation was limited to the particular circumstances. On such an interpretation the case does not stand as authority for a general restitutionary characterisation of restitution for wrongs. This view is difficult to maintain. Admittedly, it was recognised by Evans J. that the plaintiff's right to recover the bribe from the bribe giver was on the basis that the latter received a greater contract sum than he should have.[195] However, although as a result of the bribe, the plaintiff may not necessarily have received as good a price over the relevant contract, it could not be said that the bribee's gain corresponded with the plaintiff's impoverishment so as to make this a case of unjust enrichment by subtraction.[196] This much was recognised by Evans J., but he stated that he did not have to decide this issue for the purposes of characterisation.[197] Under the *lex causae*, the law of Abu Dhabi, it was held to be an essential element of the claim in unjust enrichment that, the money paid to the bribe giver as an advance payment under the contract, was in fact given to Dr Hashim as a bribe;[198] that is to say, that the bribe was paid with the plaintiff's money. This could not be demonstrated and thus the claim in unjust enrichment against Dr Hashim failed at first instance.[199] Thus, the requirement of a correspondence between the plaintiff's impoverishment and the defendant's respective gains, was a prerequisite for the *lex causae*, but not for the purposes of characterisation. This can be confirmed in the Court of Appeal's judgment, which characterised the claim against Dr Hashim for the bribe as being restitutionary, without requiring that the bribe correspond to the impoverishment.[200]

190 *Id.*, 593, *per* Nourse L.J., 597, *per* Saville L.J.

191 *Ibid.*

192 *Thahir* v. *Pertamina* [1994] 3 S.L.R. 257.

193 See Bird, p.95.

194 See Birks, pp.337–8.

195 [1993] 1 Lloyd's Rep. 543, 565.

196 *Id.*, 564.

197 *Ibid.*

198 *Id.*, 581.

199 A claim in unjust enrichment was not available against a bribe giver under the law of Abu Dhabi, something conceded by the plaintiffs: *id.*, 566.

200 [1996] 1 Lloyd's Rep. 589, 597.

Both *Arab Monetary Fund* v. *Hashim* and *Thahir* v. *Pertamina* concerned breaches of fiduciary duty, or more generally equitable wrongs. It could therefore be said that these cases only apply in relation to equitable wrongs and that they do not stand for the general proposition that all disgorgement for wrongs cases are to be characterised as wrongs. At best, they may stand for a proposition that disgorgement for equitable wrongs is to be characterised as lying in restitution. It is submitted however that equitable wrongs should not be characterised as being in restitution and that therefore these cases were wrong on this particular point.

4.3 Characterisation of Equitable Wrongs

A separate issue therefore remains in relation to the characterisation of, what under English domestic law amount to, equitable wrongs. Stevens argues that equitable wrongs should be characterised as torts.[201] He argues that it is a historical accident that such claims are seen as different in kind from torts and therefore they should be characterised accordingly. On the other hand, both Bird[202] and Barnard[203] argue that equitable wrongs should be separately characterised, attracting their own choice of law rule.[204] This latter view is difficult to maintain. There is no authority to support a separate characterisation of equitable wrongs, while there do not seem to be compelling arguments for adopting such a view. Moreover, as has already been submitted, equitable obligations should not attract a separate characterisation but instead should be characterised by reference to the particular causative event giving rise to the equitable response.[205] That is, one should look to the legal counterpart of the particular equitable issue and characterise in accordance with such issue. As such, equitable wrongs should not be characterised separately but according to their legal counterpart, namely as wrongs. It is undesirable to have a separate conflicts rule for breaches of an equitable duty merely because they are in equity and not at law.

One of Barnard's strong arguments against a tort characterisation for equitable wrongs was the inappropriateness of the double actionability rule.[206] The common law choice of law rule for torts required actionability as a tort under the *lex fori*, together with civil actionability under the *lex loci delicti*,[207] subject to a flexible proper law exception, where such law has the most significant rela-

[201] Stevens, p.189.

[202] Bird, pp.92–6.

[203] L. Barnard, "Choice of Law in Equitable Wrongs" [1992] 474, 503–7.

[204] In a somewhat similar way, Cheshire and North argue that all restitution for wrongs cases should be separately characterised and thus attract a separate own choice of law rule: pp.694–5.

[205] Above, §2.

[206] L. Barnard, "Choice of Law in Equitable Wrongs" [1992] 474, 501.

[207] See Dicey and Morris, Rule 203; *Phillips* v. *Eyre* (1870) L.R. 6 Q.B. 1; *Boys* v. *Chaplin* [1971] A.C. 356.

tionship with the occurrence and the parties.[208] According to Barnard, the *lex loci delicti* is inappropriate to determine the lawfulness of a fiduciary's or confidant's conduct because, typically, equitable wrongs are committed in the context of a prior relationship. As such, the legal system governing such relationship has a much stronger claim to determine whether the fiduciary's conduct was wrongful. Application of the *lex loci* could result in the court declaring unlawful conduct which is permitted under the law governing the relationship, or vice versa. Similar arguments apply in relation to the *lex fori*.

With the abolition of the double actionability rule, as a result of the Private International Law (Miscellaneous Provisions) Act 1995,[209] part of Barnard's argument in favour of a separate choice of law rule for equitable wrongs survives. Under s.11(1) of the Act, "[t]he general rule is that the applicable law is the law of the country in which the events constituting the tort or delict in question occur".[210] This is essentially a *lex loci delicti* rule. However, under s.12 (1), the law of another "country" may apply where it is "substantially more appropriate", bearing in mind the significance of any factors connecting the "tort" with another "country". This exception may arguably cover those equitable wrongs where the existence of the particular relationship is more significant than the *locus* of the wrong.[211] As such, the applicable law would be the law of the particular relationship rather than the law of the place where the relevant breach, or the most significant elements constituting the relevant breach, occurred. One might however consider this an unsatisfactory approach, as equitable wrongs would invariably be treated as falling within the exception rather than general choice of law rule. Surely the exception is designed to cover exceptional factual situations rather than particular categories of claims?

It is submitted that equitable wrongs should not be treated as fitting into any one single category for the purpose of private international law.[212] Not all equitable wrongs are based on the breach of a pre-existing fiduciary relationship. Different types of equitable wrongs deserve different characterisations, thereby attracting the most appropriate choice of law rule. Equitable wrongs can be divided into three general categories: first, those which are based on the breach

[208] The double actionability rule could be departed from in an appropriate case, so that a particular issue, or even the entire question of liability, might be governed by a different law with which the particular issue was more closely connected. This exception was applied in *Red Sea Insurance Co. Ltd.* v. *Bouygues S.A.* [1995] 1 A.C. 190, such that a claim which technically did not amount to a tort under the *lex fori*, on the basis that there was no actual loss, amounted to a tort under the *lex loci delicti* and was therefore actionable as a tort.

[209] Although the double actionability rule is still applicable in relation to defamation claims: s.13.

[210] In cases where the elements of such events occur in different countries, then under s.11(2)(c) the applicable law is the law of the country in which the most significant element or elements of those events occurred. Again the focus is on the events constituting the tort and not on any prior relationship which gives rise to a duty.

[211] Section 12(2) provides that the factors that may be taken into account, in determining whether the law of another country is applicable, "include, in particular, factors relating to the parties, to any of the events which constitute the tort or delict in question or to any of the circumstances or consequences of those events". Such wording presumably will include a prior equitable relationship.

[212] See also Jaffey, pp.277–8.

of a trust; secondly, those which are based on the breach of a fiduciary relationship; and finally, those which are not based around any such relationship. It is only in the case of the former two, where there is a compelling argument for applying the law of the relationship. Naturally, in the case of the third, there is no such relationship and therefore such equitable wrongs do not involve the breach of a particular relationship but rather of a more general duty.

4.3.1 Characterisation of Equitable Wrongs as Breaches of Trust

Certain equitable wrongs are breaches of trust. Where a trustee or settlor uses his fiduciary position to acquire a benefit for himself he holds such benefit on constructive trust for the beneficiary.[213] In such situations, the fiduciary duty breached is one imposed by the trust. Therefore, the law of the relevant relationship, namely the law of the trust, is the most appropriate to determine the trustee's liability, including his liability to account for any wrongful gains.[214]

4.3.2 Characterisation of Equitable Wrongs as Breaches of Contract

There are those equitable wrongs which are breaches of a fiduciary relationship outside that of a trust. Typically, these include relationships of agent and principal, partners, solicitor and client, director and company, employer and employee.[215] Such relationships are usually created through a contract and are therefore contractual. Although it has been said that the "essence" of a fiduciary relationship is that "it creates obligations of a different character from those deriving from the contract itself",[216] evaluation of contract terms between the parties is still the primary consideration in determining whether a relationship is fiduciary.[217] The contractual character of fiduciary relationships is illustrated in *Coulthard* v. *Disco Mix Club Ltd*.[218] Claims against a fiduciary, to account in the manner of a constructive trustee and for account based on wilful default, were held to fall within the contractual limitation period. Even where, as a

[213] See for example *Keech* v. *Sandford* (1728) Cas. *temp*. King 61; *Ex p. Lacey* (1802) 6 Ves. 625; *Williams* v. *Scott* [1900] A.C. 499; *Wright* v. *Morgan* [1926] A.C. 788.

[214] The governing law of a trust is determined pursuant to Articles 6 and 7 of the Hague Convention, as contained in the Recognition of Trusts Act 1987. Pursuant to Art. 8, the applicable law determines, *inter alia*: (d) the power of trustees to administer or to dispose of trust assets, to create security interests in the trust assets, or to acquire new assets; (e) the powers of investment of trustees; (g) the relationships between the trustees and the beneficiaries including the personal liability of the trustees to the beneficiaries; (j) the duty of trustees to account for their administration.

[215] See *Hospital Products Ltd*. v. *United States Surgical Corporation* (1984) 156 C.L.R. 41, 96–7 *per* Mason J, on the nature of fiduciary relationships.

[216] *Re Goldcorp Exchange Ltd*. (in receivership) [1995] 1 A.C. 74, 98, *per* Lord Mustill (P.C.). See also *United Dominions Corporation* v. *Brian Pty Ltd*. (1985) 157 C.L.R. 1, 11, *per* Mason, Brennan and Deane J.J. (H.C.A.). Also S. Worthington, "Fiduciaries: When is Self-Denial Obligatory?" [1999] C.L.J. 500.

[217] J. Glover, *Commercial Equity—Fiduciary Relationships* (Melbourne, 1995), p.45; P. Finn, "Contract and the Fiduciary Principle" (1989) 12 U.N.S.W.L.J. 76, 89–92.

[218] [2000] 1W.L.R. 707. See also *Companhia de Segura Imperio* v. *Heath (Rebx) Ltd*, 20 July 2000 (unreported) (C.A.).

matter of domestic law, there may possibly be no actual contract between the parties, the essence of the relationship is consent based.[219] Therefore it must be considered a consensual or contractual relationship for the purposes of private international law.[220] Thus, in *Upper Lakes Shipping Ltd.* v. *Foster Yeoman Ltd.*,[221] Borins J. held that a claim for breach of fiduciary duty came within the contractual provisions, in the Rules of Civil Procedure of Ontario, for service out of the jurisdiction.[222]

At common law, a relationship may be considered contractual, for the purposes of private international law, even though it may not amount to a contract as a matter of domestic law.[223] Most contractual relationships are now governed by the Contracts (Applicable Law) Act 1990, giving effect to the Rome Convention.[224] The notion of contract is also likely to receive a broad interpretation, which will not be limited to obligations which are regarded as contractual by the domestic law of the forum.[225] Such an approach has been adopted by the European Court in relation to the Brussels Convention[226] in the context of jurisdiction. An autonomous definition of contract has been adopted in relation to the phrase "matters relating to a contract".[227] A matter does not relate to a contract where "there does not exist an undertaking freely entered into by one party in relation to another".[228] It is therefore concluded, that equitable wrongs in the context of fiduciary relationships outside the field of trusts are to be characterised as contractual issues, both where the Rome Convention or the common law rules apply.

Accepting that fiduciary relationships outside of trusts are to be characterised as contractual, one still arrives at the same result in *Arab Monetary Fund* v. *Hashim*.[229] The Arab Monetary Fund's (AMF) claim for disgorgement of the bribe

219 See L. Smith, "Fiduciary Relationships—Arising in Commercial Contexts—Investment Advisor: *Hodgkinson* v. *Simms* (1995) 74 C.B.R. 714, 721–5; L. Smith, "Constructive Fiduciaries" in P. Birks (ed.), *Privacy and Loyalty* (Oxford, 1997), pp. 249, 263–4 (hereafter Smith, "Constructive Fiduciaries").

220 In *Paramasivam* v. *Flynn* (1998) 160 A.L.R. 203, 217, the full court of the Federal Court of Australia indicated in favour of characterising fiduciary relationships as contractual, where the source of the fiduciary relationship is a contract, or where it amounts to a relationship between a corporation and its officers or directors.

221 (1993) 14 O.R. (3rd) 548, 562 (O.C.J.).

222 See also *National Bank of Canada* v. *Clifford Chance* (1996) 30 O.R. (3d) 746, 761–2 (O.C.J.).

223 *Re Bonacina* [1912] 2 Ch. 394 (C.A.).

224 There are certain contractual relationships which are not covered by the Rome Convention. These are set out in Art. 1(2) and for present purposes, may include questions governed by the law of companies and other bodies corporate or unincorporate: Art. 1(2)(e).

225 Dicey and Morris, p.1204; P. Lagarde (1991) Rev. Crit. at 292–3. See also Cheshire and North, pp.543–4.

226 See generally ch. 8.2.

227 This phrase appears in Art. 5.1 which confers jurisdiction "in matters relating to a contract, in the courts for the place of performance of the obligation in question".

228 *Handte* v. *Traitements Mécano-chimiques des Surfaces* [1992] E.C.R. I–3967; see also *Peters* v. *Zuid Nederlandse Aannemers Vereniging* [1983] E.C.R. 987; *Arcado* v. *Haviland* [1988] E.C.R. 1539; *Powell Duffryn* v. *Petereit* [1992] E.C.R. I–1745; *Réunion Européene S.A.* v. *Spliethoff's Bevrachtingskantoor B.V.* (51/97) [1999] I.L.Pr.205.

229 [1996] 1 Lloyd's Rep. 589. This case was decided after the publication of Barnard's article.

was characterised as restitutionary and governed by the law of Abu Dhabi. The law of Abu Dhabi applied as the proper law of the obligation, bearing in mind a number of factors pointing to the law of Abu Dhabi. Dr Hashim's "relationship" with the Arab Monetary Fund was also governed by the law of Abu Dhabi.[230] Thus, if the disgorgement sought for Dr Hashim's breach of duty as a result of the bribe was properly characterised as contractual, nevertheless, it still would have been governed by the law of Abu Dhabi.

Finally, it should be noted that there may be instances, under certain legal systems, where a particular relationship or obligation is considered fiduciary even though it is not consensual based.[231] A relationship of guardian and minor, for example, may under some legal systems be considered fiduciary. Where particular conduct complained of is alleged to amount to a breach of such a fiduciary relationship, this should not be characterised as a contractual matter, governed by a particular law. Instead, such a breach should be characterised as a tort governed by the choice of law rules for torts. Thus, in *Paramasivam* v. *Flynn*,[232] the Federal Court of Australia did not recognise the relationship of a guardian and a minor as fiduciary. The breach of the alleged fiduciary relationship was classified as a tort.[233]

4.3.3 *Characterisation of Equitable Wrongs as "Wrongs"*

Finally, there are those equitable wrongs which do not involve an actual breach of a fiduciary relationship. Cases of knowing[234] assistance[235] are an example falling within this category.[236] Third parties may become liable if they knowingly assist a fiduciary breach his fiduciary relationship. In *Royal Brunei Airlines*

[230] *Arab Monetary Fund* v. *Hashim* [1993] 1 Lloyd's Rep. 543, 566, *per* Evans J; *Arab Monetary Fund* v. *Hashim* [1996] 1 Lloyd's Rep. 589, 597, *per* Nourse L.J. Similarly in *Arab Monetary Fund* v. *Hashim*, 15 June 1994 (unreported), a restitutionary claim relating to a breach of a fiduciary duty was held to be governed by the law governing the employment relationship between the plaintiff and the defendants. The duties owed under that legal relationship were akin to fiduciary duties and it was immaterial if the law applicable to such a relationship would describe them as such. See also *Kuwait Oil Tanker Company S.A.K.* v. *Al Bader*, 16 November 1998 (unreported) (Q.B.D.).

[231] See *M(K)* v. *M(H)* (1992) 96 D.L.R. (4th) 289; *contra Paramasivam* v. *Flynn* (1998) 160 A.L.R. 203, 218–21 (F.C.A.).

[232] (1998) 160 A.L.R. 203.

[233] *Id.*, 219. Although it was said that the law applicable to a fiduciary claim was the *lex fori* where such a fiduciary relationship was not contractual in nature, this was ultimately of little consequence given that the claim was not recognised as fiduciary but rather as tortious. Moreover, it has already been submitted that the view that equitable issues are governed by the *lex fori* is incorrect: above §2.

[234] In *Royal Brunei Airlines* v. *Tan* [1995] 2 A.C. 378 the Privy Council stated that the word "dishonest" was to be preferred from the word "knowing", to describe the liability of an accessory to a trustee's breach of trust: *id.*, 391C.

[235] See *Barnes* v. *Addy* (1874) 9 Ch. App. 244, 251–2; *Selangor United Rubber Estates Ltd.* v. *Craddock (No.3)* [1968] 1 W.L.R. 1555; *Belmont Finance Corporation Ltd.* v. *Williams Furniture Ltd.* [1979] Ch. 250 (C.A.); *Consul Development Pty Ltd.* v. *D.P.C. Estates Pty Ltd.* (1975) 132 C.L.R. 373 (H.C.A.).

[236] Another possible example is what is called *executor* or *trustee de son tort*. See C. Harpum, "The Basis of Equitable Liability" in P. Birks (ed.), *Frontiers of Liability* (Oxford, 1994) 9; P.H. Pettit, *Equity and the Law of Trusts*, 8th ed. (London, 1993), p.140.

Shn. Bhd. v. *Tan*,[237] it was said that such action is equity's version of the tort of inducing contractual breaches.[238] Such matters should clearly be characterised as torts and not as a breach of a relationship. It is inappropriate to apply the law of the particular relationship as the potential defendant is not privy to it. It is preferable to apply the rule applicable to other torts, namely a rule akin to the *lex loci delicti rule*. Subject to the application of any possible exceptions, the defaulting defendant should be liable in accordance with the law of the place where the events constituting the equitable wrong occurred.

In *Arab Monetary Fund* v. *Hashim (No.9)*[239] a claim for knowing assistance was characterised as a tort.[240] Chadwick J. stated that requirement that a claim amount to "tort" according to English law, was not confined to claims in tort "in the strict, common law, sense". Chadwick J. stated that in cases of knowing assistance the "defendant is held liable in equity not because he is, or has been, a trustee of trust property; but because his conduct in relation to trust property has been such that he ought to be liable in damages for its loss".[241]

A "tort" characterisation will apply *a fortiori* to this category of equitable wrongs, as a result of the Private International Law (Miscellaneous Provisions) Act 1995. Under the Act, the relevant choice of law rules apply to issues relating to tort.[242] What constitutes issues relating to a tort is a matter of characterisation for the courts of the forum.[243] An issue may be characterised as relating to a tort, even though it may not amount to a tort for the purposes of domestic law.[244] Therefore, there is a strong argument for saying that such equitable wrongs are now to be characterised as torts for the purposes of private international law.[245] Moreover, although it is said that s. 14(2), when read together with s. 10, limits the operation of the Act to those matters which were previously governed by the rule in *Boys* v. *Chaplin*,[246] as has already been demonstrated, equitable wrongs, such as knowing assistance, were already governed by this rule as a result of Chadwick J.'s judgment in *Arab Monetary Fund* v. *Hashim (No.9)*.[247]

[237] [1995] 2 A.C. 378.

[238] *Id.*, 387B–C. A similar parallel between knowing assistance and tort was also drawn by Hoffmann L.J. in *Polly Peck International plc* v. *Nadir* (unreported), 17 March 1993, transcript, 13. See also Smith, "Constructive Fiduciaries", pp.258–61. Meagher, Gummow and Lehane, p.881.

[239] *The Times*, 11 October 1994.

[240] See also *Grupo Torras S.A.* v. *Al-Sabah* [1999] C.L.C. 1,469 (Q.B.D.).

[241] Transcript, 42. It should be noted that the Court of Appeal in *Metall und Rohstoff AG* v. *Donaldson Lufkin & Jenrette Inc.* [1990] 1 Q.B. 391, held that a claim based on knowing assistance was not "founded on a tort" for jurisdiction purposes. It is nevertheless submitted that the approach of Chadwick J. is to be preferred.

[242] Section 9(1).

[243] Section 9(2).

[244] See Dicey and Morris, pp.1517–18; Cheshire and North, pp.618–19; A. Briggs, "Choice of law in tort and delict" [1995] L.M.C.L.Q. 519, 521–2; Fawcett and Torremans, p.150. *Cf.* however Carter (1996) 112 L.Q.R. 190, 193.

[245] See also Stevens, p.189.

[246] See A. Briggs, "Choice of law in tort and delict" [1995] L.M.C.L.Q. 519, 521–2.

[247] *The Times*, 11 October 1994. See also *Coin Controls Ltd.* v. *Suzo International (U.K.) Ltd.* [1999] Ch. 33, 43 G–H, *per* Laddie J.

4.3.4 Claims for "Knowing Receipt"

One final issue remains in relation to equitable wrongs. That is the question of how to characterise what, under domestic law, are referred to as claims for "knowing receipt", as wrongs or as matters of unjust enrichment? There are judicial statements which classify the action of knowing receipt as restitutionary. In *El Ajou* v. *Dollar Land Holdings plc*,[248] Millett J. recognised the action for knowing receipt as equity's counterpart to the common law action for money had and received, and that "both can be classified as receipt based restitutionary claims".[249] Likewise the Privy Council in *Royal Brunei Airlines* v. *Tan* compared knowing receipt and knowing assistance and stated: "Different considerations apply to the two heads of liability. Recipient liability is restitution-based; accessory liability is not".[250] More categorically, in *Koorootang* v. *A.N.Z. Banking Group*,[251] Hansen J. found "considerable persuasion" in the view that knowing receipt "is most appropriately governed and explained by the law of restitution of unjust enrichment".

It has been pointed out that "a claim can be described as restitutionary even though it is not generated by the substantive law of unjust enrichment".[252] Thus, Smith argues, knowing receipt is "equity's analogue to the claim in conversion". Liability for an unjust enrichment is strict,[253] whereas liability for knowing receipt is fault based.[254] Moreover, Smith argues that even if one were to consider knowing receipt as an exceptional case of unjust enrichment in which fault needed to be shown, the existence of "supervening liability" is consistent only with equity's conversion. A defendant who receives property without the requisite mental state is not liable; but he will become so if he acquires that mental state while he still holds the property, or its traceable proceeds. This it is argued makes knowing receipt appear more like a wrong.[255]

Nevertheless, it is submitted that matters of knowing receipt should be characterised as issues of unjust enrichment. First, although unjust enrichment does not require fault, neither does conversion. The fact that the defendant requires knowledge does not actually make the action a wrong. Secondly, although knowledge is a requisite element, the action is based upon the receipt of value and not merely by virtue of a breach of duty. Moreover, the defendant is obliged

[248] [1993] 3 All E.R. 717 (reversed on different grounds) [1994] 2 All E.R. 685.

[249] *Id.*, 736. See also *Nelson* v. *Larholt* [1948] 1 K.B. 339, 343, *per* Denning J.; *Grupo Torras S.A.* v. *Al-Sabah* [1999] C.L.C. 1,469 (Q.B.D.).

[250] [1995] 2 A.C. 378, 386F. Also *Polly Peck International plc.* v. *Nadir* (unreported) 17 March 1993, *per* Hoffmann L.J.

[251] [1998] 3 V.R. 16, 100.

[252] L. Smith, "W(h)ither Knowing Receipt?" (1998) 114 L.Q.R. 394. Moreover, the reference to "money had and received" can also be taken as also referring to the old "waiver of tort" cases.

[253] *Lipkin Gorman* v. *Karpnale Ltd.* [1991] 2 A.C. 548.

[254] There is a significant issue of what the requisite degree of knowledge is in a case of "knowing receipt" as a matter of English domestic law. This issue is beyond the scope of this work. See however S. Gardner, "Knowing Assistance and Knowing Receipt: Taking Stock" (1996) 112 L.Q.R. 56.

[255] L. Smith, "W(h)ither Knowing Receipt?" (1998) 114 L.Q.R. 394, 396.

to make restitution of what he received. Unlike cases of disgorgement for wrongdoing, the defendant's gain *will* correspond with the plaintiff's impoverishment. This factor would suggest to the liberal *lex fori* that such liability should be characterised as unjust enrichment. Thirdly, although the above *dicta* refer to "restitutionary" and not "unjust enrichment", the relevant comments were, it is submitted, made in the context of restitution as a separate form of liability, as opposed to restitution as a remedy. The relevant comments by Millett J. in *El Ajou* were followed by a reference to the choice of law rule for restitution in Dicey and Morris, as well as to *Chase Manhattan Bank N.A.* v. *Israel-British Bank (London) Ltd.*,[256] so as to ascertain the applicable law. As such, the references to the common law "action for money had and received" and to "receipt-based restitutionary liability" clearly envisaged restitution as a separate basis of liability. Likewise, the comment by the Privy Council must be read in light of its earlier comment, where it drew a parallel between the accessory liability of a person who knowingly assists a fiduciary to commit a breach and the tort of inducing contractual breaches.[257] The contrast between knowing receipt and knowing assistance becomes clearer; knowing receipt is "restitution-based" and is unlike knowing assistance, which is akin to a tort.

Fourthly, it may be argued that the element of "knowledge" in cases of knowing receipt is merely equity's way of accommodating the defence of change of position.[258] After all, this defence was only judicially recognised in 1991.[259] A defendant who no longer retains the value received, and has therefore changed his position, will only be liable for knowing receipt where he had the requisite "knowledge"; that is where he was not *bona fide*. Where the defendant is an innocent recipient he will not be liable as a constructive trustee for knowing receipt but what is referred to as a "tracing claim".[260] The extent of his liability therefore will be limited to the traceable value of the plaintiff's property which has survived in his hands. Finally, there has been growing support for the removal of the knowledge requirement in claims for knowing receipt and making such liability strictly subject to a defence of change of position.[261] This lends

[256] [1981] Ch. 105. It will be recalled that this case was concerned with a mistaken payment.

[257] *Royal Brunei Airlines* v. *Tan* [1995] 2 A.C. 378, 387B–C.

[258] See C. Harpum, "The Basis of Equitable Liability" in P. Birks (ed.), *The Frontiers of Liability*, Vol. 1 (1994), pp.9–25; P. Birks, "Misdirected Funds: Restitution from the Recipient" [1989] L.M.C.L.Q. 296, 304.

[259] *Lipkin Gorman* v. *Karpnale Ltd.* [1991] 2 A.C. 548. See ch. 1.6.1.

[260] See *Agip (Africa) Ltd.* v. *Jackson* [1990] 1 Ch. 265, 290, *per* Millett J; *Eagle Trust plc* v. *S.B.C. Securities Ltd.* [1992] 4 All E.R. 488, 500, *per* Vinelott J.; *El Ajou* v. *Dollar Land Holdings Plc* [1993] 3 All E.R. 717, 739, *per* Millett J. (reversed on different grounds) [1994] 2 All E.R. 685. In *Polly Peck International plc* v. *Nadir (No.2)* [1992] 4 All E.R. 769, Scott L.J. considered that the degree of knowledge required in relation to the knowing receipt claim, was also required in relation to the equitable tracing claim.

[261] See *Koorootang* v. *A.N.Z. Banking Group* [1998] 3 V.R. 17, 105; Goff and Jones, pp.745–6; P. Millett, "Tracing the Proceeds of Fraud" (1991) 107 L.Q.R. 71, 85; P. Birks, "The Recovery of Misapplied Assets" in E. McKendrick (ed.), *Commercial Aspects of Trusts and Fiduciary Obligations* (Oxford, 1992) 149, pp.159–61; Birks, *Restitution—Future*, ch. 2; Lord Nicholls, "Knowing Receipt: The Need for a New Landmark" in Cornish *et. al.* (ed.), *Restitution: Past, Present and Future* (Oxford, 1998) 231, pp.244–5; C. Harpum, "Knowing Receipt: The Need for a

further weight to the argument that such liability should be viewed as lying in unjust enrichment.

5 A SEPARATE ISSUE OF TRACING?[262]

Tracing is an essential component of many restitutionary claims.[263] It could be argued that tracing raises a separate issue for the purposes of characterisation. The question of international tracing, that is tracing in the context of claims involving international elements, is one for which there is no clear guidance. Is tracing to be treated as an adjunct to the related claim and thus governed by the same choice of law rule; or is it to be treated as raising a separate issue, thereby attracting its own choice of law rule?

It should be noted that not all claims involving tracing will necessarily be generated by unjust enrichment. An example of an unjust enrichment claim involving tracing is where a mistaken payer brings a claim in relation to the identifiable proceeds of a mistaken payment.[264] At the other end of the spectrum, a seller might claim proprietary rights in the proceeds of a buyer's sale of goods, where the relevant sales contract provides that the seller retains legal or equitable ownership of the goods.[265] Although tracing is relevant to both claims, it cannot be confidently said that they both raise issues of unjust enrichment. While the former is clearly a claim in unjust enrichment, the latter is not; yet both raise a potential tracing issue. The role of tracing under private international law must be addressed, as a self-contained issue, so as to properly understand restitution in private international law.

5.1 The Tracing Problem

Claims of the type set out above may contain international elements and thus the process of tracing may collide with the conflict of laws. For example, a plaintiff may wish to bring a personal or proprietary claim in relation to value received or surviving outside the jurisdiction.[266] That is, stolen moneys may

New Landmark: Some Reflections" in Cornish *et. al.* (ed.), *Restitution: Past, Present and Future* (Oxford, 1998), pp.247–50; J. Martin, "Recipient Liability after Westdeutsche" [1998] Conv. 13.

[262] See generally Smith, pp.274–6; G. Panagopoulos, "Cross-Border Tracing" [1998] R.L.R. 73.

[263] See generally ch. 5.1 and 5.2.

[264] See for example *Chase Manhattan Bank N.A.* v. *Israel-British Bank (London) Ltd.* [1981] ch. 105.

[265] See for example *Aluminium Industrie Vaasen BV* v. *Romalpa Aluminium Ltd.* [1976] 1 W.L.R. 676 (C.A.); N. Palmer, "Reservation of Title" (1992) 5 J. of Contract Law 175; B. Collier, *Romalpa Clauses: Reservation of Title in Sale of Goods Transactions* (Sydney, 1989); G. Mckormack, *Reservation of Title*, 2nd ed. (London, 1995).

[266] See for example *Chase Manhattan Bank N.A.* v. *Israel-British Bank (London) Ltd.* [1981] Ch. 105; see also *Macmillan Inc* v. *Bishopsgate Investment Trust Plc* [1996] 1 W.L.R. 387. See also the facts of *A.G. for Hong Kong* v. *Reid* [1994] 1 A.C. 324.

have been used to acquire property in a foreign jurisdiction. Alternatively, the plaintiff may need to trace through foreign jurisdictions into value received or surviving in the defendant's hands within the jurisdiction.[267] For example, stolen moneys may have been channelled through several foreign bank accounts before being returned to the jurisdiction. In such cases, a potentially separate issue of tracing may arise. Although the relevant issue in the plaintiff's claim may have been characterised in a particular way and thereby attracted its own choice of law rule, it could be argued that the question of whether the plaintiff can successfully trace is a separate issue, which could potentially attract its own choice of law rule.

In practical terms, an international tracing issue should only arise in two particular types of situations. First, there is the situation where although the *lex fori* may recognise a successful tracing exercise, it is not recognised under one of the potentially applicable foreign laws. For example, moneys may have been mistakenly paid from an English bank account into a German bank account and then transferred into an Austrian bank account. The plaintiff may therefore have to trace through, or into, foreign jurisdictions which do not recognise tracing. Secondly, there is the situation where a difference exists between the tracing rules of the *lex causae* and of the *lex fori*. That is, although tracing may be recognised by both potentially applicable laws, one may be more flexible or liberal, or allow tracing in circumstances where the other will not. For example, in this case, moneys may have mistakenly been paid from an English bank account into an Australian one. A question may arise as to whether a fiduciary relationship is required as a prerequisite to tracing in equity. There is no requirement of a fiduciary relationship to trace in equity under Australian law.[268] Thus, if the plaintiff is unable to demonstrate the existence of a fiduciary relationship, the success of the claim may depend on whether the tracing exercise is governed by Australian or English law. It will therefore be significant to determine which law applies to the tracing exercise if the success of the plaintiff's claim depends on the relevant tracing rules.

5.2 The Approaches

There are three main approaches which could be adopted in relation to the characterisation of tracing. First, it could be said that as tracing is a process and not a right or remedy, it is a procedural mechanism employed by the court to identify the whereabouts of value. That is, tracing in itself does not create any rights; it merely raises certain evidentiary presumptions. Being procedural, it therefore should be governed by the *lex fori*. Other potentially applicable laws have nothing admissible to say on the matter. Secondly, tracing could be seen as an issue

[267] See *El Ajou* v. *Dollar Land Holdings Plc* [1993] 3 All E.R. 717 (reversed on different grounds) [1994] 2 All E.R. 685.

[268] *Black* v. *Freedman* (1910) 12 C.L.R. 105, 110, *per* O'Connor J; *Australian Postal Corporation* v. *Lutak* (1991) 21 N.S.W.L.R. 584, 589.

in its own right which may attract its own choice of law rule. Finally, it could be said that although a substantive issue, tracing is an extension of rights with an independent source, and therefore, it is an issue which should be governed by the *lex causae*. In other words, the tracing issue is to be governed by the law governing the substantial issue to which the tracing exercise relates.

5.2.1 *Procedural or Substantive Issue?*

It could be argued that as tracing is merely a process, which in itself does not create any rights, it should be characterised as procedural and thus governed by the rules of the *lex fori*.[269] However, it is submitted that where a tracing issue arises, it should be characterised as a substantial issue to be governed by the *lex causae*.[270] First, tracing is not a matter which is directed at governing or regulating the mode or conduct of court proceedings. Only those issues which "[form] part of the mechanism of the machinery of litigation, or [are] directed to the regulation of the mode or conduct of court proceedings"[271] should be characterised as procedural.

Secondly, if the *lex causae* relating to the claim does not recognise tracing, the ability to trace will be pointless, irrespective of whether it is recognised by the *lex fori*. As noted above, the process of tracing and claiming are separate. However, where the law applicable to the relevant claim does not recognise claims contingent on tracing, there is nothing the *lex fori* can add to the matter. Thirdly, tracing exists both at law and in equity, each one governed by slightly different rules. Thus, the type of tracing rules which are employed will need to be determined by whether the plaintiff is claiming at law or in equity. Furthermore, some of the tracing rules and presumptions in equity, depend on whether the defendant is innocent or a wrongdoer.[272] These distinctions in the tracing rules suggest that tracing should be viewed as an issue of substance to be determined by the *lex causae* applicable to the particular claim. Moreover, whether one can trace in equity must surely depend on whether the *lex causae* recognises equitable claims. At least on present authority, a fiduciary relationship is a pre-requisite to a successful tracing exercise in equity.[273] It would be ludicrous if the *lex fori* was searching for a fiduciary relationship to allow tracing in equity, when under the *lex causae* no such requirement was necessary. The pre-requisite of a fiduciary relationship makes the tracing process seem more like an issue of substance rather than procedural. This last argument can be extended by saying that if tracing were governed by the *lex fori*, a degree of

[269] For the proposition that matters of procedure are governed by the *lex fori* see generally Dicey and Morris, Rule 17; see also *Huber* v. *Steiner* (1835) Bing N.C. 202; *Leroux* v. *Brown* (1852) 12 C.B. 801; *Mahadervan* v. *Mahadervan* [1964] p.233; *Boys* v. *Chaplin* [1971] A.C. 356; *McKain* v. *Miller* (1991) 174 C.L.R. 1 (H.C.A.); *Stevens* v. *Head* (1993) 176 C.L.R. 433 (H.C.A.).

[270] See also Smith, p.275; Bird, p.86. *Cf.* Stevens, pp.211–12.

[271] *McKain* v. *Miller* (1991) 174 C.L.R. 1, 27, *per* Mason C.J. (H.C.A.).

[272] See for example *Re Hallet's Estate* (1880) 13 Ch. D. 696; *Re Oatway* [1903] 2 Ch. 356.

[273] See above pp. 20–1.

double actionability may arise. Although a plaintiff may be able to trace the value of his property into the defendant's hands pursuant to the *lex causae's* tracing rules, his claim may fail if the tracing process is thwarted by the *lex fori's* stricter requirements. It must be contrary to common sense to defeat a claim which would succeed under the *lex causae*, but fails due to a procedural characterisation of tracing. Similarly, where the converse applied, such that the *lex causae's* tracing requirements are stricter, it would also be inappropriate to allow a claim on the basis of the *lex fori's* more liberal tracing rules, when such a claim would not succeed under the *lex causae*.

Finally, it is submitted that in *Chase Manhattan Bank N.A.* v. *Israel-British Bank (London) Ltd.*,[274] the plaintiff's ability to trace was governed by the *lex causae*, namely the law of New York.[275] Goulding J. relevantly described the issue as "whether the equitable right of a person who pays money by mistake to trace *and* claim such money under the law of New York is conferred by substantive law or is of a merely procedural character".[276] (*emphasis added*). His Lordship found that under New York law the defendant had become a constructive trustee of the moneys and that this arose "by a rule of substantive law and is not the mere result of a remedial or procedural rule".[277] Although Goulding J. further held that there was no significant difference between the law of New York and England,[278] in relation to the imposition of a constructive trust for mistaken payments, and thus that no conflict arose, the finding that the constructive trust arose as a matter of substantive law was crucial.[279] As the defendant's assets had already been impressed with a trust, as a result of the winding-up proceedings, the plaintiff needed to show that the constructive trust had arisen as a matter of substantive law and not under a remedial rule, governed by the *lex fori*. In this way, the plaintiff's money would have remained unaffected by the winding up proceedings. As it was agreed that the substantive law was that of New York, the plaintiff therefore had to show that the constructive trust had arisen by the law of New York, prior to the winding-up proceedings.[280] As already illustrated, the constructive trust which arose, comprised of both the process of tracing *and* claiming, and thus both were governed by the *lex causae*.

5.2.2 *A Separate Choice of Law Rule?*

Assuming that tracing is a not a procedural issue, the next question is whether it attracts its own separate choice of law rule. The view that tracing may attract

[274] [1981] Ch. 105.

[275] *Cf.* Smith, p.275.

[276] *Chase Manhattan Bank N.A.* v. *Israel-British Bank (London) Ltd.* [1981] 1 Ch 105, 122D.

[277] *Id.*, 127B.

[278] *Id.*, 118E, 120A, 128A–B

[279] *Cf.* Burrows, p.497.

[280] This is also consistent with Lord Browne-Wilkinson's reinterpretation of *Chase-Manhattan* in *Westdeutsche Landesbank Girozentrale* v. *Islington LBC* [1996] A.C. 669, 714–15, where he concludes that the law of New York and England were in fact different: *id.*, 837.

its own distinct choice of law rule was rejected by Millett J. in *El Ajou* v. *Dollar Holdings plc*.[281] It was recognised by his Lordship that tracing could be characterised either as procedural, and therefore governed by the *lex fori*, or as a substantive issue to be governed by the law governing the restitutionary obligation.[282] It was not necessary to give a final decision on that point in *El Ajou*, as on either footing it was to be governed by English law. What is clear is that tracing is not to be separately characterised and thus governed by its own choice of law rule. As a consequence, a plaintiff may be able to trace through jurisdictions which do not recognise tracing. It was stated that:

> [w]here [assets] have passed through many different hands in many different countries, they may be difficult to trace; but . . . neither their temporary repose in a civil law country not their receipt by intermediate recipients outside the jurisdiction should prevent the court from treating assets in the legal ownership of a defendant within the jurisdiction as trust assets.[283]

Therefore, according to Millett J., the ability to trace, at least in equity, does not require that every intermediate recipient be amenable to the court's jurisdiction but only that the defendant is. This is because the plaintiff's ability to trace is "dependent on the power of equity to charge a mixed fund with the repayment of trust moneys, not upon any actual exercise of that power".[284] Although the dicta of Millett J. are in terms of jurisdiction and tracing in equity, they nevertheless help illustrate how an international tracing issue should be treated.

It is submitted that the approach of Millett J. is correct and that an issue of tracing should not be characterised as a separate issue, attracting its own choice of law rule. First, although tracing is an issue of substance, it is not a source of rights. As discussed, tracing may be relevant to a wide variety of claims. Tracing merely extends, to other assets or defendants, rights with an independent source.[285] As noted by Birks: "Anyone can have a go at tracing. If you have a go, you may or may not succeed in locating the value of one asset in another. If you do succeed, it does not follow that you can make any claim. The background facts are important to claiming, not to tracing".[286] Thus, the most logical approach in relation to international tracing is to apply the choice of law rule relating to the relevant claim contingent on tracing.

Secondly, if a separate choice of law rule were to apply to tracing issues, what would it be? It would be difficult to imagine something other than some form of recognition by the relevant alternative jurisdictions. This would raise the fur-

[281] [1993] 3 All E.R. 717 (reversed by the Court of Appeal on different grounds).

[282] [1993] 3 All E.R. 736.

[283] *Id.*, 737.

[284] *Ibid.*

[285] Smith concludes that although a matter of substance, tracing should not attract a separate choice of law rule. Although "it is a substantive part of proving a right or claim, nonetheless it is not essentially a source of rights": Smith, p.276. Although the author agrees with this proposition, it is essentially based on our domestic law understanding of tracing. As will become apparent, there are further compelling arguments for adopting this position from a private international law perspective, as well as certain ancillary issues which also need to be addressed.

[286] Birks, *Laundering and Tracing*, p.297.

ther problem of whether the plaintiff must show a vested proprietary interest under the law of each intermediate jurisdiction, or whether he would merely need to show that the particular tracing exercise is recognised by the relevant jurisdictions. The dictum of Millett J. in *El Ajou* makes perfectly good sense. Where a plaintiff merely needs to trace *through* foreign jurisdictions, the success of his claim should not depend on whether the foreign jurisdictions recognise tracing, or that he has a valid claim under the law of each jurisdiction. Fraudsters could thereby defeat legitimate claims merely by channelling funds through the right jurisdictions.

Thirdly, a choice of law rule which reflects the interests of the foreign intermediary jurisdictions could not be said to be protecting certainty and security of transactions. One of the main policy arguments in favour of the *lex situs* rule is based on its efficacy *vis-à-vis* third parties. So as to ensure certainty in relation to real rights, a third party intending to acquire an interest in property must be protected from the risk that such a thing might be subject to a foreign law.[287] Such an argument can hardly be said to be a legitimate policy consideration in relation to funds, which often only notionally, pass through a particular jurisdiction.

Furthermore, where someone traces *into* a foreign jurisdiction, such that the value received, or surviving, is in a foreign jurisdiction, there is again no real reason for separately characterising the tracing issue. If the concern was to protect the interests of the *lex situs*, this would presumably be taken care of by any proprietary issue which might arise. For example, where stolen moneys are used to purchase a car in a foreign jurisdiction, which is then sold on to the defendant, a plaintiff's claim to the beneficial title of such a car may be met by a defence of *bona fide* purchase. This would raise an issue of title and therefore attract the choice of law rule for the transfer of tangible moveables.[288] Such an issue would raise a proprietary characterisation and therefore attract the *lex situs* or a choice of law rule reflecting the proprietary nature of the issue. Thus, the interests of the *lex situs* can be accommodated accordingly.

A separate choice of law rule for tracing issues which took into account the interests of the alternative jurisdictions would, it is submitted, be inconsistent with our understanding of tracing. What is being traced is value and not property or assets. The tracing process does not create any rights or remedies in itself. A claim may however be brought in relation to the traceable proceeds. As recognised by Millett J. in *El Ajou*, it must be the tracing rules of either the *lex fori* or the *lex causae* (of the relevant issue arising in the claim), which should apply.

5.2.3 "Characterisation" of Tracing

It is therefore submitted that tracing should neither be characterised as a matter of procedure, to be governed by the *lex fori*, nor as a separate issue attracting its

287 *Re Anziani* [1930] 1 Ch. 407, 420; *Macmillan Inc.* v. *Bishopsgate Investment Trust Plc (No.3)* [1996] 1 W.L.R. 387, 424–5, *per* Aldous L.J.; M. Wolff, *Private International Law*, 2nd ed. (Clarendon Press, Oxford, 1950), pp.511–12; Cheshire and North, p.942.

288 See above pp.76–81; also §5.3.1 below.

own choice of law rule. Tracing is best viewed as an extension of rights with an independent source. The choice of law rule governing the issue arising out of such rights must govern any tracing issues.[289] Where a restitutionary claim contingent on tracing is brought, the restitutionary choice of law rule ought to govern the ability to trace. For example, where the plaintiff's money is stolen and paid into the defendant's bank account, with which the defendant has subsequently bought bonds, the plaintiff's claim, that the defendant make restitution of the value of the bonds, may be seen as raising a restitutionary issue. If so the restitutionary choice of law rule, which governs the defendant's liability to make restitution, will also determine whether the plaintiff can trace into the bonds. Alternatively, if the issue arising out of a claim contingent on tracing is characterised as a proprietary issue, thereby attracting the *lex situs* or some other rule applicable to the particular property in question, the law applicable under that particular choice of law rule must also determine the tracing issue. The above approach applies *mutatis mutandis* to other types of claims contingent on tracing, where the relevant issue may, for example, be characterised as contractual, a wrong or a matrimonial issue.

5.2.4 Interest in the Tracing Process

It has been submitted above that when tracing internationally, the plaintiff need not show an interest under the law of each intermediary jurisdiction. There are strong arguments against such a requirement. First, the success of a tracing exercise would depend on the particular jurisdictions the traceable proceeds went through. If a fraudulent party channelled funds through a jurisdiction which did not recognise tracing, it could easily defeat a tracing exercise, and thus the relevant claim. Furthermore, the more jurisdictions involved, the more complex and costly the international claim. This would be a blessing to the fraudsters and the launderers. Secondly, where the tracing process involves funds moving through various bank accounts via electronic transfers, it becomes rather artificial to speak of the plaintiff tracing "through" a jurisdiction.

It should be noted that the above analysis is consistent with the mere power to revest theory of tracing.[290] According to this theory, the interest contingent upon tracing is an incomplete interest, that is "a mere power to revest"—or a mere equity. It is not a vested interest. There are certain advantages in adopting the mere power analysis of tracing, and this is particularly so in the context of private international law. Under this theory, the plaintiff need not show a pro-

[289] See also Smith, p.276; Bird, p.86; *Cf.* Stevens, pp.212–13. See also R.J. Millett, "Jurisdiction and Choice of Law in the Law of Restitution" in T.K. Sood, *et. al.* (ed.), *Current Legal Issues in International Commercial Litigation* (Singapore, 1997), p.203.

[290] Birks, *Laundering and* Tracing, pp.307–11; *cf.* Smith pp.358–61. *Re ffrench's estate* (1887) 21 L.R. (IR.) 283, is cited as an example of the mere power theory; *Cf. Cave* v. *Cave* (1880) 15 Ch. D. 639.

prietary interest at every intermediate link of the chain. Thus, in *El Ajou*,[291] Millett J. expressly denied that the plaintiff "must have been in a position to obtain an equitable charge against every successive account",[292] while he described the defrauded plaintiff's interest in the funds into which he traced as "entirely notional".[293] In addition to overcoming the need to establish a proprietary interest at every step in the tracing chain, the mere power analysis of tracing is consistent with the fact that tracing does not create any rights or remedies, and therefore helps explain why a tracing issue should not attract its own choice of law rule. Despite the fact that there remain some unresolved questions in relation to the power analysis, such as when and how such power is exercised,[294] it is nevertheless submitted that such an analysis should be adopted, at least as a matter of private international law.

5.3 Ancillary Issues

5.3.1 Intermediate Purchases or Acquisitions

Where one traces through a foreign jurisdiction, an ancillary proprietary issue may arise.[295] Property within the tracing chain may have been sold to an intermediary recipient, or to the defendant, and thus a purchase may have occurred. Alternatively, an accession or specification may have occurred through the process.[296] In such a case, it is submitted that a separate issue will arise of whether the ancillary proprietary issue has defeated the claim. Such ancillary issues are to be characterised separately, and are to be determined by the applicable choice of law rule for the acquisition, accession or specification of the particular type of property.[297]

An ancillary proprietary issue will often arise by way of defence, namely, the defendant may be a purchaser in good faith in relation to the property, or alternatively, the defendant may allege that a previous person in the tracing chain was a good faith purchaser. For example, the plaintiff's employee fraudulently forwards money to B who is in France. B then uses this money to purchase a car. B then sells this car to the defendant. The plaintiff claims that the defendant holds the car as trustee for the plaintiff. However, the defendant will argue that he was a *bona fide* purchaser for value. The defendant's defence, that he was a

[291] *El Ajou* v. *Dollar Land Holdings Plc* [1993] 3 All E.R. 717, 739, *per* Millett J. (reversed on different grounds) [1994] 2 All ER 685.

[292] *Id.*, 737 d–e. *Cf. El Ajou* v. *Dollar Land Holdings* (*No.2*) [1995] 2 All E.R. 213, 221g, *per* Robert Walker J.

[293] *Id.*, 737j.

[294] See Birks, *Laundering and Tracing*, p.311.

[295] See above §3.4 in relation to ancillary proprietary issues.

[296] In relation to specification or accession at private international law see for example *Borden (U.K.) Ltd.* v. *Scottish Timber Products Ltd.* [1981] Ch. 25; *Zahnrad Fabrik Passau GmbH* v. *Terex Ltd.* 1986 S.L.T. 84.

[297] See *Macmillan Inc* v. *Bishopsgate Investment Trust Plc* (*No.3*) [1996] 1 W.L.R. 387.

bona fide purchaser for value, raises an ancillary proprietary issue, which should attract the relevant choice of law rule for the particular purchase, in this case the law of the place where the tangible was at the time of transfer, namely France. The plaintiff's claim may be defeated if the ancillary proprietary question can be substantiated under the law applicable to it, and thus the claim may possibly fail.[298] Again, an analogy can be drawn here with the situation of contractual defences to tortious liability in private international law.[299] What is significant for our purposes is to note that the tracing process will still be governed by the law governing the plaintiff's claim. The fact that there has been an intermediate purchase should not affect the treatment of the tracing issue, as the considerations relating to the intermediate purchase can be dealt with as an ancillary proprietary issue.

The existence of a separate characterisation of ancillary proprietary issues, alleviates the concern of not only the situation where the defendant was a *bona fide* purchaser, but also where a previous recipient was. As a result of this safeguard, there is no reason why the plaintiff need show an interest at every link of the tracing process—that is, a "charge against every successive account".[300] It is also a logical consequence of the plaintiff not needing to establish an interest under the law of each intermediary jurisdiction. The plaintiff must be able to trace without any gaps, but the exercise of the final *in personam* or proprietary remedy must depend on the state of affairs at the end of the chain, not at every link.

5.3.2 *Tracing in Equity and at Law*

As discussed in the first chapter, the rules for tracing in equity are different from those at law.[301] The existence of this bimorphic form of tracing may add an additional problem, namely that of equity in private international law. As noted previously in this chapter, there is a view that equitable rights and remedies are administered by the court in accordance with the *lex fori*.[302] Therefore an additional argument could be raised that, irrespective of how one may characterise common law tracing, insofar as equitable tracing is concerned, this is to be governed by the *lex fori*. It has been concluded that, equitable rights and obligations should be characterised in the same way as their legal counterparts; namely

[298] A private international law matter may raise several issues each governed by a different choice of law rule: *Macmillan Inc* v. *Bishopsgate Investment Trust Plc* (*No.3*) [1996] 1 W.L.R. 387, 399, *per* Staughton L.J., 418, *per* Aldous L.J. See also above Part II, A, §2.2.

[299] *Coupland* v. *Arabian Gulf Oil Co.* [1983] 1 W.L.R. 1136. See also L. Collins, "Interaction between Contract and Tort" (1967) 16 I.C.L.Q. 103; O. Kahn-Freund, "Contractual Defences to Delictual Claims" (1968) II Hague Recueil 129–57; P. North, "Contractual Defences to Torts" (1977) 26 I.C.L.Q. 914; P. Carter (1983) 54 B.Y.I.L. 301; also A. Briggs, "From Complexity to Anticlimax: Restitution and Choice of Law" [1996] R.L.R. 88, 90.

[300] *El Ajou* v. *Dollar Land Holdings Ltd.* [1993] 3 All E.R. 717, 737, *per* Millett J. (reversed on different grounds) [1994] 2 All E.R. 685.

[301] See ch. 1.5.3.

[302] See above, §2.

according to the relevant *causative event*.[303] Therefore, when faced with an international claim contingent on equitable tracing, the court should characterise the issue arising out of the claim and the law applicable to that issue should also determine the ability to trace in equity.

There is no persuasive argument for applying a different approach to tracing in equity. As discussed above, it is pointless to apply the *lex fori* in relation to the issue of tracing where it is not recognised by the *lex causae*. Furthermore, it is inappropriate to defeat a claim contingent on tracing, which would be successful under the *lex causae*, as a result of the *lex fori's* stricter tracing requirements; or, alternatively, to allow a claim in circumstances where the *lex causae's* tracing rules would not have recognised such a claim.

6 NEGOTIORUM GESTIO

The common law does not recognise a general regime of *negotiorum gestio*. A person who intervenes to save someone's life or property does not have a general right of recovery for his expenses and services.[304] Such claims are however available under many civilian systems. The common law does allow recovery in certain discrete categories of cases such as salvage, burials and cases where there is an agency of necessity.[305] These cases have been cited as examples of recovery for necessitous intervention and as forming part of a more general category.[306] The question here is how an English court will characterise a necessitous intervention claim containing international elements.

As a matter of English domestic law, it is not apparent that necessitous intervention, or *negotiorum gestio*, forms part of the law of unjust enrichment. Although this topic is often covered in texts dealing with the law of restitution, the preferred view is that it is a separate form of liability. Birks, for example, places it in a fourth, miscellaneous category, outside contract, wrongs and unjust enrichment.[307] In most cases of necessitous intervention, the measure sought is generally not restitutionary. The measure does not focus on what the defendant has gained. Instead, it focuses on the services of the intervener. Even if one were to argue that the defendant has in fact benefited to the extent of the services rendered, the emphasis seems to be on the value of the intervener's services, rather than the benefit received by the defendant. The two do not always correspond. For example, in *Ambrose* v. *Kerrison*,[308] the benefit to the husband

[303] See above, §2.

[304] See *Falcke* v. *Scottish Imperial Insurance Co.* (1886) 34 Ch.D. 234; *Sorrell* v. *Paget* [1950] 1 K.B. 252; *The Goring* [1988] A.C. 831.

[305] See generally Burrows, pp.232-8.

[306] See Birks, pp.201-2; Burrows, p.231.

[307] P. Birks, "Definition and Division: A Meditation on Institutes 3.13", in P. Birks, *The Classification of Obligations* (Oxford, 1997), p.19. See also Burrows, pp.242-9. *Cf.* F. Rose, "Restitution for the Rescuer" (1989) O.J.L.S. 167.

[308] (1851) 10 C.B. 776.

was the basic expenses of paying an undertaker to have his late wife buried. However, the plaintiff was entitled to recover beyond the *de minimis* expenses of burying the deceased. He also recovered the additional expenses associated with having the deceased placed in the family vault in Kelvedon. Likewise, salvage awards are not measured by reference to the value of the services rendered plus outlays. They also include an element of reward. Salvage awards bear in mind the need to encourage such efforts in future, whilst they reflect the danger, the skill, and the value of what was saved.[309] As such, they go beyond a mere restitutionary measure. Furthermore, the general policy in cases of necessitous intervention is not to reverse the benefited party's enrichment but to encourage useful intervention.[310] It is therefore difficult to justify a restitutionary characterisation as a matter of English domestic law.

The charcterisation of *negotiorum gestio* as something other than restitution finds further support from civilian jurisdictions that recognise such a regime. Most civilian systems do not consider *negotiorum gestio* as part of their law of unjustified enrichment. For example, as a matter of German law, *negotiorum gestio* is a separate form of liability that is based around a contract called mandate (Auftrag).[311] Likewise, under Greek law, *negotiorum gestio* (*διοίκηση αλλοτρίων*) is dealt with in a separate chapter of the Greek Civil Code,[312] following the provisions dealing with mandate (*εντολή*).[313] It too is based around a principle of mandate and is a relationship in which all the features of mandate are present except the instructions of the principal.[314] A likely civilian position to *negotiorum gestio* in private international law is that adopted by Zweigert and Müller-Gindullis.[315] They distinguish *negotiorum gestio* from unjustifiable enrichment for the purposes of choice of law.[316] It is therefore submitted that, as *negotiorum gestio* is a distinct form of liability, it should be characterised separately and not as an issue of unjust enrichment. The liberal *lex fori* would find support for such an approach both as a matter of English domestic law and under other legal systems that recognise *negotiorum gestio*.

Where a claim for *negotiorum gestio* arises in connection with a pre-existing legal relationship, it has been suggested that the question of recovery should be governed by that legal relationship.[317] Put in another way, the issue should be

[309] See *Scaramanga* v. *Stamp* (1850) 5 C.P.D. 295 (C.A.); *The Queen Elizabeth* (1949) 82 Lloyd's. List L.R. 803; *The Telemachus* [1957] P. 47.

[310] *The Telemachus* [1957] P. 47, 59; *The St Blane* [1974] 1 Lloyd's Rep. 557, 560.

[311] See Markesinis, pp.715-16; 750-2.

[312] Chapter 23 (Art. 730-40) of the Greek Civil Code. Unjustified Enrichment is dealt with in Chapter 38 (Art. 904-13).

[313] Chapter 22.

[314] The *gestor* is under an obligation, as soon as possible, to inform the principal that he has undertaken the management of the principal's affairs. If there is no direct danger, he is obliged to await the principal's instructions: Art. 733.

[315] Zweigert and Müller-Gindullis, *Quasi-Contract*, in Lipstein (ed.), *International Encyclopedia of Comparative Law*, Vol. III, Ch. 30.

[316] *Id.* pp.20-2. *Cf.* Cheshire and North, pp.675-6.

[317] *Id.*, 20, 30-42; Stevens, p.205;

characterised as contractual, or possibly one arising under a trust, and the law applicable to the contract, or trust, should determine whether the *gestor* is able to recover. This would typically cover those cases where, as a matter of English domestic law, there existed an "agency of necessity". For example, the defendant enters into a contract with the plaintiff to transport his horse from England to France. When the plaintiff delivers the horse there is nobody there to collect it. The plaintiff incurs expenses in looking after the horse until such time as it is collected. The issue of whether the plaintiff may recover his expenses should be characterised as a contractual issue and the law of the contract would determine the question of recovery. Such an approach is consistent with the concept of agency of necessity in English law and the concept of mandate under civilian law systems. The question of whether the issue should be characterised as contractual, or otherwise, should not be based on the mere existence of a legal relationship between the parties. Where the claim for *negotiorum gestio* is sufficiently connected to a pre-existing legal relationship, such that the claim for *negotiorum gestio* is best viewed as an additional issue arising under that legal relationship, the issue should be characterised as contractual.

Where however there is no pre-existing legal relationship, sufficiently connected to the claim of *negotiorum gestio*, the question of what law should govern is a little more difficult. It has been suggested that this should be the law of the place where the *gestor* acted.[318] Alternatively, it has been suggested that the *lex situs* should apply, where the claim arises in connection with the improvement of movables or immovables.[319] These two approaches are sound in principle, however they have the disadvantage of possibly pointing to an arbitrary, or no, jurisdiction. For example, a ship may be salvaged in fortuitous territorial waters or indeed in the high seas. Recognising the difficulties involved, Cheshire and North adopt the general and unrestricted position of the proper law of the obligation.[320] Such an approach is flexible enough to deal with the variety of circumstances in which a claim for *negotiorum gestio* could arise. What is important to note is that, in cases where the *negotiorum gestio* arises outside of a sufficiently connected pre-existing legal relationship, the issue is distinct for the purposes of characterisation and therefore attracts its own choice of law rule.

[318] J. Blaikie [1984] *J.R.* 112, 119; Stevens, p.218.
[319] Stevens, p.205.
[320] Cheshire and North, p.698.

5

Theoretical Issues

I RENVOI

THERE IS NO AUTHORITY indicating whether renvoi applies in matters concerning restitution. Renvoi does not apply in the field of contract[1] or tort.[2] The argument which is often cited as to why renvoi should not apply to contract is that would be contrary to the expectation of the parties, who, when choosing the applicable law, presumably only intended that its domestic law apply. On this rationale, renvoi should generally apply unless there are compelling reasons for excluding it.[3] However, it could be alternatively argued that there is a general principle at common law that renvoi does not apply in relation to what are termed "obligations" for the purposes of private international law. This is as the doctrine has only been applied in matters concerning wills, succession, domicile and property.[4] Thus, as renvoi does not presently apply to tort or contract, there is no compelling reason why it should apply to restitution. Furthermore, the few authorities which do discuss restitution in private international law, do not make any suggestion whatsoever of the likely application of renvoi.

However, as renvoi has been held to apply to matters concerning property, it may be argued that it should apply in cases of proprietary restitution. This argument must be rejected. As matters concerning proprietary restitution will be characterised as restitutionary, then renvoi should not apply to such issues, irrespective of the fact that a proprietary remedy may be sought. Finally, it should be noted that as renvoi applies to matters concerning property, it can apply to

[1] Art. 15, Rome Convention. Renvoi does not apply to contracts at common law, and thus to matters outside the scope of the Convention: *Amin Rasheed Shipping Corp.* v. *Kuwait Insurance Co.* [1984] A.C. 50, 61–2.

[2] Section 9(5), Private International Law (Miscellaneous Provisions) Act 1995. Renvoi did not apply under the common law choice of law rule by virtue of the nature of the double actionability rule. There is Scottish and American authority that the principle of renvoi is inapplicable in the field of tort: see *M'Elroy* v. *M'Alister*, [1949] S.C. 110, 126; *Haumschild* v. *Continental Casualty Co.*, 7 Wis. 2d 130, 141–2 (1959); *Pfau* v. *Trent Aluminium Co.*, 55 N.J. 2d 511, 263 A. 2d 129, 136–7 (1970).

[3] Under French law, the position is that renvoi is generally applicable, unless there are compelling arguments for its exclusion: P. Mayer, *Droit International Privé*, 6th ed. (Paris, 1998), p.144; B. Audit, *Droit International Privé* (Paris, 1997), p.643. Thus, although the preferred view is that it does not apply in the field of contract, it theoretically may apply to delictual matters: H. Batiffol and P. Lagarde, *Droit International Privé* (Paris, 1993), t.1, pp.508–9. Likewise, under German law renvoi is generally applicable, although it specifically does not apply where the parties have chosen a particular law: Art. 4 of the Introductory Law of the German Civil Code. In contrast, renvoi is generally excluded under Greek law: Art. 32, Greek Civil Code.

[4] See Dicey and Morris, pp.72–3; Cheshire and North, pp.65–6.

the ancillary proprietary issues which may arise in cases of proprietary restitution.

2 THE INCIDENTAL QUESTION

At two particular stages in this chapter a hybrid, or two-step, characterisation process has been submitted. First, in cases where a restitutionary claim is connected with a contract, it has been proposed that the law of the contract should determine the question of the contract's validity, while the law applicable to the unjust enrichment issue should determine the right of restitution.[5] Likewise in cases of proprietary restitution it has been submitted that the law applicable to the issue of restitution should determine the availability of a proprietary remedy, while the law applicable to the transfer of the relevant property should determine any ancillary proprietary issue.[6] These two situations may appear to raise a problem of the incidental question. The incidental question arises where a court has to decide a main issue with foreign elements and, in order to do so, has to decide a subsidiary question which also contains foreign elements. The problem will occur if, by the English conflict rule, the main question is governed by a foreign law and the subsidiary question is, under the English conflict of laws, to be governed by a different law than would have applied under the conflict rules of the law governing the main question.[7]

One of the rationales for applying the incidental question, as applied in *Schwebel* v. *Ungar*,[8] is that where a main question is to be determined by a foreign choice of law rule, the secondary question should also be determined in the way the foreign court would have determined it. In this way, the English court is doing what the foreign court would have done.[9] Therefore, the law applicable to the incidental or subsidiary question should be determined by the law applicable to the main question, including its choice of law rules. To apply English choice of law rules to the subsidiary question, might provide a different result. Thus, one must apply the choice of law rule that the foreign court would have applied to the subsidiary question, if one seeks to arrive at the same result

Contractual defences to tort claims could be seen as an exception to the incidental question.[10] Each question has a choice of law rule applied to it under English law. That is, the English choice of law rule for tort determines the tortious issues and then the contractual issues are determined by the relevant English choice of law rule. It is submitted that the logical explanation for this is

[5] See above ch. 4 and 1.2.
[6] See above §§3.4, 3.4.1 and also §5.3.1.
[7] See Dicey and Morris, pp.45–7 for a more detailed description.
[8] (1964) 48 D.L.R. (2d) 644.
[9] See *Re Ross* [1930] 1 Ch. 377, 390; *Re Duke of Wellington* [1947] Ch. 506; [1948] Ch. 118 (C.A.).
[10] See *Coupland* v. *Arabian Gulf Oil Co.* [1983] 1 W.L.R. 1136.

that renvoi is excluded from contractual and tortious issues.[11] Therefore, as the aim is not to reach the same result as the foreign court, the choice of law rule is applied to the secondary issue autonomously. It is submitted that the same approach should be adopted in the case of restitutionary claims arising under ineffective contracts. Likewise, in the case of proprietary restitution, the main question is the right of restitution. As has been discussed, it will not attract renvoi. That is, where the proper law of the restitutionary issue points to a foreign law, the issue will be determined by such law, without its choice of law rules. The secondary proprietary issue will be determined by the law applicable through the English choice of law rules. Even if one accepts that property issues may attract renvoi, as the ancillary proprietary issue will never be the main issue, the problem of the incidental question will never arise.

[11] Above, §1.

PART III

CHOICE OF LAW RULES FOR RESTITUTIONARY ISSUES

6

The Existing Authorities

I INTRODUCTION

WHEREAS CHOICE OF law in contract and tort is now largely governed by statute,[1] restitution is the area of civil liability where the common law rules for choice of law still dominate. However, the applicable choice of law rule or rules for restitutionary issues is still an open matter.[2] The few English decisions dealing with this issue do not provide a definitive position. Most of these decisions deal with the topic of the applicable choice of law rule for restitution peripherally; the *ratio* of such decisions lies elsewhere. Moreover, the decisions that pre-date the English recognition of a unified law of restitution, based on the principle of unjust enrichment, must be read with this fact in mind. It may be that any previous semblance of a choice of law rule which may appear to have emerged, is based on an erroneous understanding of the law of restitution. One should reject any proposed choice of law rule to the extent that it is based on the implied contract theory. Such a choice of law rule would not truly arrive at the proper law of the restitutionary issue. It would not be based on a correct understanding of the law of restitution as a matter of domestic law, while, it would also not reflect the law of restitution under other common law systems nor under civilian systems.

At the same time, there is little, and insufficiently consistent, academic guidance on the choice of law rule for restitution. The few existing works either seek to fit the sporadic authorities within an existing theory, or to provide an account of the various theories, proposing what is usually an accommodating, yet complex, choice of law rule, moulded at the expense of certainty. The field is therefore open for a principled and reasoned approach to the question of the proper choice of law rule for restitutionary issues, placing greatest emphasis on principle and the appropriateness of the alternatives.

[1] Contracts Applicable Law Act 1990, implementing the Rome Convention (applicable to contracts made on or after 2 April 1991); Private International Law (Miscellaneous Provisions Act) 1995 (applicable to torts committed on or after 1 May 1996).

[2] See *Macmillan Inc.* v. *Bishopsgate Investment Trust Plc* (*No.3*) [1996] 1 W.L.R. 387, 408, *per* Auld L.J.

2. DICEY AND MORRIS

Dicey and Morris is undoubtedly the leading text in the English conflict of laws, if not generally in the common law world. In relation to restitutionary obligations, Dicey and Morris state in Rule 200:[3]

(1) The obligation to restore the benefit of an enrichment obtained at another person's expense is governed by the proper law of the obligation.

(2) The proper law of the obligation is (*semble*) determined as follows:
  (a) If the obligation arises in connection with a contract, its proper law is the law applicable to the contract;
  (b) If it arises in connection with a transaction concerning an immovable (land), its proper law is the law of the country where the immovable is situated (*lex situs*);
  (c) If it arises in any other circumstances, its proper law is the law of the country where the enrichment occurs.

This rule has remained largely the same ever since it first appeared in the sixth edition of *Dicey's Conflict of Laws* in 1949.[4] When the rule first appeared it was called "Quasi-Contract", which was defined as "liability, not exclusively referable to any other head of law, imposed upon a particular person on the ground of unjust benefit".[5] The addition of this rule was undoubtedly influenced by the *Fibrosa* case,[6] which is also referred to in the initial stages of the commentary. However, the rule as initially formulated was the rule for "Quasi-Contract",[7] and although today's law of restitution undeniably has its origins in the area that was referred to as "quasi-contract" the area envisaged in 1949 does not square up with the modern law of restitution.[8] "Quasi-contract" was based on the implied contract theory and was viewed as a residual category which covered those forms of liability which fell outside of contract and tort. It covered areas which might not be considered part of today's law of restitution as based on the principle of unjust enrichment. For example, in *Hodge* v. *Club Motor*

[3] Applied in *Arab Monetary Fund* v. *Hashim* [1996] 1 Lloyd's Rep. 589; also *Hong Kong and Shanghai Banking Corp Ltd.* v. *United Overseas Bank Ltd.* [1992] 2 S.L.R. 495 (H.C. of Singapore); *Kartika Ratna Thahir* v. *P.T. Pertambangan Minyak dan Gas Bumi Negara* (*Pertamina*)[1994] 3 S.L.R. 257 (C.A. of Singapore) (hereafter *Thahir* v. *Pertamina*). Also approved of in *Macmillan Inc.* v. *Bishopsgate Investment Trust Plc.* (*No.3*) [1996] 1 W.L.R. 387, 398, *per* Staughton L.J. The predecessor of Rule 201, as contained in the tenth edition of Dicey and Morris, was approved of in *Re Jogia* (*A Bankrupt*) [1988] 1 W.L.R. 484, 495, *per* Browne-Wilkinson V.-C.

[4] The main difference being that the first paragraph of the rule stated that "[t]he rights and obligations of the parties to a quasi-contractual relationship are determined in accordance with the proper law of the quasi-contractual relationship".

[5] This definition had been borrowed from P. Winfield, *Province of the Law of Tort* (Cambridge, 1931), p.119.

[6] *Fibrosa Spolka Akcyjna* v. *Fairbairn Lawson Combe Barbour Ltd.* [1943] A.C. 32.

[7] The rule was re-defined as "Restitution or Quasi-Contract" from the eighth edition in 1967 until the twelfth edition in 1993.

[8] See generally ch. I §1 and 2.

Insurance Agency Pty Ltd.,[9] Bray C.J. characterised an injured party's direct claim against the tortfeasor's insurer as quasi-contractual and applied the general choice of law rule in the eighth edition of Dicey and Morris.[10]

Despite the developments in the domestic law of restitution, the choice of law rule in Dicey and Morris has remained largely unaltered. The structure of the rule appears to be based on an understanding of "quasi-contract" as a collection of miscellaneous actions, or relationships, which arise sometimes in the context of contracts, sometimes immovable property and other times in the context of neither. One might rightly question whether a choice of law rule initially drafted to cover "quasi-contracts" should apply to issues of unjust enrichment. Moreover, would the same choice of law rule be selected if the opportunity to formulate such a rule arose today? It is submitted that one cannot ignore the quasi-contractual legacy when examining the rule in Dicey and Morris, something which has been inherited right down to the most recent edition in 2000.

According to Rule 200, restitutionary issues are divided into different categories with a different choice of law rule for each category. However, the initial approach suggested is to look for the proper law of the obligation. It is not very illuminating and rather circular to state that restitutionary obligations are governed by the proper law of the obligation. One doesn't know whether an issue is an obligation or otherwise, unless it has already been characterised and had the relevant choice of law rule applied. There is no reason to assume that the particular causative event will, under the *lex causae*, necessarily give rise to an obligation. As noted previously, the English law of restitution grants both personal and proprietary remedies.[11] It is therefore rather restrictive to speak in terms of restitutionary "obligations". The use of the word "obligation" here results from the fact that private international lawyers have traditionally used this word as a taxonomic category for matters of contract, tort and unjust enrichment, for choice of law purposes, and not as indicative of any remedial response.[12] It would be more helpful if a more neutral word, such as "issue", were used instead of obligation.

There has been some discussion of whether the "proper law" of the obligation, namely Rule 200(1), is the actual rule,[13] of which the different categories are examples, or whether it is merely a statement of the obvious.[14] In the latest edition of Dicey and Morris, the editors have indicated in the commentary that

[9] [1974] 7 S.A.S.R. 86, 89–91.

[10] Although Bray C.J. did not expressly refer to Dicey and Morris in *Hodge*, in discussing the choice of law rule for quasi-contract, he cites that part of his judgment in *Nominal Defendant* v. *Bagot's Executor & Trustee Company Ltd.* [1971] S.A.S.R. 346, where he expressly refers to the choice of law rule for quasi-contracts in the eighth edition of Dicey and Morris.

[11] See ch. 1.3.

[12] See above p.28.

[13] See McLeod, *The Conflict of Laws* (Calgary, 1983), pp.571–2 (hereafter McLeod); J. Blaikie, "Unjust Enrichment in the Conflict of Laws" [1984] J.R. 112, 125; also A. Anton, *Private International Law*, 2nd ed. (Edinburgh, 1990), p.311.

[14] See Burrows, p.491; R. Leslie, "Unjustified Enrichment in the Conflict of Laws" (1988) 2 Edinburgh Law Review 233, 236–7.

"the general choice of law rule for restitutionary obligations is that they are governed by the proper law of the obligation".[15] This is defined as the law with which the obligation has its closest and most real connection. Such an approach suggests that the sub-rules help indicate, in the various circumstances, the law with which the restitutionary obligation is most likely to have its closest and most real connection. As such, it is said that "the proper law of the obligation to make restitution may be influenced by the law which governed the anterior legal relationship, but it is an error to suppose that it must be governed by it".[16] Nevertheless, the language in Rule 200 seems more categorical than this. The various sub-rules are not put forward as mere examples of the law with which the restitutionary obligation is likely to have its closest and most real connection. The sub-rules use slightly more definite language; for example, in cases where the obligation arises in connection with a contract (*semble*) the proper law "*is* the law applicable to the contract".[17]

The basic position in 200 of Dicey and Morris is that restitutionary "obligations" are generally to be governed by the law of the place of enrichment. However, where the restitutionary matter arises in connection with a contract or an immovable, it is seen to be more appropriate to apply the law applicable to the contract or the *lex situs*, irrespective of where the enrichment occurs. The emphasis is therefore on the factual background under which the relevant restitutionary "obligation" arises, namely whether it arises in connection with a contract or an immovable. The nature of these two circumstances is presumably of such a nature as to alter the choice of law rule accordingly. As such, the essential restitutionary choice of law rule, namely the place of enrichment rule, has an apparently residual role.

In examining the above rule, certain questions arise which are relevant to determining the applicable choice of law rule for restitution. First, why is the law of the place of the enrichment seen generally as the most appropriate one to govern restitutionary obligations? That is, should the law of the place of enrichment govern restitutionary obligations in general, and if not, what should the rule be? Secondly, why is there a distinction drawn between moveables and immovables, such that a restitutionary obligation arising in connection with a transaction concerning an immovable only is governed by the *lex situs* of the immovable? Finally, to what extent must the relevant restitutionary obligation be connected with a contract for the law of the contract to apply? Is also the nature of the contractual ineffectiveness of any significance? These matters will be considered further below in the context of the various choice of law rules.

[15] Dicey and Morris, p.1490.

[16] *Ibid.*

[17] Emphasis added.

3 U.S. RESTATEMENT

The question of the choice of law rule for restitution was considered in the United States long before anywhere else in the common law world. The First Restatement in 1934 provided a place of enrichment choice of law rule. Section 452 provided that the law of the place where a benefit is conferred determines whether a right exists to have compensation. Likewise, §453 provided that the law of the place of enrichment determines whether the recipient is under a duty to repay the amount by which he has been enriched.[18] This effectively created two, almost identical, choice of law rules, one applying to "benefits" and one in relation to an "enrichment". A distinction was therefore drawn between money benefits and non-money benefits, yet in practical terms there was little difference between the two rules.

Despite the attraction of its apparent simplicity, it was felt that the place of enrichment rule could not deal with the complexity of situations arising in a cause of action in restitution.[19] Moreover, the tendency in other choice of law rules was that the governing law be that of the state which "has the most significant relationship to the occurrences and the parties" with respect to the issue. This is the general rule for torts,[20] as well as the general rule for contracts in the absence of effective choice by the parties.[21] It is thus of little surprise that the general choice of law rule in the Second Restatement for restitution is that:

> "the rights and liabilities of the parties with respect to the particular issue are determined by the local law of the state which, with respect to that issue, has the most significant relationship to the occurrence and the parties.[22]

Such choice of law rules are based on the governmental interest analysis approach which has generally influenced much of the American conflict of laws in the last fifty years or so.[23] In the Second Restatement there is a general

[18] Followed in *Wilson & Co. Inc.* v. *Douredoure* 154 F.2d 442 (3d Cir. 1946).

[19] See for example *Nissenberg* v. *Felleman* 162 N.E. 2d 304 (Mass. 1959); *Nowell* v. *Dick* 413 F. 2d 1204 (5th Cir. 1969). See also below, ch 7.1.2. *seq.* in relation to some of the criticisms of the place of enrichment rule.

[20] §145 U.S. Restatement (Second) 1971.

[21] §188 U.S. Restatement (Second) 1971.

[22] §221(1) U.S. Restatement (Second) 1971. Followed in *McAdams Inc.* v. *Boggs* 439 F. Supp. 738 (E.D. Pa.1977); *Overseas Development Disc. Corp.* v. *Sangamo Const.* 686 F. 2d 498 (7th Cir. 1982); *Phoenix Canada Oil Co. Ltd.* v. *Texaco Inc.* 560 F. Supp. 1372 (D. Del. 1983); *Aaron Ferer & Sons Ltd.* v. *Chase Manhattan Bank* 731 F. 2d 112 (2 Cir. 1984); *Gibbs-Brower International* v. *Kirchheimer Bros. Co.* 611 F. Supp. 122 (D.C. Ill. 1985); *Trinh* v. *Citibank N.A.* 623 F. Supp. 1526 (D.C. Mich. 1985); *Delaware Hurst* v. *General Dynamics Corp.* 583 A. 2d. 1334 (Del. Ch. 1990); *First Winsconsin Trust Co.* v. *Shroud* 916 F. 2d 939 (5th Cir. 1990); *Micro Data Base Systems* v. *Dharma Systems Inc.* 148 F.3d 649 (7th Cir. 1998); *Morris B. Chapman Associates Ltd.* v. *Kitzman* 706 N.E. 2d 1065 (Ill. App. 1999).

[23] A majority of the states of the United States have adopted the restatement or some variation of the interest analysis in relation to contract and tort: see S. Symeonides, "Choice of Law in the American Courts in 1997" [1998] 46 A.J.C.L. 233; also S-Symeonides, "Choice of Law in the American Courts in 1998" [1999] 47 A.J.C.L. 327.

provision in relation to choice of law principles, giving effect to the governmental interest analysis. Section 6 sets out factors relevant to the choice of the applicable law. These include the needs of the interstate and international systems; the relevant policies of the forum; the relevant policies of other interested states; the basic policies underlying the particular field of law, as well as the ease in the determination and application of the law to be applied.

Sub-rule (2) of §221 (the restitutionary choice of law rule), lists a number of contacts to be taken into account in determining the law applicable to a restitutionary issue. These are not choice of law rules. They are merely factors which may assist the court to determine the law which has the "most significant relationship to the occurrence and the parties under the principles stated in §6". They are:

(a) the place where the relationship between the parties was centred, provided that the receipt of enrichment was substantially related to the relationship,
(b) the place where the benefit or enrichment was received,
(c) the place where the act conferring the benefit or enrichment was done,
(d) the domicile, residence, nationality, place of incorporation and place of business of the parties, and
(e) the place where a physical thing, such as land or a chattel, which was substantially related to the enrichment, was situated at the time of the enrichment.

The governmental interest approach is quite foreign to the classical choice of law technique adopted in England, most other common law systems and in most continental systems.[24] It is a conflict, process of rule selecting rather than jurisdiction selecting. It finds its origins in an article published by Cavers in 1933, in which he deplored the "jurisdiction-selecting" technique, as he called it, or the traditional conflict of laws system.[25] He pointed out that to apply the law of a particular jurisdiction without regard to the content of that law was bound to lead to injustice in the individual case and to generate false problems. This was further developed by Currie, an even more revolutionary opponent of the traditional system and advocate of the method of governmental interest analysis.[26] According to this method, the way a court should proceed is to identify the governmental policy behind the forum's law and the potentially applicable foreign law. Where the forum state has no interest in the application of its policy, but the foreign state has, it should apply the foreign law. *Babcock* v. *Jackson*[27] is often cited as the case representing the shift in American conflicts thinking, wherein the New York Court of Appeals adopted a rule-selecting, as opposed to

[24] See Morris, pp.447–50. See also J. Fawcett, "Is the American Governmental Interest Analysis the Solution to the English Tort Choice of Law Problems?" [1982] I.C.L.Q. 150; G. Kegel, "The Crisis of Conflict of Laws" [1964–II] 112 Recueil Des Cours 95.

[25] D.F. Cavers, "A Critique of the Choice of Law Problem" (1933) 47 Harv. L.Rev. 173.

[26] B. Currie, *Selected Essays on the Conflict of Laws* (Durham, NC, 1963). See also W. Reese, "Conflict of Laws and the Restatement Second" (1963) 28 Law and Contemporary Problems 679.

[27] 12 N.Y. 2d 473, 191 NE 2d 279 (1963).

a jurisdiction-selecting, approach.[28] However, if at the first stage of the analysis it is discovered that both states have an interest in the application of their respective laws, one is faced with a true conflict. It is at this stage of the process for which there is no settled solution under the governmental interest analysis approach. Currie himself advocated in this case the application of the *lex fori*.[29] He explained it by saying that the forum court must primarily advance the policy of the forum, so in a case where a real conflict between a policy of the forum and that of another state arises, it must apply forum law. Other alternative methods of resolution have been proposed, such as the better law technique[30] or the comparative impairment technique.[31]

There are a number of reservations which may be raised against importing the governmental interest analysis into the English conflict of laws. First of all, it is no easy task to determine what the interest of the forum and of the foreign state is in relation to a particular law.[32] This requirement can rarely be fulfilled but in the simplest of cases.[33] The purpose of a particular law may often be unclear.[34] The determination of a state's interest in a particular piece of legislation might not be so easy. This will not always be ascertainable in the drafts of the Bill or the parliamentary debates and readings, while the latter may represent political considerations removed from the real purpose of the law. Uncertainty as to purpose means uncertainty as to outcome. If this has been recognised as a difficulty in the United States' experience, where the legal systems of the various states are similar and adopt the same language, such a difficulty must exist *a fortiori* in the case of fundamentally different legal systems, which use a different language.[35] Furthermore, it is even more difficult to

[28] The New York passenger was injured in a New York car driven by a New York host in Ontario. The plaintiff was entitled to recover damages from her New York host due to his negligent driving, despite an Ontario statute which denied a gratuitous passenger any right of recovery. There was no convincing reason why the Ontario law should have been applied.

[29] See Currie, *op.cit.*, n.26 pp.183–4, 188–9; B. Currie (1963) 63 Colum. Law Rev. 1233, 1242–3 .

[30] The main advocate of this has been Leflar: see R. Leflar, "Choice-Influencing Considerations in Conflicts Law" [1966] N.Y.U.L.R. 267.

[31] Under this approach the court seeks to weigh the interests of the states whose laws may be applicable by asking which of the states' policies would be most impaired if its laws were not applied to that issue. This approach has been adopted by the courts of California: *Bernhard* v. *Harrah's Club* 16 Cal.3d 313, 546 P. 2d 719 (1976); *Offshore Rental Co.* v. *Continental Oil Co.* 22 Cal.3d 157, 583 P. 2d 721 (1978). It has also been adopted in the Louisiana Civil Code provisions dealing with the conflict of laws: §§3519, 3539 and 3542; see S. Symeonides, "Louisiana's New Law of Choice of Law for Tort Conflicts: An Exegesis" (1992) 66 Tulane L. Rev. 677.

[32] Morris, pp.454–5; J. Fawcett, "Is the American Governmental Interest Analysis the Solution to the English Tort Choice of Law Problems?" [1982] I.C.L.Q. 150, 152–60.

[33] It takes Currie about 36 pages to identify the policy behind a statute of North Carolina which prohibited actions on the personal covenant by certain kinds of mortgagee after foreclosure proceedings: see Currie, *op. cit.*, pp.384–420.

[34] See R. Leflar, "Choice-Influencing Considerations in Conflicts Law" [1966] 41 N.Y.U.L.R. 267, 271–9; M. Rosenberg (1967) 67 Colum. L. Rev. 459, 464.

[35] Moreover, statutes in the U.S.A generally begin with a statement of the policy the statute is intended to implement, as well as the findings of the legislative committees that considered the draft bills.

ascertain the interest of a state in a rule which has been judicially created, sometimes many years ago.

Secondly, the appropriateness of examining purported governmental interests in the context of private international law has been questioned,[36] given that the latter deals mainly with private rights and obligations and is concerned with the interests of private persons.[37] Thirdly, the method of governmental interest analysis is based around the American federal context and is possibly more apt in such a situation. The various legal systems are generally alike and part of a federation. It is difficult to transpose it to international conflicts.[38] Fourthly, a methodology which applies the *lex fori* in cases where there is a conflict between the laws of two interested states encourages forum shopping. Finally, the danger of a method wherein a court is invited to choose between two different rules is that it may ultimately select what it considers to be the "better rule".[39] Over and above the arguments against the governmental interest analysis, there remains the fact that it has not caught on in England. The English courts have maintained the traditional conflicts methodology. Therefore, given the fundamentally different nature of the respective conflicts methodologies, the second American restatement can be of little, or no assistance, in determining the choice of law rule for unjust enrichment.

The overall effect of §221 is that it allows the judge a great deal of discretion in arriving at the *lex causae*. A great deal of flexibility is allowed at the ultimate expense of certainty. It therefore results in a great deal of uncertainty as to what the governing law might be in any particular case. It is only in the simplest of cases where one can confidently predict the *lex causae*. In *Nowell* v. *Dick*,[40] for example, a Texan resident engaged a New York lawyer to perform a series of legal services. The issue of whether the lawyer could recover a *quantum meruit*, in relation to such services, was held to be governed by the law of New York. This was a natural conclusion as "[t]he attorney-client relationship arose in that state and the vast majority of the attorney's work took place there".[41] In fact, there was little or no connection with any other particular state.

[36] G. Kegel, "The Crisis of Conflict of Laws" [1964–II] 112 Recueil Des Cours 95, 206–7; Morris, p.453; A. Ehrenzweig, "Choice of Law: Current Doctrine and 'True Rules'" [1961] 49 Calif. L. Rev. 240, 243–8. *Cf*. H. Baade, "Counter-Revolution or Alliance for Progress? Reflections on Reading Cavers, The Choice of Law Process" (1967) 46 Tex. L. Rev. 141, 147–50.

[37] Nevertheless, even in the case of a purely private right, an affected state may have just as much of an interest in applying its law as it would in the case of a law of a public nature. It has an interest in ensuring that contracts are enforced, that wrongs are compensated for and that unjust enrichment is reversed.

[38] This argument was recognised by Cavers in his original article advocating in favour of a rule selecting conflicts technique: D.F. Cavers, "A Critque of the Choice of Law Problem" (1933) 47 Harv. L.Rev. 173, 193.

[39] See *Clark* v. *Clark* 107 N.H. 351, 355–6, A.2d 205, 209–10 (1966). This is something that the advocates of the rule-selection approach were keen to rebuke: see Cavers, *The Choice of Law Process*, pp.75–87; Currie, *op. cit.* n.26, pp.104–6, 153–4; H. Baade (1967) 46 Tex. L. Rev. 141, 152–6. Yet this is also something which has been acknowledged by others: see R. Leflar, L. McDougal and R. Felix, *American Conflicts Law*, 4th ed. (Charlottesville, 1986), §107, pp.297–300.

[40] 413 F. 2d 1204 (5th Cir. 1969).

[41] *Id*., 1209.

By contrast, in cases where the various elements point to several jurisdictions, it is not, it is submitted, all that apparent why one particular legal system applied as opposed to another. The courts highlight the various elements of the case and select the law of the state with which the most significant elements are connected. Yet, there is no real guidance as to which elements are to be considered more significant than others, or why particular elements are highlighted while others are not even mentioned. For example, in *Phoenix Canada Oil Co.* v. *Texaco Inc*,[42] the plaintiff, a Canadian oil company, brought, *inter alia*, an action in unjust enrichment against the defendant oil companies, claiming a share of the proceeds of the defendants' interest in a concession, from the government of Ecuador, for the exploitation of petroleum and natural gas. The claim in unjust enrichment was held to be governed by the law of Ecuador. It was found that the transaction which gave rise to the alleged unjust enrichment occurred in Ecuador, concerned Ecuadorian property and payment was made through an Ecuadorian bank.[43] However, none of the parties were Ecuadorian. The plaintiff was a Canadian company, while the defendants comprised of Delaware corporations and a Pennsylvanian corporation. Moreover, the relevant payment constituting the alleged enrichment, was received in Pennsylvania. Although the case did have a significant connection with Ecuador, the judgment is unsatisfactory in its explanation as to why the elements pointing to Ecuador were more significant than those pointing to any other jurisdiction. It will be recalled that the place of enrichment, as well as the place of incorporation and residence of the parties, are two of the five contacts listed in §221(2). Finally, it is not all that clear what the interest of Ecuador would have been in regulating an alleged unjust enrichment, arising between foreign parties, in relation to a benefit received outside Ecuador.

Uncertainty as to the significance of a particular contact means uncertainty as to outcome, if not general inconsistency. In *Micro Data Base Systems Inc.* v. *Dharma Systems Inc.*,[44] the restitutionary claim was automatically assumed to be governed by the same law as that which governed the related contract, with no real discussion as to what law had the most significant relationship to the claim in restitution.[45] This decision is to be contrasted with *Caton* v. *Leach Corporation*.[46] A sales representative brought proceedings against his former employer claiming breach of contract, restitution and wrongful discharge in relation to the termination of a sales representative agreement. Although the relevant sales agreement was expressly governed by Californian law, this did not extend to the law applicable to the restitutionary claim which was to be independently ascertained. The sales representative resided in Texas, served his employer in Texas, by soliciting sales from companies in Texas, while the

[42] 560 F. Supp., 1372 (D. Del. 1983).
[43] *Id.*, 1383.
[44] 148 F.3d 649 (7th Cir. 1998).
[45] *Id.*, 653. Also *Alaska Airlines Inc.* v. *United Airlines Inc.* 902 F. 2d 1400 (9th Cir. 1990).
[46] 896 F.2d 939 (5th Cir. 1990).

employer was said to have been enriched in Texas through the obtaining of recent contract in Texas. It was held that under the most significant relationship test the law of Texas applied, while "Texas had a distinct interest in applying its restitution policy to a course of action that enriched [the employer] in Texas at the expense of a Texas citizen".[47] Nevertheless, as noted, the sales agreement was expressly governed by the law of California while the employer's principle place of business was California. The analysis in the two cases do not reveal why the law of the related contract was so significant as to apply in the one case and not in the other.

International restitutionary claims will invariably contain a fair amount of complexity. Whilst it is desirable that the choice of law method allows a degree of flexibility, it is not desirable that it be so malleable and discretionary that the only way of arriving to the *lex causae* is to litigate. It is therefore submitted that §221 of the Restatement is not an appropriate choice of law rule to adopt for restitution. It is a choice of law rule that allows for great judicial discretion not only at the expense of certainty but also at the ultimate expense of consistency. More importantly, it is a choice of law rule that is based on a conflict of laws methodology that is not only foreign to the current English conflict of laws but for which significant arguments dictate against.

4 OTHER ACADEMIC OPINION

Other academic opinion has offered little that is different from what has already been discussed. Most of the other proposed choice of law rules conform to one of three basic structures. First, there is the law of the place of enrichment which has been proposed from time to time.[48] Such a rule has the advantage of being clear and straightforward. Secondly, there are those in the form of a single, proper law of the obligation rule.[49] This is a flexible approach which focuses on the proper law of the obligation to make restitution. Finally, there is the rule consisting of multiple sub-rules which deal with the various situations.[50] Such a rule may be referred to as the *lex causae condictionis*. These various options will be considered below in relation to the various proposed choice of law rules.[51]

[47] 896 F.2d 939 (5th Cir. 1990) 943.

[48] See Gutteridge and Lipstein, "Conflicts of Law in Matters of Unjustifiable Enrichment" (1941) 7 C.L.J. 80; §§452 and 453 U.S. Restatement 1934; R. Leslie, "Unjustified Enrichment in the Conflict of Laws" (1998) 2 Edinburgh Law Review 233.

[49] See Dicey and Morris, Rule 200(1); J. Blaikie [1984] J.R. 112; Cheshire and North, p.684.

[50] See Dicey and Morris, Rule 201(2); T. Bennett, "Choice of Law Rules in Claims of Unjust Enrichment" (1990) 139 I.C.L.Q. 136; Burrows, p.492; J. Bird, "Choice of Law" in F. Rose (ed.), *Restitution and the Conflict of Laws* (Oxford, 1995), p.135; see also R. Stevens, "The Choice of Law Rules of Restitutionary Obligations" in F. Rose (ed.), *Restitution and the Conflict of Laws* (Oxford, 1995), pp.191–220.

[51] Below ch. 6.

5 THE ENGLISH CASE LAW

The English cases dealing with the possible choice of law rule for restitutionary issues do not provide a clear position. The observations made in most of these cases are not crucial to the actual decisions. They are *obiter dicta* which, at the end of the day, can only be a mere guidance. Moreover, the only case to apply a restitutionary choice of law rule so as to arrive at the governing law, was, it is submitted, wrongly characterised. Given the relatively small number of cases dealing with this issue in any significant detail, it is appropriate to examine them separately.

* *Chase Manhattan Bank N.A.* v. *Israel-British Bank (London) Ltd.*

Chase Manhattan Bank N.A. v. *Israel-British Bank (London) Ltd.*[52] is often cited in support of Rule 200(2)(c) in Dicey and Morris, namely the "place of enrichment" rule.[53] However, the case cannot be said to stand for this proposition. In *Chase Manhattan* a New York bank mistakenly paid US$2 million into the defendant's account with another New York bank. The defendant carried on business in London. The paying bank claimed that it was entitled to the mistaken payment in equity. Specifically, it argued that where a person mistakenly pays another, equity will consider that the recipient holds that money, or its traceable proceeds, as constructive trustee for the payer. It argued this because the defendant was being wound up, and it sought a priority over other creditors.

The defendant conceded the plaintiff's contention that the claim was governed by the law of New York. However, it denied that the imposition of the constructive trust formed part of the *lex causae*. The defendant argued that the constructive trust was a remedy imposed by the *lex fori*. As a constructive trust had not as yet arisen under the *lex causae*, the *lex fori* could not now impose one, as the defendant's property had already been impressed with a trust as a result of the winding up proceedings. Thus, the issue here was whether the constructive trust arose as a matter of substantive or procedural law. It was not concerned with the actual issue of which law applied and thus, with the possible choice of law rule.

Goulding J. held that under New York law the defendant had become a constructive trustee of the money. The plaintiff's equitable interest in the property and thus, the imposition of the trust on the recipient, arose as a matter of substantive law and not as a result of a remedial or procedural rule.[54] Although

[52] [1981] Ch. 105.

[53] See for example, Dicey and Morris, pp.1485, 1503; Jaffey on the Conflict of Laws, p.277; see also *Hong Kong and Shanghai Banking Corp Ltd.* v. *United Overseas Bank Ltd.* [1992] 2 S.L.R. 495, 500 (H.C. of Singapore).

[54] Goulding J. further held that there was no significant difference between the law of New York and England in relation to the imposition of a constructive trust for mistaken payments (see p.118 E and 128 A–B). Note however Lord Browne-Wilkinson's reinterpretation of *Chase-Manhattan* in *Westdeutsche Landesbank Girozentrale* v. *Islington LBC* [1996] 2 W.L.R. 802, 837 where he concludes that the law of New York and England were in fact different.

reference was made by counsel in argument to the then equivalent of Rule 200 of Dicey and Morris, this was not referred to in the judgment. The applicability of the law of New York was agreed between the parties. It was not applied through the operation of a choice of law rule.[55] The real issue was described by Goulding J. as "whether the equitable right of a person who pays money by mistake to trace and claim such money under the law of New York is conferred by substantive law or is of a merely procedural character".[56] His Lordship found that under New York law the defendant had become a constructive trustee of the moneys and that this arose "by a rule of substantive law and is not the mere result of a remedial or procedural rule".[57] The decision therefore does not assist the question of the choice of law rule for restitution.

* ***Macmillan Inc.* v. *Bishopsgate Investment Trust Plc* (No.3)**

Likewise, the decision of *Macmillan Inc.* v. *Bishopsgate Investment Trust plc (No.3)*[58] added little to the question of the choice of law rule for restitution.[59]

> The outcome of the decision was aptly described by Briggs: "Those who had harboured the hope that the law of international restitution would receive its definitive judgment on choice of law, and that it would as a result, gain the intellectual respectability which having a choice of law rule would confer, will have to wait a little longer yet".

Owing to fraud, shares which were to be held by the first defendant as trustee for the plaintiff, were used to secure debts of companies owned by the late Robert Maxwell and his family. The shares ended up in the names of the defendant banks following the collapse of the Maxwell empire. The plaintiff brought proceedings claiming restitution of these shares held by the defendant banks. In particular, it claimed that that the defendant banks held these shares on constructive trust for the plaintiff. The Court of Appeal characterised the relevant issue as whether the defendants had a defence of *bona fide* purchase for value without notice. Thus, as no issue arising in the case was characterised as restitutionary, there was no need to apply the restitutionary choice of law rule, whatever that may have been. Despite the approval of the then equivalent of Rule 200 in Dicey and Morris by Staughton L.J.,[60] parallel doubts were raised by Auld L.J.[61] who described the place of enrichment rule as "tentative" and noted that no previous decision was binding on the Court of Appeal.[62]

[55] This was noted by Auld L.J. in *Macmillan Inc.* v. *Bishopsgate Investment Trust Plc (No.3)* [1996] 1 W.L.R. 387, 408, where he specifically notes, in relation to the place of enrichment rule, that *Chase Manhattan* "does not expressly decide it".

[56] *Chase Manhattan Bank N.A.* v. *Israel-British Bank (London) Ltd.* [1981] 1 Ch. 105, 122D.

[57] *Id.*, 127B.

[58] [1996] 1 W.L.R. 387.

[59] A. Briggs, "From Complexity to Anticlimax: Restitution and Choice of Law" [1996] R.L.R. 88.

[60] *Macmillan Inc.* v. *Bishopsgate Investment Trust Plc.* (No.3) [1996] 1 W.L.R. 387, 398.

[61] *Id.*, 408.

[62] It should be noted that Aldous L.J. did not express any view on the correctness of the resitution choice of law rule in Dicey and Morris. The plaintiff's submission that the rule applied was rejected. It was said that "rule [200] is concerned with what has been called unjust enrichment, not

* *Re Jogia (A Bankrupt)*

Sir Nicolas Browne-Wilkinson V.-C. expressed approval of the then equivalent of Rule 200(2)(c) in Dicey and Morris, namely the "place of enrichment" rule, in *re Jogia (A Bankrupt)*.[63] The case however, was concerned with the service of proceedings out of the jurisdiction. In particular, the trustee in bankruptcy commenced proceedings to recover alleged excessive charges, from the bankrupt's French supplier, as money had and received and also to recover certain payments, alleging that they were void as against the trustee in bankruptcy, being made after the date of the receiving order. In order for the service to have been valid, it first had to be shown that the case fell within one of the heads of jurisdiction,[64] and secondly, that the case satisfied Order 11, rule 4(2), namely that "the case is a proper one for service out of the jurisdiction"; that is that the trustee has shown a good arguable case on the merits.[65]

In relation to the first of these requirements, it had to be shown that the claim fell within the then Order 11, rule 1(f),[66] namely that the relevant quasi-contract had been made within England. It was not necessary to form any definitive view on this question. This issue was deferred and it was held that even if the requirements of Order 11, rule 1 had been satisfied, the trustee had not shown a good arguable case on the merits. Thus, despite observations to the effect that a quasi-contract arises in the place of receipt, and that this conforms with the view of Dicey and Morris,[67] these were merely *obiter dicta*. Not only was the case one concerned with jurisdiction, but the purported choice of law rule principles were not ultimately relevant to the actual question of jurisdiction.[68]

* *El Ajou* v. *Dollar Land Holdings plc*

El Ajou v. *Dollar Land Holdings plc*[69] is also cited in support of the "place of enrichment rule".[70] The plaintiff's funds and securities were invested in a fraudulent share selling scheme without his authority. The proceeds of the fraudulent share selling scheme were channelled through several jurisdictions and some of these were invested in a London property development project in conjunction with the first defendant (DLH). DLH was unconnected with the fraud. The

a case like the present where the defendants gave value for the shares and the dispute is whether the legal titles they obtained have priority over that of the plaintiffs". *Id.*, 418.

[63] [1988] 1 W.L.R. 484.

[64] These are now contained in CPR 6.20.

[65] The test in respect of the merits of the plaintiff's claim, would now be that of a "serious issue" to be tried: *Seaconsar Far East Ltd.* v. *Bank Markazi Johmouri Islami Iran* [1994] 1 A.C. 438. Now covered by CPR 6.21(2A). See ch. 10.1 below.

[66] Now CPR 6.20(5).

[67] Dicey and Morris' view in the tenth edition was that "save in cases where the obligation arises in connection with a contract or an immovable, the proper law of the quasi-contract is the law of the country where the enrichment occurs".

[68] Although the question of choice of law possibly does enter the inquiry of whether there is a serious issue to be tried for the purposes of granting leave for service out of the jurisdiction: see ch. 10.2.1.1.

[69] [1993] 3 All E.R. 717 (reversed) [1994] 2 All E.R. 685.

[70] See Dicey and Morris, p.1485.

plaintiff brought a claim for knowing receipt against DLH to recover the traceable proceeds received by DLH. One of the issues that arose was whether the plaintiff could trace through the various civilian jurisdictions.[71] The defendant argued that this was not possible given that civil law jurisdictions did not recognise the concept of equitable ownership. It argued, that in order to succeed, the plaintiff must have been able to obtain an equitable charge against each successive account.

It was held that this argument was not open to DLH, as in the particular case, no question of foreign law had been pleaded and no evidence of foreign law had been tendered. As such, foreign law was presumed to be the same as English law.[72] Millett J. nevertheless noted that English law, including the principles of equity, would have at any rate applied to the plaintiff's claim. This was for two reasons. First, a claim for knowing receipt is to be classified as the equitable counterpart of the common law action for money had and received, namely as a receipt-based restitutionary claim. Applying the restitutionary choice of law rule in Dicey and Morris, the applicable law would be the law of the country where the defendant received the money. In this case, the proceeds received by DLH were received by it in England.[73] Alternatively, it was said that if tracing were to be characterised as procedural, then it would be governed by English law as the *lex fori*.[74] Millett J's statements in favour of the "place of enrichment rule" were *obiter dicta*. As foreign law had not been pleaded, English law applied as it was presumed to be the same as foreign law.

* *Arab Monetary Fund* v. *Hashim*

The case of *Arab Monetary Fund* v. *Hashim*,[75] is the only English authority which has applied a restitutionary choice of law rule. However, the case does not leave us any better off in understanding the content of the restitutionary choice of law rule, while it must be doubted whether the issue was correctly characterised. The Arab Monetary Fund (AMF), an international body set up through agreement by twenty Arab states, sought to recover bribes received by its former president, Dr Hashim. The claims were brought alternatively in contract, tort and unjust enrichment. As has already been discussed,[76] the Court of Appeal characterised the restitutionary claim to recover the bribe as being in unjust enrichment, thereby attracting the relevant choice of law rule.[77]

There are certain observations which need to be made in relation to this case. First, as already discussed, this case was wrongly characterised as being in unjust enrichment.[77] The case was concerned with restitution, or disgorgement,

[71] In relation to the issue of tracing in private international law, see ch. 4.5 above.

[72] [1993] 3 All E.R. 717, 736e–f.

[73] *Id.*, 736g–h.

[74] *Id.*, 736j. It has previously been submitted that tracing is a substantive issue to be governed by the law applicable to the issue arising out of the right contingent on tracing. See ch. 4, §5.2.3.

[75] [1996] 1 Lloyd's Rep. 589.

[76] See above ch. 4.4.2.

[77] [1996] 1 Lloyd's Rep. 589, 593, *per* Nourse L.J., 597, *per* Saville L.J.

[78] See above ch. 4, §§4.2 and 4.3.

for a breach of a fiduciary duty arising through Hashim's employment relationship with the AMF. This should have been characterised as a breach of a consensual relationship, namely a contract. Secondly, in any event, the alternative characterisation of the bribe in restitution was of no particular consequence, as both choice of law rules pointed to the law of Abu Dhabi.

There was an approval of the restutionary choice of law rule in Dicey and Morris. Yet, reference was only made to the general proposition, namely that ". . . the obligation to restore the benefit of an enrichment obtained at another's expense is governed by the proper law of the obligation". In applying this general choice of law rule, Saville L.J. sought to find the law under which the obligation to make restitution arose. His Lordship stated:

> in the present case the relationship between AMF and Dr Hashim was governed by the law of Abu Dhabi, as was the relationship under the building contract obtained through the bribe; and it was in Abu Dhabi that the dishonest abuse occurred; the companies obtaining the contract by putting forward a clearly dishonest low tender, and Dr Hashim being instrumental in obtaining the contract for those who had bribed him.[79]

In essence, Saville L.J. sought to find the proper law of the obligation by looking at all the circumstances surrounding the facts of the case. As most of the significant circumstances pointed to Abu Dhabi, it was concluded that the law of Abu Dhabi should apply. No single connecting factor or test was isolated which led to the law of Abu Dhabi. What is also significant is that the law of Abu Dhabi did not apply by virtue of the fact that it was the place of enrichment. In fact, the place of enrichment was not even isolated as a factor. Abu Dhabi was not the place of enrichment, as the bribes had been paid into Dr Hashim's bank account in Switzerland, whilst most of the benefits of the bribes and thus the ultimate place of enrichment was in England.[80]

6 OTHER COMMON LAW CASES

There are very few other common law cases dealing with the choice of law rule for restitution in any significant detail. Given the small number, the significant cases are dealt with individually.

* *The South Australian Motor Vehicle Contribution & Indemnity cases*

In a series of cases before the South Australian Supreme Court concerning contribution or indemnity proceedings, Bray C.J. put forward the view that the choice of law rule for "quasi-contract" is the law of the place with which the

[79] [1996] 1 Lloyd's Rep. 589, 597.
[80] [1993] 1 Lloyd's Rep. 543, 565–6.

circumstances giving rise to the obligation have the most real connection.[81] In *Nominal Defendant* v. *Bagot's Executor & Trustee Company Ltd.*,[82] a party injured in a motor vehicle accident successfully brought an action in relation to his loss against the New South Wales' Nominal Defendant. Pursuant to the New South Wales Act,[83] the nominal defendant was entitled to a claim against the owner of the vehicle and brought such proceedings against the deceased's estate in South Australia. In a dissenting judgment, Bray C.J. held that the statutory right of recovery was "an obligation to indemnify someone who has satisfied an obligation arising out of tort" and that "the right so created should be classified jurisprudentially as quasi-contractual".[84] This "Quasi-Contract" was governed by the law of New South Wales, on the basis that "the proper law of a quasi-contract is the law of the place with which the circumstances giving rise to the obligation have the most real connection".[85] Such a conclusion was based on the initial right of action against the nominal defendant under the law of New South Wales and "as a result of the judgment in New South Wales and payment pursuant to it".[86] On appeal, in the High Court of Australia, the specific question was whether the New South Wales, statute created a debt which was actionable by the Nominal Defendant in South Australia against the executor of a deceased owner. As such, the question was solely one of construction of the relevant section.

In *Stewart* v. *Honey*,[87] a person was injured as a result of a motor vehicle accident between two vehicles in Queensland. He sued both drivers in Queensland and obtained judgment. As between the two defendants, liability was apportioned forty per cent to Stewart and sixty per cent to Alexander. The injured plaintiff recovered in full from the defendant Stewart; and Stewart, in turn, obtained judgment in Queensland against the other defendant, Alexander, for his proportionate share. Alexander did not pay to Stewart the sum ordered to be paid and Stewart then brought proceedings in South Australia against Alexander's insurer, Honey, pursuant to a South Australian statute.[88] Bray C.J. stated that the right to recover against the insurer was a right *sui generis* conferred by the statute,[89] but that "it, too, I think, can be categorised for the purposes of abstract jurisprudence or private international law as quasi-contractual".[90] His previous view as to choice of law was repeated, namely that:

[81] *Nominal Defendant* v. *Bagot's Executor & Trustee Company Ltd.* [1971] S.A.S.R. 346, 366, *per* Bray C.J, reversed on other grounds (1971) 125 C.L.R. 179; *Stewart* v. *Honey* [1972] 2 S.A.S.R. 585, 592, *per* Bray C.J.; *Hodge* v. *Club Motor Insurance Agency Pty. Ltd.* [1974] 7 S.A.S.R. 86, 89–91, *per* Bray C.J.

[82] [1971] S.A.S.R. 346, revd (1971) 125 C.L.R. 179.

[83] Namely, s.32(1) of the *Motor Vehicles (Third Party Insurance) Act* 1942–1963 (N.S.W.).

[84] *Nominal Defendant* v. *Bagot's Executor & Trustee Company Ltd.* [1971] S.A.S.R. 346, 365.

[85] *Id.*, 366.

[86] *Ibid.* See further ch. 7, §2.6.below.

[87] [1972] 2 S.A.S.R. 585.

[88] Section 112 of the *Motor Vehicles Act* 1959–1971 (S.A.).

[89] Thus, following an earlier decision of *Plozza* v. *South Australian Insurance Co. Ltd.* [1963] S.A.S.R. 122, 127, *per* Hogarth J.

[90] *Stewart* v. *Honey* [1972] 2 S.A.S.R. 585, 592.

> [t]he proper law of a quasi-contract, at least in a case where the obligation is not one supervening on any real contract, is *probably* the law of the place with which the circumstances giving rise to the obligation have the most real connection.[91] (*emphasis added*)

The two different characterisations of the right to recovery, as both a *sui generis* right conferred by statute and also as quasi-contractual, seem to be at odds with one another, at least for choice of law purposes. According to Bray C.J.'s analysis, South Australian law applied on either characterisation, yet it is not altogether clear what the final basis was for its application. Furthermore, the other judge in the majority, Mitchell J., agreed with Bray C.J. that South Australian law applied to the right to recover against the insurer without specifying any reasons for his decision.[92] Yet, Bray C.J.'s concluding comment, that "[t]he question is merely one of the construction of a South Australian statute creating a new right", suggests that the earlier characterisation, namely a *sui generis* right conferred by statute, was the relevant one for the purposes of his decision.

The above views in relation to the proper law of a quasi-contract were repeated by Bray C.J. in *Hodge* v. *Club Motor Insurance Agency Pty. Ltd.*[93] The passenger of a motor vehicle being driven in South Australia, suffered injuries in an accident in which the driver was killed. The vehicle was registered in Queensland, while the insurance policy was issued under the relevant Queensland statute. Pursuant to this Act,[94] the person injured was entitled to recover from the deceased's insurer if he would have been able to recover against the insured were the latter alive. The relevant issues in the case were whether the injured person's cause of action under the Queensland statute was justiciable before the courts of South Australia and, accordingly, whether she could serve the defendant out of the jurisdiction. The majority of the South Australian Supreme Court[95] answered these questions as a matter of statutory construction and gave affirmative answers to both. Bray C.J. held that unlike a tort, the quasi-contractual obligation did not need to be actionable under the South Australian law as well as the law of Queensland. As the law of Queensland was the proper law of the quasi-contractual obligation, under the choice of law rules for quasi-contracts, such an obligation would be enforceable subject to any public policy to the contrary. Through Bray C.J.'s reference to his earlier judgment in the *Bagot's Executor* case, it can be assumed that the choice of law rule for quasi-contracts was as previously stated, namely the law of the place with which the circumstances giving rise to the obligation have the most real connection. It was noted that as the plaintiff had no connection with Queensland and the accident did not occur in Queensland, it may have been argued that there is nothing

[91] *Ibid.*
[92] *Id.*, 596.
[93] [1974] 7 S.A.S.R. 86, 89–91.
[94] Section 4A of the *Motor Vehicles Insurance Acts* 1936 1968.
[95] Bright and Zelling J.J.

under the rules of private international law to attract the law of Queensland to the situation. The answer given by Bray C.J. is quite unconvincing. The driver was permitted to drive his car in South Australia pursuant to South Australian regulations:

> if it was insured and registered in compliance with the law of Queensland. The terms of the policy contemplate that the car might be driven by him in South Australia and the defendant undertook to be responsible for damages for bodily injuries caused in South Australia by his negligence. The permission to drive in South Australia can be regarded as conditional on the acceptance of the obligation imposed under the Queensland insurance policy by the Queensland law with regard to South Australian accidents and the defendant, by the contract of insurance, impliedly undertook so to accept them.[96]

This analysis is very much influenced by notions of implied contract[97] and it is highly doubtful whether such a connecting factor, or contact, would be put forward today. Moreover, it is submitted that the issue of a an insurer's direct liability to the victim of an accident caused by the insured should not be characterised as a restitutionary matter. The preferred view, it is submitted, is that the insurer's liability should be characterised as a contractual issue, to be determined by the proper law of the contract.[98] The victim of an accident who seeks to make the insurer directly liable must establish that under the law applicable to the contract of insurance, a victim is entitled to make a claim against the insurer directly. Therefore, the law of Queensland applied to the issue of the insurer's liability as the proper law of the insurance contract. It would also therefore follow that the issue of the insurer's liability in *Stewart* v. *Honey* should also have been characterised as a contractual issue. The issue was not in relation to the obligation to contribute as between the joint tortfeasors, Stewart and Alexander.[99] Having obtained judgment against Alexander, in relation to the latter's liability to contribute, the plaintiff was seeking to rely on the South Australian statutory provision so as to recover against his co-tortfeasor's insurer. The issue of whether Stewart was entitled to recover directly against the insurer was a contractual issue. As the law of South Australia was the proper law of the insurance contract,[100] the conclusion reached by the majority was ultimately correct.

[96] [1974] 7 S.A.S.R. 86, 91.

[97] This is also apparent from Bray C.J.'s references to Munkman, *The Law of Quasi-Contracts* (1964) and Stoljar, *The Law of Quasi-Contracts* (1950) in *Nominal Defendant* v. *Bagot's Executor & Trustee Company Ltd.* [1971] S.A.S.R. 346, 365 and not to Goff and Jones, *The Law of Restitution* (1966).

[98] *Plozza* v. *South Australian Insurance Co. Ltd.* [1963] S.A.S.R. 123, *esp.* 128; *Hall* v. *National General Insurance Co. Ltd.* [1967] V.R. 355, 360; see also Dicey and Morris, pp.1527–8. For the alternative view that such issues should be characterised as tortious, see: *Li Lian Tan* v. *Durham* [1966] S.A.S.R. 143, 149; *Ryder* v. *Hartford Insurance Co.* [1977] V.R. 257.

[99] Such an obligation was founded on the *Law Reform (Tortfeasors Contribution, Contributory Negligence and Division of Chattels) Act* 1952 (Qld.). Moreover, the issue of Alexander's liability to contribute to Stewart would have been governed by the law of Queensland, as it was the law of Queensland which compelled Stewart to pay compensation to the injured party, Robinson: see below ch. 8.2.6.

[100] The policy had been issued by a South Australian company in compliance with the *Motor Vehicles Act* 1959–1971 (S.A.)

*** Pettkus v. Becker**

In *Pettkus* v. *Becker*[101] a common law wife brought a claim for proprietary restitution over immovable property situated in Ontario. The Supreme Court of Canada allowed her claim for a constructive trust on the basis of unjust enrichment.[102] It noted that, although not specifically pleaded, such a claim was arguably governed by Quebec law and not by the law of Ontario, on the basis that the parties were domiciled in Quebec up until the purchase of the properties and thus the unjust enrichment was most closely connected with Quebec.[103] It was not suggested that the law of Ontario should apply on the basis that the property was situated in Ontario. Moreover, there was no suggestion that the defendant had been enriched in Ontario.

*** Hong Kong and Shanghai Banking Corp. Ltd. v. United Overseas Bank Ltd.**[104]

In this case, an employee of the plaintiff fraudulently transferred funds, by telegraphic transfer, from the plaintiff's branch in Manila to an account at the plaintiff's branch in New York. The monies were finally transferred into an account with the defendants in Singapore. Michael Hwang J.C. recognised three possible candidates for the *lex causae*, namely, either the law of the Philippines, the law of New York or the law of Singapore. As this was an area "unexplored by judicial authority", reference was made to the "leading textbook for guidance".[105] The then equivalent of Rule 200 of Dicey and Morris[106] was accepted as the applicable choice of law rule without further question. Given that the particular claim was not connected with a contract, nor did it involve immovables, it was to be governed by the law of the place where the enrichment occurred.

A particular issue arose as to whether the place of enrichment, for choice of law purposes, was the place of immediate enrichment (i.e. New York), or whether it was the place of ultimate enrichment (i.e. Singapore). It was concluded that the *lex causae* was the place of ultimate enrichment, namely Singapore. Again, a hypothetical example set by Dicey and Morris was referred to,[107] wherein it is concluded that in cases where an enrichment is initially received in one jurisdiction but ultimately ends up in another, "the law of the country in which the immediate benefit was received is less closely connected with the obligation than the law of the country in which the ultimate enrichment occurred". Michael Hwang J.C. recognised problems which may arise in more

[101] (1981) 117 D.L.R. (3d) 257.

[102] There is an argument that cases such as *Pettkus* v. *Becker* are not really about unjust enrichment but about fulfilling expectation losses: See for example Smith, p.368; P. Birks, "Mixing and Tracing" (1992) 45(2) C.L.P. 69, 96, n.70; S. Gardner, "Rethinking Family Property" (1993) 109 L.Q.R 263; *Cf.* L. Smith [1994] R.L.R. 102,103.

[103] *Id.*, 278.

[104] [1992] 2 S.L.R. 495 (H.C. of Singapore).

[105] *Id.*, 500.

[106] At the time of the decision this was rule 203 of the eleventh edition, 1987.

[107] Dicey and Morris, 11th ed. (London, 1987), p.1354. Now to be found at p.1502 of the 13th edition.

complex scenarios where, for example, a fraudster intends to transfer funds from one jurisdiction to another, using several intermediary jurisdictions as conduits in the process.[108] In a case where the funds are injuncted by a court order in one of the intermediary jurisdictions, it would not seem clear where the place of enrichment, albeit the place of ultimate enrichment, might be. Fortunately, these issues did not arise in the present case.

Ultimately however the above observations were *obiter dicta*. It was finally concluded that the court was at any rate bound to apply Singapore law, since neither party had adduced any evidence of New York law.[109]

* ***Thahir* v. *Pertamina***[110]

Pertamina was an Indonesian state enterprise. General Thahir had been appointed general assistant to the president director of Pertamina. Two of the contractors paid General Thahir bribes to ensure better contractual terms than they would have otherwise obtained if they had tendered for the work, as well as preferential treatment where payments to them were concerned. General Thahir deposited the proceeds into several accounts at the Sumitomo bank in Singapore. Pertamina claimed to be entitled to the deposits on the basis that the moneys were bribes received by General Thahir while in its employ.

Both Lai Kew Chai J.[111] and the Court of Appeal of Singapore characterised Pertamina's claim to recover the bribes as lying in restitution. Both applied the choice of law rule in Dicey and Morris and considered that in such case, the then equivalent of sub-rule 200(2)(c), namely the place of enrichment rule, applied. Accordingly, the law of Singapore governed the determination of the claim. As already noted in relation to *Arab Monetary Fund* v. *Hashim*,[112] a bribe should not be characterised as a matter of unjust enrichment but rather as restitution, or disgorgement for a wrong, namely a breach of a fiduciary duty.[113] It should therefore have been characterised as a breach of a consensual relationship, namely a contract, and thus the law of Indonesia should have applied.

It was argued that as a result of the contract of employment between Thahir and Pertamina, and the fact that Thahir had acted in breach of his duty to the plaintiffs in his capacity as employee, sub-rule 200(2)(a) should apply. That is, the case concerned a breach of an implied obligation not to take bribes in connection with a contract. As the restitutionary claim arose in connection with a contract, one should look towards the proper law of the contract to govern the matter; namely the law of Indonesia. It was held that the place of enrichment rule, namely sub-rule 200(2)(c), was not excluded by virtue of a prior contract. For sub-rule 200(2)(a), the law of the contract, to apply, one must be seeking to

108 [1992] 2 S.L.R. 495, 500–1.
109 *Id.*, 501.
110 *Thahir* v. *Pertamina* [1994] 3 S.L.R. 257 (C.A. of Singapore).
111 *Sumitomo Bank Ltd.* v. *Thahir & ors* [1993] 1 S.L.R. 735.
112 [1996] 1 Lloyd's Rep. 589.
113 See above ch. 4, §§4.2 and 4.3.

recover money that is paid pursuant to an ineffective, illegal or other such contract. In contrast, the recovery of bribes did not fall within the category of recovery of money paid pursuant to an ineffective contract, nor did it constitute a similar case. This is therefore arguably the only common law case which actually applied the "place of enrichment rule" so as to arrive at the governing law.

7

The Various Proposed Choice of Law Rules

1 THE PLACE OF ENRICHMENT RULE

THE LAW OF the place of enrichment has been proposed as the general choice of law rule for restitution,[1] or alternatively as the choice of law rule where the issue does not arise in relation to a contract, legal relationship or in relation to land.[2] It is also the preferred choice of law rule among certain civilian systems, in relation to payments not connected with a contract.[3] For example, under French law it is said that the applicable law for quasi-contracts is the law of the place where the event giving rise to the obligation occurred and thus, in cases of unjust enrichment, the applicable law is that of the place of enrichment.[4] This is the choice of law rule which has traditionally been put forward, having the attraction of a seemingly easily identifiable *locus*.

1.1 Arguments in Favour of Place of Enrichment Rule

There are some respectable arguments which can be raised in favour of the place of enrichment as the applicable choice of law rule. First, although the action for unjust enrichment requires both impoverishment and enrichment, the enrichment may be viewed as being at the heart of the principle against unjust enrichment and is therefore at the heart of the action. Put in another way, the action is not complete until an actual enrichment has occurred. The law of the place of enrichment may therefore be the most appropriate to determine whether an

[1] See *Re Jogia (A Bankrupt)* [1988] 1 W.L.R. 484, 495–6; *El Ajou* v. *Dollar Land Holdings Plc* [1993] 3 All E.R. 717, 736, *per* Millett J. (reversed on different grounds) [1994] 2 All ER 685; *Macmillan Inc.* v. *Bishopsgate Investment Trust Plc. (No.3)* [1996] 1 W.L.R. 387, 398, *per* Staughton L.J; J.H. Beale, *A Treatise on the Conflict of Laws* (1935), pp.1429–30; Gutteridge and Lipstein, "Conflicts of Law in Matters of Unjustifiable Enrichment" (1941) 7 C.L.J. 80; *U.S. Restatement on the Conflict of Laws (1st)* (1934), Rules 452 and 453; R. Leslie, "Unjustified Enrichment in the Conflict of Laws" (1998) 2 Edinburgh Law Review 233.

[2] Dicey and Morris, Rule 200(2)(c); J. Bird, "Choice of Law" in F. Rose (ed.), *Restitution and the Conflict of Law* (Oxford, 1995), p.135 (hereafter Bird). See also *Barclay's Bank Plc.* v. *Inc. Incorporated*, 17 February 1999 (unreported).

[3] See Munchener Kommentar BGB, Vol. 8, 3rd ed. (Munich 1998), I Vor Art. 38, no. 23 *sqq*. However, in cases of enrichment by encroachment (Eingriffskondiktion), it is the place of encroachment which is relevant: *id.*, no. 24. See P. Mayer, *Droit International Privé* (6th ed., 1998), p.448 (hereafter Mayer).

[4] Mayer, *loc. cit.*

enrichment has occurred of the sort which gives rise to a right to restitution. Thus, the system of law with the closest connection to the issue may often be the law of the place in which money which was not due was nevertheless paid, or in which the *gestor* acted to avoid loss to his neighbour.[5]

Secondly, as liability is imposed on the defendant involuntarily, it is preferable to base it on law which is connected with him. The law of the place of enrichment may be more closely connected with the defendant than the law of the place of the plaintiff's impoverishment. Thirdly, the law of the place of enrichment will probably be more appropriate to determine the availability of defences, such as that of change of position. The considerations in relation to security of receipt are closely connected with those of enrichment. If a party has received an enrichment, whether it has consequentially changed its position should arguably be determined by reference to the law of the place of enrichment. Fourthly, the place of enrichment will often be the place where the relevant enrichment, if surviving, is located. As it may ultimately be in the place of enrichment that the relevant order may have to be enforced, it may be argued that it is preferable that any decision was in accordance with its laws. The courts of the place of enrichment are arguably more likely to enforce a decision determined in accordance with their law, as opposed to the law of another jurisdiction.[6]

Most significantly, the great attractiveness with the place of enrichment rule is that it seems to provide a degree of certainty. A place of enrichment, seems to have a natural *locus* of the sort to be found in a connecting factor. A parallel may be drawn with asking the question of where the damage occurred, or arose, in cases of international torts. Usually, the place of enrichment can be pointed to with some degree of certainty. Theoretically, it is not something which requires a great deal of conceptual analysis. It is merely a question of fact, namely where was the enrichment received.

1.2 Arguments Against the Place of Enrichment Rule

Despite the arguments referred to above, it is submitted that there are stronger arguments dictating against the place of enrichment as a general choice of law rule for matters of unjust enrichment. Despite its apparent simplicity and its appearance of providing a definite *locus*, as a matter of practice, the place of enrichment is often difficult to ascertain. A benefit or an enrichment may often be moved around from the moment it first leaves the plaintiff's hands until it arrives at its final place of receipt. Furthermore, the rule has little attraction when one is dealing with non-money benefits such as services or the saving of

[5] J. Blaikie [1984] J.R. 112, 119; R. Stevens,"The Choice of Law Rules of Restitutionary Obligations" in F. Rose (ed.), *Restitution and the Conflict of Laws* (Oxford, 1995), p.218 (hereafter Stevens). See however ch. 4.6 above.

[6] Although admittedly it is difficult to prove this assertion, it nevertheless may be mounted as a further practical argument in favour of the place of enrichment rule.

inevitable expenses. More importantly, the rule carries with it certain significant theoretical setbacks. It is based on an erroneous understanding of the law of restitution, tainted by notions of implied contract, while there is little theoretical basis as to why the law of the place of enrichment should in fact be the law governing restitutionary issues.

1.2.1 *Unsound foundation*

It is submitted that the English foundations for the place of enrichment, as a candidate choice of law rule, stem from the old notions of implied contract.[7] It should be rejected to the extent that it is based on the theory of implied contract, as opposed to other considerations. The theory is that an implied contract arises upon receipt of the relevant benefit. Through such receipt, the recipient impliedly agrees to restore this benefit under a contract implied at law. As it is the implied contract which creates the obligation to repay the fictitious debt, it was thought that it is created under the law of where the quasi-contract was made, namely the place where the benefit was received. Thus in *Re Jogia*[8] Browne-Wilkinson V.C. stated:

> . . . I am of the view that quasi-contractual obligations of this kind arise from the receipt of money. I find it difficult to see how such obligation can be said to be "made" or "arise" in any place other than that of receipt . . . [S]ave in cases where the obligation to repay arises in connection with a contract or an immovable, the proper law of the quasi-contract is the law of the country where the enrichment occurs.[9]

Based on the notion of implied contract, the view was taken that the quasi-contractual obligation arose where the enrichment was received and that therefore the law of the place of receipt necessarily governed such an obligation.[10] As the implied contract theory has now been abandoned,[11] a purported choice of law rule which is based on notions of an implied contract should also be viewed as inappropriate. The place of enrichment rule therefore should be adopted in its own right, on the basis of it being the most appropriate rule. Accordingly, any older authorities which purportedly applied this rule on the basis of implied contract should be discounted.

1.2.2 *No General "place of enrichment" Rule*

It is submitted that there is no general rule that restitutionary issues are to be determined by the law of the place of enrichment, where such issue is not

[7] *Re Jogia (A Bankrupt)* [1988] 1 W.L.R. 484; *Bowling* v. *Cox* [1926] A.C. 751.

[8] [1988] 1 W.L.R. 484.

[9] *Id.*, 495.

[10] *Ibid.*; *Bowling* v. *Cox* [1926] A.C. 751, 754. See also A. Briggs, "Jurisdiction Under the Traditional Rules" in F.Rose, *Restitution and the Conflict of Laws"* (Oxford,1995), p.51.

[11] *Lipkin Gorman* v. *Karpnale Ltd.* [1991] 2 A.C. 548; *Westdeutsche Landesbank Girozentrale* v. *Islington LBC* [1996] A.C. 669.

connected with a contract or an immovable. That is, there is no single English authority where such a rule was applied to determine the applicable law.[12]

First, the case of *Re Jogia*[13] is a case dealing with jurisdiction. As already discussed, the case is based on the notion of implied contract, such that jurisdiction would exist if the implied contract had been formed within the jurisdiction or were governed by the jurisdiction's law. Although Browne-Wilkinson V.-C. approved of the place of enrichment rule, stating that the place of enrichment or receipt was also likely to be the proper law of the quasi-contractual claim, this did not form part of the *ratio* of the decision.[14] As noted previously,[15] it was held that even if the case fell within one of the heads of jurisdiction, the trustee had not shown a good arguable case on the merits. Thus, despite statements to the effect that a quasi-contract arises in the place of receipt, and that this conforms with the view of Dicey and Morris—that save in cases where the obligation arises in connection with a contract or an immovable, the proper law of the quasi-contract is the law of the country where the enrichment occurs—these were merely *obiter*. Not only was the case one concerned with jurisdiction, but the actual purported choice of law rule principles were not ultimately relevant to the question of jurisdiction. At any rate, the rationale of any purported application of the "place of enrichment" rule, was essentially based on notions of implied contract which must be distinguished today.

Secondly, although *Chase Manhattan*[16] is cited as supporting the "place of enrichment" rule, the parties in that case had agreed that New York law was the *lex causae*. Therefore, no issue arose as to the applicable law and the matter was not referred to in judgment. The case therefore is of no relevance in relation to the choice of law rule. Thirdly, the applicability of the "place of enrichment" rule was questioned by Auld L.J. in *Macmillan*;[17] while although Staughton L.J. approved of the rule in Dicey and Morris generally, as possibly governing the plaintiff's claim, he did not approve of the "place of enrichment rule". Finally, the place of enrichment rule was not applied by the Court of Appeal in *Arab Monetary Fund* v. *Hashim*.[18] This was a case which was not connected with a contract, or immovable property, and thus the "place of enrichment" rule should have been applicable.

[12] The rule was applied by the Court of Appeal of Singapore in *Thahir* v. *Pertamina* [1994] 3 S.L.R. 257, 272.

[13] [1988] 1 W.L.R. 484. See also ch. 10.2.2.1 below.

[14] Auld L.J. in *Macmillan Inc.* v. *Bishopsgate Investment Trust Plc.* (*No.3*) [1996] 1 W.L.R. 387, 408, considered that the approval of the "place of enrichment rule", expressed by Browne-Wilkinson V.-C. in *Re Jogia*, was *obiter*.

[15] See above p.123.

[16] *Chase Manhattan Bank N.A.* v. *Israel-British Bank* (*London*) *Ltd.* [1981] Ch. 105.

[17] *Macmillan Inc.* v. *Bishopsgate Investment Trust Plc.* (*No.3*) [1996] 1 W.L.R. 387, 408.

[18] *Arab Monetary Fund* v. *Hashim* [1996] 1 Lloyd's Rep. 589.

1.2.3 Ignoring other Elements of a Restitutionary Claim

The "place of enrichment" rule arguably over-emphasises the importance of the "enrichment" component in a restitutionary claim. First, it is said to play down the importance of the "at the expense of" element of unjust enrichment.[19] An unjust enrichment claim by subtraction requires a correlation between the plaintiff's loss and the defendant's gain.[20] However, secondly and more importantly, it is submitted that although the enrichment is an essential component of the action for unjust enrichment, it is the fact that the enrichment is "unjust" which is at the heart of the claim. To apply a general "place of enrichment" choice of law rule might be at the expense of the "unjust factor", which will be the rationale or the reason behind the reversal of such an enrichment. The essence of a restitutionary claim is not the fact that there was an enrichment *per se*, but that such an enrichment, in the particular circumstances, was unjust and therefore gives rise to restitution. By categorically applying the law of the place of the enrichment, the law most closely connected with the reason for restitution may be denied its say.[21]

1.2.4 Arbitrary Result

The law of the place of enrichment can be arbitrary and will not always necessarily be the one most closely connected with the unjust enrichment. As argued by Dicey and Morris, where a trustee of a will, mistakenly forwards trust money to a recipient in a foreign jurisdiction, it may be considered that the payment must be seen as part of the distribution of the English trust and as being most closely connected with England. Therefore, the recipient's obligation to refund the sum should be governed by English law.[22] The arbitrariness of the place of enrichment rule was recognised by Morris, who stated:

> The place of enrichment may, for instance, have no more than the most casual connexion with the real seat of the obligation, as when the payment is made on a Saturday afternoon in a New Jersey golf club, but the transaction in respect of which the money was believed to be due was a purely New York transaction.[23]

It is said that the place of enrichment will be connected with the defendant and that therefore it is just that such law should determine the defendant's restitutionary liability. However, in many cases the place of enrichment will be quite unconnected with the defendant or indeed with the liability to make restitution. In *Arab Monetary Fund* v. *Hashim*,[24] although the place of enrichment was arguably Switzerland, being the location of Dr Hashim's account which received the bribe, neither Dr Hashim, the bribee, nor the other facts of the case

[19] Burrows, p.492.
[20] *Ibid.*
[21] See ch. 8 below.
[22] Dicey and Morris, p.1502.
[23] J. Morris, "The Choice of Law Clause in Statutes" [1946] 62 L.Q.R. 170, 182.
[24] [1996] 1 Lloyd's Rep. 589.

were particularly connected with Switzerland.[25] Not surprisingly, the Court of Appeal held that the proper law of the restitutionary obligation was Abu Dhabi; this was the law of the place which was most connected with the relevant facts surrounding the payment of the bribe. Interestingly, the Court of Appeal did not even refer to the place of enrichment as one of the indicative factors which may point to the proper law.

The notion of a "place of enrichment" is rather fictitious where the enrichment consists of an electronic transfer of funds, or where there are a variety of factors surrounding the receipt of a benefit. For example, where an English defendant channels the proceeds of fraud into his bank account in Switzerland, there is little reason why Swiss law should govern the defendant's restitutionary liability, where the only connection with Switzerland is the defendant's bank account. A place of enrichment rule in such a situation would only be a blessing to fraudsters, who might wish to regulate their potential liability by channelling funds, and thereby becoming "enriched", in the desired jurisdictions. This has been recognised in the most recent edition of Dicey and Morris where it has been added:

> But in view of the diversity of situations in which a restitutionary claim may arise, it may be that the place of enrichment will not always give an answer which corresponds to the law which has the closest connection with the claim.[26]

1.2.5 Meaning of Place of Enrichment

What the place of enrichment actually means is unclear.[27] This is especially so when the enrichment is channelled through bank accounts. Does the place of enrichment mean the place where the defendant was when the enrichment was received, the place where the enrichment was irretrievably deposited, or does it refer to the place where the defendant had access to the enrichment and was thereby enriched? The place of enrichment could refer to the defendant's location, such that it means the place of the defendant's "residence or seat".[28] However, such a technique does nothing more than apply the personal law of the defendant under a different guise and therefore should be rejected as not being particularly connected with the proper law of the restitutionary issue.

In searching for the place of enrichment, a distinction could be drawn between immediate enrichment and ultimate enrichment. Dicey and Morris give the example of a mistaken payment paid into the Paris branch of an English bank to be credited to the account of X at the London office of the same bank.[29]

[25] See *Arab Monetary Fund* v. *Hashim* [1993] 1 Lloyd's Rep. 543, 565–6, where it was noted that the benefits of the bribe were enjoyed by Dr Hashim in England. *Cf. Thahir* v. *Pertamina* [1994] 3 S.L.R. 257, 275.

[26] Dicey and Morris, p.1498. See also Cheshire and North, pp.677–8.

[27] See J. Morris, "The Choice of Law Clause in Statutes" (1946) 62 L.Q.R. 170, 182.

[28] Zweigert and Müller-Gindullis, *Quasi Contract*, in Lipstein (ed.), *International Encyclopedia of Comparative Law*, Vol. III, ch.30, p.16.

[29] Dicey and Morris, p.1502.

It is said that the proper law of the obligation would be English law, as the law of the place where the immediate benefit was received is a little less closely connected with the obligation than the law of the ultimate receipt.[30] However, the Privy Council seems to have taken a different approach in *Bowling* v. *Cox*.[31] The respondent was executor of a will in British Honduras, under which property of a bankrupt became vested in him. The respondent's attorney collected assets in British Honduras and remitted them to the respondent in Chicago. The Privy Council allowed the trustee in bankruptcy to serve proceedings out of the jurisdiction against the respondent in Chicago,[32] on the basis that British Honduras was the place of receipt, and thus where the quasi-contract was made.[33] The Privy Council therefore considered that the place of the executor's immediate receipt was the relevant receipt, or enrichment. This was British Honduras, the place where the attorney-administrator of the executor received the relevant moneys and not Chicago (or Illinois), the place where the moneys were remitted by the attorney-administrator to the executor.

The difficulties in determining the place of enrichment are accentuated in cases of claims contingent on tracing. For example, an employee forges his employer's cheques and pays them into his account in Amsterdam. Following this he draws a cheque in favour of his mistress. He gives it to her in Brussels, she in turn pays them into her account in Paris.[34] Where is the place of enrichment? It could be England, where the employee fraudulently received, or obtained, the cheque. It could also be Amsterdam, where the employee paid the cheque into his account, thereby being able to draw out moneys and so being "enriched". Alternatively, it could also be either the law of Belgium or France, as the law where the mistress received the cheque or where she paid it into her account respectively. If the employer sued the mistress as recipient, one might say that the focus should be on her particular enrichment as defendant. This would then mean that the question of *who* the plaintiff sues will effect the choice of law. Moreover, the plaintiff will have to demonstrate that the moneys in the defendant's hands are the traceable product of his original money. That is, a chain of enrichments will have to be demonstrated. Will the focus be on the first enrichment, the last, or the immediate enrichment of the defendant, or is a test

[30] See *Hong Kong and Shanghai Banking Corp Ltd.* v. *United Overseas Bank Ltd.* [1992] 2 S.L.R. 495 (H.C. of Singapore); *Sumitimo Bank Ltd.* v. *Kartika Ratna Thahir* [1993] 1 S.L.R. 735, 784–5 (affirmed by the C.A. of Singapore).

[31] [1926] A.C. 751. McLeod considers that the proper law is the law of the place where the immediate benefit was received: J. McLeod, *The Conflict of Laws* (Calgary, 1983), p.574 (hereafter McLeod). This also seems to be the position in the U.S.A.: *First Winsconsin Trust Co.* v. *Shroud* 916 F. 2d 939 (5th Cir. 1990); *Cf. Phoenix Canada Oil Co. Ltd.* v. *Texaco Inc.* 560 F. Supp. 1372 (D. Del. 1983).

[32] Service out of the jurisdiction was based on the predecessor of CPR 6.20(5) on the basis that there existed a contract which was formed within the jurisdiction, or was governed by the law of British Honduras.

[33] [1926] A.C. 751, 754; see also the discussion of *Bowling* v. *Cox* in *Re Jogia (A Bankrupt)* [1988] 1 W.L.R. 484, 495.

[34] The example is based on the facts of *Banque Belge pour l'Etranger* v. *Hambrouk* [1921] 1 K.B. 321.

to be formulated of where "in substance" the defendant was enriched? These difficulties between immediate and ultimate enrichment in relation to proprietary claims are also highlighted in *Macmillan*.[35] The plaintiffs unsuccessfully argued that the "place of enrichment" rule applied and that therefore their claim was governed by English law, as the place where the share certificates were handed over. Aldous L.J. stated that even if this rule applied, the relevant benefit or enrichment the defendants had received was the legal titles to the shares, which were obtained in New York.[36] Therefore, the law of New York was at any rate the likely applicable law under the place of enrichment rule.

The existence of various possible meanings of the place of enrichment illustrate its impracticality as a general choice of law rule. What will constitute the place of enrichment may be subject to various interpretations. Moreover, it can conceivably be interpreted in such a way as to attract the application of a particular law. For example, in many cases of international product liability, the place where the tort was in substance committed has been interpreted to mean not the place where the product was manufactured, but where it was sold without warning.[37] Such decisions were arguably based on the desire to find that the tort was committed within the jurisdiction for the purpose of service *ex juris*.[38] Until the amendment of the jurisdiction head for tort under the RSC in 1987, jurisdiction could only be assumed if the action was "founded on a tort committed within the jurisdiction". Thus, there was a tendency to define the place where the tort was committed to overcome this technical obstacle.[39] What this example illustrates is that there should be no pretence that a choice of law rule of the "place of enrichment" will provide greater certainty. The "place of enrichment" is a sufficiently malleable concept, such that it can be interpreted and applied by the courts so as to achieve a desired result. If a categorical choice of law rule is not to be applied with certainty, but is to be moulded to attract the law with the closest and most real connection, it is preferable to acknowledge this.

[35] *Macmillan Inc.* v. *Bishopsgate Investment Trust Plc.* (*No.3*) [1996] 1 W.L.R. 387.

[36] *Id.*, 418.

[37] *Distillers Co. Ltd.* v. *Thompson* [1971] A.C. 458; *Castree* v. *E.R. Squibb and Sons Ltd.* [1980] 1 W.L.R. 1248. A similar issue of where a tort was committed arises in the context of negligent misstatements. The tort is committed at the place where the representation is received and acted upon and not the place from which it was sent: *Diamond* v. *Bank of London and Montreal* [1979] 1 Lloyd's Rep. 335 (C.A.); *Cordoba Shipping Co. Ltd.* v. *National State Bank Elizabeth, New Jersey* (*The Albaforth*) [1984] 2 Lloyd's Rep. 91 (C.A.).

[38] L. Collins (1972) 21 I.C.L.C.Q. 656, 666.

[39] The twelfth edition of Dicey and Morris went so far as to suggest that the Privy Council in *Distillers Co. Ltd.* v. *Thompson*, [1971] A.C. 458, recharacterised the negligent act as negligent failure to warn rather than negligent manufacture as such: p.1511.

2 LEX FORI

It has been argued that restitutionary claims should be governed by the *lex fori*.[40] It is said that, as unjust enrichment claims are based on "conceptions of rightness and justice", these cannot "be sought in any other than the court's own legal system".[41] This theory has generally attracted disapproval from other writers.[42] The main proponent of this view, Ehrenzweig, based his view on the notion that the law of restitution is purely remedial,[43] or purely based on conscience and that the *lex fori* should therefore apply to international restitutionary issues. This rationale is fallacious on two grounds. First, the law of restitution consists of separate causes of action and is not purely remedial. Secondly, the preferred view is that remedies are questions of substance to be governed by the *lex causae* and not ones of procedure to be governed by the *lex fori*.[44] Moreover, the use of the *lex fori* as a choice of law rule for restitution rests far too much upon the accidents of jurisdiction and goes against the general internationalist trend in private international law.

However, many restitutionary claims are in equity, while almost all claims of proprietary restitution will be equitable proprietary claims.[45] There is a distinct view that equitable issues should be governed by the law of the forum. As has already been discussed, this view should be rejected.[46] Equitable issues should be characterised as issues of substance, in accordance with the causative event giving rise to the equitable response.

Short of accepting the *lex fori* as a categorical choice of law rule, Lee has argued that, in fact, the courts apply the *lex fori* on the grounds of public policy.[47] Although the courts do not directly refer to such a doctrine, they have, including by indirect means, applied their own law to either deny or uphold restitution because the result to which foreign law would lead is obnoxious to forum public policy. Lee's approach is very much influenced by, and commends, the American interest analysis: namely, that the court should apply the law of the state which has the most significant relationship to the occurrence and the parties with respect to a particular issue, having regard, *inter alia*, to the contacts

[40] A. Ehrenzweig, "Restitution in the Conflict of Laws" (1961) 36 N.Y.U.L.R. 1298. See also Gutteridge and Lipstein, "Conflicts of Law in Matters of Unjustifiable Enrichment" (1941) 7 C.L.J. 80, 91.

[41] A. Ehrenzweig, "Restitution in the Conflict of Laws" (1961) 36 N.Y.U.L.R. 1298, 1314.

[42] Gutteridge and Lipstein, "Conflicts of Law in Matters of Unjustifiable Enrichment" (1941) 7 C.L.J. 80, 91; Bird, pp.102–6.

[43] Ehrenzweig, *op. cit.*, 1302, 1314.

[44] *Chase Manhattan Bank N.A.* v. *Israel-British Bank (London) Ltd.* [1981] Ch. 105, 124; *McKain* v. *R.W. Miller & Co. (SA)* (1991) 174 C.L.R. 1, 24–5, *per* Mason CJ, 48–9, *per* Deane J. See also *Phrantzes* v. *Argenti* [1960] 2 Q.B. 37. See also *Batthyanay* v. *Walford* (1887) 36 Ch.D. 269, 284, *per* Cotton L.J.

[45] See above ch. 1.3.

[46] See above ch. 4.2.

[47] S. Lee, "Restitution, Public Policy and the Conflict of Laws" (1998) 20 U.Q.L.J. 1.

with relevant states and the policies and interests of those states in having their law applied. Yet, the "invocation of forum public policy should not depend so much on the form, content or rationale of the foreign law as it does on the *result* to which foreign law would lead as compared with the relief which is available on the evidence under forum law".[48] Lee's approach amounts to a marriage between a general *lex fori* choice of law rule and the American interest analysis, where greatest emphasis is placed on whether the forum state has an interest in applying its public policy.

As has already been submitted, there is no compelling reason why a different choice of law rule approach, whether this be in the form of a general *lex fori* rule or a forum public policy rule, should be specifically adopted in respect of restitutionary issues as opposed to other issues arising in the conflict of laws. Thus, unless a general overhaul of the entire conflict of laws is to be adopted, thereby replacing the traditional choice of law rule methodology with a public policy or interest analysis approach, it is difficult to see why such an approach should be adopted for matters of unjust enrichment and not also, for example, for matters of tort and contract.[49] Questions of forum public policy enter just as much into the inquiry of whether a contract is void for illegality, or whether particular conduct is considered negligent so as to allow compensation in respect of loss, as they might in relation to whether an enrichment should be reversed. The government interest analysis has already been discussed above, where it was concluded that it is not only contrary to the current English conflict of laws but that it also allows for too much flexibility at the expense of certainty.[50] The forum public policy approach of Lee also faces these very same criticisms[51] and therefore is not, it is submitted, an attractive alternative. The orthodox view is that public policy only applies to exclude claims to enforce or recognise rights under an otherwise applicable foreign law.[52] It does not operate as a choice of law rule. Lee's approach requires an overhaul of the entire conflict of laws, while it cannot be said to provide any clear direction.

Lee seeks to justify a number of decisions on the basis of forum public policy. At the time when almost all of these cases were decided, the law of restitution had not as yet received recognition at domestic level, let alone in private international law. It is therefore to be expected that the courts would not have recognised a distinct restitutionary issue, or indeed a separate choice of law rule. If

48 S. Lee, "Restitution, Public Policy and the Conflict of Laws" (1998) 20 U.Q.L.J. 1, 9.

49 In a similar tone to Ehrenzweig, Lee seems to justify this on the basis that "[r]estitution corrects the harsh results that might otherwise flow from rigid adherence to other legal doctrines": *id.*, 1. Yet, as has already been submitted above, a restitutionary issue, so characterised, is not about reversing enrichment on the basis of idiosyncratic notions of justice but is a specific issue concerned with the circumstances in which an enrichment may be reversed by a legal system in specifically defined circumstances.

50 See above pp.118–20.

51 Lee in fact recognises that his approach does not allow for a great deal of certainty, noting that the "full range of circumstances falling within the purview of forum public policy needs to be worked out on a case-by-case basis": *id.*, 3.

52 Dicey and Morris, Rule 2; Cheshire and North, p.123–32; Jaffey, pp.527–35.

Lee's thesis is correct, all that it tells us is that courts were able to overcome an inadequacy in the conflict of laws to deal with such topics, given the unavailability of a sophisticated, or any, choice of law rule, by applying the *lex fori*. Is it desirable that this be continued at a time when the law of restitution has received recognition domestically and is concurrently receiving such recognition in private international law? Furthermore, explaining restitution in private international law in terms of a court applying its own law where some foreign law "would violate some fundamental principle of justice, some prevalent conception of good morals, some deep-rooted tradition of common weal",[53] cannot, it is submitted, be relevant to all restitutionary claims for the purposes of private international law. Whereas public policy considerations may be relevant in some of the categories of cases recognised by Lee, such as the deliberate commission of illegal acts, fraudulent evasion of law, fraud or duress against the owner of property or other immoral conduct, many, if not most, restitutionary claims do not necessarily relate to morally unacceptable conduct on the part of one of the parties. Cases of mistake, or where a contract is void, frustrated or discharged are examples of situations where neither party is guilty of conduct justifying the public policy of the forum applying its law, or denying the application of a foreign law, so as to prevent or allow restitution. Similarly, in many cases of unauthorised transfers of property, ignorance or fraud cases, the defendant is often an innocent recipient. The law merely determines whether the defendant is unjustly enriched at the expense of the plaintiff without necessarily making a moral judgment as to his conduct. In other words, the law in such cases determines who is entitled to the "enrichment". It is doubtful whether the best way of solving these questions is through questions of public policy *via* an interest analysis.

3 MULTIPLE CHOICE OF LAW RULES

As has already been noted, there are those who propose a choice of law rule comprising several sub-rules. The variety of circumstances giving rise to unjust enrichment claims should attract different choice of law rules. The main identifiable circumstances are restitutionary claims arising in connection with a contract and those arising in connection with property. A further identifiable circumstance is where an unjust enrichment claim arises in connection with a particular relationship. These various sub-rules will be examined separately.

3.1 Law of the Contract

There is a view that the existence and the scope of the duty to make restitution of benefits acquired in connection with a contract are governed by the law which governs the contract, or by the law which would have governed the contract, if

[53] *Loucks* v. *Standard Oil Co. of New York* 224 N.Y. 99, 111 (1918) *per* Cardozo J.

the contract had been validly concluded.[54] Although the duty to make restitution does not arise under the invalid or otherwise ineffective contract, it nevertheless arises in connection with a contract. Therefore, it can be argued that the law which rendered the contract ineffective should also determine the consequential restitutionary claim. What is not agreed upon by those who advocate in favour of the *lex contractus* applying to such situations, is whether the law of the contract will apply strictly,[55] or whether it will merely apply in most cases as the law with which the duty to make restitution has its closest and most real connection.[56] That is, will the duty to make restitution be deemed to be governed by the law of the contract, irrespective of other factors? Furthermore, if the right of restitution is to be governed by the law that applied, or would have applied, to the relevant contract, how is the law of that contract to be determined? Is it to be determined pursuant to the Rome Convention or a previous common law method?

The law governing most contractual matters is determined by the Rome Convention on the Law applicable to Contractual Obligations 1980 (the "Rome Convention").[57] The governing law of a contract is that chosen by the parties, either expressly or impliedly as "demonstrated with reasonable certainty by the terms of the contract or the circumstances of the case".[58] In the event that there is no express or implied choice, the contract is to "be governed by the law of the country with which it is most closely connected".[59] Article 10(1)(e) of the Convention provides that the law applicable to the contract under the rules of the Convention shall govern "the consequences of nullity of the contract".[60]

The United Kingdom has reserved the right to not apply Article 10(1)(e) under s.2(2) of the Act; the reason is that under English and Scots law, the right to recover the consequences of nullity of the contract forms part of the law of restitution, not of contract.[61] Therefore, restitutionary obligations which may arise as a result of an invalid contract are not to be determined by the law applicable to the contract by reason of the Rome Convention.[62] The relevant choice of law rules should therefore be those applicable, as a matter of English private inter-

[54] Dicey and Morris, pp.1493–7; Bird, p.128–30; P. Brereton, "Restitution and Contract" in F. Rose (ed.), *Restitution and the Conflict of Laws* (Oxford, 1995), pp.142 *et seq*.; Stevens, pp.193–9. See also J. Blaikie [1984] J.R. 112, 123–4. *Cf*. Burrows, pp.492–4; Cheshire and North, p.686; R. Leslie, "Unjustified Enrichment in the Conflict of Laws" (1998) 2 Edinburgh Law Review 233.

[55] See Brereton, pp.161–2 *et. seq*.; Stevens, pp.197–8.

[56] See Dicey and Morris, p.1495; J. Blaikie [1984] J.R. 112, 123–4.

[57] Implemented in the Contracts (Applicable Law) Act 1990, Schedule 1 (hereafter "the Act").

[58] *Id*., Art. 3(1).

[59] *Id*., Art. 4(1).

[60] In many civilian systems the general view is that the putative proper law of the contract will govern the consequential restitutionary obligations: see Munchener Kommentar BGB, Vol. 7, I Vor Art. 38 EGBG, no. 9–22; Mayer, p.482; *Σ. Βρέλλης*, *Ιδιωτικό Διεθνές Δίκαιο* (*Αθήνα*, 1988) *σ*.150 (S. Brelles, *Private International Law* (Athens, 1988), p.150).

[61] See the Lord Advocate, Hansard (H.L.) 12 December 1989 col. 1271; Cheshire and North, pp.600, 673; Chitty on Contracts, pp.1589, 1637, 1647; Dicey and Morris, pp.1496–7; *Kleinwort Benson* v. *Glasgow City Council* [1999] 1 A.C. 153. See also Giuliano-Lagarde Report, p.33.

[62] See above ch. 4, §§1.1 and 1.2. Also *Baring Brothers & Co. Ltd.* v. *Cunninghame District Council*, *The Times*, 30 September 1996.

national law, to restitutionary, rather than those applicable to contractual, issues. However, as was discussed in the context of characterisation, there is an argument that the restitutionary consequences of breach and frustration[63] fall within Article 10(1)(c) and (d) respectively.[64] Therefore, a restitutionary claim arising after the termination of a contract, or its frustration, would be governed by the contractual choice of law. Yet, as the Rome Convention only applies to "contractual obligations",[65] it is difficult to see how Article 10(1)(c) and (d) would apply to the consequential restitutionary issues.

According to Stevens, the law of the contract should not only determine whether the contract is a nullity, but also the consequences of such a nullity.[66] The logical law to govern the restitutionary claim is that by which the contract is shown to be a nullity. Although, the contract does not actually exist, it is not the non-existent contract which governs the consequences of its non-existence, but the system of law by which it does not exist. He therefore argues that the opt out from Article 10(1)(e) is of "no practical effect". Brereton also argues that when parties enter contractual relations, they do not necessarily appreciate the distinctions between the contractual and the restitutionary issues. It is reasonable for two parties who enter an agreement to expect that the law of the contract will not only govern issues such as the terms of the agreement, but also any claims in relation to benefits received under the contract where it becomes ineffective.[67] The argument seems to advocate that the justification for allowing the parties to choose a law for their contract, should extend to any consequential claims, even though as a matter of law they arise independently of the contract. The notion of bargain has a factual unity which runs across the formal division between the law of contract and restitution.

On the other hand, while echoing the arguments raised above, Dicey and Morris have placed significant qualifications on their sub-rule.[68] It is recognised that the proper law to govern the consequential restitutionary issues will not always be the law of the connected contract. Where for example the invalidity of a contract is founded on duress, coercion or fraud, it would be inappropriate to apply the law of the contract.[69] The same applies where there is generally no meeting of the minds. Similarly, if a contract is invalidated by a law other than that of the contract, it is also inappropriate to apply the law of the contract to determine the consequential right to restitution. These examples cover a large component, if not the majority, of the situations where a restitutionary claim is brought in the context of an ineffective contract. They therefore remove much

[63] Where a contract is governed by English law, the consequences of frustration will be governed by the Law Reform (Frustrated Contracts) Act 1943.

[64] Above pp.54–5; see also Dicey and Morris, p.1487, n.16; Brereton, pp.166–7; Stevens, pp.194–5.

[65] Article 1(1).

[66] Stevens, pp.197–8.

[67] Brereton, pp.144–5. See also Dicey and Morris, p.1495.

[68] Dicey and Morris, pp.1493–7.

[69] *Id.*, pp.1494–5.

of this sub-rule's importance. The circumstances where it seems Dicey and Morris consider there to be a good argument for applying the law of the connected contract, is where the factor rendering the contract ineffective cannot be said to have impugned the parties' chosen law. This would largely cover situations where a contract is frustrated or discharged through breach. If one accepts that the law of the connected contract should generally only apply in these specifice circumstances, then this may in fact be because the consequential restitutionary issue is to be characterised as a contractual issue.[70]

The *Evia Luck* (*No.2*)[71] is cited as a possible authority for the proposition that the law of the contract also determines the consequential restitutionary issues.[72] A Panamanian flagged vessel berthed in a Swedish port and was informed by the International Transport Workers Federation (the "ITWF") that the vessel would be "blacked" unless the plaintiff owners entered into ITWF employment contracts with the crew, including, the payment of crew wages in accordance with ITWF scales, backdated to the commencement of the employment contracts. The plaintiffs submitted to the demands. Subsequently the plaintiffs sought a declaration that they had lawfully avoided the contracts on the ground of duress. They also claimed restitution of the payments made under the contracts avoided for duress.

The relevant contracts were expressed to be governed by English law. Under English law, the actions of the ITWF were unlawful, whereas under Swedish law they were lawful. Therefore the specific issue before the House of Lords was whether the actions the ITWF were legitimate or not. Lord Goff, who gave the leading speech, considered that the issue of whether the contract could be avoided for duress was to be determined by the proper law of the contract. Thus, the issue of duress was characterised as contractual. This, it is submitted, was a separate issue to the question of restitution. Lord Goff stated that "before the owners could establish any right to recover the money, they had first to avoid the relevant contract", while "once the contract was avoided, the money paid under it was recoverable in restitution".[73] No separate issue as to what law governed the right of restitution arose, as the parties had agreed that such issue was to be governed by English law.[74] In fact, as the parties had agreed that the contract would be governed by English law, the only real issue was whether contract could be avoided on the basis of duress. This much was recognised by Lord Goff, who stated that "[t]he present case is, however, concerned with the anterior question whether the pressure exerted by the ITWF constituted duress enabling the owners to avoid the contract . . .".[75] Thus, it is submitted that the case cannot be used as support for a general proposition that restitutionary

70 See above ch. 4.1.2.
71 *Dimskal Shipping Co.* v. *International Transport Workers Federation* [1992] 2 A.C. 152.
72 See Stevens, p.198; Brereton, pp.170–1. *Cf.* Dicey and Morris, pp.1494–5; Burrows, pp.498–9.
73 *Id.*, 165D.
74 [1992] 2 A.C. 152, 163.
75 *Id.*, 165E.

issues arising in connection with a contract are to be governed by the applicable law of the contract.[76] The consequential restitutionary claim, and the question of what law governed such a claim, were not in issue.

Finally, in *Baring Bros. & Co. Ltd.* v. *Cunninghame District Council*,[77] Lord Penrose held that the consequential restitutionary issues arising under a void contract are to be governed by a separate choice of law rule. It was said that a restitutionary remedy was available only because there was no contract. As the proper law of the contract had dictated that conclusion, it was not attractive to proceed then to give effect to a term of that contract when the contract had ceased to have any validity as between the parties. Such restitutionary issues are to be determined by the law of the country with which the critical events had their closest and most real connection. Any express or implied choice of law by the parties to the void contract would be relevant but not decisive. Thus, although the contract was expressly governed by English law, being the law chosen by the parties, the consequential restitutionary issue was governed by the proper law of that issue. Therefore the court was entitled to hear further argument on what the proper law might be.

There are significant arguments for not adopting the law of the contract to determine the consequential restitutionary issues. First of all, it would be defeating the aim of s.2(2) of the Contracts (Applicable Law Act) 1990 if restitutionary issues were nevertheless to be governed by the law applicable to the relevant contract. There seems to be a clear intention that the consequences of nullity of a contract, are not to be considered as contractual issues to be governed by the law applicable to the contract.[78] To nevertheless apply the law of the contract seems to be bringing in through the back door what was not brought in through the Act. Moreover, as the Rome Convention only applies to "contractual obligations", it is difficult to justify its application to restitutionary issues. Secondly, it has already been concluded that the consequential restitutionary issue is to be separately characterised, thereby attracting its own choice of law rule.[79] Such a conclusion would be defeated if this issue were simply deferred to the choice of law rule for contracts rather than to a well thought out restitutionary choice of law rule. Restitutionary liability arises by operation of law, independently of any related contract. It is therefore inappropriate that the choice of law rule in relation to a restitutionary claim connected with a contract, should be overshadowed by the contractual choice of law rule. One would not suggest that a tort claim between parties who are in a contractual relationship should be governed by the law of the contract rather than the choice of law rule for tort.

Thirdly, in many cases involving ineffective contracts, the factor which renders the contract ineffective is often a good argument for not applying the law

[76] See also above pp.50–2.

[77] *The Times*, 30 September 1996.

[78] See also Hansard H.L., vol. 513, cols 1259, 1262–3, 1271.

[79] Ch. 4.1.1.

of the contract so as to determine the consequential restitutionary issues. Thus, where a contract is void for duress, the justification for applying the law of the contract, on the basis that the parties voluntarily entered the particular agreement and thus expected the law chosen, or the law most closely connected to the contract, to govern any consequential restitutionary claims, is less obvious if not absent. *A fortiori* where such a claim does not arise *ex contractu*. Moreover, it may well be that a law other than the law of the contract might render the relevant contract ineffective. For example, in *Baring Bros. & Co. Ltd.* v. *Cunninghame District Council*, the relevant interest rate swap was specifically governed by English law. However, the contract was *ultra vires* the Scottish council and accordingly void pursuant to Scottish law.[80] Likewise a contract which is perfectly valid under its applicable law, may be held to be void or otherwise ineffective on the basis that it is contrary to the public policy of the forum,[81] or on the basis that it is illegal in the place of performance.[82]

Finally, a restitutionary claim arising in the context of an ineffective contract is usually put forward on the basis of "failure of consideration". Such a claim is based on the fact that the plaintiff has provided consideration for which the defendant has not provided counter-consideration. Claims for failure of consideration may also arise outside of a contractual context.[83] It is submitted that it is inappropriate to apply a different choice of law rule according to whether such a claim arises "in the context of a contract". Surely the same choice of law rule should apply to what are essentially identical liabilities, namely liabilities to make restitution on the basis of failure of consideration? We would be losing sight of the legal system out of which the liability to make restitution arises if we were to apply the law of the contract and this is highlighted by the fact that we would be applying different choice of law rules to almost identical situations.

Clear situations exist where the law chosen, or allegedly chosen, by the parties, or the proper law of the actual or purported contract, will be quite unconnected with the restitutionary issues. Suppose, for example, that building works are to be performed in Australia under a contract expressly governed by English law. Neither of the parties are English. The building contract is ineffective due to local regulations. If the builder sued to recover on a *quantum meruit*, should the law applicable to the contract also determine the restitutionary issues? For

80 This was as a result of *Morgan Guaranty Trust Co. of N.Y.* v. *Lothian Regional Council* 1995 S.L.T. 299, where it was held that interest rate swaps are *ultra vires* the local council. Although it is suggested in the report of *Baring Bros.* that the contract was ineffective under its proper law, namely English law, it is submitted that the ineffectiveness of the contract arose as a result of the Scottish Council's incapacity as a matter of Scottish domestic law: see R. Stevens, "Restitution and the Rome Convention" (1997) L.Q.R. 249, 252.

81 At common law see *Rousillon* v. *Rousillon* (1880) 14 Ch.D. 351; *Kaufman* v. *Gerson* [1904] 1 K.B. 591; *Trendtex Trading Corp.* v. *Crédit Suisse* [1982] A.C. 679; under the Rome Convention see Art. 16.

82 See *Foster* v. *Driscoll* [1929] 1 K.B. 470 (C.A.); *Lemenda Trading Co. Ltd.* v. *African Middle East Petroleum Co. Ltd.* [1988] Q.B. 448.

83 See Birks, pp.219–20, 223–6; Burrows, pp.250–3, 320–1.

example, should the *lex contractus* determine whether there was in the circumstances an incontrovertible benefit, thereby allowing the plaintiff to recover. This is not a contractual question but one that goes to the question of enrichment in a restitutionary claim. Such an issue is quite unconnected with England. A well thought out restitutionary choice of law rule may be better equipped to answer this question. Moreover, the contract in this example is not ineffective under its law but under the law of the place where the consideration was to be provided. It is inappropriate that the restitutionary issues should *ipso facto* be determined by the law applicable to the contract, especially where connecting factors, other than the law chosen for the contract, point towards other legal systems. This was recognised by Lord Penrose in *Baring Bros.*,[84] where despite an English choice of law clause, evidence was to be heard as to whether there was in reality only one centre with which the transaction had any material connection, namely London, and thus that the law of England was the appropriate system of law to regulate the parties' restitutionary rights and obligations.

To conclude, as has already been discussed in relation to characterisation, the issue of whether a contract is ineffective is a contractual issue, to be determined by the law applicable to the contract, whereas the issue of whether the defendant is liable to make restitution is a restitutionary issue to be governed by the applicable law. The fact that there may be a contractual relationship looming in the background is a factual setting which does not alter the nature of the restitutionary liability. It is submitted that the choice of law rule applicable to restitutionary issues arising in connection with contracts is an independent choice of law rule. Furthermore, such choice of law rule should be governed by the same principles as would govern choice of law rules for restitutionary issues in general.

3.2 Law of the Relationship

It has been suggested that an alternative method of determining the proper law of an unjust enrichment is the law of the place where any relevant relationship is centred.[85] This may be particularly relevant in situations where the restitutionary liability does not arise in connection with a contract, but with a particular relationship. Thus, it is said that where a trustee mistakenly pays trust property, the relevant relationship will be that of the trust. It has therefore been argued that the law applicable to the trust is the proper law giving rise to restitution. Likewise, a pre-existing fiduciary relationship may be connected with a particular legal system, such that where a breach of that fiduciary duty occurs, through the accepting of a bribe, the restitutionary issue should be governed by such legal relationship. A parallel can therefore be drawn with situations where

[84] *Baring Brothers & Co. Ltd.* v. *Cunningham District Council*, *The Times*, 30 September 1996.

[85] Bird, pp.130–2; see also §221(2)(a), U.S. Restatement (Second) 1971; *Cf.* R. Leslie, "Unjustified Enrichment in the Conflict of Laws" (1998) 2 Edinburgh Law Review 233.

the law of a related contract may be the law with which the unjust enrichment is most closely connected.

One has to be careful to distinguish those cases where the existence of a particular relationship is an essential component of the issue in dispute and those where the particular relationship is a mere circumstantial fact. As has already been discussed in the context of characterisation, certain claims which arise in connection with a breach of trust, are cases of restitution for wrongdoing and therefore are not to be characterised as being in unjust enrichment.[86] They are to be characterised as breaches of trust. Thus, where a trustee makes some form of gain in breach of trust, the beneficiaries' right to seek disgorgement of this gain should be determined by the law applicable to the trust.[87] Likewise, where a trustee, for example, overpays a beneficiary, it may be considered that the issue of the beneficiary's liability to repay is to be characterised as an issue concerning the relationship between the trustee and the beneficiary[88] and thus governed by the law applicable to the trust.[89] Furthermore, where a fiduciary makes a gain in breach of a fiduciary duty this too should not be characterised as unjust enrichment. It has been submitted that these matters should be characterised as consensual or contractual matters and thus the law applicable to the particular relationship should apply.[90]

In contrast, where a trustee, for example, mistakenly pays trust money to a third-party recipient, unconnected with the trust, the issue of the recipient's restitutionary liability is to be characterised as being in unjust enrichment. The fact that such a cause of action arises in the context of a particular legal, or other, relationship, should not alter the applicable choice of law rule. The existence of, for example, a trust is merely a factual backdrop. The mistaken payer may have been a bank clerk, an employee, or an agent. The fact that the payer happened to be a trustee, should not alter the choice of law rule which might be applied in relation to the respective rights between the payer and the payee. The recipient's liability arises independently of such a relationship, so therefore the law of such a relationship should not govern the recipient's liability. The trustee's claim to recover is still in unjust enrichment. One must be careful not to allow the existence of circumstantial relationships to confuse the choice of

[86] See above ch. 4.4.3.1.

[87] See Art. 8(g) of the Hague Convention on Trusts, as contained in the Recognition of Trusts Act 1987. It provides that the law applicable to the trust shall govern: "the relationships between the trustees and the beneficiaries including the personal liability of the trustees to the beneficiaries". This is essentially the position taken by Goff and Jones in the first edition of *The Law of Restitution* where they examined the conflict of laws: Goff and Jones, *The Law of Restitution* (London, 1966), pp.507–8.

[88] See Art. 8(g) of the Hague Convention on Trusts. Although, it might be argued that such an interpretation should not be taken as paragraph (g) suggests that, although the applicable law might determine issues of the trustee's liability, it does not necessarily apply to issues of any restitutionary liability a beneficiary may have towards the trust. In such an event, the issue of the beneficiary's restitutionary liability towards the trust would attract an independent restitutionary characterisation and therefore be governed by the relevant restitutionary choice of law rule.

[89] This is determined by Articles 6 and 7 of the Hague Convention on Trusts.

[90] See above ch. 4.4.3.2. Goff and Jones, *op. cit.*, p.508.

law process. Moreover, applying the law of the relationship would mean that a different choice of law rule may apply if the mistaken payer happened to be a trustee as opposed to someone else. It is inappropriate to apply a different choice of law rule to essentially identical forms of liability. Therefore, the law of a particular relationship will only be relevant where the relevant issue is, for example, characterised as a breach of trust or a breach of a fiduciary relationship. In such an event the proper law of the trust, or the proper law of the contract,[91] will apply respectively.

3.3 Lex Situs of Immovables

Dicey and Morris submit that where a restitutionary obligation arises in connection with an immovable, the proper law will be the *lex situs* of such immovable.[92] They cite *Batthyanay* v. *Walford*[93] as authority for the general proposition that the restitution of a benefit obtained in connection with a person's ownership of land is governed by the *lex situs* of the land. The plaintiff in that case was the successor of certain lands in Austria and Hungary. He brought an action against the executrix and trustees of his predecessor's estate, in relation to the deterioration which the property had suffered. Under the law of Austria and Hungary, the relevant land was subject to a *fidei commis* and the possessor was liable to hand the property to his successor in the same state as he received it. Failure to do so resulted in liability to the successor for any deterioration. The Court of Appeal characterised the plaintiff's action as one in implied contract and not in tort. Had the matter been characterised as tort, the *actio personalis* rule would have prevented the plaintiff from suing the defendant's estate. The court applied Austrian law to the action without any real discussion as to why such law applied.

It is submitted that this case does not support a general principle that restitutionary obligations arising in connection with immovables are to be governed by the *lex situs* of such an immovable. First, the action was arguably incorrectly characterised as one in implied contract.[94] Secondly, it is submitted that the implied-contract characterisation was essentially made in order to overcome the operation of the *actio personalis* rule. The Court of Appeal stated that the claim according to Austrian law was not in the nature of damages for default, and thus

[91] This is as a breach of a fiduciary relationship should be characterised as a breach of a contract: see ch. 4.4.3.2.

[92] Rule 200(2)(b). See also Bird, p.135; Cheshire and North, pp.677–8. The U.S. 2nd Restatement also raises a similar consideration in relation to both land and chattels in §221(2)(e): see ch. 5, §2 above.

[93] (1887) 36 Ch. D. 269. The U.S. 2nd Restatement also cites *Batthyanay* v. *Walford* as authority for this proposition.

[94] There was no suggestion that Austrian law would have characterised the action as being in implied contract or as quasi-contractual. North J., in the court of first instance, had recognised that the English counterpart of the relevant action existed in the doctrine of waste: (1886) 33 Ch.D. 624, 630.

did not attract a tort characterisation. However, this was despite the fact that there would be no liability if the deterioration was not caused by the fault of the defendant.[95] Furthermore, liability was to make good any loss.[96] One must query whether this action was correctly characterised as being in implied contract. Moreover, it is almost certain that a court of today would not characterise this as unjust enrichment. It need only be pointed out that there was no indication that the defendant was enriched as a result of the deterioration to the property. Liability was for loss, namely deterioration, and not for gain.

At any rate, even if one accepts that the issue was properly characterised as quasi-contractual, there is no indication that Austrian law applied *ipso facto* as the *lex situs* of the relevant land. Undoubtedly, one of the relevant factors in that case was the *situs* of the land. It could equally be argued that Austrian law applied as the proper law of the issue, having in mind the *situs* of the land, the place where the alleged deteriorations had taken place and the law which created the *fidei commis*, namely the obligation to maintain the properties. In fact, the only connection with England was the fact that the deceased's will had been proved in England and thus the executrix was also English.

Nevertheless, it could be argued that in cases affecting property, or proprietary interests, particularly in the case of immovables, a choice of law rule should be applied which takes these issues into account. Therefore, the choice of law rule for proprietary restitution should be different from that affecting ordinary, *in personam*, restitutionary obligations. However, as discussed in the fourth chapter, the issue of whether a restitutionary right exists, of the sort which may give rise to a proprietary remedy, should be characterised as restitutionary. The rationale is that the law of unjust enrichment creates the proprietary remedy.[97] If the relevant choice of law rule for restitutionary claims connected to property was to be the *lex situs*, the purpose of such a restitutionary characterisation would be defeated.

Moreover, the concerns which may be raised in favour of a *lex situs* choice of law rule become less compelling when one has the following in mind. Where the relevant issue has been characterised as proprietary,[98] the *lex situs*, or similar proprietary choice of law rule, will apply in relation to moveables, whereas in relation to immovables the court will not have jurisdiction to hear the matter.[99] Where however the relevant issue has been characterised as restitutionary, the issue will not be one of title, but whether a right of restitution is available of the

[95] Cotton L.J. dealt with this point by holding that the possessor was *prima facie* liable for deterioration, but that the law allowed him to be excused if it had occurred without his fault: *id.*, 281–2. With respect, this distinction is rather unconvincing.

[96] *Id.*, 278.

[97] See ch. 4.3.2, 4.3.3 *seq.*

[98] On the characterisation of matters concerning property, see ch. 4.3.1.1.

[99] This principle applies both as a matter of common law: *British South Africa Co.* v. *Comphania de Moçambique* [1893] A.C. 602; *Hesperides Hotels Ltd.* v. *Aegean Turkish Holidays Ltd.* [1979] A.C. 508; *Re Polly Peck International Plc.* (*No.2*) [1998] 3 All E.R. 812; and also under Art. 16(1) of the Brussels Convention: see ch. 9.4.3.3. See also Dicey and Morris, Rule 114.

sort which may give rise to proprietary restitution.[100] The issue focuses on the events giving rise to the unjust enrichment including the proprietary remedy. To borrow a phrase from the European Court of Justice, the immovable nature of the property held in trust and its location, are irrelevant to the issues to be determined.[101] Although a proprietary remedy will be claimed, the court will have characterised the issue by reference to the causative event. Such claims will be in equity and, thus, the court will be exercising its *in personam* jurisdiction over the defendant. The significance of the *lex situs* as the applicable law is diminished. The relevant issue is one of restitution and thus the same choice of law rule which would apply to other restitutionary matters should apply.

4 PROPER LAW OF THE OBLIGATION

The proper law of the obligation is also put forward as a choice of law rule for restitutionary issues,[102] particularly in Dicey and Morris. This is explained as being the law with which the obligation to make restitution has its closest and most real connection.[103] The view is that, as restitutionary claims arise in such a wide variety of situations, no single choice of law rule can adequately deal with all of them. As such, the applicable law will depend on the circumstances and facts giving rise to the claim in restitution. It is often the case that this rule is qualified through certain presumptions as to what the proper law might be. For example, where a claim arises in connection with a contract, the proper law is said to be that of the contract. These presumptions are usually along the lines of the sub-rules examined above, with the difference that they do not apply categorically but are indicia of the proper law.

One disadvantage or difficulty with this rule is that it is circular and vague. It begs the question to state that a restitutionary obligation is governed by the proper law of the obligation. The choice of law rule is applied so as to determine whether a right of restitution exists under the applicable law, including whether restitution is effected through an obligation or otherwise. If we do not as yet know whether such a right exists, how are we to ascertain this "obligation" so as to find out its proper law? Presumably, we have to find out the law that is

[100] In relation to the characterisation of proprietary restitution as a restitutionary issue, see ch. 4, §§3.2–3.4.

[101] *Webb* v. *Webb* (294/92) [1994] E.C.R. I–1717. It should be noted that this case was concerned with the issue of jurisdiction under the Brussels Convention. However, the particular analysis is, it is submitted, helpful to the question of choice of law.

[102] See Dicey and Morris, Rule 200(1); Cheshire and North, p.684; McLeod, p.571; J. Blaikie, "Unjust Enrichment in the Conflict of Laws"[1984] J.R. 112; *Arab Monetary Fund* v. *Hashim* [1996] 1 Lloyd's Rep. 589. See also *Nominal Defendant* v. *Bagot's Executor & Trustee Company Ltd.* [1971] S.A.S.R. 346, 366, *per* Bray C.J.; reversed on other grounds, 125 C.L.R. 179; *Stewart* v. *Honey* [1972] 2 S.A.S.R. 585, 592, *per* Bray C.J.; *Hodge* v. *Club Motor Insurance Agency Pty. Ltd.* [1974] 22 F.L.R. 473, 477, *per* Bray C.J.; *Barclay's Bank Plc.* v. *Inc. Incorporated*, 17 February 1999 (unreported).

[103] See Dicey and Morris, p.1490.

applicable to the relevant issue, namely the right of restitution, so as to ascertain whether restitution is available and if so, in what form. It is the *lex causae* which must point us to the obligation and not the obligation to the *lex causae*. Moreover, restitution may be effected through either a personal or proprietary remedy. Therefore, the use of the expression "a restitutionary obligation", might be taken as implying that such choice of law rule is limited to restitutionary obligations and thereby excludes matters of proprietary restitution. Yet, this does not seem to be the intention in Dicey and Morris, where cases such as *Chase Manhattan Bank N.A.* v. *Israel-British Bank (London) Ltd.*[104] and the imposition of proprietary remedies, such as constructive trusts, are discussed in the context of the restitutionary choice of law rule, without a distinction being drawn between issues of obligation and property.[105] It would therefore be more helpful if such a rule were framed along the lines of:

> The issue of liability to restore the benefit of an enrichment obtained at another person's expense is governed by the law that has the closest and most real connection with the relevant events and circumstances.

The advantage of a proper law rule is that it allows a great deal of flexibility so as to deal with the choice of law question on a case-by-case basis. The disadvantage is that it does not provide a great deal of certainty. Often, parties will need to litigate so as to find out what the proper law of the obligation is. It may be that by having certain presumptions in the form of the sub-rules already examined, a degree of predictability can be achieved. That is, in the case where a restitutionary claim arises in connection with a contract, the proper law of the restitutionary issue will *generally* be the law of the contract; where a restitutionary issue arises in other circumstances, the proper law of the restitutionary issue will generally be that of the place of enrichment, and so on. Yet, it will be difficult to know what weight the various connecting factors, or sub-rules, are to carry. Further fine tuning can only be achieved on a case by case basis.

The only English authority which actually applied a choice of law rule so as to arrive at the *lex causae* of a restitutionary obligation is *Arab Monetary Fund* v. *Hashim*.[106] The Court of Appeal examined the various factors and found that the law of Abu Dhabi applied as the proper law of the obligation. The applicable choice of law rule, if any, was the proper law of the obligation rule. As already discussed, the case was wrongly characterised as being in restitution.[107] It was a case concerning a bribe and therefore a breach of a fiduciary duty. It should have been characterised as a breach of a consensual or contractual relationship. Yet, leaving aside the erroneous characterisation of the issue, there was no doubt that the law of Abu Dhabi was the applicable law to such a claim.

[104] [1981] Ch. 105.

[105] Dicey and Morris, pp.1485, 1502–3. The distinction drawn in Dicey and Morris is on the question of whether proprietary remedies are a matter of substance, which arise under the *lex causae*, or a matter of procedure, which arise under the *lex fori*.

[106] [1996] 1 Lloyd's Rep. 589. See above, ch. 5, §4.

[107] See above ch. 4.4.2.

Almost all of the circumstances pointed to Abu Dhabi. The view expressed by the Court of Appeal that restitutionary obligations are governed by their proper law does not leave us any better off in the quest for finding the proper law in future cases. As such, the proper law of the obligation rule is merely a statement of the obvious. It is all very well to examine all the events and circumstances surrounding a claim, in an attempt to identify the law with the closest and most real connection to the issue of unjust enrichment. However, in so doing, we may potentially isolate a myriad of factors. Unless they all point to one jurisdiction, it will be necessary to apply different degrees of importance to the respective factors. How are we to know what weight is to be placed on these various factors? Some of them may only be circumstantially relevant to the issue, whilst others may not pertain to the issue of restitution. Uncertainty as to the significance of a particular factor means uncertainty as to outcome. Such an approach does not provide any clear guidance for future cases.

5 PROPOSED CONVENTION ON THE LAW APPLICABLE TO NON-CONTRACTUAL OBLIGATIONS

The European Group for Private International Law has prepared a proposal for a European Convention on the law applicable to non-contractual obligations.[108] This has been informally referred to as "Rome II Convention" as it is considered a complement to the Rome Convention of 1980.[109] This draft has been prepared by the European Group for Private International Law, so as to assist the working party which has been set up by the Council of the European Union to prepare a convention on the law applicable to non-contractual obligations. As such, the draft is at this stage a mere proposal. It may be a significant period of time before an actual convention is, if at all, adopted by the working group, let alone before it is implemented by statute in the United Kingdom.

5.1 Scope of the Draft Proposal

The draft proposal applies to "non-contractual obligations in any situation involving a choice between the laws of different countries".[110] It states that it is not applicable to non-contractual obligations arising out of special rules of family law;[111] the personal liability of officers, members and statutory auditors, for the obligations of a company or other body corporate or incorporate;[112] and also liability connected with the exercise of public authority.[113]

[108] This proposal was adopted by the Group at its eighth session, held in Luxembourg from 25 to 27 September, 1998.
[109] The proposed draft can be found in (1998) 45 N.I.L.R. 465.
[110] Article 1.
[111] Article 1(2)(a).
[112] Article 1(2)(b).
[113] Article 1(2)(c).

Under the draft proposal, obligations are divided into two main categories: obligations arising out of a harmful event,[114] and obligations arising out of an event other than a harmful event.[115] The former category generally covers the law of wrongs. A question arises as to whether this includes the area of restitution for wrongs. It arises out of a "harmful event" and would, under English law, fall within this category. However, as already noted, a German or a Greek court is likely to characterise a claim for restitution for wrongdoing as lying in unjustified enrichment.[116] Presumably an autonomous notion of "obligations arising out of a harmful event" will need to be developed, something which is absent from the draft. The latter category covers, *inter alia*, claims of unjust enrichment. Before examining the proposed choice of law rules, there are a few preliminary observations which need to be made. As previously discussed, the use of the word "obligation" is an inappropriate word, particularly when discussing the law of unjust enrichment from an English perspective.[117] The English law of restitution, as well as that of most other common law systems, grants both personal and proprietary remedies,[118] while proprietary remedies are also available in relation to certain wrongs.[119] It is therefore restrictive to speak in terms of choice of law rules for particular obligations. Is the intention to limit the application of the choice of law rules to particular remedies? Moreover, describing the subject matter to which the choice of law rule applies as an "obligation" is circular and vague. If we do not as yet know whether a right of restitution exists and therefore need to turn to the *lex causae* for this answer, it is pre-emptive to have already defined our subject-matter as an obligation. It would be more appropriate to speak in terms of an "issue".

5.2 Choice of Law Rule

The proposed choice of law rule in the draft is similar to Rule 200 in Dicey and Morris.[120] The general rule in Article 7(1) is that "[a] non-contractual obligation arising out of an event other than a harmful event shall be governed by the law of the country with which it is most closely connected". A parallel may be drawn between this rule and the proper law of the obligation rule contained in Rule 200(1) in Dicey and Morris, which is said to equate with the law with which the obligation has its closest and most real connection.[121]

114 Title II, Articles 3–6.
115 Title III, Art. 7.
116 See pp.83–4.
117 See above pp.113, 153–4.
118 See ch. 1.3.
119 See *A.G. for Hong Kong* v. *Reid* [1994] 1 A.C. 324; *Thahir* v. *Pertamina* [1994] 3 S.L.R. 257 (C.A. of Singapore); *L.A.C. Minerals Ltd.* v. *International Corona Resources Ltd.* (1989) 61 D.L.R. (4th) 14. See also *Boardman* v. *Phipps* [1967] 2 A.C. 46.
120 See p.112 above.
121 Dicey and Morris, p.1490. See also *Arab Monetary Fund* v. *Hashim* [1996] 1 Lloyd's Rep. 589 and the general discussion of this case above pp.154–5.

The rule then provides certain presumptions of what the most closely connected law will be. When a non-contractual obligation is connected to a pre-existing or contemplated relationship between the parties, Article 7(2) provides that "it shall be presumed that the obligation has the closest connection with the law which governs or would govern that relationship". The scope here is wider than that in Rule 200(2)(a) of Dicey and Morris, extending beyond contracts to relationships in general. Presumably, relationships here means pre-existing or contemplated legal relationships. The effect of this is to defer the choice of law question to that of the relationship's applicable law. Although there exists a uniform regime for determining the law applicable to most contractual issues, namely the Rome Convention, such is not the case for relationships in general, as well as those falling outside of the Rome Convention. The applicable law to relationships beyond contract must presumably be determined by the *lex fori's* rules of private international law. It seems odd that a proposed convention which seeks to bring uniformity to questions of choice of law hands back a significant component to the individual states' rules of private international law.

The reference to the law of a relationship is more in line with a civilian rather than a common law way of thinking. Apart from trusts, common law lawyers are not used to thinking of legal relationships outside of contract. In contrast, the civilian tradition is more prepared to recognise other relationships as legal,[122] governed by a particular legal regime; therefore their courts are more well equipped at isolating the *lex causae* of a particular relationship. Thus, it may be better that the term "relationship" be avoided, or at least more clearly defined if the proposed convention truly intends to apply uniformly among both civilian and common law systems.

A fundamental question arises as to the meaning of the word "connected". Certainly where a contract is frustrated, the consequential restitutionary claim which may follow can be said to be connected with a pre-existing or contemplated relationship. What happens however where a bank mistakenly pays money into an account in another jurisdiction? Under many systems of law, a recognisable "relationship" arises by virtue of the payment. Will the law of that relationship govern the right of restitution or will this be said to fall outside the scope of Article 7(2)? In fact it will be very difficult to find situations where a restitutionary claim is not somehow connected to a relationship of some sort. In light of the choice of a broad phrase such as "existing or pre-existing relationship", the term "connected" needs to be carefully defined.

A question also arises in relation to a "contemplated" relationship; what does this actually mean? Presumably this would cover situations where, for example, a contract is void *ab intitio*, such that there was no actual contract. There is however a difference between a purported relationship which is void *ab initio* and one which is merely contemplated. What degree of contemplation is necessary? Must it be contemplated by all parties to the relationship, or is it sufficient

[122] See Markesinis, pp.31–4, 726–7; Zimmerman, pp.498–507.

if it is contemplated by the plaintiff? It is submitted that, although the intention behind this phrase is clear, the word "contemplated" gives rise to certain ambiguities. It is one that requires further particularisation.

Article 7(3) provides "that an obligation to make restitution based on unjust enrichment is most closely connected with the country in which the enrichment occurs". The first question which arises is whether this provision is intended to apply as a general rule, or merely as a residual rule? Given that Article 7(2) refers to "non-contractual obligations", whereas Article 7(3) refers to "an obligation to make restitution based on unjust enrichment", it seems logical to conclude that all unjust enrichment claims are intended to fall with Article 7(3), irrespective of whether they are connected with an actual or contemplated relationship. If this view is correct, then the draft convention does no more than propose a general "place of enrichment rule" subject to a flexible exception in Article 7(5), "when it appears from the circumstances as a whole that the obligation is more closely connected with another country". It has been previously submitted that unjust enrichment claims should not be subject to a different choice of law rule depending on whether they arise in connection with a contract.[123] This interpretation of the draft convention is to be welcomed, namely, that matters of unjust enrichment are not to be distinguished by virtue of an actual or contemplated relationship. The "place of enrichment rule" has already been examined and it was concluded that it is not a satisfactory rule for matters of unjust enrichment.[124] Over and above the criticisms against this rule, it might be noted once again that, for the reasons already highlighted above, it is pre-emptive, circular and inappropriate to define the issue as "an obligation to make restitution based on unjust enrichment". Surely it is better to refer to the "issue" of restitution based on unjust enrichment, or simply to matters of unjust enrichment.

[123] See pp.148–9 above.
[124] Ch. 7.1.2 *et seq.*

8

Preferred Choice of Law Rule

1 THE ESSENTIAL ELEMENT OF THE UNJUST FACTOR

AT A GENERAL level, it can be said that matters of unjust enrichment are governed by the proper law of the alleged unjust enrichment. This in itself does not tell us very much. The quest here is to identify a more specific rule which will point us to the proper law. Given the lack of authority on this question, the field is open for a principled and reasoned solution to the question of the choice of law rule for matters of unjust enrichment. The essential question in developing such a choice of law rule, is to ascertain the element in a restitutionary claim which might be isolated as being of such significance that it should be used to determine the applicable law. It is submitted that the most significant element, for the purposes of choice of law, is the "unjust factor"; that is to say, the circumstance which renders the receipt of a benefit unjust at the expense of another. A connecting factor which focused on this element would be both sensitive to the nature of unjust enrichment claims and the variety of circumstances in which such claims arise.

The unjust factor is at the heart of an unjust enrichment, being the means by which the law determines the various circumstances where enrichment should be reversed. It is this element which triggers the reason or cause for restitution; and, in principle, the system of law most closely connected with the unjust factor should govern any restitutionary duty. Although important legal issues may arise in relation to whether there has been "enrichment" and whether such enrichment was "at the expense of the plaintiff",[1] these are predominantly factual questions. These are simply questions of whether there has in fact occurred a shift of value or wealth from the plaintiff to the defendant, such that a *prima facie* claim in unjust enrichment may be available. They are similar to the question of whether there was loss or damage in contractual or tortious claims. The law may of course assist by determining whether there was for example enrichment, especially in certain borderline situations. However, it is the issue of whether the receipt of such enrichment is in fact "unjust" which ultimately gives rise to a restitutionary duty; this is where the law imposes *its* values. That is to say, the unjust factor isolates the circumstances where an enrichment may be reversed. As such, it is only logical that, as a matter of principle, the proper law of the alleged unjust factor should govern the right of restitution. It is that legal system which should have the most to say on the matter, whether this be the law

[1] See Ch. I, §§2.1 and 2.2.

of the place with the closest and most real connection with, or alternatively the law most closely connected to, the alleged unjust factor.

For the purposes of private international law, the closest analogy with unjust enrichment is tort. Both are non-consensual rights and obligations imposed by operation of law. They are both imposed in circumstances independently of the parties' wishes. The imposition or non-imposition of these liabilities ultimately reflects the legal values of a particular legal system. Unlike contracts, they are not consensually created by express or implied reference to a particular legal system. Tort and unjust enrichment are rights and obligations which are imposed by a legal system *ex post facto* so as to remedy a wrong or to reverse an unjust enrichment, respectively.

In cases of torts, the general approach is to apply the *lex loci delicti*, namely the law of the place where the wrong occurred.[2] The Private International Law (Miscellaneous Provisions) Act 1995 (the "Act") has essentially adopted the *lex loci delicti* rule as its basic tenet.[3] The general rule under s.11(1) of the Act is that in cases of torts, the applicable law is the law of the country in which the events constituting the tort in question occurred, namely, where the wrong occurred. In cases where the events constituting the tort have occurred in different countries, there are more specific rules. In a cause of action in respect of personal injury, the applicable law is the law of the country where the individual was when he sustained the injury;[4] in relation to damage to property, the applicable law is the law of the place where the property was when it was damaged;[5] while in all other cases this is the "law of the country in which the most significant element or elements of those events occurred".[6] Thus, where for example, A, an Australian, negligently injures B, an Englishman, in a motor vehicle accident in France, the applicable law will be the law of France.[7] This is the law of the place where the wrong was committed. Admittedly, in relation to causes of action in respect of personal injury or damage to property, the Act deems the applicable law. Although such a law will generally also amount to the law of the place of the wrong, such a rule is not necessarily the same as a *lex loci delicti* rule. This

[2] The *lex loci delicti* rule was recently adopted in Canada in *Tolofson* v. *Jensen*; *Lucas* v. *Gagnon* (1994) 120 D.L.R. 4th 289; and in Australia: *John Pfeifer Pty. Ltd.* v. *Rogerson*, 21 June 2000 (unreported) (H.C.A.). It is the general choice of law rule for torts in most continental systems: see Appendix, Law Com. W.P. No. 87 (1984). It remains the choice of law rule for torts in ten states of the U.S.A., namely, Alabama, Georgia, Kansas, Maryland, Montana, New Mexico, North Carolina, Virginia, Wyoming (also possibly West Virginia): see S. Symeonides, "Choice of Law in the American Courts in 1997" [1998] 46 A.J.C.L. 233; also S. Symeonides, "Choice of Law in the American Courts in 1998" [1999] 47 A.J.C.L. 327.

[3] See Dicey and Morris, p.1544; Jaffey, p.257. See also Cheshire and North, p.629; A. Briggs, "Choice of law in tort and delict" [1995] L.M.C.L.Q. 519, 521; C.Morse, "Torts in Private International Law: A New Statutory Framework" (1996) 45 I.C.L.Q. 888, 896. One commentator has described the approach under the Act as a "*statutory lex loci delicti*": B. Rodger, "Ascertaining the Statutory *Lex Loci Delicti*"(1998) 7 I.C.L.Q. 205.

[4] Section 11(2)(a).

[5] Section 11(2)(b).

[6] Section 11(2)(c).

[7] See s.11(2)(a) of the Private International Law (Miscellaneous Provisions) Act 1995.

situation is largely based on practical and policy considerations in the ascertainment of the applicable law in cases of personal injury and damage to property.[8] The general rule contained in s.11(1), as well as the residual, "in any other case", rule contained in s.11(2)(c), are essentially *lex loci delicti* rules and it is these more general rules which are of assistance in determining the choice of law rule for unjust enrichment. Finally, it should be noted that there is a general exception to the tort choice of law rule in s.12. Where in the circumstances[9] it is "substantially more appropriate for the applicable law for determining the issues arising in the case" to be the law of another country, then its law will apply.

One might point out, however, that, in the case of torts, the question is not where the wrong was committed as such. It is a question of where the events constituting the tort occurred, or, where these events have occurred in several jurisdictions, it is where the most significant element or elements of the events constituting the tort occurred. The occurrence of damage may in itself be considered a significant element. The place where such damage occurred may not correspond with where the "wrong" itself was committed. The current English position, it may be argued, is not a *lex loci delicti* rule as such. It may therefore be said that, in cases of international restitution, one should also look for the most significant element or elements, which may in certain situations be, for example, the place of enrichment.

However, it is submitted that the most significant element in a tort will almost invariably be the commission of the wrong or wrongful conduct.[10] First, the general intention of the Act was to effectively replace the double actionability rule with a *lex loci delicti* rule,[11] while this is also how the majority of commentators have interpreted it.[12] Secondly, although the residual rule concentrates on the most significant element or elements constituting the alleged tort, it is submitted that the courts will invariably have to ask where the wrong was committed. Guidance may be found from the "substance" test which is used to determine the place of commission of a tort at common law. According to this view, one had to look at the sequence of events constituting the tort and ask the question, where in substance did the cause of action arise?[13] In formulating this test, Lord Pearson added:

[8] See for example, Law Commission Working Paper No. 87 (1984), para 4.70.

[9] Namely "the significance of factors which connect a tort or delict with the country whose law would be the applicable law under the general rule; and . . . the significance of any factors connecting the tort or delict with another country": see s.12(1).

[10] See also P. Birks, "The Concept of a Civil Wrong" in D. Owen (ed.), *Philosophical Foundations of Tort Law* (Oxford, 1995) pp.31, 37–45.

[11] See Law Commission Working Paper No.87, *Choice of Law in Tort and Delict* (1984); Law Commission No. 193, *Choice of Law in Tort and Delict* (1990).

[12] See Dicey and Morris, p.1544; Jaffey, p.257; B. Rodger, "Ascertaining the Statutory *Lex Loci Delicti*"(1998) 47 I.C.L.Q. 205; C. Morse, "Torts in Private International Law: A New Statutory Framework" (1996) I.C.L.Q. 888. See also Cheshire and North, p.629; A. Briggs, "Choice of law in tort and delict" [1995] L.M.C.L.Q. 519, 521.

[13] *Distillers Co. Ltd.* v. *Thompson* [1971] A.C. 458, 468, *per* Lord Pearson (P.C.).

> It is not the right approach to say that, because there was no complete tort until the damage occurred, therefore the cause of action arose wherever the damage happened to occur.[14]

It would therefore follow that, where the acts on the part of the defendant which give rise to the alleged tort and the resultant damage occur in different jurisdictions, the wrong, it is submitted, is, as a general rule, committed in the former.[15] In *Jackson* v. *Spittall*, it was held that the question of whether a cause of action was to be classified as local or foreign is to be answered by ascertaining the place of the "act on the part of the defendant which gives the plaintiff his cause of complaint".[16] In *Distillers Co. Ltd.* v. *Thompson*,[17] the cause of action arose in the place where the failure to warn of the dangers of a product occurred.[18] This also happened to be the jurisdiction where the damage occurred. Yet, the emphasis was placed on the tort arising where the failure to warn occurred. In isolating the failure to warn, Lord Pearson stated:

> That is the act (which must include omission) on the part of the English Company [the defendant] which has given the plaintiff a cause of complaint in law.[19]

This, together with Lord Pearson's view that a defendant should have to answer for his wrongdoing in the country where he did the wrong, suggests that, if the damage had occurred in a third jurisdiction, for example if the product had been used in a jurisdiction other than that of purchase, the tort would have occurred in the place where the failure to warn occurred. This view is confirmed by the High Court of Australia's interpretation in *Voth* v. *Manildra Flour Mills Pty Ltd.*, "[o]ne thing that is clear from *Jackson* v. *Spittall* and from *Distillers* is that it is some act of the defendant, and not its consequences, that must be the focus of attention".[20] It has therefore been held that an action in relation to the negligence of an accountant arises in the place where the accountancy services are provided,[21] while the negligent services of a law firm are committed in the place where the firm operated.[22] In cases of fraudulent or negligent representations, the cause of action arises at the place where the communication is received, not necessarily the place where the statement is acted upon or where the relevant

[14] *Distillers Co. Ltd.* v. *Thompson* [1971] A.C. 458, 468, *per* Lord Pearson (P.C.).

[15] *Jackson* v. *Spittal* (1870) L.R. C.P. 542, 552; *Distillers Co. Ltd.* v. *Thompson* [1971] A.C. 458, 467–8 *per* Lord Pearson; *Voth* v. *Manildra Flour Mills Pty Ltd.* (1990) 171 C.L.R. 538, 567. *Cf. Metall und Rohstoff AG* v. *Donaldson Lufkin & Jenrette Inc.* [1990] 1 Q.B. 391.

[16] (1870) L.R. C.P. 542, 552. See also *Anderson* v. *Nobels Explosive* (1906) 12 O.L.R. 644; *Paul* v. *Chandler and Fisher Ltd.* [1924] 2 D.L.R. 479; *Koop* v. *Bebb* (1951) 84 C.L.R. 629; *Buttigeig* v. *Universal Terminal and Stevedoring Co.* [1972] V.R.626. *Cf. Jenner* v. *Sun Oil Co.* [1952] 2 D.L.R. 526; *Pindling* v. *National Broadcasting Corp.* (1984) 14 D.L.R. (4th) 391.

[17] [1971] A.C. 458.

[18] Also *George Monro Ltd.* v. *American Cynamid and Chemical Corp.* [1944] K.B. 432, 439.

[19] *Distillers Co. Ltd.* v. *Thompson* [1971] A.C. 458, 469. See also *Castree* v. *Squibb Ltd.* [1980] 1 W.L.R. 1248.

[20] (1990) 171 C.L.R. 538, 567, *per* Mason C.J., Deane, Dawson and Gaudron J.J.

[21] *Voth* v. *Manildra Flour Mills Pty Ltd.* (1990) 171 C.L.R. 538, 568–9 (H.C.A.).

[22] *National Bank of Canada* v. *Clifford Chance* (1996) 30 O.R. (3d) 746 (Ont. C.J.).

loss arises.[23] As the statement is directed to a recipient, it is, in substance, made at the place to which it was directed. In a sense, the statement is "incomplete" until it is received.[24] An even more restrictive approach has been taken as to where misstatements occur in the context of Article 5(3) of the Brussels Convention. In *Domicrest Ltd.* v. *Swiss Bank Corporation*,[25] the "place where the harmful event occurred" has been held to be where the misstatement occurs.[26] Rix J. justified this as "[i]t is there that the negligence, even if not every element of the tort, is likely to take place".[27] Likewise, in the case of defamation, it has been held that, as publication is the material element in such cases, the tort occurs where the statements are disseminated, rather than where they are first written.[28] Contrary to the above decisions, in *Metall und Rohstoff AG* v. *Donaldson Lufkin & Jenrette Inc.*,[29] it was held that the tort of inducing a breach of contract was committed in England, where the breach and the resulting damage occurred, and not in New York, where the acts of inducement occurred.

In determining the applicable law to an action for passing off, Scott V.-C. in *Waterford Wedgwood plc.* v. *David Nagli Ltd.*[30] sought to determine where the actual passing off had occurred. Having identified the essential ingredient of misrepresentation to the public,[31] it was considered that passing off had arguably[32] occurred in Spain and New York, as it was passed off to particular individuals in Spain, while it found its way into the retail market in New York.[33] Scott V.-C.'s statements are consistent with the proposition that torts are governed by the place where the alleged wrong is committed. In looking at "the events constituting the tort or delict", he did not focus on the place where the counterfeit Waterford Crystal was manufactured, namely Ireland, or the place where the trademarks were registered, namely the U.K., or the place where the alleged loss or damage arose.[34] In conclusion, it is submitted that the most

23 *Diamond* v. *Bank of London & Montreal* [1979] Q.B. 333 (C.A.); *The Albaforth* [1984] 2 Lloyd's Rep. 91 (C.A.); *Voth* v. *Manildra Flour Mills Pty Ltd.* (1990) 171 C.L.R. 538, 568. A similar approach has been taken in relation to defamation under Art. 5(3) of the Brussels Convention. The entire tort has been held to have occurred where the publisher was established, whereas the specific damage is suffered in each state in which the publication was distributed: *Shevill* v. *Press Alliance S.A.* (68/93) [1995] E.C.R. I–415.

24 *Diamond* v. *Bank of London & Montreal* [1979] Q.B. 333, 346, *per* Stephenson L.J.

25 [1999] 1 W.L.R. 364.

26 See also *Cordova Land Co.* v. *Victor Bros. Inc.* [1966] 1 W.L.R. 793, 798, 800.

27 *Id.*, 382.

28 *Bata* v. *Bata* [1948] W.N. 366; *Church of Scientology* v. *Metropolitan Police Commissioner* (1976) 120 Sol. Jo. 690.

29 [1990] 1 Q.B. 391.

30 [1998] F.S.R. 92.

31 *Id.*, 105.

32 As no evidence of foreign law was presented before the court, there could be no finding of passing off.

33 See also *Intercontex* v. *Schmidt* [1988] F.S.R 575, 578; Cheshire and North, p.636.

34 In *Modus Vivendi Limited* v. *The British Products Sanmex Company Limited* [1997] I.L.Pr. 654, Knox J. drew a distinction between the place where the damage occurred and the place where the loss was suffered in cases of passing off, in the context of Art. 5(3) of the Brussels

significant element or elements are those which give rise to the wrongful event and not the resulting damage.

Why is it that the law of the place where the wrong is committed should generally govern liability? This was aptly described by Lord Pearson in a jurisdictional context, stating that it is "manifestly just and reasonable that a defendant should have to answer for his wrongdoing in the country where he did the wrong".[35] *A fortiori* in the choice of law context, the defendant's liability should generally be governed by the law of the place where his wrongdoing was committed.[36] A defendant should not be made liable pursuant to a particular law, where his acts are either legitimate, or attract a different level of liability, under the law of the place where such acts were committed. A defendant is therefore able to regulate his acts according to the law of the various places where such acts occur.

We may draw an analogy between the commission of the wrong and the circumstances making the relevant enrichment unjust, namely the unjust factor. A plaintiff should also not be able to recover an enrichment from a defendant, where, according to the law of the place where the alleged unjust factor arose, no such restitutionary liability attaches. The liability of an enriched party should generally be governed by the law of the place where the events which allegedly render such an enrichment unjust occurred, or alternatively, the law most closely connected to the alleged unjust factor. It is submitted that this is the proper law of the duty to make restitution of an unjust enrichment.

The analogy between tort and restitution can be drawn even further. The "damage" element in tort finds its parallel in the "enrichment" element in restitution.[37] Both these elements complete the action and are both questions of an essentially factual nature. In international torts, the place where the damage occurred is not viewed as being of such importance that its law should govern liability. Such an argument should likewise extend to restitution and the place of enrichment. As already seen, the place of enrichment is often arbitrary, unconnected with the circumstances surrounding the claim for restitution and often difficult to determine. Likewise an analogy may be drawn between the "at the expense of" element and that of causation. Both these elements provide the necessary nexus between the plaintiff and the defendant. While being undeniably important elements to a claim in tort, the "damage" and "causation" elements are not of such significance as to dictate the tort choice of law rule.

It might be considered that the commission of the wrong finds its parallel with the more general question of where the cause of action for unjust enrich-

Convention. The place where the damage occurred was held to have also been the place where the passing off was effected, for the purpose of establishing "the place of the harmful event".

[35] *Distillers Co. Ltd.* v. *Thompson* [1971] A.C. 458, 468 (P.C.).

[36] See also *Phillips* v. *Eyre* (1869) L.R. 4 Q.B. 225, 239; (1870) L.R. 6 Q.B. 1, 28; *Canadian Pacific Ry.* v. *Parent* [1917] A.C. 195, 205, *per* Lord Haldane; *Boys* v. *Chaplin* [1971] A.C. 356, 389, *per* Lord Wilberforce; *Metall und Rohstoff AG* v. *Donaldson Lufkin & Jenrette Inc.* [1990] 1 Q.B. 391, 445.

[37] Although certain torts do not actually require damage, the analogy is nonetheless helpful.

ment arose and not merely the unjust factor component of it. However, as illustrated in the cases discussed above, where the resultant damage or loss arise in a jurisdiction other than where the relevant acts constituting the wrong occurred, the *lex causae* will generally be that of the latter. Thus, where a tort comprises events in several jurisdictions, the question of where the wrong was committed will not focus on where the entire cause of action arose, but rather on the question of where the alleged wrongful conduct arose. By focusing on the place where a wrong is committed, the choice of law rule isolates the legal system most closely connected with the reason as to why the alleged wrong should be redressed, namely, because the acts complained of are wrongful under the legal system of where they occurred, or with which they are most closely connected. Such a choice of law rule seeks to identify the *locus* of the relevant acts constituting the alleged wrong, because they go to the reason for liability.

As it is through the commission of the alleged wrongful conduct that the law determines the circumstances in which damage must be compensated, so too in cases of unjust enrichment, it is through the "unjust" factor that the law determines the circumstances in which enrichment received must be reversed. In tort, it is the *lex loci delicti's* legal values which are applied and not the law connected with any other factor. The tortfeasor's liability is measured by reference to the law of the place where the relevant conduct occurred. These are the key elements in the two actions and the reasons behind the two actions: that which makes the act "wrongful" or the enrichment "unjust". Just as the *lex loci delicti* determines liability for torts, so too the proper law of the unjust factor should determine restitutionary liability. It is these two elements (the commission of the wrong and the unjust factor) which are the essential ingredients in these two forms of liability and through which a legal system imposes its particular legal values. This is a significant consideration, given that both tort and unjust enrichment arise by operation of law. The preferred choice of law rule should therefore focus on these two elements if it is to arrive at the most appropriate law to govern the issue.

The parallel with torts can ultimately only be a guide. In examining a cause of action in unjust enrichment, we note that the fundamental tenet of the case and the essential reason for restitution is that which makes the enrichment unjust, namely, the unjust factor. Put in another way, the gist of the action is the circumstances which allegedly make the enrichment unjust. The choice of law rule therefore must focus on the proper law of the alleged unjust factor. Thus, where the event, or events, which allegedly make the enrichment unjust, namely the unjust factor, and the enrichment occur in different jurisdictions, the proper law of the unjust factor should determine the issue of restitutionary liability. The place of enrichment merely completes the cause of action. If the place where the damage occurs is not adopted as the *locus* of a tort, *a fortiori* the place of enrichment should not be adopted as the choice of law rule for unjust enrichement. As discussed previously, there are compelling arguments for not adopting the place of enrichment rule.[38] It is arbitrary; it gives a deceptively simple *locus*, yet is often difficult to determine; it may not necessarily be connected with either of the parties, or events; and, finally, but most importantly, it can be manipulated by *mala fide* parties, who might ensure that they are "enriched" in jurisdictions with rules that will suit their aims. On the other hand, the events connected with the unjust factor will lie more at the heart of the cause of action. It is therefore submitted that the choice of law rule for matters of unjust enrichment should be the proper law of the unjust factor.

Such a choice of law rule creates a degree of predictability. Affairs can be regulated accordingly. For example, a bank or other financial institution which engages in business in England estimates that, in any particular financial year, a certain number of mistaken payments are made. If the applicable law is that connected with the events giving rise to the unjust factor, namely the mistaken payment, it can determine its position, as English law will apply to all these mistaken payments. If on the other hand the law of the place of enrichment applied, its position would have to be determined each and every time a mistaken payment was made to a different jurisdiction. It would be left in an uncertain position. All would depend on the fortuity of where payments might be made. Greater uncertainty will arise if the proper law of the obligation applied. The answer would depend on all the relevant circumstances, which will vary from case to case. Ultimately much would depend on a degree of judicial discretion, with the result that parties may be forced to litigate so as to find out the "proper law". The example referred to in relation to mistaken payments could apply *mutatis mutandis* to businesses who need to know their position in relation to fraud or other such activities.

At the same time, the proposed choice of law rule also allows for a degree of flexibility. In searching for the law, or the law of the place, with which the alleged unjust factor has its closest and most real connection, one must necessarily pay attention to the events and circumstances of the particular case. It does not focus on a particular arbitrary event such as the "place of enrichment" which may often be unrelated to the alleged reason for restitution. However, unlike the "proper law of the obligation", the inquiry is more specific. It is not a vague, abstract and broad notion such as that of the "proper law of the obligation". Instead, it is more specific, focusing on the circumstances which give rise to the alleged right of restitution.

2 DETERMINING THE PROPER LAW OF THE UNJUST FACTOR

As has already been discussed in the first chapter, the law of restitution operates through certain defined "unjust" factors. These are the categories of cases or circumstances in which an enrichment will be reversed. The proper law of the

[38] See above ch. 7.1.2 *et seq.*

unjust factor will invariably depend on the particular circumstances giving rise to the alleged restitutionary liability. The circumstances therefore help identify the *lex causae*. Therefore, although as a simple proposition the choice of law rule searches for the law most closely connected with the unjust factor, as a matter of practice, it is necessary to consider the various "unjust" categories separately.

Up until now we have referred to the proper law of the unjust factor. This concept conveys two specific meanings. First, it may refer to the *law of the place* with which the alleged unjust factor has its closest and most real connection. Secondly, it may alternatively refer to *the law* with which the alleged unjust factor has its closest and most real connection. Under the first meaning, we would be looking for the place with which the various circumstances giving rise to the alleged unjust factor have their closest and most real connection. Under the second, we would be looking for the legal system with which the alleged unjust factor has its closest and most real connection irrespective of any *locus*. Certain unjust factors may be better at identifying a place whereas others may be more suited to directly identifying a legal system. As will be shown, both these interpretations have a role to play in arriving at the proper law of the unjust factor.

For choice of law purposes, unjust factors can be put into two broad categories. First, there are those cases where the unjust factor is event-based, thereby providing a particular *locus*. Secondly, there are those cases where the unjust factor is in the form of a legal rule. Such unjust factors are more suited to pointing to a legal system. In the first category, the event-based unjust factors, the choice of law rule must seek to find the place with which the alleged unjust factor has its closest and most real connection which will be able to point us to the *lex causae*. This covers cases such as mistake, illegitimate pressure and failure of consideration. In such cases, the proper law to govern the issue of restitutionary liability is the law of the place most closely connected with the particular event and thus the reason for restitution. In the second, and narrower, category, the law-based unjust factors, the choice of law rule will seek the law with which the alleged unjust factor has its closest connection. This will cover cases such as *ultra vires* demands or legal compulsion. In such cases, the unjust factor is connected to a particular legal system rather than a place. That is, a particular legal system rendered the demand *ultra vires*, or compelled the plaintiff to provide a benefit. Such a legal system is the most appropriate also to determine the issue of restitution. The unjust factor is therefore more suited to finding a law rather than a place, as it has no real *locus*. **Therefore, the general choice of law rule, in terms of the proper law of the unjust factor, may be restated: restitutionary issues are governed by the law, or the law of the place, with which the unjust factor has its closest and most real connection.**

A few observations now need to be made. The two categories of unjust factors mentioned above need not necessarily square up with any taxonomy of unjust factors for the purposes of domestic law.[39] Our present categorisation is

[39] In relation to the taxonomy of unjust factors as a matter of domestic law, see P. Birks, "The Law of Restitution at the End of an Epoch" (1999) 28 U.W.A.L.R. 13.

one made to assist us with arriving at the *lex causae*. Owing to their nature, certain unjust factors are better at identifying a place, whereas others are better at directly identifying a legal system. If we wish to arrive at the law most closely connected with the reason for restitution, we must acknowledge such a distinction. Having said that, it may be noted that the two categories mentioned may nevertheless be matched with existing categories as a matter of domestic law. The "event-based" category covers the two categories described as non-voluntary transfer and unconscientious receipt.[40] The law-based category roughly covers what is referred to as policy motivated restitution, namely that the law considers that there should be restitution.

The specific categories of unjust factors listed below are not put forward as separate choice of law rules. They are merely examples of the general choice of law rule's application. Where the court has characterised a matter as giving rise to an issue of restitutionary liability, its next task is to identify the factor which allegedly makes the enrichment unjust or unjustifiable. In any cause of action in unjust enrichment, there is always a reason why the plaintiff alleges the enrichment is unjust. That is, particular events or circumstances are relied upon. It is these circumstances or events which will point us to the proper law. Where a new or domestically unrecognised unjust factor arises, the general principles should be applied so as to determine the *lex causae*. The court will look towards the circumstances and events surrounding the alleged unjust factor, or reason for restitution, and will identify the proper law. The examination of the specific unjust categories best illustrates how the choice of law rule operates, in the variety of circumstances in which a claim for unjust enrichment might arise.

2.1 Mistake

In cases of mistake, the plaintiff's reason for shifting his wealth, and thus his impoverishment, arises as a result of a mistake. That is, but for the mistake, the plaintiff would not have made the relevant payment or provided the relevant service. Owing to this mistake, it is unjust for the defendant not to make restitution of the relevant benefit. As a general rule, the *lex causae* in mistake cases will be the law of the place where the mistake occurred, namely, the law of the place where the plaintiff acted on the relevant mistake.[41] Often, this will coin-

[40] In the former category, the circumstances reveal that the plaintiff did not mean the defendant to have the particular enrichment. He either had an imperfect, a qualified or no intention to transfer value to the defendant and therefore such circumstances render the enrichment unjust. In the case of unconscientious receipt, the defendant's conduct is such as to make the particular enrichment unjust. Both these two categories essentially point to events. The law of the place with which these events have their closest and most real connection is, it is submitted, the proper law of the unjust enrichment.

[41] Mistake here covers both mistakes of fact and law. Given that we are concerned with finding the law of the place with which the mistake has its closest and most real connection (generally the law of the place where the mistake occurred), the question of whether the plaintiff was mistaken as to a fact or a law is inconsequential to such an inquiry. As such, the particular law to which the plaintiff was mistaken is as irrelevant as is, for example, the mistaken location of a recipient.

cide with the place where the relevant acts giving rise to the shift of wealth occurred, as the mistake is the cause for the execution of the payment or service. Thus, where a New York bank mistakenly pays a sum into the defendant's account with another New York bank, the defendant carrying on business in England, the mistake will have its closest and most real connection with New York, where the mistaken payment was made.[42] Likewise, where a payer in England mistakenly makes a payment, via telegraphic transfer, to the wrong recipient in New York, the relevant mistake has its closest and most real connection with England, where the payer mistakenly provided the English bank with the wrong information as to the recipient. In both these examples, the place where the mistake occurred coincides with that of the relevant acts giving rise to the enrichment because the plaintiff was mistaken at the time he executed the relevant acts; that is, at the time when he made the payment or when he authorised his bank to transfer funds to the wrong recipient respectively.

In certain situations, the mistake will not necessarily arise in the same place as where the shift of wealth occurred. Thus, if the plaintiff in England mistakenly instructs his employee to deliver goods to the wrong recipient in France, the place where the mistake occurred is England, whereas the relevant acts giving rise to the shift of wealth, namely the delivery of goods, arises in France. The plaintiff acted on, or suffered from, the mistake in England.

As already discussed, there are strong commercial arguments for adopting the law of the place where the mistake occurred.[43] Banks and other financial institutions can know their position in advance in relation to inevitable mistakes. Moreover, they can ensure that overseas payments are executed in a particular manner so as to ensure that a particular law will apply in the event of a mistake. Adopting the proper law of the obligation as a choice of law rule does not leave them in a satisfactory position. They may often need to litigate to find the proper law. Adopting the place of enrichment also fails to allow the desired level of predictability. Over and above the problems already discussed in relation to such a choice of law rule,[44] the place of enrichment will vary depending on where the mistaken payment, or other benefit, was received. It is precisely because the payment was made mistakenly that it is inappropriate to apply the law of the place of enrichment. Such a place may often be a fortuity, unconnected with the place where the plaintiff acted upon the relevant mistake.

2.2 Illegitimate Pressure

The term illegitimate pressure here is used as a generic phrase to describe those cases where restitution is granted as a result of duress or undue influence. In

[42] See *Chase Manhattan Bank N.A.* v. *Israel-British Bank (London) Ltd.* [1981] 1 Ch 105. See also *Barclay's Bank plc.* v. *Inc. Incorporated*, (1999) 242 A.R. 18 (Alberta Q.B.D.).

[43] See above p.166.

[44] See the criticisms of the place of enrichment as a choice of law rule discussed above: ch. 7.1.2 *et seq*.

such cases, it is the fact that pressure was exercised, which is considered by the law as illegitimate, that makes the retention of the enrichment by the defendant unjust. In cases of illegitimate pressure, the *lex causae* will generally be the place where the illegitimate pressure was exercised or exerted. This will generally be the law of the place where the plaintiff succumbed to the illegitimate pressure. It might not necessarily coincide with the place where the defendant committed the relevant acts which amount to illegitimate pressure.

What is important to note here is that the defendant is not being held liable as a result of his exercising such pressure *per se*. Instead the defendant is made liable to restore an enrichment as a result of his exercising illegitimate pressure *upon* the plaintiff. As such, an argument along the lines that the defendant should be made liable according to the law of the place where he committed the relevant acts, does not hold in such cases. A defendant should be made liable to make restitution on the basis of illegitimate pressure according to the place of where such acts had their effect. An analogy may be drawn here with cases of negligent misrepresentation in tort.[45] The plaintiff would not have ordinarily intended the defendant to receive such an enrichment but for the illegitimate pressure. It is therefore just to apply the law of the place where the plaintiff succumbed to the illegitimate pressure.

In *The Evia Luck (No.2)*,[46] a Panamanian flagged vessel berthed in a Swedish port and was informed by the International Transport Workers Federation (the "ITWF") that the vessel would be "blacked" unless the plaintiff owners entered into ITWF employment contracts with the crew. In addition, the payment of crew wages in accordance with ITWF scales, backdated to the commencement of the employment contracts, was also demanded. Such pressure was considered lawful under the law of Sweden, yet it amounted to illegitimate pressure, in the form of economic pressure, under English law. The plaintiffs submitted to the demands. Subsequently they sought a declaration that they had lawfully avoided the contracts on the ground of duress. They also claimed restitution of the payments made under the contracts avoided for duress.

The relevant contracts were expressed to be governed by English law, while the parties had agreed that the consequential restitutionary claims were governed by English law as their proper law. Therefore, the specific issue before the House of Lords was whether the contract could be avoided on the basis of duress given that the acts of the ITWF were legitimate in Sweden. No separate issue as to what law governed the restitutionary obligation arose, as the parties had agreed that question of entitlement to restitution was to be governed by English law. Nevertheless, English law would have applied as the law most closely connected to the unjust factor. It was in England that the owners suc-

[45] See for example *Diamond* v. *Bank of London & Montreal* [1979] Q.B. 333 (C.A.); *The Albaforth* [1984] 2 Lloyd's Rep. 91 (C.A.). *Cf. Voth* v. *Manildra Flour Mills Pty. Ltd.* (1990) 171 C.L.R. 538, 568–9.

[46] *Dimskal Shipping Co.* v. *International Transport Workers Federation* [1992] 2 A.C. 152.

cumbed to the pressure and made the relevant payments into the ITWF's account.[47]

The example of the *Evia Luck* is a good one with which to analyse the potentially applicable laws. Precisely because a certain type of pressure is considered legitimate in a particular jurisdiction may be a reason for the cross-border exercise of such pressure. It is not surprising that the pressure in the *Evia Luck* was exercised in Sweden and not in England. It is proper that a plaintiff's right to recover be judged according to the law of the place where he succumbed to such pressure, especially where this does not coincide with the place where such acts of pressure were exercised. If however the plaintiff chose to conduct his affairs in a particular jurisdiction and receives a particular form of pressure which is legitimate there, he cannot complain of the legitimacy of such pressure. This is to be distinguished from the case where a plaintiff receives pressure from jurisdiction A and succumbs to such pressure in jurisdiction B. A plaintiff who succumbs to such pressure should not be judged according to the legal rules of A but that of B. Moreover, if the place of the enrichment rule were to apply, a defendant such as the ITWF could direct that the payments be received in a jurisdiction that would recognise the legitimacy of such demands.

2.3 Failure of Consideration

In cases of failure of consideration, or failure of basis,[48] the *lex causae* will generally be the law of the place with which the failure of consideration has its closest and most real connection. Cases of failure of consideration fall into two broad categories. First, there are those cases where the failure of consideration arises in the context of a contract which is ineffective. Secondly, there are those cases where the failure of consideration arises outside of a contractual setting.[49] In both these types of cases, the unjust factor arises because the plaintiff has enriched the defendant on a basis which has failed. The plaintiff has provided his side of the bargain but, in the circumstances, has not received the defendant's reciprocation. In cases where, for example, a contract is void or discharged, the obligation to make restitution does not arise from the contract as such, but from the fact that the defendant did not provide the consideration agreed upon.

The plaintiff is not suing to enforce the contract but rather is seeking to recover the enrichment received by the defendant on the basis that, as a result of the failure of consideration, it would now be unjust for the defendant to retain this enrichment. As already noted, it is undesirable to have two different choice of law rules in relation to cases of failure of consideration, depending on

[47] See the judgment of the judge at first instance [1989] 1 Lloyd's Rep. 167, 168–9.

[48] Certain commentators consider the term "failure of basis" as a better phrase to describe the unjust factor of "failure of consideration": see P. Birks, "Restitution after Void Contracts" [1993] U.W.A.L.R. 195; Burrows, pp.251–3.

[49] See Birks, pp.219–20, 223–6; Burrows, pp.250–3, 320–1.

whether there was or there was not a contract in the factual setting.[50] Both claims are based on a failure of consideration or basis and it is therefore proper that the same principles apply in determining the applicable law. Although a contract may be a relevant factual setting to the claim, the actual claim revolves around the failure of basis.

The unjust factor's *locus* will be the law of the place with which the failure of basis has its closest and most real connection. In cases where the failure of basis is the defendant's failure to provide an agreed reciprocation, such place is generally where the agreed reciprocation was due to be received or performed. Thus, if one considered the relevant unjust factor in *Baring Bros. & Co. Ltd.* v. *Cunninghame District Council*[51] to have been failure of consideration, the bank's entitlement to restitution of the payments made under the purported interest-rate swap agreement was to be governed by English law. The basis for the bank's claim was that it had made payments in relation to which the council had failed to provide consideration, namely to make alternate payments. Such consideration was to be received or performed in England and therefore the unjust factor's closest and most real connection was with England. Were it the other way around, such that the Scottish council were suing the English bank for its failure to make alternate payments, it is just that the claim be governed by Scottish law as the place with which the failure of basis, or the event which rendered the enrichment unjust, has its closest and most real connection. Furthermore, in cases where consideration was to be received or performed in several jurisdictions, the *lex causae* will be the law of the place of the principal, or predominant, performance.[52] This, it is submitted, will be the law of the place with which the failure of basis has its closest and most real connection.

To take another example, in *Etler* v. *Kertesz*,[53] a foreign exchange contract governed by Austrian law was illegal and void under that law. The Court of Appeal of Ontario considered that since the contract was illegal under Austrian law, the plaintiff was not entitled to recover the moneys forwarded, either upon the purported contract or on the basis of unjust enrichment. The Court of Appeal's treatment of the consequential unjust enrichment issue is most unsatisfactory. It did not separately characterise this issue and apply a separate choice of law rule, nor was its decision to disallow restitution arrived at because Austrian law dictated such a conclusion. It considered that the result followed from the fact that the contract was illegal. Had the Court of Appeal of Ontario separately characterised the issue of unjust enrichment, and thus proceeded to apply the above choice of law rule, it would have been apparent that the unjust

[50] See above ch. 6, §3.1.

[51] *The Times*, 30 September 1996.

[52] Guidance to this inquiry may be found from the jurisprudence of the European Court of Justice in relation to the question of the "place of performance of the obligation in question", in the context of Art. 5(1) of the Brussels Convention. See *De Bloos* v. *Bouyer* (14/76) [1976] E.C.R. 1497; *Shenavai* v. *Kreischer* (266/85) [1987] E.C.R. 239; *Moulox IBC* v. *Geels* (125/92)[1993] E.C.R. I-4075.

[53] (1961) 26 D.L.R. (2d) 209.

factor was a failure on the part of the defendant to provide the agreed repayment. This was to be performed in Switzerland[54] and thus Swiss law applied to the separate issue of unjust enrichment. Nevertheless, even if Swiss law would have allowed recovery, the ultimate decision of the Court of Appeal of Ontario may have been justified on the basis that it was contrary to its public policy to allow restitution in the case of such an illegal contract. Indeed, it was noted that, "[t]his law is similar in its effect to the law in force in Canada . . . prohibiting dealings in foreign exchange except through certain authorized dealers".[55]

2.4 Unauthorised Transfer

The term unauthorised transfer here is used as a generic phrase to describe those cases where restitution is effected on the basis of "ignorance", or alternatively on the basis of an interference with another's interest or property. These cases arise where, as a result of fraud, or some other form of unauthorised appropriation, the value of the plaintiff's wealth ends up in the hands of the defendant. The important facts to keep in mind here are that, first, an actual appropriation or interference has occurred; secondly, the plaintiff has not authorised the relevant shift of wealth.

In cases of an unauthorised transfer, the relevant unjust factor is that there has been an unauthorised interference or appropriation. It therefore follows that, the *lex causae* in such cases, will be the law of the place where the relevant interference or appropriation occurred. For example, E, an employee in England forges his employer's cheques and pays them into his account in England. He subsequently withdraws the cheques making them payable to his mistress in France. She pays them into her account in France. In an action for restitution by the employer, the applicable law will be the law of England as the law of the place where the relevant appropriation occurred. Likewise, if a case such as *Lipkin Gorman*[56] had an international perspective to it, such that Cass, the partner addicted to gambling, had gambled money belonging to the partnership in an overseas casino, the firm's *prima facie* right to restitution would be governed by English law, as the law of the place where the unauthorised appropriation occurred. However, if the casino raised a defence akin to that of *bona fide* purchaser for value, this would be an ancillary proprietary issue which would be separately characterised and determined by the law applicable to the transfer of the particular moveable, presumably that of the *lex situs*.[57]

El Ajou v. *Dollar Land Holdings plc*[58] is another case dealing with an unauthorised transfer of funds. The plaintiff owned significant investments in Switzerland. His investment manager in Geneva was bribed to invest such

[54] *Id.*, 210, 212.
[55] *Id.*, 223.
[56] *Lipkin Gorman* v. *Karpnale Ltd.* [1991] 2 A.C. 548.
[57] See ch. 4, §§3.4 and 5.3.1 above in relation to ancillary proprietary issues.
[58] [1993] 3 All E.R. 717, reversed [1994] 2 All E.R. 685.

money in a fraudulent share selling scheme, without the the plaintiff's authority. The proceeds of the fraudulent share selling scheme were channelled through several jurisdictions and some of these were invested in a London property development project in conjunction with the first defendant (DLH). No question of foreign law had been pleaded, while no evidence of foreign law was tendered in this case. However, as the unauthorised transfer arguably occurred in Switzerland, Swiss law should have theoretically applied to the defendant's liability to make restitution. This was the place where the unauthorised appropriation occurred, and thus, its law will be most closely connected with the restitutionary liability.

2.5 Restitution for Wrongs

It has been previously submitted that restitution for wrongs cases should be characterised as either issues of contract, breach of trust or as torts.[59] They should not be characterised as being in unjust enrichment. However, one further advantage of adopting the choice of law rule proposed, namely that of applying the law of the place most closely connected with the unjust factor, is that in restitution for wrongs cases the same result should theoretically be reached even if one adopted an unjust enrichment characterisation. The relevant "unjust" factor would be the fact that an alleged wrong had been committed, namely, the defendant had become enriched by committing a wrong against the plaintiff. Accordingly, the proper law would be the law of the place most closely connected with such a wrong. As a result, the question of how such matters should be characterised becomes one of little practical consequence.

Assuming that cases of restitution for wrongs are characterised as unjust enrichment matters, we could then say the following. Where a plaintiff seeks disgorgement of the defendant's gain in connection with a tort, the applicable law would be the law of the place where the tort was committed. Where the elements constituting the tort occurred in more than one jurisdiction, it would be desirable to adopt a similar approach to that in the *Private International Law (Miscellaneous Provisions) Act* 1995. Such torts would be said to have occurred in the place where the most significant element or elements were committed. Likewise, a similar approach should be adopted to equitable wrongs which are not breaches of trust or contract. For example, in a case of knowing assistance, the question would be to find the place connected with the relevant wrong. Where was the wrong committed, and if it occurred in more than one place, where did the most significant element or elements arise?

In cases of equitable wrongs which amount to a breach of trust or a fiduciary duty, it would preferable to adopt the law most closely connected with the trust or "contract" constituting the fiduciary relationship. If the law of the place

[59] See above ch. 4.4.1 *seq*.

where the relevant breach occurred were to be adopted, we would arrive at a different law from that if the relevant issue had been characterised as a breach of trust or contract.[60] It is submitted that the law most closely connected with the trust or contract is more appropriate to govern the issue of disgorgement than the law of the place where the breach occurred. The latter may often be fortuitous.

2.6 Legal Compulsion

Legal compulsion is used here to describe cases where a person seeks restitution in respect of payment which he was legally compelled to make. In certain situations, the law may consider that the plaintiff should nevertheless be entitled to restitution. The compulsory discharge of another's liability is an example. Contribution proceedings are another. Different legal systems may provide a different answer to the same set of facts. For choice of law purposes, the unjust factor in these situations is legal compulsion and it identifies a legal system rather than a place. In some situations it may be that the alleged compulsion is not in fact legal. The unjust factor is therefore a factual compulsion, in which case the choice of law rule must look for the law of the place with which the compulsion had its closest and most real connection.

Where someone discharges another's liability in circumstances where he was legally compelled to do so, the person whose liability was discharged may be unjustly enriched at the expense of the payer. The legal system under which the plaintiff was compelled to make the payment should be the applicable law to govern restitutionary liability. After all, given that the particular demand was lawful, restitution should only follow where it is allowed by the same legal system. This will be the legal system with which the facts surrounding the plaintiff's alleged compulsion have occurred or are most closely connected.[61] It should determine, for example, whether the plaintiff's right of restitution requires the defendant to be primarily liable and not merely liable in the same degree. It will also determine whether the plaintiff is entitled to restitution in relation to the entire amount paid or merely in relation to his degree of liability.

It is difficult to envisage cases where the elements for a compulsory discharge of another's liability will have much connection with a legal system other than that which compelled the plaintiff to make the payment. For example, a Canadian defendant may have exported goods to England which are stored in the plaintiff's warehouse. The goods are stolen, yet the plaintiff is nonetheless obliged under the Customs Act to pay the import duty to customs.[62] The plaintiff's right of recovery from the defendant in respect of the duties so paid will be

[60] See above ch. 4.4.3 *seq*.

[61] See Goff and Jones, *The Law of Restitution* (London, 1966), p.506.

[62] This example is based on *Brook's Wharf & Bull Wharf Ltd.* v. *Goodman Bros.* [1937] 1 K.B. 534.

governed by English law, as the compulsion arose under English law, or had its closest and most real connection with England. This will be despite the fact that the defendant was arguably enriched in Canada. A more difficult question might arise in the situation where two English joint-owners of a property in France are jointly and severally liable for certain local rates. The plaintiff discharges the entire amount due. Should his right of recovery be governed by English or French law? The plaintiff was legally compelled to make the payment under French law and thus French law has the closest and most real connection with the event which rendered the payment unjust. Therefore, French law should govern the right of restitution.[63] Nevertheless, it might be argued that as both parties are English, the rights between these two parties should be determined under English law. The existence of a property in France is coincidental and thus an exception should possibly apply. An analogy might be drawn with *Boys* v. *Chaplin*.[64] A tort committed between two British servicemen in Malta should nevertheless be governed by English law as an exception, as there is no reason why one should deny the application of English law to the parties. However, unlike the cases of tort, in the example cited French law is far more connected with the rights of the parties than the circumstantial *locus* of a tort. After all, it is French law that compelled the plaintiff to discharge the entire liability and thus made this a *prima facie* unjust enrichment. The right of restitution should accordingly be determined under French law.

In *Nominal Defendant* v. *Bagot's Executor & Trustee Company Ltd.*,[65] a party injured in a motor vehicle accident successfully brought an action against the Nominal Defendant of New South Wales. The Nominal Defendant then brought proceedings in South Australia against the executor of the driver seeking reimbursement. Bray C.J. held that the executor's liability to the Nominal Defendant was governed by the law of New South Wales on the basis that it was "the place with which the circumstances giving rise to the obligation [had] the most real connection".[66] A closer analysis reveals that the Nominal Defendant of New South Wales was obliged to compensate the injured party for his loss under the law of New South Wales. Therefore, it was correct that the issue of the Nominal Defendant's right of restitution, against the party whose liability had been discharged, be governed by the law of New South Wales. This was the law with which the circumstances had their most real connection because the plaintiff had been legally compelled to discharge the defendant's liability under New South Wales' law.

[63] This is the view Goff and Jones come to in an almost identical example given in the first edition of their book, where they devoted a chapter to the conflict of laws: Goff and Jones, *The Law of Restitution* (London, 1966), p.506.

[64] [1971] A.C. 356.

[65] *Nominal Defendant* v. *Bagot's Executor & Trustee Company Ltd.* [1971] S.A.S.R. 346, see also ch. 5, §5.

[66] *Id.*, 366.

Another example of legal compulsion is in the field of contribution. A particular worker insured in, for example, Victoria, is insured for workers' compensation liabilities through a Victorian insurer. He is also insured against public risks through an insurer in England. The contracts are expressly governed by Victorian and English law respectively. A particular event occurs which falls within the risks insured under both policies, thereby entitling the insured to recover under either policy. The insured chooses to recover under the English public risks' policy and not the workers' compensation policy. This discharges the Victorian insurer's liability. The English insurer seeks contribution in relation to its payment. It argues that its payment has unjustly enriched the defendant insurer in that it is no longer obliged to pay the insured. It therefore seeks a contribution in relation to the proportion of the loss which its insurance bears to the aggregate amount insured by both policies. Assuming that such a contribution claim is unavailable under Victorian law, or that it would, for example, make the contributions between the insurers equal, even though the Victorian insurer had insured for a greater sum, a question will arise as to what law governs the right of contribution. The liberal *lex fori* will presumably characterise this as an issue of unjust enrichment,[67] even though it might not strictly amount to such a claim as a matter of domestic law. The English insurer was compelled to make this payment under a contract governed by English law; its right to restitution should also be governed by English law. The Victorian insurer cannot complain about the fact that Victorian law was not applied to its restitutionary liability, as the law of its insurance contract. It has had its liability discharged through the operation of English law compelling the English insurer to make the relevant payment. Similarly, if matters were the other way around, such that the Victorian insurer had paid out first and was now seeking contribution from the English insurer, it is appropriate that Victorian law now apply, as the law which compelled the Victorian insurer to make the payment. The Victorian insurer would ordinarily not have had an entitlement to a contribution, or to as generous a contribution. It made its payment under a contract of insurance which was governed by Victorian law. Why should it now be entitled to claim the operation of English law merely by virtue of the fortuity that the other insurance contract happened to be governed by English law?

In *Arab Monetary Fund* v. *Hashim (No.9)*,[68] Chadwick J. held that a contribution claim brought in relation to a liability under the Civil Liability (Contribution) Act 1978 (the "Act") is *sui generis* and therefore the availability

[67] See Dicey and Morris, pp.1488, 1533; A. Briggs, "The International Dimension to Claims for Contribution" [1995] L.M.C.L.Q. 437; Stevens, p.209; *Nominal Defendant* v. *Bagot's Executor & Trustee Company Ltd.* [1971] S.A.S.R. 346, 365, *per* Bray C.J; reversed on other grounds (1971) 125 C.L.R. 179; *Stewart* v. *Honey* [1972] 2 S.A.S.R. 585, 592, *per* Bray C.J.; *Hodge* v. *Club Motor Insurance Agency Pty. Ltd.* [1974] 22 F.L.R. 473, 477, *per* Bray C.J. *Cf. Plozza* v. *S.A. Insurance Co.* [1963] S.A.S.R. 122, 127; *Baldry* v. *Jackson* [1977] 1 N.S.W.L.R. 494; *Lucas* v. *Gagnon* (1992) 99 D.L.R (4th) 125, 137–8, *per* Tarnopolsky J.A., 141–2, *per* Carthy J.A., reversed but on different grounds (1994) 120 D.L.R. (4th) 289 (S.C.C.).

[68] *The Times*, 11 October 1994.

of such a claim is a question of statutory interpretation.[69] Its availability does not depend on whether, under the rules of private international law, the contribution claim is governed by English law so as to allow a claim under the Act. Instead, the question to be asked is "whether under the rules applicable in an English court, which include the provisions of the Act itself, the contribution claim ought to succeed".[70] Effectively, this means that so long as the court has jurisdiction over the defendant, the Act permits and requires it to order contribution in accordance with the Act. This decision has received academic criticism[71] and is also contrary to the views expressed by the Law Commission.[72]

If *Arab Monetary Fund* v. *Hashim* (*No.9*) is correct, then choice of law questions only arise in relation to contribution claims which fall outside the scope of the Act.[73] However, it is submitted that this decision is wrong and that where an English court has jurisdiction to hear a contribution claim it should not automatically apply its own domestic law to the issue without regard to choice of law.[74] First of all, there is no indication in the Act that it is to apply notwithstanding any international elements which may be present in a contribution claim. Given the absence of any intention to the contrary, the Act must be presumed to define the rules of English domestic law.[75] The question of applicable law in the context of a particular contribution claim is beyond the scope of the Act, one that is to be determined by the rules of English private international law and in particular the restitutionary choice of law rule. Secondly, it cannot be said that a contribution claim is a matter of procedure, and not of substance, to be automatically governed by the *lex fori*. Moreover, such an argument is inconsistent with Chadwick J.'s view that where a claim for contribution falls outside

[69] In support of this approach see also *Plozza* v. *S.A. Insurance Co.* [1963] S.A.S.R. 122, 127; *Nominal Defendant* v. *Bagot's Executor & Trustee Company Ltd.* [1971] S.A.S.R. 346, 356, *per* Bright J.; *Cf. Stewart* v. *Honey* [1972] 2 S.A.S.R. 585, 592, *per* Bray C.J.

[70] Transcript, 11.

[71] A. Briggs, "The International Dimension to Claims for Contribution" [1995] L.M.C.L.Q. 437. See also R. Stevens, "The Choice of Law Rules of Restitutionary Obligations" in F. Rose (ed.), *Restitution and the Conflict of Laws* (Oxford, 1995), p.210; C. Mitchell, "The Civil Liability (Contribution) Act 1978" [1996] R.L.R. 27, 52.

[72] Law Com. W.P. No.75 (1980), paras. 7378; Law Com.W.P. No.87 (1984), para. 2.83.

[73] The scope of the Act is quite broad. The claimant and the contributor must both be liable "in respect of the same damage (whether jointly . . . or otherwise)": s.1(1). Such liability is not limited to tort but extends to "whatever the basis of . . . liability, whether tort, breach of contract, breach of trust or otherwise": s.6(1). The liability may, therefore, not only be owed by a tortfeasor, but also a trustee, a partner or an independent contractor whose act causes damage "to another person". It has even been held that liability extends to a claim for restitution: *Friends' Provident Life Office* v. *Hillier Parker May & Rowden* [1997] Q.B. 85, 102, *per* Auld L.J; but *Cf.* Goff and Jones, pp.395–7. It does not extend to situations where the parties are jointly liable for the same debt, nor does it extend to situations where the liability is in the form of a penalty, tax or other public liability: *Customs and Excise Commissioners* v. *Bassimeh* [1995] S.T.C. 910, 919. It is unclear whether the Act applies to contribution claims between co-sureties or between indemnity insurers: Goff and Jones, p.397; Mitchell, *op. cit.*, p.29.

[74] See also A. Briggs, "The International Dimension to Claims for Contribution" [1995] L.M.C.L.Q. 437.

[75] On the interpretation of statutes and the conflict of laws, see generally Dicey and Morris, pp.16–18.

the scope of the Act, it is governed by its proper law.[76] Thirdly, the preferred view is that an issue arising under the Law Reform (Contributory Negligence) Act 1945 is one of substance, and should therefore be governed by the law applicable to the main claim.[77] Given that the wording of the two statutes is similar, a consistent approach is called for.

Finally, applying the law of the forum to contribution matters, notwithstanding the law applicable to the primary liability owed, cannot be said to always reach the most just result. For example, D1 is an American car manufacturer. One of its vehicles is rented out to D2, an English tourist holidaying in Greece. While driving such vehicle, D2 injures P. The accident was largely due to D2's careless driving but also partly due to certain manufacturing faults in the vehicle. If one had to apportion fault, D2 was ninety per cent whereas D1 was only ten per cent to blame. P brings a successful claim against D1 in the courts of Greece and D1 is held liable in respect of P's loss. D1 now brings a contribution claim against D2. Suppose that under Greek law, no consequential contribution claim may be brought, or that a contribution claim would automatically apportion liability equally. Why should D1 have the advantage of the more generous English contribution law in a case where, its initial liability is governed by Greek law and, its contribution claim is not connected with England other than it being the defendant's domicile? It is submitted that it is proper for the law which determines liability to also determine the question of contribution and that such a matter should not depend on the fortuity of venue. Such an approach encourages forum shopping.

To alter the facts a little, suppose that proceedings where brought against both D1 and D2 and the Greek court held that D1 was not liable to P, in circumstances where the English courts would have held the contrary.[78] Would it be correct to suggest that D2 should nevertheless be entitled to a contribution claim against D1 merely on the basis that the claim falls within the scope of the Act? If the contribution claim by D2 were governed by Greek law, being the law which compelled D2 to make the payment which allegedly enriched D1, such a problem would not arise. It is therefore submitted that contribution claims are issues of substance whose applicable law is the law which compelled the person seeking contribution to make the relevant payment, namely, the law which made him liable.

[76] Transcript, 29.

[77] Dicey and Morris, pp.1527–8; P. North (1967) 16 I.C.L.Q. 379; C. Morse, "Torts in Private International Law" (Amsterdam, 1978), pp.180–1; also Briggs, *op. cit.*, 439.

[78] This it is suggested might occur by reason of a different choice of law rule.

2.7 Ultra Vires Payments

A plaintiff may be entitled to restitution where moneys are paid pursuant to an *ultra vires* statute, regulation, or other unlawful public demand.[79] In such a case the relevant unjust factor is the fact that the demand was *ultra vires* and thus the payment was not owing. This is clearly illustrated in *Woolwich Equitable B.S.* v. *I.R.C.*,[80] where the building society paid the relevant tax even though it considered it invalid. Accordingly, the payment could not be said to have been made under a mistake. Nevertheless, the House of Lords held that the building society was entitled to restitution in such circumstances because where a public authority receives a payment pursuant to an unlawful demand, it is unjustly enriched.

The unjust factor here has its closest and most real connection with the law that determines the lawfulness or otherwise of the public demand. Thus, the right to restitution will be governed by the law that has determined the *ultra vires* nature of the relevant law or demand. This is appropriate for a number of reasons. First, restitution can only follow where the demand is *ultra vires*. Secondly, it is appropriate that the public body be liable to make restitution in accordance with the law that made its law or demand *ultra vires*. Thus, if a defence of "passing on" is recognised under its law,[81] it should be entitled to such a defence. Thirdly, the question of whether the relevant public body has available a defence that it changed its position, and its extent, should be determined under the same law.

2.8 Illegality and Incapacity

There may be situations where a contract or other transaction is rendered void by operation of law, for example, due to illegality or incapacity. A consequent claim in unjust enrichment may be brought, not on the basis of failure of consideration but, because the legal system which rendered the contract void specifically allows for such a claim. In such cases, the law which rendered the contract void should also govern the consequential restitutionary claim. For example, suppose an Australian insurer agrees to insure a Singaporean assured. The contract of insurance is expressed to be governed by the law of England. Let us

[79] See for example *Woolwich Equitable B.S.* v. *I.R.C.* [1993] 1 A.C. 70; *British Steel Plc* v. *C.&E. Commissioners* [1997] 2 All E.R. 366 (CA). See also *Air Canada* v. *British Columbia* (1989) 59 D.L.R. (4th) 161; *David Securities Pty Ltd.* v. *Commonwealth Bank of Australia* (1992) 175 C.L.R. 353; *Commissioner of State Revenue (Victoria)* v. *Royal Insurance Australia Ltd.* (1994) 182 C.L.R. 51; *SCI Operations* v. *Cwth of Australia* (1996) 139 A.L.R. 595.

[80] [1993] 1 A.C. 70

[81] This defence will deny restitution where the relevant taxpayer passed on the cost of a tax to consumers and thus was not impoverished: see *Air Canada* v. *British Columbia* (1989) 59 D.L.R. (4th) 161; *Cf. Commissioner of State Revenue (Victoria)* v. *Royal Insurance Australia Ltd.* (1994) 182 C.L.R. 51.

assume that under Australian law, it is illegal for insurers to enter into contracts of insurance of that particular nature. After the insured period, it is established that the contract of insured was in fact illegal and therefore void under its proper law. The assured claims restitution of the premiums. Let us further assume that under English law, there is no right to restitution as there has been no failure of consideration, while under Australian law however, restitution is allowed merely by virtue of the fact that the insurance contract was void. It is submitted that the right to restitution is governed by Australian law, being the law which rendered the contract void on the basis of illegality. It should be stressed that the unjust factor here is not failure of consideration.

Suppose a Scottish local council enters into a swap agreement with an English bank.[82] The contract is *ultra vires* the council and thus void due to the council's incapacity. Although the swap is completed, one of the parties brings a claim seeking restitution of the overpayments made by it. The claim here is not brought on the basis of failure of consideration as the swap has been completed; there has been no failure of basis. The unjust factor here is incapacity,[83] which arises under Scottish law. Therefore, the issue of restitutionary liability must be determined under Scottish law.

TABLE 2: Summary of circumstances giving rise to restitution(unjust factors for choice of law rule purposes) and the type of choice of law rule applicable

Unjust Factor	Law of the Place Rule	Rule Legal System most closely connected
Mistake	√	
Illegitimate Pressure	√	
Failure of Consideration	√	
Unauthorised Transfer	√	
Restitution for Wrongs	√	
Legal Compulsion		√
Ultra Vires Payments		√
Illegality and Incapacity		√

3 UNJUST AND UNJUSTIFIED

There is a final matter which must be considered. Although the law of unjust enrichment under most common law systems is based around specific unjust factors or categories, this is not necessarily the case under other legal systems.

[82] See *Baring Bros. & Co. Ltd.* v. *Cunninghame District Council*, *The Times*, 30 September 1996; *Kleinwort Benson* v. *Glasgow City Council* [1999] 1 A.C. 153.

[83] See A. Dickinson, "Incapacity and Choice of Law" [1997] R.L.R. 66, 70–1; see also Dicey and Morris, p.1496.

Specifically, under many civilian systems this subject is the law of unjustified enrichment.[84] An enrichment is reversible where it is received without legal cause.[85] At first sight, this may seem to pose a problem. Where an English court is faced with a claim for unjust enrichment, said to be governed by German law for example, how is it to determine the unjust factor? Although such foreign claims will not be based around a specific unjust factor as a matter of law, they will as a matter of fact. There will be a reason as to why the relevant enrichment is unjustified which will accord with an unjust factor. There will be an alleged mistake, duress, failure of consideration or other event of the sort described above which, in the circumstances, makes the enrichment without legal cause and therefore gives rise to a claim in restitution. Enrichment is unjustified in specific categories of cases or circumstances under civilian systems as it is under English law.[86] This is apparent when one considers the origins of the civilian law of unjustified enrichment in the Roman *condictiones*.[87] These were specific categories of claims which roughly square up with the unjust factors.

The way a court should proceed is as follows. When applying the choice of law rule to an international restitutionary claim, the court should do this independently of any particular legal system. After all, the purpose of applying a choice of law rule is to arrive at the applicable law. It should ask itself the reason why it is alleged that the particular enrichment should be reversed; that is, it should identify the unjust factor. The relevant unjust factor will point the court to the *lex causae*, pursuant to which it may determine the plaintiff's claim to restitution. Under this process, it is inconsequential whether the law ultimately applicable recognises specific unjust factors or not. The unjust factor here is a connecting factor which guides the court to the applicable law, it is not a legal pre-requisite.

The German decision of the Bundesgerichtshof, concerning the minor's flight, may be used as an illustration.[88] In that case, the defendant joined the transit passengers in Hamburg and entered a plane for a flight to New York without

[84] Hobhouse J. and Dillon L.J. in *Westdeutsche Landesbank Girozentrale* v. *Islington L.B.C.* [1994] 4 All E.R. 890 and the Court of Appeal in *Guinness Mahon & Co. Ltd.* v. *Kensington L.B.C.* [1998] 2 All E.R. 272 put forward "absence of consideration" as a basis for restitution; *Cf. Westdeutsche Landesbank Girozentrale* v. *Islington L.B.C.*[1996] A.C. 669, 683. This has been strongly criticised and is inconsistent with the general English law of restitution: see Goff and Jones, pp.500–2; P. Birks, "No Consideration: Restitution after Void Contracts" (1993) 23 U.W.A.L.R. 195; A. Burrows, "Swaps and the Friction Between Common Law and Equity" [1995] R.L.R. 15; P. Millett (1998) 114 L.Q.R. 395, 414.

[85] See ch. 1.2.3.

[86] German law draws a distinction between enrichment by performance and enrichment in another way. Where performance is "undone", it will be based on a factor akin to the unjust factors under English law. Likewise performance in another way covers both restitution for wrongs and ignorance or unauthorised transfers of wealth. Moreover, the provisions in the German civil code recognise several special *condictiones*: see Markesinis, pp.713–20, 725–31. Stathopoulos recognises specific categories of, or circumstances giving rise to unjustified enrichment under Greek law: see Stathopoulos, pp.337–40.

[87] See Zimmerman, ch.26.

[88] BGH 7 January 1971, N.J.W. 1971, 609 (Markesinis, p.771).

being in possession of a valid ticket for this journey. Having been refused entry into the U.S., the plaintiff air-carrier agreed to carry the defendant back to Germany on the basis that the defendant sign a document acknowledging that he owed the plaintiff US$256. The agreement was unenforceable under German law, as the defendant's mother, as his statutory agent, refused to grant consent to legal transactions concluded between the defendant and the plaintiff. Assuming that the plaintiff air-carrier was not German, say for example British, and that the unenforceable agreement provided that the payment was to be made in Germany upon the defendant's return, the question may arise as to the law applicable to the plaintiff's claim for unjustified enrichment.

First of all, the issue of the alleged contract's validity would be a separate contractual issue, to be determined by the law applicable to the contract.[89] Assuming that under the *lex contractus* the contract was unenforceable, the claim for unjustified enrichment would be characterised as raising an issue of unjust enrichment. The reason for restitution here, or the alleged unjust factor, is failure of consideration; that is, the minor was allowed to fly back on the basis that he would pay the specified sum. This was to be paid back in Germany. The failure of consideration, namely the failure to make the payment occurred in Germany, or is most closely connected with Germany. Thus, German law should govern the issue of restitution.

Certain observations need to be made here. German law would not consider there to be an "unjust factor" of failure of consideration. In fact, a German court would consider the enrichment of the minor as unjustified on the basis that given the contract's unenforceability, it was without legal cause. Yet, for the purposes of identifying the *lex causae*, the English court can look at the particular claim and objectively identify the alleged "unjust factor" or reason for restitution. Having done this, it can identify the legal system with the closest and most real connection to the alleged unjust factor. It should also be observed that the *lex causae* of the restitutionary issue, applies irrespective of the law applicable to the related, unenforceable contract. The applicable law to the unjust enrichment is determined by identifying the legal system most closely connected with the alleged reason for restitution and not by deferring this question to the law of a related contract, whose applicable law is not necessarily connected with the alleged duty to make restitution.

[89] See ch. 4.1.2.

PART IV

JURISDICTION IN RESTITUTIONARY CLAIMS

9

Jurisdiction under the Brussels Convention

I BACKGROUND TO THE CONVENTION

WHERE AN ENGLISH court is faced with a jurisdictional question, it must first consider the possible application of the Brussels Convention.[1] If the case falls within the subject matter scope of the Convention, it will govern the taking of jurisdiction. The Convention is therefore the starting point, as the rules of common law apply in those circumstances where the Convention points one to such rules.[2] The Brussels Convention has in fact been amended on several occasions.[3] The Contracting States to the Convention are Belgium, Denmark, France, Germany, Greece, Ireland, Italy, Luxembourg, the Netherlands, Portugal, Spain and the United Kingdom. A Convention for the accession of the newer European Union states, namely, Austria, Finland and Sweden, was signed in 1996,[4] however this has not yet been ratified in the United Kingdom.[5]

In addition to the Brussels Convention, the Lugano Convention is a convention entered into between the states of the then European Community and the six states of the European Free Trade Association (EFTA),[6] namely, Austria, Finland, Iceland, Norway, Sweden and Switzerland. The Lugano Convention is substantially identical to the Brussels Convention as amended. It is however distinct from the Brussels Convention as it is not within the interpretative jurisdiction of the European Court of Justice. It applies in cases where a defendant is domiciled in an EFTA state, or where Articles 16 or 17 of the Lugano Convention confer jurisdiction on the courts of such an EFTA state.[7]

[1] The Brussels Convention, as amended, is contained in the Civil Jurisdiction and Judgments Act 1982, as amended (hereafter the "1982 Act").

[2] See Briggs and Rees, pp.3–5, 11–12.

[3] For a summary of the various amendments to the Brussels Convention, see Briggs and Rees, pp.5–7.

[4] [1997] O.J. C.15/2.

[5] The application of the Brussels Convention to these three states is due to take effect under the Civil Jurisdiction and Judgments Act 1982 (Amendment) Order 2000. (S.I. 2000/1824).

[6] Printed in [1988] O.J. L.319/9. It also appears as Schedule 1 to the Civil Jurisdiction and Judgments Act 1991 and Schedule 3C to the 1982 Act.

[7] Article 54B of the Lugano Convention provides that it shall not prejudice the Member States of the EC from applying the Brussels Convention. Where a defendant is domiciled in a Contracting State which is a member of the EC, or where Articles 16 or 17 of the Brussels Convention confer jurisdiction on the courts of such a Contracting State, the Brussels Convention applies to matters or

In relation to intra-UK matters, ss. 16 and 17 of the 1982 Act give effect to a modified version of the Brussels Convention, contained in Schedules 4 and 5, for the allocation of jurisdiction within the United Kingdom. These rules are a matter of internal United Kingdom law and not a matter whose interpretation is within the European Court of Justice's ("ECJ") competence pursuant to the 1971 Protocol to the Convention.[8] Nevertheless, in interpreting the intra-UK Convention, the courts of the United Kingdom are required to pay regard to any relevant principle or interpretation of any provision laid down by the ECJ in connection with the Brussels Convention.

For present purposes, unless a specific convention is referred to, the phrases the "Convention" or "the Brussels Convention" will be used. Unless otherwise indicated, references to the Convention are based on the consolidated version of the Brussels Convention.[9]

2 INTERPRETING THE CONVENTION

There are a number of observations to be made in relation to the interpretation of the Convention. First, the jurisprudence of the ECJ is the relevant path in the interpretation of the treaty. It has been given jurisdiction to make preliminary interpretive rulings[10] upon the Brussels Convention as amended.[11] Secondly, the Conventions are written in all the official languages of the European Community at the relevant time. All these texts are "equally authentic".[12] As such, it is wrong to apply the same process of literal statutory interpretation as would be applied to a domestic English statute. Thirdly, the Conventions are

jurisdiction. Where however a defendant is domiciled in a Contracting State which is not a member of the EC, or where Articles 16 or 17 of the Lugano Convention confer jurisdiction on the courts of such a Contracting State, the Lugano Convention applies.

[8] *Kleinwort Benson Ltd.* v. *City of Glasgow District Council* (*346/93*) [1995] I–615; [1996] Q.B. 57. *Cf.* however *Leur-Bloem* [1998] 2 W.L.R. 27, where certain provisions contained in an EC fiscal Directive had been voluntarily incorporated by the Netherlands into its own purely domestic law. The ECJ held that it had jurisdiction to give an interpretative ruling where the national legislature had transposed the provisions of a Directive into domestic law and had chosen to apply the same treatment both to purely internal situations and to those governed by the Directive. *Kleinwort Benson* v. *Glasgow City Council* was distinguished by the ECJ, although the distinction drawn seems very fine, if not unconvincing.

[9] Printed in [1998] O.J. C.27/1.

[10] This is pursuant to the 1971 Protocol to the Convention as contained in Schedule 2 of the 1982 Act.

[11] The ECJ does not have interpretive jurisdiction over the Lugano Convention. However, annexed to the Lugano Convention is a declaration from the representatives of the EFTA states that, in interpreting the Lugano Convention, their courts pay due account to the rulings of the ECJ, and of the courts of the Member States of the European Community, in respect of the provisions of the Brussels Convention which are substantially reproduced in the Lugano Convention: see [1988] O.J. L.319/40. There is a parallel declaration from the Member States of the European Community that, in interpreting the Brussels Convention, the ECJ pay due account to the decisions concerning the Lugano Convention: see [1988] O.J. L.319/37. Finally, it should also be noted that Art. 1, of Protocol 2, provides that the courts of the Contracting States to the Lugano Convention are required to take account of any principles laid down in any relevant decision of a court of any other Lugano Contracting State concerning the interpretation of the Convention.

[12] Article 68.

each supplemented by a report, written by experts, to provide a background and explanation to the text.[13] These reports are of great importance in the interpretation of the Conventions and are given significant weight.[14]

Finally, the ECJ has generally adopted a teleological approach to the interpretation of the Conventions. That is, an interpretation is adopted which promotes the aims and objectives of the Conventions; namely, the furtherance of a truly internal market through the adoption of common rules of jurisdiction allowing for increased harmonisation of laws, providing greater legal certainty, avoiding discrimination and facilitating the "free movement" of judgments. As such, the ECJ has generally given "autonomous" meanings to various terms and concepts, as opposed to the meaning such a term may have under national law.[15] Such an approach minimises the problems which might otherwise arise due to a multiplicity of interpretations and helps ensure a uniform application of the Convention throughout the Contracting States.

3 THE SCOPE OF THE CONVENTION

The Convention applies to "civil and commercial" matters.[16] It does not extend "in particular to revenue, customs or administrative matters". The term "civil and commercial matter" has been given an autonomous meaning.[17] It does not therefore matter that the action may be classified as, for example, a tort as a matter of domestic law.[18] The scope of the Convention is limited to private matters and does not cover the exercise of powers which are of a public nature, nor does it extend to matters concerning public law.

[13] The reports are: the Jenard Report [1979] O.J. C.59/1; the Schlosser Report [1979] O.J. C.59/71; the Evrigenis and Kerameus Report [1986] O.J. C.298/1; the Almeida Cruz, Desantes Real and Jenard Report [1990] O.J. C.189/35; the Jenard and Möller Report [1990] O.J. C.189/57.

[14] The English courts are entitled to consider the Reports and to give them such weight as is appropriate in the circumstances: see for example s.3 of the 1982 Act.

[15] Autonomous or Convention meanings have been adopted in relation to "civil and commercial matters" in Art. 1: *LTU GmbH* v. *Eurocontrol* (29/76) [1976] E.C.R. 1541; *Netherlands State* v. *Rüffer* (814/79) [1980] E.C.R. 3807; the meaning of "branch, agency or other establishment" in Art. 5(5): *Somafer S.A.* v. *Saar-Ferngas A.G.* (33/78) [1978] E.C.R. 2183; "contract" in Art. 5(1): *Peters Bauunternehmung GmbH* v. *Zuid Nederlandse Aannemers Vereneging* (34/82) [1983] E.C.R. 987, 1002 (para. 9); *Handte GmbH* v. *Société Traitements Mécano-chimiques des Surfaces* (26/91) [1992] E.C.R. I–3967; "matters relating to tort, delict or quasi-delict" in Art. 5(3): *Kalfelis* v. *Schroeder, Munchmeyer, Hengst & Co.* (189/87) [1988] E.C.R. 5565; "place where the harmful event occurred" in Art. 5(3): *Bier* v. *Mines de Potasse d'Alsace S.A.* (21/76) [1976] E.C.R. 1735. *Cf.* however the national approach adopted in relation to the "place of performance of the obligation in question" in Art. 5(1): *Industrie Tessili Italiana Como* v. *Dunlop AG* (12/76) [1976] E.C.R. 1473; *Custom Made Commercial Ltd.* v. *Stawa Metallbau GmbH* (288/92) [1994] E.C.R. I–2913.

[16] Article 1.

[17] *LTU GmbH* v. *Eurocontrol* (29/76) [1976] E.C.R. 1541; *Netherlands State* v. *Rüffer* (814/79) [1980] E.C.R. 3807.

[18] Thus, in *Netherlands State* v. *Rüffer*, *id.*, a claim by a Dutch public authority to recover the costs relating to the compulsory removal of a sunken barge in a public waterway, administered by the state, was held not to be a civil and commercial matter. It was irrelevant that as a matter of Dutch law, this was characterised as a tort. The removal of the wreck was exercised pursuant to a public power.

Nearly all restitutionary claims will clearly amount to "civil and commercial" matters and thus fall within the scope of the Convention. Some difficulties may however be encountered in cases where a plaintiff seeks to recover, for example, moneys paid pursuant to an *ultra vires* statute, regulation, or other unlawful public demand,[19] or a contract entered into with a public body which is *ultra vires* the body.[20] In such a case, it may be argued that the recovery is based on an essentially public law doctrine, namely that of promoting government legality.[21] Such actions may be said to differ from ordinary actions for restitution and therefore fall outside the scope of the Convention. Such an argument may apply *a fortiori* in relation to *ultra vires* taxes, as matters of revenue and customs are expressly excluded from the scope of the Convention. Likewise, as the Convention does not apply to matters of "social security",[22] a claim to recover money wrongly paid by way of social security might also be said to fall outside the scope of the Convention.

It is submitted that the ECJ's autonomous interpretation of "civil and commercial" matters extends to actions to recover *ultra vires* payments. The fact that it is the *ultra vires* public demand or payment that renders the enrichment unjust does not render the claim of a sufficiently public nature, so as to bring it outside the autonomous meaning ascribed by the ECJ to "civil and commercial" matters. Such restitutionary claims are not particularly exercised by a public body nor are they an exercise of a public power. They are claims of a private nature, brought in relation to erroneous exercises of public power by public, or governmental, bodies. The public flavour is a factual backdrop but not the actual basis of the claim. The distinction adopted by Briggs and Rees in relation to whether a matter falls within the scope of the Convention is helpful. They state:

> [I]f the claim made is one by, or against, a public law body, which only a public law body could make (or which could lie against only a public law body), the claim will not fall within the Convention. If instead it is a claim which could be brought by any other legal person, but which just happens to be brought by a public law body, it will fall within the scope of the Convention.[23]

Therefore, in *Sonntag* v. *Waidmann*,[24] a claim for compensation brought against a schoolteacher was held to fall within Article 1, despite the contention

[19] See for example *Woolwich Equitable B.S.* v. *I.R.C.* [1993] 1 A.C. 70; *British Steel Plc* v. *C&E Commissioners* [1997] 2 All E.R. 366 (CA). See also *Air Canada* v. *British Columbia* (1989) 59 D.L.R. (4th) 161; *David Securities Pty Ltd.* v. *Commonwealth Bank of Australia* (1992) 175 C.L.R. 353; *Commissioner of State Revenue (Victoria)* v. *Royal Insurance Australia Ltd.* (1994) 182 C.L.R. 51; *SCI Operations* v. *Cwth of Australia* [1996] 139 A.L.R. 595.

[20] See for example *Westdeutsche Landesbank Girozentrale* v. *Islington London Borough Council* [1996] A.C. 669; *Kleinwort Benson Ltd.* v. *Glasgow City Council* [1999] 1 A.C. 153.

[21] See Burrows, pp.348–52.

[22] Article 1(3).

[23] Briggs and Rees, p.31.

[24] (172/91) [1993] E.C.R. I–1963.

that, as a German state employee, the schoolteacher owed public law and not private law duties. The ECJ held that:

> . . . the fact that a teacher has the status of civil servant and acts in that capacity is not conclusive. Even though he acts on behalf of the State, a civil servant does not always exercise public powers.[25]

It was not an action brought by or against a public law body acting as such. It was one brought as any private individual would. A claim for unjust enrichment in relation to an *ultra vires* payment is, in this sense, no different from any other claim for unjust enrichment. Just as a schoolteacher who concurrently exercises public powers may become civilly liable for compensation, so too a public authority which becomes unjustly enriched might also become civilly liable to make restitution. The fact that such liabilities were incurred by an individual or body which concurrently exercised public powers does not diminish the "civil and commercial" nature of the claim.

The opportunity to examine *ultra vires* payments in relation to the Brussels Convention has presented itself in several cases and, although no definitive answer can be derived, they indicate that such claims will generally fall within the scope of the Convention. In the *Kleinwort Benson* v. *City of Glasgow* litigation,[26] claims were brought to recover payments made to a local authority pursuant to several interest rate swap agreements. These agreements were void by virtue of their being *ultra vires* the local authority. It was not disputed that such claims were civil and commercial and therefore within the scope of the Convention. It was evidently assumed that the Convention applied to such claims. Nor was the application of the Convention to such claims objected to in the abortive reference to the ECJ.[27]

Furthermore, in *Menten* v. *The Federal Republic of Germany*,[28] the Gerechtshof, in the Hague, held that the Brussels Convention was applicable to a claim for compensation by the Federal Republic of Germany (FRG). The German authorities had paid compensation to an individual for pecuniary damage suffered by him as a result of acts of war. On an application by the FRG, the Landgericht Berlin declared the settlement null and void and ordered the individual to repay the amounts received with interest, on the basis that he had wrongfully obtained the money from the German authorities. The individual appealed against the enforcement of the proceedings served upon him in the Netherlands and, *inter alia*, the issue arose as to whether this was a "civil and

[25] *Id.*, 1996 (para. 21).

[26] *Barclays Bank Plc* v. *Glasgow City Council* [1993] Q.B. 429; *Kleinwort Benson Ltd.* v. *Glasgow City Council* [1996] Q.B. 678 (C.A.); *Kleinwort Benson Ltd.* v. *Glasgow City Council* [1999] 1 A.C. 153 (H.L.).

[27] *Kleinwort Benson Ltd.* v. *Glasgow City Council* [1995] E.C.R. I–615. However, it may be argued that, as the ECJ held that it did not have any jurisdiction to make a ruling in relation to the intra-UK Convention, the case is of little weight in relation to the issue of the Convention's application to these types of claims.

[28] N.I.P.R. 1987, No. 281; [1991] I.L.Pr. 259.

commercial" matter so as to attract the application of the Brussels Convention. The Gerechtshof held that the present matter concerned a claim brought by a creditor to recover compensation in relation to damage wilfully caused.[29] The fact that the claim was one brought by a public authority, did not place the matter beyond the scope of the Convention. It was not a claim which derived from the creditor's position as a public authority. Moreover, it made no difference that the claim was originally based on payments made by the German authorities pursuant to a war compensation scheme.

Although it is submitted that claims to recover *ultra vires* payments will generally fall within the scope of the Convention, a particular qualification needs to be made. Such claims will fall outside the scope of the Convention where the plaintiff also seeks to establish the *ultra vires* nature of the relevant demand. To fall within the scope of the Convention, the claim must be one relating to the private right to restitution. The *ultra vires* nature of the law, regulation, contract or demand is an issue which cannot be said to fall within the scope of the Convention. Such issue must be a premise for the claim and not a question to be answered in the proceedings.[30] The objection might be taken that jurisdiction becomes an accident of the case being heard; namely, whether or not the case also concerns the *ultra vires* issue as a threshold question to restitution. This is an inevitable consequence of rules of jurisdiction which seek to exclude public matters and are limited to "civil and commercial" matters. Ultimately a line has to be drawn somewhere between those matters falling within and those outside of the Convention.

4 APPLICATION OF THE CONVENTION

4.1. The General Rule

Assuming that a case falls within the scope of the Convention, the general rule is to be found in Article 2. Where a defendant is domiciled in a Contracting State, the defendant shall be sued in the courts of that Contracting State. This applies irrespective of his nationality. There is therefore a general principle adopted under the Convention that persons should be sued in the Contracting State in which they are domiciled. Such principle, referred to also as the principle of *actor sequitur forum rei*, is of fundamental importance to the overall scheme and purpose of the Convention.[31]

[29] Specifically, the claim was based on Art. 826, German Civil Code, which is to be found in the section dealing with delicts. It provides: "A person who wilfully causes damage to another in a manner contrary to public policy is bound to compensate the other for damage".

[30] See *British Steel plc* v. *Customs and Excise Commissioners* [1996] 1 All E.R. 1002, 1013, *per* Laws J. See also Burrows and Mckendrick, pp.560–2; Burrows, pp.354–6.

[31] See Jenard, p.18; Lando, p.26; Briggs and Rees, p.15; Dicey and Morris, p.341.

The question of whether an individual is domiciled in the Contracting State whose courts are seised of a matter is determined by that state's internal law. When a person is not domiciled in the state whose courts are seised of a matter, the question of whether that person is domiciled in another state is determined by the law of that other state.[32] Thus, the question of whether an individual is domiciled in the United Kingdom is determined by the law of the United Kingdom;[33] the question of whether that individual is domiciled in Italy is determined by Italian law, and so on. In relation to legal entities, Article 53 provides that the seat of a company or other legal person or association of natural persons shall be treated as its domicile. Such seat is to be determined by the national court applying its rules of private international law.

The provisions which allow a defendant to be sued in a court other than that of his domicile apply by way of exception.[34] As such, the ECJ has repeatedly emphasised that such provisions are to be interpreted strictly, both in the context of the exclusive jurisdiction provisions[35] and the special jurisdiction provisions.[36] Characteristically, it has been said:

> the "special jurisdictions" enumerated in Articles 5 and 6 of the Convention constitute derogations from the principle that jurisdiction is vested in the courts of the State where the defendant is domiciled and as such must be interpreted restrictively.[37]

It therefore follows that a defendant's right to be sued in the courts of his domicile is a fundamental principle of the Convention. Jurisdiction is granted to courts other than the defendant's domicile by way of exception, which is interpreted no wider than is necessary to achieve the purposes of the Convention.

Where a restitutionary claim is brought against a defendant who is domiciled in a Contracting State, the courts of such a state will, subject to Articles 16 and 17, have jurisdiction to hear the claim. Therefore, a plaintiff bringing a restitutionary claim will generally have the option of suing a defendant in the courts of the defendant's domicile. As a matter of practice, however, the plaintiff may wish to sue in his own courts, or perhaps the courts of a third Contracting State.

[32] Article 52.

[33] This is to be determined pursuant to s.41 of the Civil Jurisdiction and Judgments Act 1982. Section 41(3) determines whether an individual is domiciled in a particular part of the United Kingdom; that is in Scotland, Northern Ireland or England and Wales.

[34] *Kalfelis* v. *Schröeder, Munchmeyer, Hengst & Co. (189/87)* [1988] E.C.R. 5565, 5585 (para. 19); *Dumez France* v. *Hessische Landesbank (220/88)* [1990] E.C.R. I–49, 79 (para. 17).

[35] *Saunders* v. *van der Putte (73/77)* [1977] E.C.R. 2383, 2391 (paras. 17–18); *Reichert* v. *Dresdner Bank* [1990] E.C.R. I–27, 41 (para. 9); *Reichert* v. *Dresdner Bank (No.2) (261/90)* [1992] E.C.R. I–2149, 2182 (para. 25).

[36] *Kalfelis* v. *Schröeder, Munchmeyer, Hengst & Co. (189/87)* [1988] E.C.R. 5565, 5585 (para. 19); *Dumez France* v. *Hessische Landesbank (220/88)* [1990] E.C.R. I–49, 79 (para. 17).

[37] *Kalfelis* v. *Schröeder, Munchmeyer, Hengst & Co. (189/87)* [1988] E.C.R. 5565, 5585 (para. 19). See also *Kleinwort Benson Ltd.* v. *Glasgow City Council* [1999] 1 A.C. 153, 163–4, *per* Lord Goff in relation to the intra-UK version of the Convention as contained in Schedule 4 of the 1982 Act. This principle has been echoed in relation to the Consumer Contract provisions contained in Title II, Section 4 of the Convention; see *Shearson Lehman Hutton* v. *TVB (89/91)* [1993] E.C.R. I–139, 187 (para. 17); *Benincasa* v. *Dentalkit Srl (269/95)* [1997] I E.C.R. 3767, 3794–5 (para. 14).

The next issue therefore is determining the circumstances under which a plaintiff may be able to sue a defendant in unjust enrichment, in courts other than that of the defendant's domicile. This is a particularly important issue given the fact that, unlike in matters of tort and contract, there is far less international harmony as to the choice of law rule for restitutionary matters.

4.2 Special Jurisdiction

Articles 5 and 6 of the Convention[38] set out particular circumstances in which a plaintiff may sue a defendant domiciled in a Contracting State, in the courts other than that of his domicile. These allow for alternative jurisdiction in a number of defined situations as there will generally be a close connection between the dispute and the courts which are chosen under these jurisdiction rules.[39] The ECJ stated in *Dumez*:

> As the Court has already held . . . those cases of special jurisdiction, the choice of which is a matter for the plaintiff, are based on the existence of a particularly close connecting factor between the dispute and courts other than those of the State of the defendant's domicile, which justifies the attribution of jurisdiction to those courts for reasons relating to the sound administration of justice and the efficacious conduct of proceedings.[40]

Although there are specific provisions allowing for special jurisdiction in cases of contract[41] and tort,[42] no such specific provision exists in relation to unjust enrichment. *Prime facie* therefore, one might say that, as the Convention does not envisage the existence of a special jurisdiction in unjust enrichment cases, jurisdiction in such actions is to be limited to the courts of the defendant's domicile.[43] This argument was put by Lord Goff in *Kleinwort Benson Ltd.* v. *Glasgow City Council*:

> No express provision is made in article 5 in respect of claims for unjust enrichment as such; and it is legitimate to infer that this omission is due to the absence of any close connecting factor consistently linking such claims to any jurisdiction other than the

38 Section 2 of the Convention.

39 Jenard Report, p.22; *Industrie Tessili Italiana Como* v. *Dunlop AG* (12/76) [1976] E.C.R. 1473; *Dumez France* v. *Hessische Landesbank* (220/88) [1990] E.C.R. I–49, 79 (para. 17). The jurisdiction rules will apply even where the court chosen is not particularly closely connected with the dispute. There is a general hostility to considerations of *forum conveniens* in relation to the special jurisdiction provisions: see *Custom Made Commercial Ltd.* v. *Stawa Metallbau GmbH* (288/92) [1994] E.C.R. I–2913; *The Tatry (cargo owners)* v. *Maciej Rataj (owners)* (406/92) [1994] E.C.R. I–5439; *Boss Group Ltd.* v. *Boss France SA* [1997] 1 W.L.R. 351, 358D. *C f. Marinari* v. *Lloyd's Bank plc* (364/93) [1995] E.C.R. I–2719, 2738 (para. 10).

40 *Dumez France* v. *Hessische Landesbank* (220/88) [1990] E.C.R. I–49, 79 (para. 17).

41 Article 5(1).

42 Article 5(3).

43 Jaffey, pp.80–1; C. McLachlan, "Restitution", in McLachlan and Nygh (eds.), *Transnational Tort Litigation: Jurisdictional Principles* (Oxford, 1996), p.230 (hereafter McLachlan).

defendant's domicile. Article 2 therefore provides the appropriate jurisdiction for such claims.[44]

Accordingly, a majority of the House of Lords held that a claim to restitution of moneys paid under a void contract did not fall within Article 5(1). It was a claim in unjust enrichment to which Article 2 provided the relevant jurisdiction.[45] Likewise, in *Colorificio Paulin SpA* v. *Soc. Sogeref Artlin*,[46] the Corte di cassazione held that a claim to recover the price paid under a contract of sale which had been declared null and void and thus inoperative *ex tunc* did not fall within Article 5(1). The general rule in Article 2, that jurisdiction lay with the courts of the place where the defendant was domiciled, applied.

The argument that the Convention does not envisage special jurisdiction in matters of unjust enrichment might find further support in the fact that restitution does make a small appearance in Article 5(4). A defendant may be sued "as regards a civil claim for damages or restitution which is based on an act giving rise to criminal proceedings, in the court seised of those proceedings". Therefore, it could be argued, that although the Convention grants special jurisdiction for restitutionary claims in cases where there are parallel criminal proceedings, the absence of any special jurisdiction for restitutionary claims in general evinces a clear intention that only the courts of the defendant's domicile are to have jurisdiction in matters of unjust enrichment. However, a claim under Article 5(4) for "restitution" might not necessarily lie in unjust enrichment, but might also cover a claim for restitution in relation to a wrong. Therefore, it may alternatively be argued that, Article 5(4) refers generally to claims which give rise to a remedy of restitution and not specifically to matters of unjust enrichment. This latter argument diminishes the significance of the reference to restitution in Article 5(4).

Despite the absence of any specific provision, views have been expressed that unjust enrichment claims nevertheless fall within one of the alternative bases of special jurisdiction. In line with the autonomous approach adopted for many concepts in the Convention, it has been argued that the absence of any specific provision for unjust enrichment matters is of no practical effect. Peel has therefore argued:

> [U]ntil such time as the Contracting States decide to draft a specific basis of jurisdiction over restitutionary claims, it seems legitimate to attempt to accommodate them somewhere in order to fulfil one of the objectives of the Convention that claims may be heard not only before the defendant's domicile but also before those best qualified territorially to take cognisance of an action.[47]

[44] [1999] 1 A.C. 153, 167. It should however be noted that this decision was concerned with the interpretation of the Intra-UK Convention as contained in Schedule 4 of the 1982 Act. See also *Davenport* v. *Corinthian Motor Policies at Lloyd's* 191 S.L.T. 774.

[45] *Kleinwort Benson Ltd.* v. *Glasgow City Council* [1999] 1 A.C. 153, 167, *per* Lord Goff, 184–5, *per* Lord Clyde, 195, *per* Lord Hutton.

[46] No. 5224, Mass. foro it. 1989, 731 (Corte di cassazione, Sezioni unite).

[47] E. Peel, "Jurisdiction Under the Brussels Convention" in F. Rose (ed.), *Restitution and the Conflict of Laws* (Oxford, 1995), p.6 (hereafter Peel).

The question here is whether unjust enrichment claims generally fall within one of the main bases for special jurisdiction, namely those dealing with contract or tort. This is concerned with whether either of these bases can catch *all* matters of unjust enrichment. It is not concerned with the related question of whether certain claims, for example a restitutionary claim connected to a contract, may, owing to their particular circumstances, fall within one of the bases for special jurisdiction. This latter issue, of whether specific types of restitutionary claims may fall under alternative bases for jurisdiction, will be examined at a later point.[48]

4.2.1 Article 5(1)—Matters Relating to a Contract

Article 5(1) of the Convention provides that a person domiciled in a Contracting State may be sued in the courts of another Contracting State "in matters relating to a contract, in the courts for the place of performance of the obligation in question". The expression "matters relating to a contract" has been given an autonomous interpretation. It is not therefore limited to what constitutes a contract as a matter of domestic law. The ECJ ruled in *Handte* that a matter could not relate to a contract "in a situation in which there does not exist an undertaking freely entered into by one party in relation to another".[49] As such, the enforcement of the obligations of membership of an association have been held to fall within the expression "matters relating to a contract",[50] whereas the right of a sub-buyer to sue the manufacturer was not a contractual matter.[51]

Upon this understanding of "matters relating to a contract", it is quite clear that claims in unjust enrichment do not fall within such an autonomous definition. Such obligations are not created by consent but are imposed by operation of law. This is not a view of unjust enrichment particularly based on domestic law criteria but one that would be accepted more generally.[52] The ruling in *Handte* is in negative terms, namely that there cannot be a matter relating to a contract where there does not exist an obligation freely entered into by one party with another. It may not necessarily follow that there will always be a contractual matter in every case where there is such an obligation.[53] However, even if one accepts a limited reading of the autonomous definition in *Handte*, it cannot be said that it encompasses matters of unjust enrichment. As such, unjust enrichment as an entire category does not fall within Article 5(1).

[48] See §4.3 below.

[49] *Handte GmbH* v. *Société Traitements Mécano-chimiques des Surfaces* (26/91) [1992] E.C.R. I–3967, 3994 (para. 15). See also *Réunion Européene S.A.* v. *Spliethoff's Bevrachtingskantoor B.V.* (51/97) [1998] E.C.R. I–6511.

[50] *Peters Bauunternehmung GmbH* v. *Zuid Nederlandse Aannemers Vereniging* (34/82) [1983] E.C.R. 987.

[51] It should be noted that such a matter was characterised as contractual under French law, as well as under the law of Belgium.

[52] This would be what we may describe as an autonomous definition of unjust enrichment.

[53] See Briggs and Rees, pp.94–7.

4.2.2 Article 5(3)—Matters Relating to Tort, Delict or Quasi-Delict

Article 5(3) of the Convention allows a person domiciled in a Contracting State, to be sued in the courts of another Contracting State: "in matters relating to tort, delict or quasi-delict, in the courts for the place where the harmful event occurred". *Prima facie*, such a reading suggests that this provision intends to allow for special jurisdiction in cases of torts and other related wrongs and that it does not apply to matters of unjust enrichment.

As in the case of "matters relating to a contract", the phrase "matters relating to a tort . . ." has been ascribed an autonomous meaning. In *Kalfelis* v. *Schröeder*,[54] the ECJ ruled that "matters relating to a tort, delict or quasi-delict" has an autonomous meaning and that this meaning applied to "all actions which seek to establish liability of a defendant and which are not related to contract within the meaning of article 5(1)". At its broadest, this ruling suggests that Article 5(3) is a residual provision. All forms of civil obligation which do not fall within Article 5(1), in that they are not consensual, or "freely entered into", fall within Article 5(3). Naturally, this would include restitutionary obligations as they arise by operation of law. Such a reading, namely that Article 5(3) might cover restitutionary obligations, is supported by the fact that the claims brought in *Kalfelis* included one for unjust enrichment. As such, the issue of unjust enrichment was a relevant consideration and one in the EC J's mind when it formulated its ruling.

The view that, as a result of *Kalfelis*, unjust enrichment claims fall within the scope of Article 5(3) has further support. First, the Danish and Portuguese versions of the Convention, at least, make general reference in Article 5(3) to non-contractual matters.[55] Moreover, it could be argued that this is particularly relevant in the case of the Portuguese version which was adopted under the San Sebastián Convention in 1989,[56] after the decision in *Kalfelis*. Secondly, Advocate-General Darmon expressed the view in *Shearson Lehman Hutton* v. *TVB*[57] that the autonomous definition of matters relating to tort includes claims based on unjust enrichment. It is of particular significance that he was the Advocate-General in the *Kalfelis* case. Thirdly, in describing the subject matter of Article 5(3) in *Marinari* v. *Lloyd's Bank plc*,[58] the ECJ made use of the expression "non-contractual civil liability". Finally, several works[59] have commented

[54] (*189/87*) [1988] E.C.R. 5565, 5585 (para. 17). See also *Reichert* v. *Dresdner Bank (No.2)* (*261/90*) [1992] E.C.R. I–2419; *Réunion Européene S.A.* v. *Spliethoff's Bevrachtingskantoor B.V.* (*51/97*) [1998] E.C.R. I–6511.

[55] In Danish, the phrase "i sager om erstatning uden for kontrakt" and in Portuguese "Em matéria excontractual" is used.

[56] The San Sebastián Convention was entered into with the accession of Spain and Portugal into the European Community on 26 May 1989: [1989] O.J. L.285/1. It incorporated Spain and Portugal into the scheme and also made some changes to the text of the existing Brussels Convention.

[57] (*87/91*) [1993] E.C.R. I–139 (para. 102 of the opinion).

[58] (*364/93*) [1995] E.C.R. I–2719, 2740–1 (para. 18).

[59] See Peel, pp.20–3; Briggs and Rees, pp.112–13, 117; Cheshire and North, pp.212–13. *Cf.* Jaffey, pp.80–1; McLachlan, pp.226–30.

favourably towards the view that unjust enrichment claims are caught by Article 5(3).[60]

There are however as many, if not more, compelling arguments for not seeking to place[61] unjust enrichment claims within the framework of Article 5(3). As has been commented:

> "[i]t does considerable violence to the language of the Article to treat restitutionary claims, which in many jurisdictions are accepted as a head of civil liability wholly distinct from both contract and tort, as merely a species of tort".[62]

First of all, placing unjust enrichment claims within Article 5(3) was rejected by all of the judges in the *Kleinwort Benson* litigation,[63] including the House of Lords. Secondly, it would appear from the language of Article 5(3) that it is aimed at wrongs and not matters of unjust enrichment. The English version of the Convention refers to "tort, delict or quasi-delict". Likewise, apart from the Portuguese and Danish versions, all the other language versions refer to a concept akin to torts[64] and not one that is generally non-contractual. Furthermore, although the Danish version uses the expression "unden for kontrakt", literally meaning "out of contract", it is preceded by the word "erstatning". This word best translates as "compensation" or "replacement" and under Danish law, it refers to that area concerned with tort or delict. The argument that particular note should be taken of the Portuguese version in light of the time in which it was drafted, that is, that it was drafted after the decision in *Kalfelis*, runs into the counter-argument that the Spanish version, which is also post-*Kalfelis*, makes reference to delictual or quasi-delictual matters.[65] Moreover, despite its

[60] The Italian decision of *Volksbank Alfred eG* v. *Banca di Credito Agrario SpA*, Giust. civ. 1991, I, 71 (Corte de cassazione, Sezioni unite) might also be cited as supporting the view that matters of unjust enrichment fall within Art. 5(3); however such a view is difficult to maintain. Although the facts surrounding the case concerned a mistaken payment, it was held by the Corte de cassazione that the plaintiff's claim did not satisfy the requirements of unjust enrichment (Art. 2033 of the Codice civile). The defendant's conduct constituted a tort or delict under Italian law and therefore jurisdiction lay in Art. 5(3) of the Convention. It should also be noted that the Italian court did not refer to *Kalfelis*, nor was its decision based on an autonomous definition of "tort, delict and quasi-delict". It would seem that Art. 5(3) was applicable on the basis that the facts constituted a tort or delict as a matter of Italian domestic law.

[61] More aptly one might say "force".

[62] McLachlan, p.226.

[63] *Barclays Bank Plc* v. *Glasgow City Council* [1993] Q.B. 429 (H.C.); *Kleinwort Benson Ltd.* v. *Glasgow City Council* [1996] Q.B. 678 (C.A.); *Kleinwort Benson Ltd.* v. *Glasgow City Council* [1999] 1 A.C. 153 (H.L.). This litigation was concerned with the intra-UK version of the Convention as contained in Schedule 4 of the 1982 Act. It was held in all of the judgments that matters of unjust enrichment do not fall within Art. 5(3) of the intra-UK Convention.

[64] The German version refers to "eine unerlaubte Handlung oder eine Handlung, die einer unerlaubten Handlung gleichgestellt ist"; the French version refers to "en matière délictuelle ou quasi délictuelle"; the Italian version refers to "in materia di delitti o quasi-delitti"; the Dutch version refers to "ten aanzien van verbinstenissen uit onrechtmatige daad"; the Greek version refers to "*ως προς ενοχές εξ αδικοπραξίας ή οιονεί αδικοπραξίας*"; the Gaelic version refers to "in ábhair a bhaineann le tort, mighnníomh nó samhail mhighnímh"; and in the Spanish version: "en materia delictual o cuasidelictual".

[65] The Spanish version of Art. 5(3) states: "en materia delictual o cuasidelictual".

reference to matters "excontractual", the Portuguese version adopts the connecting factor of the place of occurrence of the harmful fact.[66] This, it might be said, gives the Portuguese version an overall delictual flavour. Likewise, the Danish version uses the word "skadetilføjelsen" meaning the "place of harm". To a Danish lawyer, the word "skade" connotes loss or harm in a delictual context.

Thirdly, Article 5(3) grants jurisdiction "to courts for the place where the harmful event occurred". The phrase "matters relating to tort, delict or quasi-delict" cannot be interpreted independently of the remainder of Article 5(3). It is difficult to justify a jurisdictional rule with such a framework for matters of unjust enrichment. They are not dependent on there being a harmful event as such, but rather on there being an enrichment at the plaintiff's expense which is in the circumstances unjust or unjustified. Common sense would dictate that a jurisdictional rule with such a connecting factor is not designed to accommodate matters or unjust enrichment. Moreover, it would be particularly difficult to identify the "harmful event" in cases of unjust enrichment. This much was recognised by both Lords Goff and Hutton in *Kleinwort Benson*,[67] who stated that as "a claim for unjust enrichment does not, apart from exceptional circumstances, presuppose either a harmful event or a threatened wrong,"[68] therefore "it would be inappropriate to apply the words 'where the harmful event occurred' to a claim for unjust enrichment".[69]

It has also been suggested that matters of unjust enrichment may be construed to amount to wrongs and therefore warrant the application of Article 5(3). Briggs and Rees cite the example of "a claim that a recipient of a sum, the retention of which unjustly enriches him, must hand it over may require a prior demand, with which the defendant has failed to comply".[70] It is suggested that this may be construed as a wrongful act. This approach is placing square pegs in round holes. On such a basis all forms of liability may be construed as a wrongful act. For example, a claim for damages in respect of a breach of contract could amount to a wrongful act in two different ways. First, the breach of contract can be viewed as a wrong, yet there is no suggestion that cases of breach of contract are to fall within Article 5(3). Alternatively, according to the above example, the defendant's refusal to pay damages for breach of contract is also a wrong. Although a plaintiff may have previously made a request for restitution, the obligation does not arise from the defendant's refusal to make restitution but rather by the fact that the defendant has been unjustly, or unjustifiably, enriched at the plaintiff's expense.[71] This is not a distinction that is particularly limited to an understanding of unjust enrichment as a matter of

[66] The Portuguese version states "do lugar onde ocorreu o facto danoso".

[67] *Kleinwort Benson Ltd.* v. *Glasgow City Council* [1999] 1 A.C. 153.

[68] *Id.*, 172, *per* Lord Goff.

[69] *Id.*, 196, *per* Lord Hutton.

[70] Briggs and Rees, pp.113, also 117, 124–5. See also Peel, p.25.

[71] See P. Birks, "The Concept of a Civil Wrong" in D. Owen (ed.), *Philosophical Foundations of Tort Law* (Oxford, 1995), pp.48–9.

English domestic law, but is an ecumenical one that would be accepted under the legal systems of most Contracting States.[72]

If one were to construe matters of unjust enrichment as wrongs there would be the problem of locating the place of the harmful event. Presumably, the place of the harmful event would be the place where the defendant is due to perform the restitutionary obligation, the failure of which constitutes a harmful event. Yet, this is something for which there would be no clear answer. We would therefore need to identify the place of performance of the restitutionary obligation. In the early days of its jurisprudence, the ECJ resolved this question in matters relating to contract by allowing the *lex causae* to determine the place of performance of the obligation in question. In *Tessili* v. *Dunlop*,[73] it was held that it is for the court before which the question has arisen to determine the place for the performance of the contractual obligation. This is to be done by applying its own private international law to ascertain the law governing the legal relationship in question, and determining under such law the place of performance of the relevant obligation. Such an approach is possible in matters of contract as there is greater consensus as to the applicable choice of law rules, especially as a result of the Rome Convention.[74] There is therefore greater chance of uniformity. Quite the opposite is the case in matters of unjust enrichment. As such, the approach of allowing the court before which the question has arisen to determine the place where the defendant was due to perform the restitutionary obligation, by applying its rules of private international law, is a very unattractive and uncertain approach.[75]

Alternatively, it may be considered that the place of performance of the obligation to make restitution might have an autonomous meaning. An analogy could be drawn with the place of performance of a debtor's obligation to a creditor. The problem with such an analogy is that there is no consensus among the legal systems of the Contracting States as to where a debtor is liable to pay a creditor. On the one hand, it could be deemed to the place of business, or domicile, of the plaintiff, in that the obligation of the defendant is to make restitution in such a place. Such an approach is unsatisfactory, as it would merely substitute the jurisdiction of the defendant's domicile with that of the plaintiff's without there necessary being a close connection with the dispute. It would also be contrary to the *actor sequitur forum rei* principle under the Convention. Alternatively, the place of performance of the restitutionary obligation could be deemed to be the place of business, or domicile, of the defendant. In such an

[72] See for example Zimmerman, pp.15–18, 20–4, 834–901; Zweigert and Kötz, pp.537–94.

[73] *Industrie Tessili Italiana Como* v. *Dunlop A.G.* (*12/76*) [1976] E.C.R. 1473. This decision was subsequently confirmed in *Custom Made Commercial Ltd.* v. *Stawa Metallbau GmbH* (*288/92*) [1994] E.C.R. I–2193.

[74] The Convention on the Law Applicable to Contractual Obligations (the Rome Convention) is to be found in the Contracts (Applicable Law) Act 1990. See also above pp. 144–5.

[75] Correlating the place of the harmful event with the place of performance of the obligation to make restitution has one further disadvantage in that it does not fit well with claims for proprietary restitution. Such claims do not actually involve an obligation.

event, the special jurisdiction in Article 5(3) is rendered largely redundant for restitutionary claims, as the defendant may, in any event, be sued in the courts of his domicile by virtue of Article 2.

Peel has submitted that the concept of the place of the harmful event may be adapted to cover restitutionary claims for the purposes of jurisdiction.[76] This essentially would correspond with the place of the plaintiff's impoverishment, namely where the plaintiff suffered his loss. However a distinction, it is said, should be drawn between the place where the plaintiff suffered his loss and the place where the event which produced the loss occurred—usually the transfer from the plaintiff to the defendant. The place where the loss was suffered should be rejected as a basis for jurisdiction, where at least it does not coincide with the place of the transfer. This is because it carries the risk of awarding jurisdiction to a court with little or no connection with the dispute and generally to the courts of the plaintiff's domicile.[77] Instead, the place of the transfer should be adopted as the relevant connecting factor. An analogy is drawn with *Dumez France and Tracoba* v. *Hessische Landesbank*[78] and its analysis in identifying the place of the harmful event, in cases of wrongs, where the consequential loss has been suffered in a subsequent jurisdiction. The ECJ held that this was the place where the causal event "directly produced its harmful effects upon the person who is the immediate victim of that event".[79] A distinction is therefore made between the place of occurrence of the damage and the place where the damage was suffered.[80] Looking at the restitutionary analogy, the place where the damage was merely suffered would translate as that of the place where the plaintiff was impoverished, whereas the place of the occurrence of the damage translates as that of the place of the transfer; that is, the event that gives rise to the defendant's enrichment.

The above analysis is an ingenious way of accommodating matters of unjust enrichment within the framework of Article 5(3). Furthermore, if one accepts that *Kalfelis* does in fact stand for the proposition that matters of unjust enrichment fall within Article 5(3), there may be no other practical way of making such an accommodation. However, the above analysis would not give matters of unjust enrichment the same degree of predictability, or certainty, as does the "place of the harmful event" in matters of tort or delict. This, after all, is one of the prime aims of the Convention.[81] Identifying the *locus* of a transfer is not an easy task. It is not as obvious as locating the harmful event in the case of wrongs. For example, if a bank in England mistakenly pays money into the defendant's account held by a bank in Paris, where has the "transfer" occurred? It might be

[76] Peel, pp.23–31.
[77] Peel, pp.23–4.
[78] (*220/88*) [1990] E.C.R. I–49.
[79] *Id.*, 80 (para. 20).
[80] *Id.*, 66, *per* Darmon A.G.
[81] *Handte GmbH* v. *Société Traitements Mécano-chimiques des Surfaces* (*26/91*) [1992] E.C.R. I–3967, 3995 (para. 18).

said that this was England. If however the moneys have gone through a clearing house located in a third jurisdiction, is the place of the transfer still in England or in that third jurisdiction? Particular types of claim will require individual rulings so that the place of the transfer may be identified accordingly. Where would the place of the harmful event lie in a case of a fraudulent transfer of funds? In a sophisticated case of fraud, the process of transferring funds may have consisted of several transfers.[82] In matters of unjust enrichment, the place of the harmful event, albeit in the form of the place of the transfer, is unlikely to share the same degree of predictability and certainty as it will in cases of wrongs. As has been noted by the ECJ:

> The objective of strengthening legal protection of persons established in the Community, which is one of the objectives which the Convention is designed to achieve, also requires that the jurisdictional rules which derogate from the general principle of the Convention should be interpreted in such a way as to enable a normally well-informed defendant reasonably to predict before which courts, other than those of the State in which he is domiciled, he may be sued.[83]

To adopt the place of impoverishment, even in the form of the place of the transfer, as the corresponding connecting factor to the place of the harmful event, is to adopt a fiction. The fact of the matter is that the place of the transfer is not a harmful event as such. The ECJ has ruled that the place where the harmful event occurred means "both the place where the damage occurred and the place of the event giving rise to it.[84] It does not seem that this autonomous and independent meaning is intended to cover the element of impoverishment in matters of unjust enrichment. An impoverishment merely refers to a shift of wealth and not damage, or events which result in damage. It is unlikely that a separate definition of the place where the harmful event occurred would be adopted specifically to deal with matters of unjust enrichment. It is also of significance that the harmful event in cases of wrongs is that which generally completes the action, whereas the transfer, or more generally the impoverishment, occurs prior to the completion of the action. Additional events, namely in the form of enrichment, are required before a claim for unjust enrichment can be made out.

Furthermore, the place of the impoverishment does not have the same degree of connection with a claim for unjust enrichment such as to warrant the granting of jurisdiction in courts other than that of the defendant's domicile. The ECJ has stated on several occasions that the provisions in Article 5 allow for special jurisdiction:

[82] See for example the facts of *El Ejou* v. *Dollar Holdings Ltd.* [1993] 3 All E.R. 717. See also C. Howard, *Butterworths Money Laundering Law* (1997) Div. 2.

[83] *Handte GmbH* v. *Société Traitements Mécano-chimiques des Surfaces* (26/91) [1992] E.C.R. I–3967, 3995 (para. 18).

[84] *Bier* v. *Mines de Potasse d'Alsace SA*(21/76) [1976] E.C.R. 1735, 1748 (para. 24).

> because of the existence in a number of clearly defined situations, of a particularly close connecting factor between a dispute and the court which may be called upon to hear it, with a view to the efficacious conduct of the proceedings.[85]

In the situation of torts, the place where the harmful event occurred in obviously a close connecting factor. Where a harmful event occurs in a particular jurisdiction—that is either where the immediate damage occurs, or where the event giving rise to such damage occurs—the courts of such jurisdiction are generally a closely connected forum to such a dispute. The same cannot be said in matters of unjust enrichment. The relevant connecting factor between the dispute and the court which may be called upon to hear it, is not only not particularly close, but, more importantly, artificial. As a connecting factor, the place of impoverishment, under the guise of the place of the harmful event, does not share the same closeness between the dispute and the courts chosen. The provisions of special jurisdiction require an interpretation of the key phrases with the likely jurisdictional result in mind. If such result is one which would generally give jurisdiction to the courts of a place having no real connection with the underlying dispute, such an interpretation must be rejected.[86]

There is a final argument against including matters of unjust enrichment within the framework of Article 5(3). It is submitted that a proper reading of *Kalfelis*[87] does not suggest that unjust enrichment matters fall within Article 5(3). This is based both on the language of the case and on the questions actually answered by the ECJ. Considering the language of the case, the concept of "liability" in *Kalfelis* has a narrower meaning than simply being on the receiving end of a writ.[88] The language of the case in *Kalfelis* was in German. The key word used in the ECJ's ruling on the autonomous definition of tort was "Schadenshaftung" which has a narrower meaning than "liability".[89] It connotes the obligation to compensate for wrongdoing. This was also the view of Lord Hutton in *Kleinwort Benson*.[90] Liability in *Kalfelis* "must be interpreted as meaning liability within the scope of Article 5(3), namely liability in tort, delict or quasi-delict".[91] Accordingly, the obligation on a defendant to make

[85] *Somafer* v. *Saar-Ferngas AG (33/78)* [1978] E.C.R. 2183, 2191 (para. 7); *Peters Bauunternehmung GmbH* v. *Zuid Nederlandse Aannemers Vereneging (34/82)* [1983] E.C.R. 987, 1002 (para. 11); *Kleinwort Benson Ltd.* v. *Glasgow City Council* [1999] 1 A.C. 153, 164, *per* Lord Goff, 173, *per* Lord Nicholls, 180, *per* Lord Clyde, 189, *per* Lord Hutton.

[86] See also A. Dickinson, "Restitution and the Conflict of Laws in the House of Lords: *Kleinwort Benson* v. *Glasgow City Council*" [1998] R.L.R. 104, 116.

[87] *Kalfelis* v. *Schröeder, Munchmeyer, Hengst & Co. (189/87)* [1988] E.C.R. 5565.

[88] Briggs and Rees, p.113.

[89] Lord Clyde in *Kleinwort Benson Ltd.* v. *Glasgow City Council* [1999] 1 A.C. 153, 185, held that the argument that *Kalfelis* supports the incorporation of unjust enrichment within Art. 5(3) is in fact based "upon an imprecise translation of the passage in *Kalfelis*". Similarly, Lord Goff stated that this argument is based on a "misreading of paragraph 2(a) of the ruling of the Court of Justice in *Kalfelis* v. *Bankhaus Schröder*": *id.*, 172.

[90] *Kleinwort Benson Ltd.* v. *Glasgow City Council* [1999] 1 A.C. 153.

[91] *Id.*, 196.

restitution of an unjust enrichment will not *per se* fall within Article 5(3)[92] as it is not liability in the sense of compensation for wrongdoing.

It has been pointed out that to draw a distinction between liabilities which compensate for wrongdoing and other forms of liability may raise greater practical difficulties than it solves.[93] The significant point here however is not to suggest that the nature of "liability" be the test as to whether a matter falls within the scope of Article 5(3) or not. Rather, the narrower notion of liability in the original text helps demonstrate that the autonomous definition of tort is not so wide as to cover matters of unjust enrichment. The ECJ in *Kalfelis* was more concerned about drawing the line between Articles 5(1) and 5(3). The narrower notion of liability helps demonstrate that the autonomous definition of tort cannot roam unfettered into the other direction. A line must also exist which separates matters within the autonomous definition of tort from other forms of liability which do not arise from obligations freely entered into.

Furthermore, there is an argument that, upon examining the actual questions answered by the ECJ in *Kalfelis*, it cannot be said that the case stands for the proposition that matters of unjust enrichment fall within Article 5(3). There is an apparent conflict between paragraphs 18 and 19 of the judgement. Question 2(b) in the case was, as put by the court:

> intended to essentially ascertain . . . in the case of an action based concurrently on tortious or delictual liability, breach of contract and unjust enrichment, whether the court having jurisdiction by virtue of article 5(3) may adjudicate on the action in so far as it is not based on tort or delict.[94]

Before answering this question the ECJ gave its ruling on the autonomous definition of the phrase "matters relating to tort, delict or quasi-delict" in paragraph 18.[95] After then observing that Articles 5 and 6 must be interpreted restrictively, in paragraph 19 the ECJ ruled that "a court which has jurisdiction under Article 5(3) over an action in so far as it is based on tort or delict does not have jurisdiction over that action in so far as it is not so based". It would seem that this ruling stands for the proposition that only actions based on "tort or delict" fall within the scope of Article 5(3). Actions for breach of contract and unjust enrichment were clearly in the court's mind as they were referred to in the question. Their omission in the ruling would suggest that they are not within the ambit of Article 5(3). Moreover, the court emphasised that this ruling must be read restrictively. This reconciliation of the rulings was one adopted by the

[92] There may be instances where a given set of facts may give rise to an alternative analysis; that is, both a claim for autonomous unjust enrichment and restitution for wrongdoing. In such a case, the claim may fall within the scope of Art. 5(3) by virtue of the fact that it jointly gives rise to a wrong.

[93] Briggs and Rees, p.113.

[94] *Kalfelis* v. *Schröeder, Munchmeyer, Hengst & Co.* (*189/87*) [1988] E.C.R. 5565, 5584 (para. 14).

[95] Namely, that it covers "all actions which seek to establish the liability of a defendant and which are not related to a 'contract' within the meaning of Article 5(1)": *id.*, 5585 (para. 17).

House of Lords in *Kleinwort Benson*[96] in the context of the intra-UK version of the Convention.

It may however be pointed out that the ruling in relation to Question 2(b) must be read subject to the previous ruling, in response to Question 2(a), which gave an autonomous definition of tort; namely, that Article 5(3) covered "all actions which seek to establish the liability of a defendant and which are not related to a 'contract' within the meaning of Article 5(1)".[97] A counter-argument may therefore be raised, that the court's reference to "tort and delict" in answering Question 2(b) must be read subject to the autonomous definition of tort already given. Thus, the court's ruling insofar as it limits a court of a Contracting State, which has jurisdiction under Article 5(3) from having concurrent jurisdiction over an action in so far as it is not based on Article 5(3), is limited to matters that fall outside of the autonomous definition of tort; namely, liability which relates to a contract within the meaning of Article 5(1).

In conclusion, it is submitted that matters of unjust enrichment do not fall within Article 5(3). Despite the arguments supporting an embracement of unjust enrichment within the autonomous definition of tort, it is submitted that this autonomous definition should be restricted to liabilities akin to tort or delict. Such an approach is consistent with the vast majority of the language versions of the Convention and consequently one which is dictated by common sense. Moreover, when one bears in mind the restrictive interpretation which is to be placed on the special jurisdiction provisions in Article 5, in that they constitute derogations to the general domiciliary rule, together with the general inappropriateness and irrelevance of the connecting factor contained in Article 5(3), including the fact that it cannot be said to constitute a particularly close connecting factor, one should reject including matters of unjust enrichment within Article 5(3).

4.3 Particular Types of Restitutionary Claims

Proceeding from the proposition that matters of unjust enrichment do not entirely fall within any of the specific provisions of the Convention, particular types of restitutionary claims may nevertheless be caught by one of the jurisdictional provisions. As has been examined previously, a restitutionary claim may arise in connection with a contract, it may be based on a wrong or it may give rise to a proprietary remedy. These various situations may provide a separate basis for jurisdiction. Thus, although there is no single provision of the Convention to cover *all* restitutionary claims, certain categories of restitutionary claims may be caught, owing to their particular circumstances.

[96] *Kleinwort Benson Ltd.* v. *Glasgow City Council* [1999] 1 A.C. 153.

[97] *Kalfelis* v. *Schröeder, Munchmeyer, Hengst & Co.* (189/87) [1988] E.C.R. 5565, 5585 (para. 18).

4.3.1 Restitutionary Claims Connected with a Contract—Article 5(1)

Article 5(1), it will be recalled, provides that a person domiciled in a Contracting State may be sued in the courts of another Contracting State "in matters relating to a contract, in the courts for the place of performance of the obligation in question". There are three steps in applying this provision: first, it must be a "matter relating to a contract": secondly the "obligation in question" must be identified; while finally "place of performance" of that obligation must be identified.

Restitutionary claims may arise in connection with a contract. A contract may, for whatever reason, have become "ineffective", such that a consequential restitutionary claim might follow.[98] As a matter of English domestic law,[99] as well as under the legal systems of most civilian systems,[100] the consequential restitutionary claim which follows is not contractual. It arises independently, by operation of law, through the principle of unjust enrichment. The question here is whether a restitutionary claim will fall within Article 5(1) where it follows an ineffective contract. Will the plaintiff be entitled to bring the action before the courts of the place of performance of the obligation in question, or will he be limited to the courts of the defendant's domicile?

* *The Approaches*

There are four basic approaches in relation to the question of whether consequential restitutionary claims which follow an ineffective contract fall within the scope of Article 5(1); two in favour and two against. All of them appear in at least one of the judgments in the litigation between *Kleinwort Benson* and the *Glasgow City Council* which went to the House of Lords. First, one might say that where a contract is void *ab initio* there was no contract. As such, the matter cannot be said to relate to "a contract" (Approach 1).[101] The place where the contract was, or would have been performed, if it had been enforceable, is quite

[98] See the discussion of restitution and contract in the context of characterisation: ch. 4.1.1.

[99] *Ibid.*

[100] Under German law, where a contract is rescinded (i.e. where a contract is entered into by mistake (Art. 119 BGB) or has been induced by fraud (Art. 123 BGB)), or where a contract is void, the consequential restitutionary claim lies in unjust enrichment. The recipient is bound to effect restitution of any benefits received as they were received without legal cause (Art. 812(1)I). On the other hand, where a contract is terminated as a result of a breach, the preferred view is that the contract comes to an end *ex nunc* and the parties' rights to restitution are governed by the special contractual rules in the BGB dealing with the restoration of benefits Arts. 346 to 361: see Markesinis, pp.641–5, 716. Under French law, where a contract is annulled, or terminated, through résolution, a retrospective termination of the contract follows. In such an event, a consequential restitutionary may be available: see Terré, Simler, Lequette, *Les obligations* (Dalloz, 1999), p. 387; Bell, *et. al.*, *Principles of French Law* (Oxford, 1998), pp.420–7.

[101] Approach adopted by Hirst J. in *Barclays Bank Plc* v. *Glasgow City Council* [1993] Q.B. 429; also Leggatt L.J. in *Kleinwort Benson Ltd.* v. *Glasgow City Council* [1996] Q.B. 678, 689–91. However, the judgment of Leggatt L.J. could be seen to go even further. Although he states that a claim connected to a void contract is not a "matter relating to a contract, he then goes as far as saying that 'it is impossible to regard a claim for unjust enrichment as a matter relating to a contract' ": *id.*, 691. This approach was also adopted by Lord Clyde in *Kleinwort Benson Ltd.* v. *Glasgow City Council* [1999] 1 A.C. 153, 181; and Lord Hutton, *id.*, 195.

irrelevant. However, in such an event where a contract is not void *ab initio* but has become void *in futuro* or discharged, there was a "contract". The matter would therefore still relate to these types of contracts.[102] Secondly, it might be said that the "obligation in question" must be a contractual obligation. As the consequential restitutionary obligation does not arise *ex contractu* but under the law of unjust enrichment, such claims cannot fall within Article 5.1 (Approach 2).[103] These first two approaches can of course be combined. On the other side of the debate there are two basic possibilities. The phrase "matters relating to a contract" merely gives a contextual basis. That is, the claim merely relates to a contract or arises in connection with a contract. As such, thirdly, it could be argued that when a consequential restitutionary claim is brought the "place of performance of the obligation in question" is the place of performance of the particular restitutionary obligation on which the plaintiff relies (Approach 3).[104] Finally, it might alternatively be argued that, where a contract is ineffective, the "place of performance of the obligation in question" includes the place of performance of the supposed obligation under the ineffective contract (Approach 4).[105]

* *Kleinwort Benson* v. *Glasgow City Council*

This question was examined by the House of Lords in *Kleinwort Benson Ltd.* v. *Glasgow City Council*.[106] Kleinwort Benson (the "Bank"), entered into numerous interest rate swap transactions[107] with Glasgow City Council (the "Council"). Throughout the course of these agreements, the Bank made payments to the Council totalling £807,230.31 and the Council made payments to the Bank totalling £79,152.41. Therefore, the Council had effectively received a total of £728,077.90 pursuant to the swap transactions. In 1991, the House of Lords ruled that swap contracts with local authorities were void as they were

[102] However, Art. 5(1) would presumably not apply to contracts which have become void *in futuro*, or discharged, under the interpretation given by Lord Clyde, who paid attention to the fact that the English wording of this provision adopts the phrase "relating to a contract" and not "related" to a contract.

[103] This approach was also adopted by Hirst J. in *Barclays Bank Plc* v. *Glasgow City Council* [1993] Q.B. 429, 439; also Leggatt L.J. in *Kleinwort Benson Ltd.* v. *Glasgow City Council* [1996] Q.B. 678, 691; also Lord Goff in *Kleinwort Benson Ltd.* v. *Glasgow City Council* [1999] 1 A.C. 153, 167; Lord Clyde, *id.*, 182; Lord Hutton, *id.*, 195. See also Gaudemet-Tallon, *Les Conventions de Bruxelles et de Lugano*, 2d. ed. (Paris, 1996), pp.114–16; Mclachlan, pp.229–30; O'Malley and Layton, *European Civil Practice* (London, 1980), p.391; P. Kaye, *Civil Jurisdiction and Enforcement of Foreign Judgments* (Oxford, 1987), p.490.

[104] This approach was adopted by Roch L.J. in *Kleinwort Benson Ltd.* v. *Glasgow City Council* [1996] Q.B. 678, 694–5.

[105] This was the approach adopted by Millett L.J. in *Kleinwort Benson Ltd.* v. *Glasgow City Council* [1996] Q.B. 678; also Lord Nicholls, with whom Lord Mustill agreed, in *Kleinwort Benson Ltd.* v. *Glasgow City Council* [1999] 1 A.C. 153, 175. See also Briggs and Rees, p.103.

[106] [1999] 1 A.C. 153.

[107] On the nature of interest rate swaps, see: P. Birks, "No Consideration: Restitution after Void Contracts" (1993) U.W.A.L. Rev. 195, 200–1; A. Burrows, "Swaps and the Friction Between Common Law and Equity" [1995] R.L.R. 15.

beyond the powers of the local authorities.[108] Accordingly, the Bank commenced proceedings in the English High Court claiming restitution of the net payments made by it to the Council. The Bank served the writ upon the Council in Scotland without leave,[109] arguing that the English courts had jurisdiction pursuant to the provisions of the intra-UK version of the Convention. The Council challenged the jurisdiction of the English High Court, arguing that it should have been sued in Scotland, the place of its domicile. The issue of jurisdiction was keenly fought as the limitation period in England was longer than that in Scotland.[110] This naturally made England a more attractive jurisdiction for the Bank, while, together with the fact that it might naturally prefer to defend proceedings in its own courts, a less attractive jurisdiction for the Council.

The House of Lords held by a majority (3–2)[111] that the consequential restitutionary claim did not fall within either Articles 5(1) or 5(3) and that consequently, the English courts did not have jurisdiction to hear the claim by *Kleinwort*. The majority considered that the dispute must essentially be about the performance of a contractual obligation so as to fall within the ambit of Article 5(1). As already noted, the House of Lords unanimously rejected the proposition that restitutionary claims fall within Article 5(3). As such, the claim was one which had to be pursued in the courts of the defendant's domicile, namely Scotland. The particular decision concerned the intra-UK version of the Convention. A different approach may be taken by the ECJ in relation to the Brussels Convention. Moreover, the decision cannot be said to resolve all issues concerning claims of unjust enrichment in connection with contracts.

The reasoning of the majority was not identical. However, certain common principles on the interpretation of Article 5(1) were stated in their judgments. First of all, although the case concerned the interpretation of the intra-UK Convention,[112] their Lordships' judgments were made in accordance with and subject to the jurisprudence of the ECJ.[113] As will be recalled, when dealing with

[108] *Hazell* v. *Hammersmith and Fulham London Borough Council* [1992] 2 A.C. 1.

[109] Pursuant to Order 11, rule 1(2) of the Rules of the Supreme Court. Now CPR 6.19.

[110] It might seem odd that the issue of jurisdiction between England and Scotland was so fiercely contested, given that, pursuant to s.1(1)(a) of the Foreign Limitation Periods Act 1984 and under the Scottish equivalent, namely the Prescription and Limitation Act 1985, the limitation period of the *lex causae* would have been applicable. It therefore may seem logical to assume that the question of the applicable law would have been the real point of difference. Yet, the battle as to jurisdiction goes to show that the parties considered there to be significant strategic advantages in pursuing their claims in the respective courts. In particular the English and Scottish courts were likely to adopt a different approach as to the choice of law rule for restitution and therefore possibly apply a different *lex causae*, consequently applying a different limitation period, as well as a possibly different interpretation to such a limitation period.

[111] Lords Goff, Clyde and Hutton; Lords Nicholls and Mustill dissenting.

[112] Contained in Schedule 4 of the 1982 Act; see §1 above.

[113] It might be said that ultimately this was not so in the case of Lord Clyde, who placed particular emphasis on the language of the provisions. Moreover, he actually noted that despite the differences with the language of the French text, the particular language used may be a significant consideration in the context of Schedule 4 of the 1982 Act: [1999] 1 A.C. 153, 180–1.

the intra-UK Convention, the court is merely required to have regard to, and not make a decision in accordance with, the relevant principles evolved by the ECJ.[114] There was however some acknowledgment that a different approach may be warranted in particular circumstances.[115] Secondly, the majority emphasised the basic principle that the defendant is to be sued in the courts of his own domicile and that any derogation from this principle is to be construed restrictively. Thirdly, it was stressed that the provisions in Article 5 exist "because of the existence, in certain clearly defined situations, of a particularly close connection factor between a dispute and the court which may be called upon to hear it, with a view to the efficacious conduct of the proceedings".[116] Finally, it was held that the "obligation in question" referred to the particular contractual obligation on which the claim is based. Where the particular obligation is not contractual, the claim does not fall within Article 5(1).

Millett L.J., in the Court of Appeal, had held that the word "contract" in Article 5(1) includes a void contract, and that the expression "place of performance of the obligation in question" includes the intended place of performance of the supposed obligation under a void contract (Approach 4).[117] Therefore, the Bank's claim to recover money paid under a contract, which was *ultra vires* the recipient and void, fell within Article 5(1). It was said that the intended place of performance is no less relevant a connecting factor merely because the contract is afterwards held to be void. The judgment of Millett L.J. requires some particular attention. After all, despite not agreeing with it, Lord Goff describes it as "most impressive". Moreover, it was the judgment with which the minority of their Lordships agreed.

Millett L.J. noted that the question of whether a claim is to be regarded as falling within Article 5(1) is to be distinguished from that of whether a claim would be characterised as contractual or tortious under domestic law.[118] The Convention applies to a number of Contracting States with different national laws and systems of characterisation. He further stated:

> [J]urisdiction is not allocated by reference to the cause of action. The words "matters relating to a contract" are intentionally indefinite. They are designed to get away from technical classifications of causes of action in national laws, which may well differ. The expression "matters relating to a contract" is not, in my opinion, to be equated with "contractual causes of action" or "the enforcement of contractual obligations" or even "claims based on contract".

Millett L.J. was not persuaded by the "powerful" arguments along the lines that a restitutionary claim which follows a void contract lies in restitution and not in

[114] Contrast for example s.16(3) with s.3 of the 1982 Act.

[115] Lord Goff, for example, left open the possibility of a different approach being taken in particular circumstances: [1999] 1 A.C. 153, 163F, 171C; also 178F–G, *per* Lord Clyde.

[116] *Kleinwort Benson Ltd.* v. *Glasgow City Council* [1999] 1 A.C. 153, 164, *per* Lord Goff, 173, *per* Lord Nicholls, 180, *per* Lord Clyde, 189, *per* Lord Hutton.

[117] [1996] Q.B. 678, 699. This was also the approach adopted by Lord Nicholls, with whom Lord Mustill agreed, in the House of Lords: [1999] 1 A.C. 153, 175.

[118] *Id.*, 698.

contract; that it is not a contractual claim. The Convention, he said, requires a broad and unanalytical approach and not the kind of analysis employed by a national law to classify causes of action for domestic purposes.[119]

Beyond the issue of how one might classify matters relating to a contract for the purposes of the Convention, there is a consideration of significant practical convenience. The court which has jurisdiction to rule on the validity of a contract should also have jurisdiction to decide the consequences, including the consequential restitutionary claims.[120] This seems to be one of the most compelling arguments for extending Article 5(1) jurisdiction to include restitutionary claims which arise in connection with a contract. As some of the aims of the Convention are to provide legal certainty, consistency and the avoidance of the multiplicity of closely related proceedings in different Contracting States, this may be best achieved by ensuring that all matters relating to a contract, even those which may not be strictly contractual, be heard in the same courts. Along the same lines, Lord Nicholls cited the example of where a plaintiff may seek restitution as an alternative to damages for breach of contract. For example, a plaintiff may have made payments pursuant to a contract under which the defendant refuses to perform or return the part-payments.[121] There is a great practical advantage in hearing both these alternative claims in the same jurisdiction and therefore ascribing Article 5(1) with the scope to encompass both.

Although there are significant practical considerations in favour of the arguments raised by Millett L.J. and Lord Nicholls, it is submitted that their approach fails properly to take into account the operation of Article 5(1) and how the special jurisdiction provisions fit within the framework of the Convention. First of all, it is always open to the plaintiff to pursue all the claims arising in connection with a contract before the courts of the defendant's domicile pursuant to Article 2. Thus, it cannot be said that related claims cannot be brought before the same courts. However, insofar as Article 5 is concerned, it will not automatically follow that the mere relation ship between one claim and another justifies bringing both before the same courts, on the basis that one of them falls under Article 5. Thus, where the same set of facts amount to both a claim in contract and tort, special jurisdiction must be established in relation to each claim separately.[122] Likewise, where a claim is brought in tort in relation to damage suffered by the plaintiff in several jurisdictions, the courts of a particular Contracting State will only have jurisdiction over so much of the claim

[119] [1996] Q.B. 678, 699.

[120] *Kleinwort Benson Ltd.* v. *Glasgow City Council* [1996] Q.B. 678, 700, *per* Millett L.J.; *Kleinwort Benson Ltd.* v. *Glasgow City Council* [1999] 1 A.C. 153, 175, *per* Lord Nicholls, with whom Lord Mustill agreed. See also A. Briggs [1997] B.Y.I.L. 331, 336–7; G. Virgo, "Jurisdiction over Restitutionary Claims" [1998] L.M.C.L.Q. 22, 25–6; R. Stevens, "Jurisdiction over Unjust Enrichment Claims" (1998) 114 L.Q.R. 386, 388–9; *Cf.* S. Pitel, "Jurisdiction Over Restitutionary Claims" [1998] 57 C.L.J. 19, 21–2; A. Dickinson, "Restitution and the Conflict of Laws in the House of Lords: *Kleinwort Benson* v. *Glasgow City Council*" [1998] R.L.R. 104, 111–14.

[121] *Kleinwort Benson Ltd.* v. *Glasgow City Council* [1999] 1 A.C. 153, 175.

[122] *Kalfelis* v. *Schröeder, Munchmeyer, Hengst & Co.* (*189/87*) [1988] E.C.R. 5565; *Shearson Lehman Hutton* v. *TVB* (*89/91*) [1993] E.C.R. I–139.

as was derived from damage occurring within that jurisdiction.[123] The ECJ has clearly rejected an approach of "channelling". That is to say, allowing a related claim to be "channelled" with a primary claim, thereby allowing the courts with jurisdiction to hear the primary claim to also hear the related claim.[124] In *Kalfelis*,[125] it was held that jurisdiction under Article 5(3) in relation to a tort claim did not grant jurisdiction for related claims in unjust enrichment and contract.[126] Secondly, as noted by Dickinson,[127] Lord Nicholls' reference to the need to avoid a multiplicity of closely related proceedings[128] is not pertinent in construing Article 5(1). Admittedly one of the key objects of the Convention is to avoid the risk of conflicting judgments, to ensure the effective reciprocal enforcement of judgments within the Contracting States.[129] The Convention contains provisions specifically aimed at avoiding such a conflict.[130] However, Article 5 does not share such an aim. Its main purpose is to ensure the efficacious conduct of proceedings by conferring jurisdiction upon the courts of a place having a close connection with the dispute.[131] It is therefore submitted that the question of whether claims related to a contract fall within Article 5(1) will not be based on pragmatic considerations or questions of convenience, but rather on the question of whether the claim actually falls within the spirit of the provision.

This brings us to the final point against the arguments raised by Millett L.J. and Lord Nicholls. The intended place of performance of the supposed obligation under an ineffective contract cannot be said to be a close connecting factor in the case of a restitutionary claim. As has been previously noted, the ECJ has emphasised that the provisions in Article 5 are in the Convention:

> because of the existence, in certain clearly defined situations, of a particularly close connecting factor between a dispute and the court which may be called upon to hear it, with a view to the efficacious conduct of the proceedings.[132]

[123] *Shevill* v. *Presse Alliance S.A.* (68/93) [1995] E.C.R. I–415. See also *Leathertex Divisione Sintetici SpA* v. *Bodetex BVBA* [1999] 2 All E.R. (Comm) 769 (ECJ); in the context of contractual obligations to be performed in different jurisdictions.

[124] In *Kalfelis* v. *Shröeder, Munchmeyer, Hengst & Co.* (189/87) [1988] E.C.R. 5565 and *Shearson Lehman Hutton* v. *TVB* (89/91) [1993] E.C.R. I–139, Advocate-General Darmon took the view that a claim in tort should be "channelled" into the jurisdictional provision for contractual claims. This was expressly rejected in *Kalfelis* while it received no support in *Shearson Lehman*. *Cf.* however *Peters Bauunternehmung GmbH* v. *Zuid Nederlandse Aannemers Vereneging* (34/82) E.C.R. 987, 1003 (para. 14).

[125] *Kalfelis* v. *Schröeder, Munchmeyer, Hengst & Co.* (189/87) [1988] E.C.R. 5565.

[126] *Id.*, 5586 (para. 21).

[127] A. Dickinson, "Restitution and the Conflict of Laws in the House of Lords: *Kleinwort Benson* v. *Glasgow City Council*" [1998] R.L.R. 104, 114.

[128] A point also raised by Millett L.J.: *Kleinwort Benson Ltd.* v. *Glasgow City Council* [1996] Q.B. 678, 698.

[129] See above p.189; see also *Gubisch Maschinenfabrik KG* v. *Palumbo* (144/86) [1987] E.C.R. 4861.

[130] See Articles 6, 21–2.

[131] *Peters Bauunternehmung GmbH* v. *Zuid Nederlandse Aannemers Vereneging* (34/82) [1983] E.C.R. 987, 1002 (para. 11).

[132] *Peters Bauunternehmung GmbH* v. *Zuid Nederlandse Aasnnemers Vereneging* (34/82) [1983] E.C.R. 987, 1002 (para. 11); *Kleinwort Benson Ltd.* v. *Glasgow City Council* [1999] 1 A.C. 153, 164, *per* Lord Goff, 173, *per* Lord Nicholls, 180, *per* Lord Clyde, 189, *per* Lord Hutton.

Where the parties enter into a contract, the place of performance of the contractual obligation which forms the basis of the claim is clearly a close connecting factor to such proceedings. After all, this is something the parties chose. However, where a restitutionary claim is brought, the place of performance of the supposed obligation is more removed. It is not the obligation which forms the basis of the claim. It is an obligation under an ineffective contract which merely forms the background to the dispute. As put by Lord Goff:

> No such a close connecting factor can, in my opinion, exist in a case where the contract is void *ab initio* and the only question at issue relates to the recovery of money paid under it on the ground of unjust enrichment.[133]

Moreover, in many cases involving ineffective contracts the factor which renders the contract ineffective is often a good reason for excluding the agreed place of performance as a basis of jurisdiction; *a fortiori* where such claim does not arise *ex contractu*.

In delivering his speech, Lord Goff placed emphasis on the previous interpretation of the "obligation in question". His Lordship stated:

> We know from the jurisprudence of the *de Bloos* case that reference in article 5(1) to the "obligation in question" is to "the contractual obligation forming the basis of the legal proceedings" (para. 11, p.1508), and is that obligation "which corresponds to the contractual right on which the plaintiff's action is based". It was that principle which was reaffirmed by the court in *Shenavai* v. *Kreischer*, where it was stated that uncertainty was avoided if "regard is had solely to the contractual obligation whose performance is sought in the judicial proceedings".[134]

Thus, Lord Goff relied heavily on the jurisprudence of the ECJ and noted that, apart from the case of *Ivenel*,[135] the obligation in question has not, before either the ECJ or the courts of the United Kingdom:

> been construed to mean anything other than the particular contractual obligation upon which the plaintiff's claim is based, the performance or non-performance of which is relied upon to support the plaintiff's claim.[136]

[133] *Peters Bauunternehmung GmbH* v. *Zuid Nederlandse Aasnnemers Vereneging (34/82)* [1983] E.C.R. 987, 1002 (para. 11) 169.

[134] *Kleinwort Benson Ltd.* v. *Glasgow City Council* [1999] 1 A.C. 153, 169. See also *Leathertex Divisione Sintetici SpA* v. *Bodetex BVBA* [1999] 2 All E.R. (Comm) 769, para. 31 (ECJ).

[135] *Ivenel* v. *Schwab (133/81)* [1982] E.C.R. 1891. This case was concerned with the particular situation of employment contracts, which were distinguished by virtue of their particularities. The relevant obligation in such cases is that of the employee to work because that is considered to be "characteristic" of the contract. The effect of this ruling was codified in the San Sebastián Convention, which amended Art. 5(1).

[136] *Kleinwort Benson Ltd.* v. *Glasgow City Council* [1999] 1 A.C. 153, 169. In *Agnew* v. *Länsförsäkringsbølagens AB*, [2000] 2 W.L.R. 497, a majority of the House of Lords (Lords Nicholls, Woolf and Cooke) held that a claim to set aside a contract of re-insurance, on the basis of pre-contractual obligations to avoid misrepresentation and non-disclosure, did fall within Art. 5(1) of the Lugano Convention. Although the obligation did not arise "under" the contract, it could still be regarded as a contractual obligation, given that it arose "from" the contract. The majority did not consider their decision to be in any way inconsistent with the *Kleinwort Benson* decision.

* *The preferred Approach*

It is submitted that the approach of Lord Goff is to be preferred (namely Approach 2 above), that the phrase "obligation in question", in Article 5(1), refers to the particular contractual obligation which forms the basis of the claim.[137] As such, it will generally not be possible to bring an unjust enrichment claim, following an ineffective contract, under Article 5(1). There are strong reasons for adopting such an approach and rejecting the others. As already discussed, equating the "obligation in question" with the intended place of performance of the supposed obligation under a void contract (Approach 4), should be rejected. First, the argument that Article 5(1) should extend to cover consequential restitutionary claims, so that all related claims arising in connection with a contract should be heard in one jurisdiction, is contrary to some of the key purposes of Article 5 as well as the jurisprudence of the ECJ. Secondly, there is no necessary connection between the place of performance of the supposed obligation under an ineffective contract and a claim for restitution under such a contract. Moreover, where a restitutionary claim is brought, there will be greater difficulties in identifying the obligation in question than in the case of a contractual claim. It will not be possible to rely on the obligation on which the plaintiff bases his claim, as the plaintiff will not be relying on a contractual obligation. The ineffective contract may have comprised several obligations to be performed in more than one jurisdiction.[138] The plaintiff may be seeking restitution in relation to some or all of them. Which of these obligations will the court focus on so as to identify the place of performance? Where there are several obligations, will it focus on the principal obligation under the contract?[139] What if the principal obligation under the contract is not the one with which the plaintiff's claim to restitution is connected? Such an approach does not provide the degree of certainty required by the jurisdictional rules in Article 5.[140]

There is some attraction in the argument that the "obligation in question" can include the restitutionary obligation on which the plaintiff bases his claim (Approach 3). Such an approach overcomes, at least, the argument that there is not a connection between the place of performance of the obligation in question and the actual claim. Indeed, the obligation in question would be the subject matter of the claim. However, there is no reason to suppose that the place of

In contrast, the minority (Lords Hope and Millett) held that the expression "obligation in question" must be limited to an obligation, the non-performance of which gives rise to contractual liability, and does not extend to what is merely a condition precedent to the formation of a fully binding contract.

[137] See also *De Bloos* v. *Bouyer* (14/76) [1976] E.C.R. 1497; *Leathertex Divisione Sintetici SpA* v. *Bodetex BVBA* [1999] 2 All E.R. (Comm) 769 (ECJ).

[138] See Briggs and Rees, pp.100–2, in relation to the application of Art. 5(1) to multiple obligations under a contract. Also G. Panagopoulos "Jurisdiction in Relation to a Contract split between two States" [2000] L.M.C.L.Q. 150.

[139] This was the approach adopted by the ECJ in *Shenavai* v. *Kreischer* (266/85) [1987] E.C.R. 239 where it isolated the main obligation.

[140] *Handte GmbH* v. *Société Traitements Mécano-chimiques des Surfaces* (26/91) [1992] E.C.R. I–3967, 3995 (para. 18).

performance of the obligation to make restitution will necessarily have a close connection with the claim for restitution. As has already been analysed in relation to Article 5(3), there are significant disadvantages in adopting the place of performance of the restitutionary obligation as a connecting factor.[141] There would be great uncertainty and unpredictability if one were to allow the individual court to determine the *locus* of the place of performance, applying its rules of private international law. Alternatively, adopting an autonomous meaning of the place of performance of the restitutionary obligation would invariably result in substituting the courts of the defendant's domicile with those of the plaintiff's. Moreover, if one were to accept that the obligation in question in Article 5(1) extends to the restitutionary obligations, such an approach would carve up, for jurisdictional purposes, those unjust enrichment claims which arise in connection with a contract from those that do not. That is, where a claim for restitution arises in connection with a contract, the courts of the place of performance of the relevant restitutionary obligation will have jurisdiction. Where however a claim for restitution is brought outside a contractual context, for example, a claim to recover a mistaken payment, such a claim would not fall within Article 5(1) and therefore Article 2 would apply; the courts of the defendant's domicile would have jurisdiction. Yet, there is no reason why the courts of the place of performance of the restitutionary obligation should have jurisdiction only in those cases where the claim relates to an ineffective contract. Such an arbitrary division of unjust enrichment matters for the purpose of jurisdiction cannot be something the Convention intended. Surely, it is the purpose of the Convention to treat like cases alike. Dividing similar claims on the basis of their factual background cannot further the aims and purposes of the Convention.

Finally, the argument that where a contract is void *ab initio* there is no contract, and thus, the matter cannot be said to relate to a "contract" (Approach 1), also faces certain problems. This was essentially the approach taken in *Kleinwort Benson* v. *Glasgow City Council* by Lord Clyde, where great emphasis was placed on the language of Article 5(1).[142] By focusing on whether there was actually a "contract", one focuses essentially on how the contract became ineffective; was it void or merely voidable? One gets bogged down in the intricacies of contract law from a domestic point of view. Different legal systems will take different views as to when and how a contract became ineffective. It would fly contrary to the spirit of the autonomous interpretation which has been given to "matters relating to a contract" if such a definition rested upon the way a contract became ineffective under its *lex causae*. The question of whether there is a "matter relating to a contract" is not to be determined by the particular rules of any state, but through an

[141] See above, pp. 200–1.

[142] Something which has not received positive support: see E. Peel, "Jurisdiction over Restitutionary Claims" [1997] L.M.C.L.Q. 22, 24 n.18; A. Briggs [1997] B.Y.I.L. 331, 334; A. Dickinson, "Restitution and the Conflict of Laws in the House of Lords: *Kleinwort Benson* v. *Glasgow City Council*" [1998] R.L.R. 104, 109–10. However, Lord Clyde's interpretation was directed at the intra-UK Convention as contained in Schedule 4 of the 1982 Act.

autonomous definition of contract. Thus, a matter may be a contractual matter[143] even though no such contract exists as a matter of domestic law.[144]

It is therefore submitted that the approach of Lord Goff is to be preferred. The question of whether a claim relating to a contract falls within Article 5(1) is to be determined by whether the obligation in question, upon which the plaintiff's action is based, is a "contractual obligation". An autonomous definition of what constitutes a "contractual obligation" is to be applied. Thus, Lord Goff noted that, a plaintiff's claim to recover, on the ground of failure of consideration, money paid under a valid contract (i.e. where such a contract is discharged), may be a contractual obligation for the purposes of Article 5(1). This is on the basis that it is capable of so being classified under some systems of law and on the autonomous principle of a contractual matter as recognised in *Peters*.[145] Likewise, a claim based on certain pre-contractual obligations, for example the duty to avoid misrepresentations, may also fall within the autonomous definition of a "contractual obligation".[146] Most restitutionary claims brought consequent to an ineffective contract will therefore fall outside Article 5(1), on the basis that the plaintiff's action will not be based on a "contractual obligation".

* *Consumer Contracts*

The question remains whether the above approach is applicable to Section 4 of Title II of the Convention, namely the consumer contract provisions. They provide that "in proceedings concerning a contract" which falls within the definition of a consumer contract in Article 13, a consumer may bring proceedings against the other party to the contract, in the courts of the Contracting State in which either that party is domiciled or in which the consumer is domiciled.[147] If, for example, a consumer were to claim relief for breach of contract together with an alternative claim for restitution of his money where the supposed contract were found to be a nullity, would he be able to bring both claims before the courts of the place in which the consumer is domiciled? If the same approach were to be adopted as in the case of Article 5(1) the answer would be no. It might be said that it would be contrary to the intention of the consumer contract provisions if a consumer could only avail himself of the benefit of these provisions, where his claim was founded on a contractual obligation and did not extend to consequential restitutionary claims. However, it should not be assumed that the interpretation applicable to Article 5(1) is automatically applicable to the consumer contract provisions. First, it is quite significant that Article 14 does not

[143] To adopt the French wording of *matière contractuelle*.

[144] See *Peters Bauunternehmung GmbH* v. *Zuid Nederlandse Aannemers Vereneging* (*Case 34/82*) [1983] E.C.R. 987.

[145] *Ibid*.

[146] See for example *Agnew* v. *Länsförsäkringsbølagens AB*, [2000] 2 W.L.R. 497 (H.L.).

[147] Article 14.

contain the same connecting factor as Article 5(1); the connecting factor in Article 14 is the domicile of either the consumer or the other party to the contract. Jurisdiction is not determined by a legal criterion in the form of the "place of performance of the obligation in question". The interpretation which has been given to this last phrase, limiting it to the contractual obligation which forms the basis of the plaintiff's claim, is clearly not applicable in the case of Article 14. As such, there is no reason to suppose that the jurisdiction available in the consumer contract provisions is intended to be limited to situations where a contractual claim is brought. Secondly, the consumer contract provisions have a different objective from that of Article 5. Unlike Article 5, their aim is not the efficacious conduct of proceedings by enabling them to be brought before a court having a close connection with the claim. Their aim is to protect consumers who are presumably in a weaker position.[148] Accordingly, the consumer is afforded a choice between the two relevant domiciles.[149] He is not discouraged from bringing an action by being compelled to only sue in the courts of the defendant's domicile; or indeed from having to sue in the place of performance of the obligation in question, or merely in relation to a contractual obligation.

* *Restitution for Breach of Contract*

Two final points need to be raised. First, it would follow from the above analysis that where a plaintiff seeks restitutionary damages for breach of contract,[150] such a matter would fall within the scope of Article 5(1). In such a case, restitution is merely a remedial response. The relevant causative event is the breach of contract and not unjust enrichment.[151] The plaintiff's claim is based on a contractual obligation and as such clearly falls within Article 5(1) on any of the approaches raised above.

* *Declarations of Non-liability*

The second point is a little more difficult. There remains the question of whether Article 5(1) extends to cover the issue of whether there was a valid contract in the first place. Irrespective of whether the issue of a contract's validity or existence falls within Article 5(1), the possible consequential restitutionary claim will not. Nevertheless, it is necessary to know how, for jurisdictional purposes, the question of a contract's validity might be dealt with given that such an issue might be closely connected with a claim for restitution.

In *Kleinwort Benson*, the actual validity of the contract was not in issue. It was accepted that the relevant contract was void. A different situation may arise

[148] In *Benincasa* v. *Dentalkit Srl* (269/95) [1997] I–E.C.R. 3767, 3796 (para. 18), the ECJ described the consumer contract provisions as "protective rules".

[149] See A. Dickinson, "Restitution and the Conflict of Laws in the House of Lords: *Kleinwort Benson* v. *Glasgow City Council*' [1998] R.L.R. 104, 115.

[150] See for example *A.G.* v. *Blake* 27 July 2000 (unreported) (HL).

[151] See also ch. 4.1.3.

where the validity or existence of the contract is in dispute. In *Effer* v. *Kanter*[152] the ECJ held that, where a defendant raises a defence which denies the existence of a contract, such a matter still falls within Article 5(1). The Court of Appeal went further in *Boss Group Ltd.* v. *Boss France SA*,[153] by holding that where there was a dispute as to the existence of a contract, it did not matter which of the parties denied or affirmed such existence. Even a claim for a negative declaration was still held to be a "matter relating to a contract" falling within Article 5(1). In *Kleinwort Benson*, the minority considered that a claim that there is no contract falls within Article 5(1).[154] Out of the majority, Lord Clyde expressed a similar view[155] and explicitly supported the decision in *Boss Group*. A majority of their Lordships therefore took the view that declarations of contractual non-liability fall within Article 5(1). Lord Hutton was not so clear on this point. His Lordship drew a distinction for the purposes of Article 5(1):

> between a case where one party claims that the contract is, or was, in existence and the other party claims that the contract never existed or has ceased to exist, and a case such as the present one where both parties accepted before the commencement of the action that the contract was void *ab initio*.

This statement could be interpreted as supporting the proposition that the issue of a contract's validity is a "matter relating to a contract" and therefore within Article 5(1).[156] However, such an interpretation is difficult to maintain in the light of Lord Hutton's agreement with Lord Goff that "jurisdiction under Article 5(1) only arises when the claim is to enforce an obligation arising under a contract".[157] Lord Goff on the other hand expressly cast "serious doubt whether, as a general rule, a court can have jurisdiction under article 5(1) to rule upon the validity of a contract".[158]

If one were to accept the approach of Lord Goff and Lord Hutton as being correct, it would follow that the question of a contract's validity would not fall within Article 5(1), as such a claim would not be based on a contractual obligation. Such a conclusion might be an inevitable consequence of a connecting factor which looks for the "place of performance of the obligation in question". How would one identify the "obligation in question" in a claim for a declaration that no contract existed? This is especially a problem given that the obligation in question has been interpreted by the ECJ as that upon which the

152 *(38/81)* [1982] E.C.R. 825.

153 [1997] 1 W.L.R. 351.

154 *Kleinwort Benson Ltd.* v. *Glasgow City Council* [1999] 1 A.C. 153, 172, *per* Lord Mustill, 173–4, *per* Lord Nicholls.

155 *Id.*, 182.

156 See A. Dickinson, "Restitution and the Conflict of Laws in the House of Lords: *Kleinwort Benson* v. *Glasgow City Council*" [1998] R.L.R. 104, 111; *Cf.* A. Briggs [1997] B.Y.I.L. 331, 335, 336, n.32.

157 *Kleinwort Benson Ltd.* v. *Glasgow City Council* [1999] 1 A.C. 153, 195E.

158 *Id.*, 169H, 170E. In *Agnew* v. *Länsförsäkringsbølagens AB*, 17 February 2000 (unreported), Lord Millett expressed doubt as to whether Art. 5(1) confers jurisdiction in respect of the validity of a contract, while Lord Hope expressed a contrary view.

plaintiff's claim is based.[159] According to *Boss Group*, the answer to this must be to look to the obligation in dispute, [160] and in cases where there are several obligations, the principal obligation in dispute between the parties.[161] Under such an approach, the connecting factor would point to a jurisdiction that was close to the dispute from the point of view of the party seeking to affirm the contract. The same will not necessarily be the case for the party seeking to deny the contract. As the claimant of non-liability alleges that there is no contract, the place of performance of the principal obligation in dispute cannot be said to be a close connecting factor. Yet, in such cases it will be the plaintiff who will be seeking to rely on this connecting factor as a basis for jurisdiction other than that of the defendant's domicile. The defendant therefore, who affirms the contract, can hardly complain that the courts of the place of performance of the relevant obligation should not have jurisdiction. After all he is the one asserting that there is a contract and that it does have a principal obligation which presumably was, is, or is to be, performed in the place in whose courts the plaintiff has commenced such proceedings. Although such analysis might not be based on the general method of interpretation given to the Convention, it helps illustrate why there might be little argument for denying the closeness of the connecting factor in a negative declaration claim.

It is submitted that the question of a contract's existence or validity should fall within Article 5(1). First, there is clear support for such a view by the Court of Appeal in *Boss Group* and by a majority of their Lordships in *Kleinwort Benson*. Secondly, the decision in *Effer SpA* v. *Kanter* should not be read as merely being limited to the situation where a defendant disputes the existence or validity of a contract, but should apply generally to the situation where there is a dispute as to the existence or validity of a contract. This is apparent from the language of the ruling, which states:

> The plaintiff may invoke the jurisdiction of the courts of the place of performance in accordance with Article 5(1) . . . even when the existence of the contract on which the claim is based in dispute between the parties.[162]

Moreover, it was noted that there might be a danger of Article 5(1) "being deprived of its legal effect, since it would be accepted that, in order to defeat the rule contained in that provision it is sufficient for *one of the parties* to claim that the contract does not exist" (*emphasis added*).[163] This envisages something

[159] *De Bloos* v. *Bouyer* (14/76) [1976] E.C.R. 1497.

[160] This is arguably based on an adaptation of *De Bloos* v. *Bouyer* (14/76) [1976] E.C.R. 1497, although no reference was actually made to this case in *Boss Group*. See E. Peel, "Jurisdiction Over Non-Existent Contracts" (1996) L.Q.R. 541, 542–3. See also *Agnew* v. *Lansförsäkringsbølagens AB* [1997] 4 All E.R. 937, 940, *per* Evans L.J.

[161] Saville L.J., who gave the main judgment in *Boss Group Ltd.* v. *Boss France SA* [1997] 1 W.L.R. 351, 357 reached this conclusion by applying the *obiter dictum* in *Shenavai* v. *Kreischer* (266/85) [1987] E.C.R. 239. It should be noted that the ECJ's statements in *Shenevai* concerned a situation where the plaintiff's claim related to multiple obligations.

[162] *Effer SpA* v. *Kanter* (38/81) [1982] E.C.R. 825, 835 (para. 8).

[163] *Id.*, 834 (para. 7).

beyond the mere facts of *Effer* v. *Kanter*, where the defendant denies the existence of a contract to a more general situation of where there is generally a dispute as to the existence of a contract.

4.3.2 Choice of Court Agreements—Article 17

Article 17 of the Convention provides, *inter alia*, that if there is an agreement "that a court or the courts of a Contracting State are to have jurisdiction to settle any disputes which have arisen or which may arise in connection with a particular relationship, that court or those courts shall have exclusive jurisdiction". The question here is whether Article 17 may operate in the context of a claim for unjust enrichment. In particular, where a restitutionary claim arises in connection with a contract, which contains a choice of court clause that satisfies the requirements of Article 17, will the jurisdiction conferred by such a clause extend to the claim for restitution?

There are many issues which arise in relation to Article 17, most of which do not concern us for present purposes.[164] As such, the question of whether there is in fact a choice of court agreement and its particular scope will not be examined. More importantly for present purposes is the question of whether, and when, such choice of court agreements might catch restitutionary claims. On a first reading, the reference in Article 17, to a court or courts having jurisdiction to settle "any disputes which have arisen or may arise", seems broad enough to catch restitutionary claims.[165] The only limitation seems to be that such disputes must be connected "with a particular relationship". It is not necessary that such relationship be contractual, or that the particular claim must be contractual; it is sufficient that it arises in connection with a particular relationship. This has, for example, been held to extend to corporate obligations arising between shareholders and a company.[166]

Further support for the above proposition may be found in paragraph 2 of Article 17, which provides that:

> The court or courts of a Contracting State on which a trust instrument has conferred jurisdiction shall have exclusive jurisdiction in any proceedings brought against a settlor trustee or beneficiary, if relations between these persons or their rights or obligations under the trust are involved.

Many of the types of claims envisaged by this provision may well be restitutionary. It would follow that if a jurisdiction clause in a trust is capable of applying to such restitutionary claims, there is no reason why the same cannot apply in the case of a jurisdiction clause contained in a contract, or indeed any other relationship which comes within the scope of Article 17.

[164] See however Briggs and Rees, pp.63–79.

[165] Assuming that the jurisdiction clause is accordingly worded so as to catch restitutionary claims.

[166] *Powell Duffryn plc* v. *Petereit* (*214/89*) [1992] E.C.R. I–1745.

Support for the proposition that restitutionary claims might be covered by a choice of court agreement may be found in two decisions of the ECJ concerning Article 17. In *Meeth* v. *Glacetal*,[167] it was held that a court which had jurisdiction under Article 17 to hear a main claim would also have jurisdiction to hear an incidental set-off claim. It might therefore be argued that if the court has jurisdiction to hear a claim not arising under the particular contract, *a fortiori* it should have jurisdiction to hear a restitutionary claim arising under, or connected with, the particular contract.

More significantly, in *Benincasa* v. *Dentalkit Srl*,[168] it was held that the courts chosen under an Article 17 choice of court agreement have exclusive jurisdiction even where an action is brought seeking a declaration that the contract is void. The ECJ described the jurisdiction clause as something "procedural", governed by the provisions of the Convention. It is therefore separate, or ancillary, to the main contract in which that clause is incorporated; the contract is governed by the *lex causae*, as determined by the rules of private international law of the State of the court having jurisdiction.[169] This it is said is in the interests of legal certainty, "that the court seised should be able to readily decide whether it has jurisdiction on the basis of the rules of the Convention, without having to consider the substance of the case".[170] Thus, where a negative declaration is brought in the context of Article 17, the court will have exclusive jurisdiction where the requirements under Article 17 are satisfied. It therefore would follow that such legal certainty may also extend to restitutionary claims which arise under a contract containing an exclusive jurisdiction clause. Yet, ultimately this will depend on the scope of the actual jurisdiction clause; that is, whether the particular jurisdiction clause is intended to also cover restitutionary claims. Such an issue is to be determined by the national court, which is to interpret the clause conferring jurisdiction invoked before it.[171] Presumably this will be done in accordance with its rules of private international law.

There is a serious objection which may be raised against extending the scope of Article 17 to claims of unjust enrichment, particularly when they arise in connection with a contract. In many cases where claims for unjust enrichment are brought in the context or ineffective contracts, the factor which rendered the contract ineffective, and thus gives rise to a consequential claim in restitution, is often a good reason for excluding the matters agreed to by the parties, including any choice of court agreement. Where, for example, a contract is entered into through mistake, or duress, and is subsequently rescinded, there is a good argument for not giving effect to the particular jurisdiction clause, as there may have been no true consensus or agreement. One response to such an objection is

[167] (*23/78*) [1978] E.C.R. 2133.

[168] (*269/95* [1997] I E.C.R. 3767.

[169] *Id.*, 3797 (para. 25).

[170] (*269/95*) [1997] I E.C.R. 3767, 3797 (para. 27).

[171] *Id.*, 3798 (para. 31); *Powell Duffryn plc* v. *Petereit* (*214/89*) [1992] E.C.R. I–1745, 1778 (para. 36–7).

based on the interpretation given to Article 17 jurisdiction clauses in *Benincasa*. As already noted, jurisdiction clauses are viewed differently from the actual contract. They were said to be "merely procedural". Consequently, according to Advocate-General Ruiz-Jarabo Colomer, "any grounds of nullity which might affect the substantive elements of a contract should not have any impact on jurisdiction clauses".[172] Thus:

> if one party alleges that there was no consensus *ad idem*—for example, that there was a mistake as to essential aspects of the subject-matter, rendering the mutual obligations void—the jurisdiction clause is not necessarily affected because the mistake does not extend to the express choice of the competent court.[173]

This is not all that convincing. After all, a jurisdiction clause may well depend on the same economic and legal factors which form the basis of the rest of the contract. A choice of court agreement is capable of being negotiated as is any other term of a contract and forming part of the bargaining process. It is a little fictitious to render it something that is merely procedural and somehow disconnected from the rest of the contract. An alternative, or at least additional, response to this objection is, it is submitted, more convincing. Where as a result of a particular vitiating factor, such as mistake for example, there was in fact no *consensus ad idem*, the requirements of Article 17 will not have been satisfied. There will not have been an *agreement* for the purposes of Article 17. The comments of Advocate-General Ruiz-Jarabo Colomer must read as proceeding from the assumption that the particular jurisdiction clause satisfied the requirements of Article 17. In such a case, it is no answer to allege that the particular contract was void due to a particular vitiating factor. Thus, Advocate-General Ruiz-Jarabo Colomer commented that a jurisdiction clause "applies *a fortiori* where the alleged grounds of nullity of the contract relate to its compatibility or otherwise with the substantive law of a particular legal system".[174] In such a case, it will be beyond dispute that the parties have *agreed* that a court or courts of a Contracting State are to have jurisdiction.

4.3.3 Proprietary Restitutionary Claims in Relation to Land in a Contracting State—Article 16(1)

Where a claim of proprietary restitution is brought in respect of land in a Contracting State, the question of jurisdiction may be governed by Article 16(1). This provision provides that:

> in proceedings which have as their object rights *in rem* in immovable property or tenancies of immovable property, the courts of the Contracting State in which the property is situated,

[172] *Benincasa* v. *Dentalkit Srl* (269/95) [1997] E.C.R. I–3767, 3785 (para. 75).
[173] *Id.* (para. 76).
[174] *Ibid.*

shall have exclusive jurisdiction, regardless of domicile. This jurisdictional rule is practical and sensible. The courts of the Contracting State where land is situated should have exclusive jurisdiction to hear proceedings wherein the plaintiff seeks to establish that he has a title to immovable property which is good against the whole world. What is more controversial and more difficult to answer is the question of jurisdiction where land is the object of a proprietary remedy. For example, the plaintiff in England claims that the defendant holds land in France on constructive trust for his benefit, on the basis that such land is the traceable proceeds of his money fraudulently removed from his account. Should the courts of France nevertheless have exclusive jurisdiction to hear such a claim, on the basis that the proceedings have as their object rights *in rem* in immovable property? Or would such a claim be distinguished and thereby not attract the operation of Article 16, owing to its restitutionary character—namely, that the constructive trust is a means of reversing an unjust enrichment?

An issue along such lines was examined by the ECJ in *Webb* v. *Webb*.[175] A father purchased a flat in France; however, the legal title was vested in his son. The father and son had a falling out, and the father sought to obtain the property. Proceedings were brought in England for a declaration that the son held the property on resulting trust, and for an order requiring the son, as trustee, to execute the necessary documents to vest legal title in the father. The son challenged the jurisdiction of the English court on the ground that the action related to a right *in rem* in immovable property and that, accordingly, the French courts had exclusive jurisdiction by virtue of Article 16(1) of the Brussels Convention. The son argued that the ultimate purpose of the father's action was to establish rights over the flat which would be enforceable against the whole world. Therefore, the action came within the exclusive jurisdiction of the French courts. The father argued that his claim was based on a fiduciary relationship between himself and his son, and was not seeking a declaration that he was the legal owner, or an order for possession or rectification of any register. Thus, his claim did not relate to rights *in rem* in immovable property, within the meaning of Article 16(1). The father's submissions were supported by the Advocate-General who submitted that the jurisdiction *ratione materiae* of a court must necessarily be assessed in the light of the subject matter of the claim, as defined in the application, without looking at the purpose.

The ECJ held that Article 16(1) did not apply and that therefore the matter did not come within the exclusive jurisdiction of the French Courts. Exclusivity of jurisdiction in the courts of the *lex situs* is justified where the dispute concerns property. Such a jurisdiction rule is justified because "actions concerning rights *in rem* in immovable property often involve disputes frequently necessitating checks, inquiries and expert assessments which must be carried out on the spot".[176] Here, the father did not "claim that he already [enjoyed] rights directly

175 (294/92) [1994] E.C.R. I–1717; [1994] Q.B. 696.
176 *Id.*, 1738 (para. 17); 717.

relating to the property which are enforceable against the whole world, but [sought] only to assert rights as against the son".[177] the Immovable nature of the property held in trust and its location, were irrelevant to the issues to be determined.[178] The issue was whether the father could enforce a personal right against the defendant.

As noted in the context of characterisation, there is a respectable view that resulting trusts arise so as to reverse an unjust enrichment.[179] Although the case does not describe the claim by the father in favour of a resulting trust as being restitutionary, if one accepts that resulting trusts arise by operation of law and that they form part of the law of restitution, then *Webb* v. *Webb* may well stand for the general proposition that Article 16(1) does not cover claims for proprietary restitution; at least, insofar as a plaintiff seeks to assert a proprietary remedy against a particular defendant.

Irrespective of how one might characterise resulting trusts as a matter of domestic law, *Webb* v. *Webb* may more generally stand for the proposition that claims for proprietary remedies in relation to land, which are sought to be exercised against a particular defendant, are not caught by Article 16(1). This would apply particularly in cases where an equitable interest is asserted which arises by operation of law and not through a consensual transaction. In such cases, there may be little justification for granting jurisdiction to the *lex situs*, as the immovable nature of the property, over which an equitable interest is claimed, is irrelevant to the issues to be determined. The true issues in dispute may, for example, centre around the fiduciary relationship between the parties and/or the events giving rise to the unjust enrichment. As noted by the ECJ, the issues to be determined in such proceedings "would have been the same if the dispute had concerned a flat situated in the United Kingdom or a yacht".[180] This suggests that like cases are to be treated alike, and where therefore a proprietary remedy is sought to be exercised against a defendant, it makes no difference whether the particular property is moveable or immovable.

The above view is possible owing to two main considerations. First of all, Article 16(1) is given a strict interpretation.[181] It confers exclusive jurisdiction to the courts where the immovable property is situated and constitutes a derogation from the general principle in Article 2. It may compel litigation to take place in a state in which neither party is domiciled and inflict considerable inconvenience. The ECJ has therefore refused "to extend the scope of this provision to cover claims which only indirectly or incidentally concern rights *in rem*".[182] The

[177] *Id.*, 1738 (para. 15); 716.

[178] *Cf.* A. Briggs (1994) 110 L.Q.R. 527; P. Birks, "In rem or in personam?" (1994) 8 Trust.L.Int., 99.

[179] See p.73, n. 136.

[180] (294/92) [1994] E.C.R. I–1717, 1739 (para. 18); [1994] Q.B. 696, 717.

[181] *Saunders* v. *van der Putte* (73/77) [1977] E.C.R. 2383, 2391 (para. 17–18); *Reichert* v. *Dresdner Bank* (No.2) [1992] E.C.R. I–2149, 2182 (para. 25). See also *Reichert* v. *Dresdner Bank* [1990] E.C.R. I–27, 41 (para. 9).

[182] *Id.*, 1725 (para. 32), *per* Advocate-General Darmon. Also *Lieber* v. *Göbel* [1994] E.C.R. I–2550 (paras. 13–14).

fact that the action may ultimately affect immovable property is irrelevant. As Briggs and Rees note, the plaintiff must essentially be relying on rules peculiar to land law.[183] The second consideration is a little more controversial. It is often said that for the purposes of private international law, equity acts *in personam.*[184] As a result, equitable jurisdiction has historically been exerciseable in relation to immovables overseas[185] and thus the rule that English courts had no jurisdiction to hear claims concerning title to foreign land[186] was side-stepped. This analysis helps explain the decision in *Webb* and why proprietary restitution over immovables, which will invariably involve equitable interests,[187] is not caught by Article 16(1).[188] It should be welcomed that the same approach is adopted under the Brussels Convention as has been under the traditional rules.[189] It has been submitted elsewhere in this work that certain proprietary equitable interests are characterised as if they were obligations, or *in personam* rights for choice of law purposes.[190] That is to say, those equitable proprietary interests which arise by operation of law should be characterised by reference to the causative event which allegedly creates them. Most commonly this will be as wrongs or unjust enrichment. Those equitable interests which are created through consensual transfers should be characterised as proprietary issues or issues of title. The decision in *Webb* is, it is submitted, consistent with this theory as the proprietary interest the plaintiff sought to assert arose by operation of law. Therefore, it was characterised as an *in personam* right and not one *in rem.* This final consideration is an essential component of the decision in *Webb*, which was not merely based on a requirement of interpreting Article 16(1) strictly. As noted by Birks, if this was the case, the ECJ could have concentrated on the question of whether the claim in *Webb* was such an assertion

[183] Briggs and Rees, pp.43, 44–5. In *Re Hayward* [1997] Ch. 45, a claim by the trustee in bankruptcy to be entitled to the debtor's share of a villa in Spain was held to fall within Art. 16(1). This was a legal claim to the immovable, while the order sought was for rectification of the land register in Spain. See also *Ashurst* v. *Pollard* [2000] 2 All E.R. 772 (Ch.D.).

[184] See ch. 4.3.3.1.

[185] *Penn* v. *Lord Baltimore* (1750) 1 Ves. Sen. 444; 27 E.R. 1132; *Re Courtney, ex parte Pollard* (1840) 4 Deac. 27; *British South Africa Co.* v. *De Beers Consolidated Mines Ltd.* [1910] 2 Ch. 502, reversed on different grounds [1912] A.C. 52 (H.L.); *Re Smith*; *Lawrence* v. *Kitson* [1916] 2 Ch. 206; *In re Anchor Line (Henderson Bros.)* Ltd. [1937] 1 Ch. 483, 488; *Richard West* v. *Dick* [1969] 2 Ch. 424.

[186] *British South Africa Co.* v. *Companhia de Moçambique* [1893] A.C. 602; *Hesperides Hotels Ltd.* v. *Aegean Turkish Holidays Ltd.* [1979] A.C. 508.

[187] See ch. 1.3.

[188] In *Re Hayward* [1997] Ch. 45, a claim by a trustee in bankruptcy to be entitled to the debtor's share of a villa in Spain, was held to fall within Art. 16(1) of the Brussels Convention and thus subject to the exclusive jurisdiction of the Spanish Courts. *Webb* v. *Webb* was distinguished on the basis that the relevant claim in that case was equitable and therefore personal: *id.*, 57. As the trustee in bankruptcy's claim was to a legal right "it [was] difficult to contemplate any right more clearly a right in rem than a right to legal ownership such as is claimed by the trustee in the present case": *ibid.*

[189] See however A. Briggs (1994) 110 L.Q.R. 527; P. Birks, "In rem or in personam?" (1994) 8 Trust.L.Int., 99; Peel, pp.33–6.

[190] See ch. 4, §§3.3.2 and 3.3.3.

of rights *in rem* as fell within the mischief for which exclusive jurisdiction was supposed to be the remedy.[191] The ECJ clearly went beyond this.

It has been questioned whether the ECJ would have arrived at the same decision if the defendant had been insolvent and that the aim of the proprietary claim was to defeat the claims of third parties.[192] It is submitted that this would have made no difference to the outcome of the decision. The plaintiff would have been claiming an equitable interest in property which coincidentally would have been land. The immovable nature of the property, held on trust and its location, would have been irrelevant to the issues to be determined. The ultimate aim of such proceedings may have been to obtain priority in the distribution of the defendant's assets. Yet, assuming such proceedings sought to exercise the proprietary remedy against the defendant, there is no reason why such proceedings should have been caught by Article 16(1). They would still amount to *in personam* proceedings for the purposes of the conflict of laws.

4.4 Other Particular Types of Restitutionary Claims

Up until now we have examined the question of whether restitutionary claims, some or all, fall within any of the particular provisions contained within the Convention. It is also necessary to consider how the jurisdictional questions facing certain types of restitutionary claims might be treated under the Convention.

4.4.1 Claims in Equity

It will be recalled that many restitutionary claims are in equity. It has been submitted elsewhere in this work that claims in equity should not be treated any differently from their common law counterparts in private international law.[193] Their different historical origin should be of no consequence. It is submitted that this general approach should also apply in relation to matters of jurisdiction concerning the Brussels Convention.[194] Such an approach is an inevitable consequence of the fact that various terms and concepts under the Convention have been given an autonomous definition. It therefore would follow that the jurisdictional origin of a claim as a matter of domestic law, namely whether it is in equity or at law, should be irrelevant. Those equitable claims which arise to reverse an unjust enrichment should be characterised as matters of unjust enrichment for the purposes of the Convention and treated as one would treat any other claim for unjust enrichment. Therefore, the equitable "action to follow moneys impressed with an express trust, or with a constructive trust owing to a fiduciary relationship", is the legal equivalent of "an action for money had

[191] P. Birks, "In rem or in personam?" (1994) 8 Trust.L.Int., 99.
[192] Peel, p.34.
[193] See ch. 4.2.
[194] See also Briggs and Rees, p.116; Peel, p.37.

and received or damages for conversion of a cheque".[195] Thus, where as a result of a mistaken payment, the plaintiff brings an equitable claim in relation to the moneys received by the defendant,[196] this should still be classified as a matter of unjust enrichment, irrespective of the fact that the claim is in equity. Jurisdiction for such a claim falls within Article 2, namely the courts of the defendant's domicile.

Certain equitable claims may not, as a matter of substantive law, fit within any of the recognised categories. Such may be the case for certain equitable obligations or rights derived from unconscionable conduct. Briggs and Rees note that, for the purposes of the Convention, they have to be classified as either contract or tort: "as one or the other".[197] It is submitted that such equitable claims should not automatically be classified as either torts or contract for the purposes of the Convention. A third option should be added here, namely of possibly classifying some equitable claims as unjust enrichment. Although, matters of unjust enrichment are not expressly dealt with in the Convention as a separate category, this is not to say that such matters must automatically fall within contract or tort. It is clear from the ECJ's jurisprudence that matters of unjust enrichment are a separate category, standing alongside tort and contract.[198] Therefore, where a particular equitable claim is best classified as a matter of unjust enrichment, it should be treated as one would treat any other matter of unjust enrichment.

4.4.2 Proprietary Restitution

The English law of unjust enrichment grants both personal and proprietary remedies.[199] Apart from Ireland, a proprietary remedy is something which would be foreign to most of the legal systems of the other Contracting States.[200] Matters of contract, tort and unjust enrichment only give rise to obligations. The question is whether, for the purposes of the Convention, a claim for restitution should be classified differently on the basis that it gives rise to a proprietary and not an *in personam* remedy. It is submitted that matters of unjust enrichment should be classified in a uniform manner, irrespective of whether or not they may give rise to a proprietary remedy. Significantly, apart from the fact that most of the legal systems of the other Contracting States do not recognise

[195] *Nelson* v. *Larholt* [1948] 1 K.B. 339, 343, *per* Denning J.; see also *El Ajou* v. *Dollar Holdings Ltd.* [1993] 3 All E.R. 717, 736, *per* Millett J. (reversed by the Court of Appeal on different grounds) [1994] 2 All E.R. 685.

[196] See for example *Chase Manhattan Bank N.A.* v. *Israel-British Bank (London) Ltd.* [1981] Ch. 105.

[197] Briggs and Rees, p.116.

[198] See *Kalfelis* v. *Schröeder, Munchmeyer, Hengst & Co.* (189/87) [1988] E.C.R. 5565, *esp.* 5584 (para. 14), 5585 (para. 19); see also the discussion of *Kalfelis* above, §4.2.2.

[199] See generally ch. 1.3.

[200] The availability of proprietary restitution, or an *in rem* response, to reverse an unjust enrichment would be unavailable under most civilian systems: *ibid.*

proprietary restitution, there is no apparent reason in the text of the Convention why such claims should, for the purposes of jurisdiction, be treated differently.

We have already examined the situation of proprietary restitution in relation to immovables.[201] In *Webb* v. *Webb*,[202] the ECJ held that proprietary claims in relation to land, which are sought to be exercised against a particular defendant, are not caught by Article 16(1). One reading of this case may simply be that Article 16(1) is to be interpreted strictly.[203] Yet, the ECJ went beyond the question of whether the claim in *Webb* was an assertion of rights *in rem* as would fall within the mischief for which exclusive jurisdiction was supposed to be the remedy.[204] It held that such a claim essentially amounts to an *in personam* right where such a claim is exercised against a particular defendant. It is submitted that this should apply *a fortiori* where such a claim is brought in relation to property other than immovables. Therefore, given that claims for proprietary restitution will invariably be in equity, they are likely to be viewed as *in personam* claims for the purposes of the Convention. Such claims will therefore be treated as one would treat any other claim for unjust enrichment. At any rate, even if such claims are not treated as *in personam* proceedings, owing to the particular nature of proprietary restitution, one should focus on the causative event giving rise to the proprietary remedy and not the question of property itself. Where the relevant causative event is an unjust enrichment, a claim for proprietary restitution should be classified accordingly. Where, however, a proprietary restitutionary claim is brought against a "settlor, trustee or beneficiary" in connection with a trust,[205] such a claim will fall within Article 5(6). In such a case, the defendant may be sued in the courts of the domicile of the trust.[206]

Ultimately, it is submitted, it will rarely be of consequence whether a claim for proprietary restitution is classified as a matter of unjust enrichment or one of title. It has been previously submitted that matters of unjust enrichment are not specifically dealt with in the Convention and therefore such claims fall within the general provision in Article 2; that is, the defendant must be sued in the courts of his domicile. Where a claim is brought by the plaintiff asserting title to his moveable property, such a claim will ordinarily come within Article 2 of the Convention. As such, until the Convention is amended so as to provide a specific jurisdictional basis for matters of unjust enrichment, the present question is of no practical significance.

201 See above, §4.3.3.

202 (294/92) [1994] E.C.R. I–1717; [1994] Q.B. 696.

203 See *Saunders* v. *van der Putte* (73/77) [1977] E.C.R. 2383, 2391 (para. 17–18); *Reichert* v. *Dresdner Bank* (No.2) [1992] E.C.R. I–2149, 2182 (para. 25). See also *Reichert* v. *Dresdner Bank* [1990] E.C.R. I–27, 41 (para. 9).

204 P. Birks, "In rem or in personam?" (1994) 8 Trust.L.Int., 99.

205 It should be noted that the trust must be "created by the operation of statute, or by a written instrument, or created orally and evidenced in writing", in order for Art. 5(6) to apply.

206 The domicile of a trust is ascertained by the domestic law of the contracting state whose courts are seised of the case: see Art. 53. Section 45 of the 1982 Act provides that a trust is domiciled in a part of the United Kingdom, "if and only if the system of law of that part is the system of law with which the trust has its closest and most real connection".

4.4.3 Restitution for Wrongs

As already discussed, the law may allow restitution, or disgorgement in relation to a wrong.[207] The preferred view is that such matters do not, as a matter of English domestic law, form part of the law of unjust enrichment but instead belong to the law of wrongs. It has been submitted in the context of characterisation for choice of law purposes that restitution for wrongs should be classified as wrongs; namely as issues of tort, breach of contract and also possibly equitable wrongs.[208] In relation to equitable wrongs, they should be classified as either a breach of trust, breach of contract, or as a tort.[209] It is submitted that the same general approach should be adopted in relation to their classification for the purposes of the Brussels Convention. Therefore, those restitution for wrongs cases which amount to a breach of a fiduciary relationship, or other consensual relationship, will fall within Article 5(1). Those restitution for wrongs cases which amount to "wrongs" (such as torts or cases of knowing assistance) will fall within Article 5(3). Finally, those restitution for wrongs cases which amount to breaches of trust, and such claim is brought against a settlor, trustee or beneficiary of trust,[210] will fall within Article 5(6).[211]

Of course, the interpretation of the Convention is not based on the taxonomic understanding of restitution for wrongs as a matter of English domestic law but will apply a Convention or autonomous approach. The legal systems of certain Contracting States classify such cases as forming part of the law of unjustified enrichment.[212] Moreover, even as a matter of English law, the same set of facts may amount to both a restitution for wrongs case and a case of autonomous unjust enrichment. Judging from the jurisprudence of the ECJ to date, an autonomous definition of matters or unjust enrichment will need to be developed, in order to determine the line between unjust enrichment and matters

[207] See ch. 1.4.

[208] See generally ch. 4.4.1.

[209] See ch. 4, §4.3 *seq*.

[200] It should be noted that the trust must be created by operation of statute, by a written instrument or evidenced in writing, in order for Art. 5(6) to apply.

[211] Where the particular trust does not satisfy the requirements of Art. 5(6), in that it is not created by statute or created or evidenced in writing, such a claim should fall within Art. 5(1) where it amounts to a breach of a consensual arrangement. Where on the other hand Art. 5(6) does not apply, on the basis that the claim is not brought against a "settlor, trustee or beneficiary of [the] trust", such claim should be classified as a matter of unjust enrichment, as it would be brought against a party who is a stranger to the trust such as a third party recipient: see for example *Re Diplock* [1948] Ch. 465. Art. 5(1) would not be applicable in such a case as the claim would not amount to a breach of a consensual arrangement: *Handte GmbH* v. *Société Traitements Mécano-chimiques des Surfaces* (*26/91*) [1992] E.C.R. I–3967, 3994 (para. 15); *Peters Bauunternehmung GmbH* v. *Zuid Nederlandse Aannemers Vereneging* (*Case 34/82*) [1983] E.C.R. 987.

[212] Under German law the defendant may be enriched other than by performance, as contained in the second limb of the general limb in Art. 812(1) of the German Civil Code. This, *inter alia*, includes "Eingriffskondiktion", which covers much of what in English law is called restitution for wrongs: see Markesinis, pp.741, 743–7. Art. 904 of the Greek Civil Code, which is the general unjust enrichment provision, provides that a person may be enriched, *inter alia*, through causing damage to another.

relating to "tort, delict and quasi-delict", in connection with restitution for wrongs. Alternatively, the autonomous definition of "matters relating to tort, delict or quasi-delict" will have to be further developed. It is submitted that, upon the current version of the Convention, the answer to this problem lies in the connecting factor in Article 5(3) of the "place of the harmful event". Irrespective of whether a claim is classified as a wrong or unjust enrichment as a matter of domestic law, it will amount to a "tort, delict or quasi-delict" for the purposes of Article 5(3) if it comprises of a harmful event. For example, a claim for restitution, or disgorgement, is brought against a German defendant, in relation to the infringement of the plaintiff's intellectual property right in copying a particular product and selling it in England. The infringement is the harmful event. Therefore, irrespective of the fact that a German court is likely to characterise such a claim as a matter of unjustified enrichment,[213] while an English court is likely to characterise the same claim as a tort,[214] the relevant claim consists of a "harmful event" and therefore should fall within an autonomous definition of "tort, delict or quasi-delict". The relevant connecting factor can readily point to a particular jurisdiction which will be closely connected with the claim, irrespective of whether such claim seeks restitution, or disgorgement, rather than damages. It therefore makes good sense to classify claims that comprise of an alleged harmful event as "matters of tort, delict and quasi-delict".

[213] See for example BGH 9 March 1989, BGHZ 107, 117 (to be found in Markesinis, p.802, case 137).

[214] The infringement of intellectual property is characterised as tortious: see *House of Spring Gardens Ltd.* v. *Waite* [1991] 1 Q.B. 241, 253 (copyrights); *Mölnlycke AB* v. *Proctor & Gamble Ltd.* [1992] 1 W.L.R. 1112, 1117 (patents). See also Fawcett and Torremans, p.150.

10

Jurisdiction under the Traditional Rules

WHERE THE JURISDICTIONAL rules contained in the Brussels Convention do not apply, the plaintiff[1] must base his claim under the common law rules of jurisdiction so as to bring an international restitutionary claim. Generally, this will be either where the claim does not fall within the Convention's scope, or where the relevant claim falls within Article 4 of the Convention.[2] Naturally, the common law rules have less significance today than prior to the operation of the Convention. However, they will be particularly prominent in cases where the defendant is not domiciled in one of the Contracting States of either the Brussels or Lugano Conventions,[3] where the courts of one of the Contracting States do not have jurisdiction by virtue of Article 16 or 17, or where the claim does not fall within the subject matter of the Convention.[4] Moreover, a variation of these rules is still the sole basis of jurisdiction in non-European, common law countries which have not become a party to either the Brussels or Lugano Conventions.

Unlike the Convention, the common law rules do not seek to determine the question of jurisdiction among competing jurisdictions. The question is asked from an English point of view and that is whether the English courts have jurisdiction to hear a matter. Is the particular defendant and/or claim sufficiently connected with England, irrespective of whether it is also connected with another jurisdiction?

I SERVICE OUT OF THE JURISDICTION

Where a defendant is not present within the jurisdiction[5] the plaintiff must serve process outside of the jurisdiction; this has been described as "exorbitant"[6] or

[1] The term "claimant" has been adopted under the new Civil Procedure Rules. However, as almost all of the cases that will be dealt with here pre-date the new rules, it has been considered more convenient, generally, to use the traditional word plaintiff.

[2] See further Briggs and Rees, p.187.

[3] i.e., in one of the European Union or EFTA Member States.

[4] See above, ch. 9.3.

[5] A claim may always be brought against a defendant who is present within the jurisdiction. The defendant need not be domiciled, nor present for some significant period of time; a temporary presence is sufficient: *Maharanee of Baroda* v. *Wildenstein* [1972] 2 Q.B. 283 (C.A.).

[6] See for example, L. Collins (1991) 107 L.Q.R. 10; Briggs and Rees, p.219. See also *The Siskina*

"long-arm" jurisdiction.[7] The new rules dealing with service out of the jurisdiction are set out in Part 6 of the Civil Procedure Rules ("CPR").[8] They came into force on 2 May 2000 and are largely based on RSC Order 11. In interpreting the new rules, guidance is sought from the previous case law, subject to any specific changes to the wording of a particular provision.

In order to serve outside of the jurisdiction, the claimant must both serve in accordance with Part 6 of the CPR and also obtain permission[9] of the court to do so.[10] Where permission is granted and the defendant has been served, the defendant may either enter an appearance without more and thereby submit to the jurisdiction; or enter an appearance and then apply under CPR 11[11] to challenge the jurisdiction of the court.[12] As a matter of practice, it is where a challenge is brought to the granting of permission, that the issues of jurisdiction will be properly argued.

The are two basic steps in determining whether permission will, or should have been, granted:

(1) It must be shown that the claim, or each claim if there is more than one, falls within one or more of the sub-rules in CPR 6.20, namely it must fall within one or more of the specific "heads", or bases, for jurisdiction. The standard of proof here is that the plaintiff must show a "good arguable case" that the claim falls within one of the specific heads.[13] If this is satisfied, the court will have jurisdiction to allow service *ex juris*.
(2) The claimant must show that England is the proper place in which to bring the claim for the court to exercise its discretion in favour of granting such permission. This involves two basic steps:
    (a) Does the claim satisfy the doctrine of *forum conveniens*, namely:
        (i) is England clearly and distinctly shown to be the most appropriate forum for the action; and

v. *Distos Compania Naviera S.A.* [1979] A.C. 210, 254, *per* Lord Diplock; *Amin Rasheed Corp.* v. *Kuwait Insurance Co.* [1984] A.C. 50, 65 *per* Lord Diplock.

[7] Although Lord Goff expressed the view: "I myself feel that the word 'exorbitant' is, as used in the present context, an old-fashioned word which perhaps carries unfortunate overtones: it means no more than that the exercise of the jurisdiction is extraordinary in the sense explained by Lord Diplock in the *Amin Rasheed* case": *Spiliada Maritime Corp.* v. *Cansulex Ltd.* [1987] A.C. 460, 481.

[8] The Civil Procedure Rules were made pursuant to s.2 of the Civil Procedure Act 1997. They came into force on 26 April 1999, by virtue of Civil Procedure Rules 1998 (S.I. 1998/3132), replacing the Rules of the Supreme Court (RSC). The relevant order of the RSC for service *ex juris*, namely Order 11, was repealed by The Civil Procedure (Amendment) Rules 2000 (S.I. 2000/221), and was replaced by Section III of Part 6.

[9] The term "permission" has been adopted under the CPR instead of "leave".

[10] See also Briggs and Rees, pp.218–20.

[11] Formerly RSC Order 12, rule 8.

[12] The grounds for challenge are: first, that service was not effected properly; secondly, that the court does not have jurisdiction over him on the basis that the courts of a Contracting State under the Brussels or Lugano Convention have jurisdiction; or thirdly, that leave should not have been granted for service out of the jurisdiction and that it should be set aside. The court may set aside the order granting leave for service pursuant to CPR 23(10), formerly RSC Order 32, rule 6.

[13] *Seaconsar Far East Ltd.* v. *Bank Markazi Johmouri Islami Iran* [1994] 1 A.C. 438.

(ii) is there nevertheless any overriding injustice in allowing to the claimant to proceed in England, or by bringing the defendant to England for the litigation;

(b) Does the claimant's claim establish that there is a serious issue to be tried on the merits?

Under RSC Order 11, rule 4 (2), permission would not be granted "unless it shall be made sufficiently to appear to the court that the case is a proper one for service out of the jurisdiction". This had been interpreted to require the two steps set out in 2(a) and (b) above.[14] This exact provision does not appear in CPR 6. Instead, CPR 6.21(2A) provides that "[t]he court will not give permission [for service of the jurisdiction] unless satisfied that England and Wales is the proper place in which to bring the claim".[15] It is submitted that the effect of this new provision is substantially the same as that of RSC Order 11, rule 4(2). Accordingly, the two steps set out in 2(a) and (b) above have been preserved.

Assuming that all the above are satisfied, permission will be granted in the plaintiff's favour. In the context of restitutionary claims, we are particularly concerned with step (1), namely the possible heads of jurisdiction in CPR 6.20 which might form a jurisdictional basis for a restitutionary claim. Step (2) involves nothing particularly unique to the bringing of restitutionary claims but applies equally to all claims. As such, this step will not be examined.[16] It is therefore important to focus on the different jurisdictional bases upon which a restitutionary claim may be brought under the Rules. The relevant sub-rules, in CPR 6.20, which are likely "heads" of jurisdiction for restitutionary claims are:

6.20

. . .

Claims in relation to contracts

(5) a claim is made in respect of a contract where the contract-

(a) was made within the jurisdiction;

(b) was made by or through an agent trading or residing within the jurisdiction;

(c) is governed by English law; or

(d) contains a term to the effect that the court shall have jurisdiction to determine any claim in respect of the contract.

(6) a claim is brought in respect of a breach of contract committed within the jurisdiction.

(7) the claim is made for a declaration that no contract exists where, if the contract was found to exist, it would comply with the conditions set out in paragraph (5).

Claims in tort

(8) a claim is made in tort where-

(a) damage was sustained within the jurisdiction; or

(b) the damage sustained resulted from an act commited within the jurisdiction.

[14] *Ibid.*

[15] The provision was added by the Civil Procedure (Amendment No. 2) Rules (S.I. 2000/940).

[16] For an examination of the principles involved, see: Briggs and Rees, pp.191–218, 238–45.

Claims about property within the jurisdiction

(10) the whole subject matter of a claim relates to property located within the jurisdiction.

Claims about trusts etc.

(14) a claim is made for a remedy against the defendant as constructive trustee where the defendant's alleged liability arises out of acts committed within the jurisdiction.

(15) a claim is made for restitution where the defendant's alleged liability arises out of acts committed within the jurisdiction.

In granting permission, the jurisdiction of the court is in part discretionary. The courts have generally expressed a degree of caution in the process of exercising jurisdiction to grant leave.[17] Moreover, the provisions in the Rules which allow for jurisdiction are to be interpreted strictly. Lord Diplock stated in *The Siskina* v. *Distos Compania Naviera S.A.*:

> In several of the cases specified in the sub-rules . . . the jurisdiction exerciseable over foreigners by the High Court is wider than that which is recognised in English law as being possessed by courts of foreign countries. These are "exorbitant" jurisdictions which run counter to the normal rules of comity amongst civilized nations. For this reason it has long been held that where there is any room for doubt as to their meaning the provisions of the sub-rules are to be strictly construed in favour of the foreigner.[18]

These considerations may be borne in mind when examining whether restitutionary claims fall within the provisions of the Rules for service out of the jurisdiction. However, such a degree of caution may no longer be warranted with the recognition of the doctrine of *forum conveniens*.[19] The above comments were made prior to the acceptance of such a doctrine. As such, the courts accommodated such considerations by applying a degree of strictness in their interpretation of the jurisdictional provisions. There had to be a strong basis before a foreigner could be brought before the courts of the jurisdiction. Such considerations may now be accommodated for through the second step examined above, whether the claim is a proper one for service out of the jurisdiction, which now includes the question of whether the claim satisfies the doctrine of *forum conveniens*. It is therefore submitted that the same degree of strictness is no longer applicable when examining the issue of whether a restitutionary claim falls within one of the heads of jurisdiction, contained in CPR 6.20.

[17] See *Société Générale de Paris* v. *Dreyfus* (1885) 29 Ch.D. 239, 242, *per* Pearson J. Also *The Hagen* [1908] P. 189, 201, *per* Farwell L.J.; *The Siskina* v. *Distos Compania Naviera S.A.* [1979] A.C. 210, 254–25, *per* Lord Diplock; *Amin Rasheed Corp.* v. *Kuwait Insurance Co.* [1984] A.C. 50, 65, *per* Lord Diplock; *Spiliada Maritime Corp.* v. *Cansulex Ltd.* [1987] A.C. 460, 481, *per* Lord Goff. See also Dicey and Morris, p.317.

[18] [1979] A.C. 210, 254–5. Also *The Hagen* [1908] P. 189, 201, *per* Farwell L.J. See also Dicey and Morris, pp.307–8.

[19] Recognised in *Spiliada Maritime Corp.* v. *Cansulex Ltd.* [1987] A.C. 460.

2 HEADS OF JURISDICTION

2.1 Sub-rule (15): claim for restitution

This is the most obvious sub-rule which might form the jurisdictional basis of a restitutionary claim and is therefore the most appropriate one to start with. This provision was added in 2000, together with the general overhaul of the rules on jurisdiction.[20] The addition of this sub-rule is testimony to the increasing recognition of the law of restitution, particularly in the field of private international law. In part, it replaces the former RSC Order 11, rule 1(1)(t), which provided for jurisdiction where "the claim is brought for money had and received or for an account or other remedy against the defendant as a constructive trustee, and the defendant's alleged liability arises out of acts committed, whether by him or otherwise, within the jurisdiction".

It is peculiar that sub-rule (15) appears under the sub-heading "claims about trusts etc.". Although restitutionary claims may arise in the context of a trust, many such claims will not arise in such a context.[21] As such, it would have been more appropriate to have this sub-rule under a separate sub-heading. One may take the view that the sub-rules following the sub-heading "claims about trusts etc." are intended to deal with claims connected to trusts and, as such, the provision dealing with claims for restitution is limited to this factual situation. Such an interpretation would be unfortunate. It would deprive sub-rule (15) of any real effect, while it would create a more limited scope for this sub-rule than that of its predecessor in RSC Order 11, rule 1(1)(t). Moreover, there is nothing in the actual wording of sub-rule (15) to suggest such a limited reading. It is submitted that sub-rule (15) is to apply generally to restitutionary claims.

Sub-rule (15) applies to claims "made for restitution". It is not necessarily limited to claims for restitution of an unjust enrichment. As such, it may also apply to claims for restitution for wrongdoing; that is, unless one accepts that restitution for wrongdoing is really concerned with disgorgement for wrongdoing and should be thus described.[22] What is not clear is whether the phrase "a claim . . . made for restitution" includes proprietary claims as well as personal claims. The wording of the sub-rule does not suggest that the type of restitution claimed is to be limited to, for example, *in personam* claims. Furthermore, assuming that the connecting factor in sub-rule (15) were satisfied (i.e., that "the defendant's alleged liability arises out of acts commited within the jurisdiction"), there would be no justifiable reason for limiting the scope of this provision. Even if the

[20] The Civil Procedure (Amendment) Rules 2000 (S.I. 221).

[21] See generally Ch. I.

[22] See L. Smith, "The Province of the Law of Restitution" (1992) 71 C.B.R. 672, 694–9; Smith, pp.19–21, 297–9; J. Edelman, "Gain-Based Remedies For Wrongdoing" [2000] A.L.J. 231. See also *Cadbury Schweppes Inc.* v. *F.B.I. Foods* [1999] 1 S.C.R. 142.

scope were to be limited to personal claims, a claimant could alternatively rely on the provision in sub-rule (14), which deals with claims "against the defendant as constructive trustee"[23] and contains an identical connecting factor. This leads us to a significant reason as to why sub-rule (15) should be read as allowing both personal and proprietary restitutionary claims. If sub-rule (15) were to be limited to personal claims, a claimant would have to resort to sub-rule (14) so as to bring a claim for proprietary restitution. Such a situation would then limit the claim to situations where the proprietary remedy claimed is a constructive trust. Claims for other kinds of proprietary remedies would not be covered. As previously noted, there is a respectable view that many resulting trusts are restitutionary and arise so as to reverse an unjust enrichment.[24] Secondly, a lien may also be imposed as a means of reversing an unjust enrichment.[25] If, however, the general restitutionary sub-rule extended to claims for proprietary restitution, it would not be limited to particular kinds of proprietary remedies, such as constructive trusts, but would extend to all claims for proprietary restitution.

The connecting factor in sub-rule (15) is that the "defendant's alleged liability arises out of acts committed within the jurisdiction". The provision does not state that all relevant acts were committed within the jurisdiction, but only that "acts" were so committed. This would suggest that it is sufficient if one or more of the acts which constitute the alleged liability occurred within the jurisdiction. Such acts would need to be substantial to justify the jurisdictional basis. Thus, where a bank in England makes a mistaken payment to a bank in New York,[26] a significant act, namely the act of payment, occurred within England, even though the receipt occurred outside the jurisdiction, and the event which occurred within the jurisdiction was not an act committed by the defendant. Likewise, where a union exercises economic duress over the plaintiff, by blacking his vessel in Russia,[27] the plaintiff's claim to recover moneys paid pursuant to such economic duress will fall within sub-rule (15) where such payment was made from England, or where England was the place where the plaintiff was subjected to such pressure.[28]

[23] The phrase "a remedy against the defendant as constructive trustee" includes both a personal claim against a constructive trustee, such as an order that there be an account, as well as a proprietary claim, namely, an order that the defendant holds property on constructive trust: see *Ghana Commercial Bank* v. *C. & ors*, *The Times*, 3 March 1997.

[24] See above p.73, n. 136.

[25] *Re Hallett's Estate* (1880) 13 Ch.D. 696; *Re Oatway* [1903] 2 Ch. 356; *Roscoe Ltd.* v. *Winder* [1915] 1 Ch. 62; *Re Diplock* [1948] Ch. 465. *Re Hallet's Estate* suggests that, where a trustee or other fiduciary uses trust money to purchase property for himself, the beneficiary will have a choice between a beneficial interest or a lien on the relevant asset as security for the trust money used to purchase it: (1880) 13 Ch.D. 696, 708–9. See also Goff and Jones, pp.44–5, 72, 85; Birks, pp.88, 370, 375–7, 389–93; Burrows pp.29, 40–5, 369. On liens and charges generally, see Smith, pp.347–56.

[26] See for example *Chase Manhattan Bank N.A.* v. *Israel-British Bank (London) Ltd.* [1981] Ch. 105.

[27] *Dimskal Shipping Co. S.A.* v. *I.T.W.F.* (*The Evia Luck* (No.2)) [1992] 2 A.C. 152 (H.L.).

[28] This would include the situation where the pressure might be exercised from outside the jurisdiction but the plaintiff is subjected to the pressure, or the pressure's adverse effect is felt, within the jurisdiction.

Nevertheless, the phrase "liability arises out of acts committed" was interpreted by Millett J. to mean that all the acts necessary to impose liability should have been committed within the jurisdiction in *ISC Technologies Ltd.* v. *Guerin*.[29] It was therefore held that RSC Order 11, rule 1(1)(t) covered a claim for knowing participation by acts in England in a fraudulent breach of trust committed in England, but not a claim for knowing receipt abroad of the proceeds of such a fraud. This is an unfortunate interpretation which would limit the effect of sub-rule (15) as a jurisdictional basis.[30] It would restrict it to restitutionary claims whose only international element is that the defendant is not domiciled, or present, within the jurisdiction; that is, where all the acts which go to constitute the claim, which are "necessary" to impose liability, have occurred within the jurisdiction. It might be argued that Millett J. sought to limit the operation of RSC Order 11, rule 1(1)(t) merely to cases where the relevant enrichment was received within the jurisdiction. This is as liability does not arise until there has been enrichment or receipt and therefore it is these acts which are "necessary" to impose liability. Even if this was what was intended by Millett J., it is submitted that this would still give rise to an unsatisfactory situation. Again, jurisdiction in restitutionary matters would be unnecessarily limited. They would be restricted to cases where the relevant enrichment was received within the jurisdiction and would exclude cases where significant acts had been committed within the jurisdiction but the enrichment had, coincidentally or deliberately, been received elsewhere. Thus, for example where, through acts of fraud committed within the jurisdiction, the defendant channelled the value of the plaintiff's money into his bank account in the Cayman Islands, the English courts would not have jurisdiction to hear the claim for restitution. This would be either on the basis that not all the necessary acts which give rise to restitutionary liability were committed within the jurisdiction, or alternatively because the enrichment had been received outside the jurisdiction. On either interpretation, the result cannot be condoned.

A contrary approach was taken by Hoffmann J. in *ISC Technologies Ltd.* v. *Guerin*,[31] where he expressed the view that Millett J. "may have construed (t) too narrowly". In Hoffmann J.'s opinion:

> [T]he case for which (t) was primarily designed was the foreign entity which has not participated in the fraud but has been used as a receptacle for the proceeds by the natural persons who controlled it. I would be inclined to construe "arise out of" as meaning "be founded upon" without requiring that every act necessary to create liability should have been committed within the jurisdiction.[32]

[29] Unreported, 7 December 1990. This case is discussed in *ISC* v. *Guerin* [1992] 2 Lloyd's Rep. 430, 433.

[30] The decision has not received support, see: *ISC Technologies Ltd.* v. *Guerin* [1992] 2 Lloyd's Rep. 430, 433, *per* Hoffmann J; *Polly Peck International plc.* v. *Nadir* unreported, 17 March 1993. See also A. Briggs, "Jurisdiction under the Traditional Rules" in Rose (ed.), *Restitution and the Conflict of Laws* (Oxford, 1995), pp.61–2 (hereafter Briggs); Briggs and Rees, pp.236–7.

[31] [1992] 2 Lloyd's Rep. 430.

[32] *Id.*, 433.

However, Hoffmann J.'s views were *obiter dicta*, as it was held that the tenth defendant could be served in relation to the claims for equitable restitutionary remedies[33] under RSC Order 11, rule 1(1)(c), on the basis that he was a "necessary or proper party" to the action.[34] It was therefore unnecessary to give a final view on whether the restitutionary claims could be brought under sub-rule (t). Nevertheless, these views were restated by Hoffmann L.J.,[35] this time in the Court of Appeal and as part of the *ratio decidendi* of his decision, in *Polly Peck International plc.* v. *Nadir*.[36] A purposive approach was taken to the construction of sub-rule(t):

> it is sufficient if a substantial part of the acts, viewed as a whole, on the part of the original fiduciary and the defendant which give rise to the alleged liability, took place within the jurisdiction.

Hoffmann L.J., drew an analogy with the construction given to sub-rule (f)(the tort sub-rule)[37] by the Court of Appeal in *Metall & Rohstoff A.G.* v. *Donaldson Lufkin & Jenrette Inc.*[38] It was held that the requirement that damage in a tort claim has "resulted from an act committed, within the jurisdiction" is met if the damage resulted from "substantial and efficacious acts" committed within the jurisdiction. It was however pointed out by counsel in *Polly Peck* that the wording in sub-rule (f) and (t) differed. Hoffmann L.J. stated:

> Mr Heslop . . . drew attention to the use of the plural "acts" in sub-paragraph (t) instead of "an act" in (f). This meant, he said, that although damage could obviously be the combined result of a number of acts, sub-section (f) expressly required only one of them to be within the jurisdiction. But the use of the plural in (t) suggested that all the acts necessary to found liability should have been within the jurisdiction. I agree that if one has no regards to the consequences, this is a construction which the language will bear, but I think that if it had been intended, the rule would have said "wholly" or some such word after "arises". It seems to me more significant to consider the results of the rival constructions than minor differences in language and these lead me to the conclusion that a broader construction would reflect a more consistent purpose.

It is not therefore necessary that all the acts which gave rise to the defendant's alleged liability were committed within the jurisdiction. What is required is that a "substantial part of the acts" occurred within the jurisdiction. That is to say, the restitutionary claim must be based on substantial acts occurring within the jurisdiction. Finally, it is submitted that the word "acts" should extend to omissions. Such an interpretation would be in line with Hoffmann L.J.'s purposive

[33] There were also claims for damages for fraudulent misrepresentations which came within Order 11, rule 1(1)(f), being claims founded on tort.

[34] This is now covered by CPR 6.20(3)(b).

[35] With whom Glidewell and McCowan L.JJ. expressly agreed.

[36] 17 March 1993 (unreported).

[37] This is now covered by CPR 6.20(8).

[38] [1990] 1 Q.B. 391, 437.

construction of RSC, Order 11, rule 1(1)(t) in *Polly Peck International plc.* v. *Nadir*. On such a construction, a failure to provide consideration within the jurisdiction, for example, would fall within sub-rule (15). It would be unfortunate if a plaintiff were, for example, to be denied jurisdiction in a claim based on the defendant's failure to provide counter-performance within the jurisdiction.

2.1.1 *Questions of Choice of Law*

There is one further point which needs to be considered in relation to CPR 6.20(15). That is whether questions of choice of law enter into the examination of jurisdiction under this provision. In *Metall und Rohstoff A.G.* v. *Donaldson Lufkin & Jenrette Inc.*,[39] it was held that, for a claim to be founded on a "tort" for the purposes of RSC Order 11, rule 1(1)(f), it had to be founded on conduct which amounted to a tort for the purposes of private international law.[40] In other words, it was not sufficient that the claim was founded on what constituted a tort as a matter of English domestic law; if the tort was in substance committed overseas, it had to amount to a tort under the double actionability rule.[41] It could therefore be argued that this principle is not limited to sub-paragraph (f) under the old rules, but that it applies generally to all jurisdictional provisions under CPR 6.20. Indeed, this was also the approach adopted in relation to the question of whether there was a "contract" for the purpose of the old rules.[42] As such, so as to fall within CPR 6.20(15), a plaintiff's claim must be based not only on the fact that substantial acts were committed within the jurisdiction; it must also be shown that "liability" is present under the *lex causae*. There must not merely be a claim, but a claim of substance.

It is not exactly clear whether the heads of jurisdiction in CPR 6.20, and in particular sub-rule (15), are to be interpreted in accordance with the rules of private international law. Dicey and Morris have in the past expressed doubt as to whether *Metall und Rohstoff* is correct in relation to this issue.[43]

[39] [1990] 1 Q.B. 391.

[40] *Id.*, 443. See also Briggs and Rees, pp.221–2, 231. *Cf. The TS Havprins* [1983] 2 Lloyd's Rep. 356; R. Fentiman, "Tort—Jurisdiction or Choice of Law?" [1989] C.L.J. 191.

[41] This was the choice of law rule for torts commited outside the jurisdiction at common law. It had to be shown that the alleged conduct would have been actionable as a tort under English domestic law and that it gave rise to civil liability under the law of the place where the alleged tort occurred: see *Boys* v. *Chaplin* [1971] A.C. 356. The double actionability rule could be departed from in an appropriate case, so that a particular issue, or even the entire question of liability, might be governed by a different law with which the particular issue was more closely connected. This exception was applied in *Red Sea Insurance Co. Ltd.* v. *Bouygues S.A.* [1995] 1 A.C. 190, such that a claim which technically did not amount to a tort under the *lex fori*, on the basis that there was no actual loss, amounted to a tort under the *lex loci delicti* and was therefore actionable as a tort. The choice of law rule for torts is now to be found in the Private International Law (Miscellaneous Provisions) Act 1995.

[42] *Amin Rasheed Shipping Corp.* v. *Kuwait Insurance Co.* [1984] A.C. 50; *Bank of Baroda* v. *Vysya Bank Ltd.* [1994] 2 Lloyd's Rep. 87.

[43] Dicey and Morris, *The Conflict of Laws* (12th ed. by L. Collins, London, 1993), p.341, n.88; curiously, the 13th edition does not comment on the correctness or otherwise of *Metall und Rohstoff*

Furthermore, even if one were to adopt such an approach this is not to say that it automatically applies in relation to sub-rule (15). First of all, there is no indication in the cases which dealt with RSC Order 11, rule 1(1) (t) that issues of choice of law enter into the question of whether a claim fell within this provision.[44] Secondly, the wording of RSC Order 11, rule 1(1)(f) was different from that in the restitutionary provision in sub-rule (15).[45] Whereas the former was concerned with claims "founded on a tort", the latter is based on "alleged liability". The view could be taken that, as the former required "a tort", this necessarily imported with it the question of the actual existence of a tort. When dealing with an international tort such a question was answered by the *lex causae*. The restitutionary provision merely requires "alleged liability" and not actual liability. To fall within this provision there merely needs to be a claim of the sort envisaged, namely, a claim for restitution; and substantial acts must have occurred within the jurisdiction.

As examined above, in order to obtain permission to serve out of the jurisdiction, the plaintiff must show that the claim has a reasonable prospect of success (step 2 above). *Inter alia*, this requires the plaintiff to show that his claim establishes a serious issue to be tried on the merits. If the plaintiff has no claim under the *lex causae*, there cannot be a serious issue to be tried. Put in another way, the issue of whether the plaintiff's claim establishes a serious issue to be tried on the merits presupposes an element of choice of law; namely, that under the *lex causae* the plaintiff has a claim. As issues of choice of law inevitably enter the inquiry of whether permission should be granted for service out of the jurisdiction, it will ultimately make little difference if such issues also fall to be examined in the first step of the inquiry, namely in the context of whether the claim falls within one of the heads of jurisdiction in Rule 6.20.[46] It is therefore perfectly legitimate to consider questions of choice of law in examining whether a claim falls within sub-rule (15). This can only further confirm the necessary jurisdictional connection between the claim and the English courts.

Importing questions of choice of law in the context of sub-rule (15) would add an additional step in determining whether a claim falls within this provision. Unlike sub-rules (6) or (8), one may not necessarily be dealing with a discrete type of claim, namely "torts" or "contracts", for which there is a specific choice of law rule. As already noted, sub-rule (15) applies generally to claims for restitution and is not specifically limited to claims for restitution of an

on this issue: see p.330. See also R. Fentiman, "Tort—Jurisdiction or Choice of Law?" [1989] C.L.J. 191. *Cf.* however Briggs and Rees, p.231.

[44] See *ISC Technologies Ltd.* v. *Guerin* [1992] 2 Lloyd's Rep. 430; *Polly Peck International plc.* v. *Nadir* unreported, 17 March 1993.

[45] Indeed it is different from the wording of CPR 6.20(8), which merely requires that "a claim is made in tort".

[46] However, the necessary standard of proof will be different depending on whether the choice of law issues are dealt with in the first or second step of the inquiry. There must be a "good arguable case" that the claim falls within the relevant jurisdictional head, while in relation to the merits, the claim must establish a "serious issue to be tried".

unjust enrichment. It may extend to restitution for wrongdoing, namely a tort, an equitable wrong or possibly other circumstances. As such, it would be necessary at the outset to characterise the plaintiff's claim so as to be directed to the relevant choice of law rule. This would add a step which may not be present in the context of sub-rules (6) or (8), at least not to the extent where the only issue is, for example, whether the claim is "in tort" or otherwise. Presumably the plaintiff's claim will ordinarily disclose the basis of the remedy sought. Nevertheless, the court will need to characterise, in accordance with the general analysis examined in the context of characterisation. It will need to establish whether the plaintiff's claim for restitution raises an issue of unjust enrichment, a tort, an equitable wrong or otherwise for the purposes of characterisation. This is an inevitable consequence of applying questions of choice of law into the inquiry of whether a claim falls within one of the jurisdictional heads in CPR 6.20.

2.2 Sub-rules (5) and (6): claims in relation to contracts

The traditional jurisdictional basis for restitutionary claims was to be found in those provisions dealing with contracts.[47] This was based on two significant factors. First, the prevailing view at the time was that restitutionary claims were quasi-contractual and based upon the implied contract theory. As such, they were viewed as contracts and were accommodated within a contractual framework. Secondly, there was no independent jurisdictional head for restitutionary claims. Rule 6.20(15) came into existence in 2000, while its predecessor, RSC Order 11, rule 1(1)(t), only came into being into 1990.[48] It was therefore inevitable that jurisdictional refuge had to be found for restitutionary claims elsewhere. The combination of the implied contract theory, together with the unavailability of an alternative jurisdictional basis, made the jurisdictional provisions for contracts the only available home for, what were viewed as, "quasi-contractual" actions or actions for money had and received. Given that these two factors no longer apply, the contractual provisions may cease to hold their previous significance. Furthermore, as a result of the acceptance of the doctrine of unjust enrichment as the unifying principle for unjust enrichment claims, as well as the express rejection of the implied contract theory,[49] the previous cases dealing with jurisdiction for quasi-contractual claims can no longer be

[47] See for example *Bowling* v. *Cox* [1926] A.C. 751; *Rousou's (A Bankrupt) Trustee* v. *Rousou* [1955] 1 W.L.R. 545; *Re Jogia* [1988] 1 W.L.R. 484; *Finnish Marine Insurance Co. Ltd.* v. *Protective National Insurance Co.* [1990] 1 Q.B. 1078. See also *Durra* v. *The Bank of N.S.W.* [1940] V.L.R. 170; *Earthworks & Quarries Ltd.* v. *F.T. Easement & Sons Pty Ltd.* [1966] V.R. 24; *Campus Holidays Ltd. (in liquidation)* v. *Charles Porter and Sons Pty. Ltd.* (1990) 8 A.C.L.C 1.226 (WA.S.C.).

[48] This was through rule 12 of The Rules of the Supreme Court (Amendment No.2) 1990 (S.I. 1990/1689).

[49] See ch. 1.1.

considered particularly relevant.[50] Nevertheless, it is still useful briefly to examine these decisions, particularly in light of the fact that leading texts still make reference to quasi-contracual claims being brought pursuant to the contractual provisions.[51] Moreover, the contractual provisions remain relevant to those restitutionary claims which arise in connection with a contract.

2.2.1 Implied Contract Made within the Jurisdiction

Jurisdiction has been justified in a number of cases concerning "quasi-contractual" claims on the basis of a contractual analogy. The old theory was that, through the receipt of the relevant benefit, the recipient impliedly agrees to restore this benefit under a contract implied at law. Where the enrichment has been received within the jurisdiction, the view has been taken that this amounts to a claim relating to a contract which "was made within the jurisdiction". As such, the equivalent of Rule 6.20(5)(a) has been available for service out of the jurisdiction on the basis that the "quasi-contract" was made within the jurisdiction. In *Bowling* v. *Cox*,[52] Plummer had been made bankrupt and went to live in British Honduras where he remained till his death, undischarged from bankruptcy. His executor had paid large sums to the trustee in bankruptcy but a good deal was still owing. The executor's attorney paid large sums of money, out of the estate of Plummer, to the respondent in Chicago, being under the mistaken belief that the creditors had been satisfied and that the money was free. Having issued proceedings in British Honduras against the attorney for money had and received, the trustee sought to also issue proceedings against the recipient of the moneys in Chicago. The Privy Council held that the implied contract was one made within British Honduras and that therefore the appellant was entitled under the Rules of British Honduras[53] to serve the respondent in Chicago. Viscount Haldane stated:

> The surplus of the estate in British Honduras, in the hands of the respondent and his attorney, might well be money had and received to the use of the appellant. If so, this title to it arose when the respondent and his attorney received it, and not in England or at the time of the bankruptcy in 1869. The money was rather money had and received, in which case the title to it arose, when it was got in by the executor, under

[50] See *Ansett Transport Industries (Operations) Pty. Ltd.* v. *Alenia Aeritalia & Selenia SpA* (1991) 105 F.L.R. 169. See also Burrows, p.490.

[51] See Dicey and Morris, p.318; Cheshire and North, p.303; *Cf.* Briggs and Rees, p.226.

[52] [1926] A.C. 751.

[53] These provided that: "Service out of the jurisdiction . . . may be allowed by the Court . . . whenever the contract which is sought to be enforced or rescinded, dissolved, annulled or otherwise affected in any such action, or for the breach whereof damages or other relief are or is demanded in such action, *was made or entered into within the jurisdiction*, and whenever there has been a breach within the jurisdiction of any contract wherever made, and whenever any act or thing sought to be restrained or removed, or for which damages are sought to be recovered, was or is to be done, or is situate within the jurisdiction" (*emphasis added*). To be found at *id.*, 753.

> an implied contract which the law imputes, and which renders him liable to proceedings in the nature of an assumpsit at common law.[54]

The views expressed by Viscount Haldane should come as no surprise. After all it was he who in *Sinclair* v. *Brougham* stated:

> [B]roadly speaking, so far as proceedings *in personam* are concerned, the common law of England really recognizes (unlike Roman law) only actions of two classes, those founded on contract and those founded on tort. When it speaks of actions arising *quasi ex contractu*, it refers merely to a class of action in theory based in a contract which is imputed to the defendant by a fiction of law. The fiction can only be set up with effect if such a contract would be valid if it really existed.[55]

Such views have since been rejected by the House of Lords.[56] Nevertheless, even accepting the implied contract theory for a moment, the analysis of *Bowling* v. *Cox* is most unsatisfactory. The claim for which service out of the jurisdiction was sought was against the recipient of the moneys in Chicago. Thus, the relevant implied contract to repay such moneys must have arisen upon the receipt of such money in Chicago and not when the executor and his attorney received the moneys in British Honduras. It is submitted that, although the overall outcome of the decision is correct,[57] the basis for such a decision cannot be because the obligation to repay such moneys, or indeed the implied contract, arose in British Honduras. Yet, guided by the instinct that the courts of British Honduras should have had jurisdiction in such a matter, the fictitious contractual basis of jurisdiction was justified by moulding the implied contract theory accordingly. The case did not leave one with any clear picture as to when and where implied contracts are created, other than that they depend on the receipt of moneys somewhere. It sufficed that an implied contract existed prior to the payment of the moneys to the recipient in Chicago and that such pre-existing obligation was not owed by the recipient. The case illustrates the unsatisfactory nature of the implied contract theory in identifying jurisdiction for restitutionary claims.

The decision in *Bowling* v. *Cox* formed the basis of other decisions which adopted, or were bound by, the fiction that quasi-contractual claims amount to "contracts" for jurisdictional purposes. An attempt to uncover this fiction was made in *Rousou's (A Bankrupt) Trustee* v. *Rousou*,[58] a case with similar facts. In the initial application for leave, Danckwerts J. stated:

[54] *Id.*, 754.

[55] [1914] A.C. 398, 415.

[56] *Westdeutsche Landesbank Girozentrale* v. *Islington London BC*. [1996] A.C. 669, 687B–C, *per* Lord Goff, 710, *per* Lord Browne-Wilkinson, 718, *per* Lord Slynn, 738, *per* Lord Lloyd.

[57] The courts of British Honduras should have had jurisdiction in relation to the claim by the trustee in bankruptcy to recover the payment made to the recipient in Chicago. This is because the alleged liabilty arose out of substantial acts committed within the jurisdiction, for the purposes of Rule 6.20(15).

[58] [1955] 1 W.L.R. 545.

> it seemed to me at first sight, that this had very little, if anything, to do with the law of contract at all. The rights given to the trustee were in each case as it seemed to me rights arising under some statute.[59]

However, on the authority of *Bowling* v. *Cox*, leave was allowed. A more valiant attempt was made in the application to set aside leave, again before Danckwerts J. The Official Solicitor, as guardian of the infant recipients, argued:

> that there is no sort of contract in respect of any obligation by the infant defendants to repay any money which they may have received as a result of any transaction which may be set aside by the courts of this country. There is no consensus of any sort or description.[60]

Danckwerts J. recognised that an implied contract "quite plainly . . . is not a contract in the ordinary sense of the term",[61] and that it is essentially "an obligation which is imposed against the will of one of the parties and really without any desire or wish on his part to undertake such an obligation at all".[62] Nevertheless, upon the authority of *Bowling* v. *Cox*, it was held that an implied contract fell within the rule allowing service *ex juris* in respect of a contract and thus the application to set aside leave was dismissed. However, in *Rousou* it could not easily be said that the relevant quasi-contract was entered within the jurisdiction. Unlike *Bowling* v. *Cox*, the relevant moneys in *Rousou* were never within the jurisdiction. They were in a church fund in Cyprus and were transferred into an account in Cyprus in the names of the bankrupt's children. How could it be said that the implied contract to repay such money was "made within the jurisdiction"? This question was not adequately dealt with. Danckwerts J. tackled this question by saying that one must treat the word "made", in the phrase "made within the jurisdiction", as being equivalent, in the case of quasi-contract or obligation of that kind, to "arising". Thus, there must be a quasi-contract or other obligation arising within the jurisdiction, or one which by its terms or by its implication should be governed by English law.[63] In *Rousou*, it was held that the obligation to repay the money was one which arose in England and was also governed by English law. Presumably this was as the obligation to repay the money was one imposed by the Bankruptcy Act of England and through English bankruptcy proceedings, although this was not clearly spelt out.

The inconsistency between *Bowling* v. *Cox* and *Rousou* was recognised by Browne-Wilkinson V.-C. in *Re Jogia*.[64] The view that quasi-contracts are made or arise in the place where money is received was reinforced. It was stated:

59 *Id.*, 548.
60 [1955] 3 All E.R. 486, 490.
61 *Ibid.*
62 *Id.*, 492.
63 *Ibid.*
64 [1988] 1 W.L.R. 484. *Cf. Campus Holidays Ltd.* (*in liquidation*) v. *Charles Porter and Sons Pty. Ltd.* (1990) 8 A.C.L.C 1.226 (WA.S.C.)

> . . . I am of the view that quasi-contractual obligations of this kind arise from the receipt of money. I find it difficult to see how such obligation can be said to be "made" or "arise" in any place other than that of receipt . . . [S]ave in cases where the obligation to repay arises in connection with a contract or an immovable, the proper law of the quasi-contract is the law of the country where the enrichment occurs.[65]

Doubt was expressed as to the correctness of Danckwerts J.'s decision in *Rousou*, given that the relevant moneys were never within England. Ultimately, however, Browne-Wilkinson V.-C.'s views in relation to the contract jurisdiction rule were *obiter*, as no final view was given on this point. The trustee was unable to show a good arguable case on the merits[66] and thus leave for service out of the jurisdiction was denied.[67]

2.2.2 *Breach of Implied Contract within the Jurisdiction*

Jurisdiction has also been justified, in a number of Australian decisions on the basis of non-compliance with the obligation to perform under an implied contract which amounted to a breach or alleged breach within the jurisdiction, thus falling within the equivalent of RSC Order 11, rule 1(1)(e) (now CPR 6.20(6)). In *Durra* v. *The Bank of New South Wales*,[68] O'Bryan J. allowed service out of the jurisdiction in relation to a claim for money had and received in respect of payments made by the plaintiff under protest for the release of his goods.[69] The obligation to pay, or repay, under the imputed contract was within Victoria and therefore the action was founded on a breach or alleged breach committed within the jurisdiction which ought to have been performed within the jurisdiction.[70] It was argued that the wording of the jurisdictional rule only sought to cover contracts which are actual agreements and not those which are fictional agreements imputed by law.[71] However, on the authorities of *Bowling* v. *Cox* and *Sinclair* v. *Brougham*, the word "contract" in the relevant provision of the Victorian civil procedure rules was interpreted as also covering implied contracts. This approach was followed in a number of subsequent Australian decisions.[72]

[65] *Id.*, 495.

[66] The test would now be one of whether there is a serious issue to be tried on the merits: *Seaconsar Far East Ltd.* v. *Bank Markazi Johmouri Islami Iran* [1994] 1 A.C. 438.

[67] *Re Jogia* [1988] 1 W.L.R. 484, 496.

[68] [1940] V.L.R. 170.

[69] The relevant rule was contained in the Rules of the Supreme Court of Victoria 1938, Order XI, rule 1(e), which is similar, though not identical, to the wording of RSC Order 11 rule 1(1)(e). It allowed for service out of the jurisdiction where: "the action is founded on any breach or alleged breach within the jurisdiction of any contract wherever made which according to the terms thereof ought to be performed within the jurisdiction".

[70] [1940] V.L.R. 170, 179.

[71] *Id.*, 175.

[72] *Earthworks and Quarries Ltd.* v. *F.T. Eastment and Sons Pty Ltd.* [1966] V.R. 24; *Wilson Electric Transformer Co. Pty. Ltd.* v. *Electricity Commission of N.S.W.* (1967) 12 F.L.R. 314, 317 (Vic.S.C.); *Campus Holidays Ltd. (in liquidation)* v. *Charles Porter and Sons Pty. Ltd.* (1990) 8 A.C.L.C 1.226 (WA.S.C.).

2.2.3 The Preferred Approach

A commendable departure from the above approach occurred in the decision of the Supreme Court of the Australian Capital Territory in *Ansett Transport Industries (Operations) Pty. Ltd.* v. *Alenia Aeritalia & Selenia SpA.*[73] Miles C.J. held that a claim for *quantum meruit* is not a claim in contract and thus did not fall within the jurisdiction provision dealing with claims for damages in general.[74] The basis for his decision was the decision of the High Court of Australia in *Pavey & Mathews Pty. Ltd.* v. *Paul*,[75] where it was recognised that the obligation to make restitution is based on the principle of unjust enrichment and not on implied contract. Although the plaintiff in *Ansett (Operations)* did not base its *quanum meruit* claim on the jurisdictional provisions for contracts,[76] the decision of Miles C.J. necessarily implies that such a claim can no longer be brought under such provisions.[77] It is submitted that the approach of Miles C.J. should be adopted in England. As there has now been clear acceptance of the principle of unjust enrichment and rejection of the implied contract theory as the basis for restitution, such claims do not fall generally within the contractual provisions for jurisdiction contained in CPR 6.20 (5) and (6). Such a view applies *a fortiori* now, in light of the existence of an independent jurisdictional basis covering claims for restitution. Many of the previous cases which relied on the contractual provisions can be justified under the new jurisdictional provision for restitution. For example, the claims brought in *Bowling* v. *Cox*[78] and *Durra* v. *The Bank of New South Wales*[79] would nowadays fall within the jurisdictional provision in CPR 6.20 (15). In both these cases, substantial acts had been comitted within the jurisdiction and thus, jurisdiction had been rightly made available. In *Bowling* v. *Cox*, the act of payment of the sums had occurred from the jurisdiction, even though the receipt occurred outside of the jurisdiction. In

[73] (1991) 105 F.L.R. 169 (S.C.A.C.T.).

[74] Section 11(1)(d) of the Service and Execution of Process Act (Cth) 1901, provided jurisdiction for: "any act . . . for which damages are sought to be recovered, was done . . . within that State or part". This provision formed the jurisdictional basis for torts committed within the state, yet it went beyond claims in tort and extended to any claim for damages in which there is an act of the type contemplated, which has been done or is still to be done within the relevant state: (1991) 105 F.L.R. 169, 173.

[75] (1987) 162 C.L.R. 221.

[76] These would have been ss. 11(1)(c) and (d) of the Service and Execution of Process Act (Cth) 1901.

[77] It should also be noted that s.11 of the Service and Execution of Process Act 1901 (Cth) did not contain a specific provision that would cover a *quantum meruit* claim under some alternative head of jurisdiction. It might therefore be argued that the effect of the decision of the High Court of Australia in *Pavey & Mathews* v. *Paul* should not deprive the court of jurisdiction it would have had before. However, the Service and Execution of Process Act 1901 (Cth) has been repealed and replaced by the Service and Execution of Process Act 1992 (Cth). Service of process from one Australian jurisdiction in another is possible without any need for a territorial nexus with the issuing jurisdiction.

[78] [1926] A.C. 751.

[79] [1940] V.L.R. 170.

Durra, money had been paid by the plaintiff within the jurisdiction under protest for the release of his goods. As such, there would be no need to justify such cases on the fiction that there was a "quasi-contract" made within the jurisdiction, or that a breach of a quasi-contract had occurred within the jurisdiction.

Over and above the rejection of the implied contract theory, there are a number of other practical reasons why restitutionary claims should not be treated as implied contract claims for the purposes of jurisdiction and thereby accommodated within the contractual provisions of the Rules. First, the rationale for the jurisdictional provisions dealing with actual contracts does not necessarily extend to implied contracts. Jurisdiction is justified in a case where parties enter a contract within the jurisdiction, or where a breach, or the intended performance which was breached, occurred within the jurisdiction on the basis that the parties voluntarily entered into such an agreement. There is a connection between the jurisdiction and the dispute between the parties, as they chose to execute such an agreement within the jurisdiction or stipulate, expressly or impliedly, that performance was to occur within the jurisdiction.[80] Such rationale does not extend to restitutionary claims, or "implied contracts", which arise by operation of law and not through the actual agreement of the parties. Put in another way, the jurisdictional rules for contracts are not designed for restitutionary claims. The latter were only seen as "contractual" as a result of the historical accident that they largely grew out of the old *indebitatus assumpsit*.

Secondly, there is a great deal of ambiguity, if not conflict, as to where an implied contract arises. In *Bowling* v. *Cox* it was said that the implied contract arose in British Honduras by virtue of the fact that the executor and his attorney received such moneys in British Honduras. However, the claim related to moneys received by the recipient in Chicago. Presumably the obligation arose upon the receipt of the moneys by the recipient and was an implied contract between the recipient in Chicago and the trustee in bankruptcy in England. It is difficult to see how this implied contract arose in British Honduras, at least insofar as it arose upon the receipt of the moneys, and why such an implied contract was based on the executor and his attorney receiving the money in British Honduras. Unless of course the obligation had already arisen prior to the money being paid to the recipient in Chicago and that the money somehow remained impressed with this implied contract, somehow akin to a beneficial interest arising in moneys which can then be traced to the recipient. However, this was not made clear in the decision. In *Rousou*, a conflicting result arose, which nevertheless purported to rely on the authority of *Bowling* v. *Cox*. The money never was in England and was in fact, at all relevant times, in Cyprus. As such, it could

[80] Such an argument was raised by counsel in *Durra* v. *The Bank of N.S.W.* [1940] V.L.R. 170, 175.

not be said that it was received within the jurisdiction.[81] Yet, it was stated that the implied contract had been "made", or had "arisen" within the jurisdiction.[82] It was said to arise as a result of English bankruptcy law and therefore was both governed by English law and arose in England.[83]

The antithesis between *Rousou* and *Bowling* v. *Cox* was discussed by Browne-Wilkinson V.-C. in *Re Jogia*. He stated:

> I have considerable doubts whether this latter part of the decision in Rousou was correct. It seems to me inconsistent with the decision in *Bowling* v. *Cox*. If the view of Danckwerts J. were right, the quasi-contractual obligations in *Bowling* v. *Cox* would have arisen not in British Honduras but in England, being the law of the relevant bankruptcy. Yet, the Privy Council plainly thought that the obligation was either made or governed by the law of British Honduras.[84]

Browne-Wilkinson V.-C. emphasised that implied contracts arise in the place of receipt of the money and are accordingly also governed by the law of the place of receipt or enrichment.

The above cases do not leave us with any clear picture as to where, if it makes any sense to ask the question, implied contracts are made or arise.[85] There is a clear inconsistency between *Bowling* v. *Cox* and *Rousou*. Furthermore, in *Bowling* v. *Cox* it was held that the implied contract had been made within the jurisdiction even though the relevant moneys had not been received by the recipient within the jurisdiction. The only decision which is technically binding is that of *Rousou*, as *Bowling* v. *Cox* is a decision of the Privy Council while the statements in *Re Jogia* are *obiter*. It is therefore submitted that the inconsistencies and ambiguities in these cases is a further reason for no longer following them.

Finally, allowing jurisdiction on the basis of a breach of an implied contract occurring within the jurisdiction is somewhat artificial. The obligation to which the breach relates is that of making restitution under the implied contract.[86] Inevitably this will amount to the plaintiff's jurisdiction as the defendant will generally be obliged to make payment in the residence or place of business of the

[81] This argument was actually raised by counsel in the case. Danckwerts J. acknowledged that the facts of *Rousou* were different from *Bowling* v. *Cox*, yet did not deal with this point. He merely noted that the only reason why this latter case was referred to him was so as to demonstrate that quasi-contractual obligations are capable of being treated as contracts for the purposes of jurisdiction under the Rules of the Supreme Court: [1955] 3 All E.R. 486, 491.

[82] [1955] 3 All E.R. 486, 492.

[83] *Ibid*.

[84] [1988] 1 W.L.R. 484, 495.

[85] Cheshire and North state that a "quasi-contract" is deemed to have been made in England "if quasi-contractual liability arises from something that has occurred in England": p.303. This, it is submitted, is a most ambiguous guide and further illustrates the inappropriateness of using the test of whether an implied contract was made in England as a basis for jurisdiction.

[86] See *Durra* v. *The Bank of N.S.W.* [1940] V.L.R. 170; *Earthworks & Quarries Ltd.* v. *F.T. Easement & Sons Pty Ltd.* [1966] V.R. 24; *Campus Holidays Ltd.* (*in liquidation*) v. *Charles Porter and Sons Pty. Ltd.* (1990) 8 A.C.L.C 1.226 (WA.S.C.).

creditor/plaintiff.[87] Such an obligation will be one imposed by operation of law. The place of payment of such an obligation may not necessarily be connected with the facts surrounding the obligation to make restitution. It is akin to allowing jurisdiction in matters of tort, or contract, merely on the basis that the defendant's obligation to pay compensation is to do so within the jurisdiction, regardless of the fact that there may be no other connection with the jurisdiction. Such an analysis is an unsatisfactory basis for jurisdiction as it will invariably allow the plaintiff to assert jurisdiction merely on the basis that the plaintiff resides or carries on business within the jurisdiction. Admittedly, the court must also ask whether the claim has a reasonable prospect of success,[88] which includes the question of whether England is the proper forum. As such, the issue of whether the claim is closely connected with the jurisdiction will be dealt with. Nevertheless, this is no reason for adopting an artificial interpretation for one of the heads of jurisdiction, which will allow claims even where there is no real factual connection with the jurisdiction. Moreover, the purpose of the heads of jurisdiction in CPR 6.20 are different from those of the doctrine of *forum conveniens*. The former justifies exorbitant jurisdiction in particular categories of claims because of a particular connection with the jurisdiction. For example, where a breach has occurred within the jurisdiction, this shows a connection with the jurisdiction either because the relevant event occurred within the jurisdiction or because the parties chose the jurisdiction as a place of performance. In the case of the doctrine of *forum conveniens*, the question is whether England is clearly and distinctly the most appropriate forum for the resolution of the dispute and also whether there is any overriding injustice to the defendant in proceeding with the matter in England. These factors focus on the expedient hearing of the trial and the appropriateness of the jurisdiction as a venue. They include, for example, where the parties reside or carry on business, the availability of witnesses, the applicable law, the possibility of a *lis alibi pendens*, related proceedings and the availability of a fair trial in the foreign court.[89]

2.2.4 *Restitutionary Claims Connected with a Contract*

The next question to be asked is whether certain restitutionary claims may nevertheless fall within CPR 6.20(5) and (6) where they arise in connection with a contract. Although restitutionary claims will not generally fall within the rules dealing with contracts, the contractual backdrop may nonetheless form the jurisdictional basis for a consequential restitutionary claim; that is, a

[87] See for example *Robey* v. *Snaefell Mining Co.* (1887) 20 Q.B.D. 152; *The Eider* [1893] P. 119; *Thompson* v. *Palmer* [1893] 2 Q.B. 80; *Reading Trust Ltd.* v. *Spero* [1930] 1 K.B. 492; *Fincham* v. *Spencer* (1901) 26 V.L.R. 665; *Earthworks & Quarries Ltd.* v. *F.T. Easement & Sons Pty Ltd.* [1966] V.R. 24.

[88] See Step 2 on p.232 above.

[89] See generally *Spiliada Maritime Corp.* v. *Cansulex Ltd.* [1987] A.C. 460. See also *Charm Maritime Inc.* v. *Kyriakos* [1987] 1 Lloyd's Rep. 433; *The Nile Rhapsody* [1992] 2 Lloyd's Rep. 399, aff'd [1994] 1 Lloyd's Rep. 382; *Mohammed* v. *Bank of Kuwait and the Middle East* [1996] 1 W.L.R. 1483.

restitutionary claim that arises in connection with a contract. An ineffective contract may give rise to a consequential restitutionary claim.[90] For example, an interest rate swap agreement may have been entered in England between an English local authority and an Australian bank. The contract is *ultra vires* the local authority. Where the local authority seeks to bring a restitutionary claim against the bank so as to recover payments made under the agreement, may it serve the defendant in Australia on the basis that, either the alleged contract was entered within England, was governed by English law, or that it contained an English choice of court agreement? Alternatively, suppose the bank had failed to make its payments and the local authority decided to terminate the contract on the basis that the defendant bank's breach amounted to a repudiation of the contract. In a claim for restitution of the moneys paid by the local authority under the swap agreement, would the local authority be entitled to serve out of the jurisdiction on the basis that the claim is brought "in respect of a breach committed within the jurisdiction"? It should be stressed that the claims in the examples above would not be contractual claims; that is, they would not arise under the relevant contract. Although they would relate to the contract, they would be based on an independent obligation to make restitution of an unjust enrichment.

Part of the answer to the above question lies in the wording of the two relevant provisions. Sub-rule (5) applies to claims made "in respect of a contract". This is to be contrasted with its predecessor, namely RSC Order 11, rule 1(1)(d), which applied to claims

> "brought to enforce, rescind, dissolve, annul or otherwise affect a contract, or to recover damages or obtain other relief in respect of the breach of contract".

Under the old sub-rule (d), a consequential restitutionary claim, other than a claim for rescission, could only be justified if one accepted that the word "affect" carried a broad interpretation.[91] As such, it was unclear whether claims for restitution could be brought under the old sub-rule. However, the language of the new version of this jurisdictional provision may have clarified this uncertainty. The use of the words "claim . . . in respect of a contract" is a compelling reason to conclude that consequential restitutionary claims arising in connection with an ineffective contract fall within sub-rule (5).

The key inquiry is ascertaining what the words "in respect of" mean. It has been held that:

> The words "in respect of" are difficult of definition, but they have the widest possible meaning of any expression intended to convey some connection or relation between the two subject-matters to which the words refer.[92]

[90] See generally the discussion of restitution and contract in the context of characterisation: ch. 4, §§1, 1.1 and 1.2.

[91] See *B.P. Exploration Co Ltd.* v. *Hunt* [1976] 1 W.L.R.788, 795–6, *per* Kerr J.; *Gulf Bank K.S.C.* v. *Mitsubishi Heavy Industries Co* [1994] 1 Lloyd's Rep. 323, 328, *per* Hobhouse J.

[92] *The Trustees Executors & Agency Co. Ltd.* v. *Reilly* [1941] V.L.R. 110, 111, *per* Mann C.J. Approved in *State Government Insurance Office (Queensland)* v. *Crittenden* (1966) 117 C.L.R. 412, 416, *per* Taylor J.

A similarly wide approach has also been taken by the English courts. It has been held that, where moneys had been paid by the plaintiff, at the defendant's request, to persons with whom the defendant had lost bets, such payments could not be recovered as they amounted to payments made "in respect of a contract or agreement rendered null and void" by the Gaming Act 1845.[93] Upon such a wide interpretation, a restitutionary claim brought in connection with an ineffective contract would fall within Rule 6.20 (5). Similarly, Rule 6.20 (6) applies where "a claim is brought in respect of a breach". On the above interpretation of "in respect of", it could be safely concluded that this jurisdictional provision extends to consequential restitutionary claims brought upon a contract's termination, as a result of a breach.[94]

In *B.P. Exploration Co Ltd.* v. *Hunt*,[95] it was held that the phrase "claim brought to . . . otherwise affect a contract" in the then equivalent of RSC Order 11, rule 1(1)(d)[96] not only covered a claim for a declaration that a contract had become frustrated but also the consequential claim for benefits received under s.1(3) of the Law Reform (Frustrated Contracts) Act 1943. As such, leave was allowed for service in relation to both claims. Kerr J. stated that a claim under s.1(3):

> is clearly one which "affects" such a contract. Here again, the contrary construction would produce undesirable results, which I do not think can have been intended. The consequence would be that an English court would have jurisdiction to give leave to serve a defendant out of the jurisdiction where the plaintiff claims that a contract governed by English law has become frustrated, but, . . . the English court would then have to leave it to a foreign court to decide the consequences between the parties which flow from the Act of 1943.[97]

A broad interpretation was given to the word "affect" so as to cover a consequential claim brought upon the frustration of a contract. Strictly speaking, the claim in *B.P. Exploration Co Ltd.* v. *Hunt* was not a claim in unjust enrichment, but one that arose under statute. As such, the case may be distinguished on the basis that the Act applied generally to contracts governed by English law[98] and therefore included the claim for consequential relief. Nevertheless, the case shows that the court was willing to extend the phrase "otherwise affect a contract" to cover consequential claims. It would follow that, *a fortiori*, the phrase "in respect of" in sub-rule (5), will apply to a consequential claim brought upon the frustration of a contract. Yet, as Kerr J. observes, there are further arguments supporting such an analysis. Where an English court has jurisdiction to

[93] *Tatam* v. *Reeve* [1893] 1 Q.B. 44. Approved of in *Saffrey* v. *Mayer* [1901] 1 K.B. 11 (C.A.). *Cf. Heyman* v. *Darwins Limited* [1942] A.C. 356.

[94] A claim for restitutionary damages as a result of a breach of contract would also fall within sub-rule(6): see also ch. 4.1.3.

[95] [1976] 1 W.L.R. 788.

[96] Namely RSC, Order 11, rule 1(f).

[97] *B.P. Exploration Co Ltd.* v. *Hunt* [1976] 1 W.L.R. 788, 796. In *Spiliada Maritime Corp.* v. *Cansulex Ltd.*[1987] A.C. 460, 481, Lord Goff considered that Kerr J. "rightly granted leave to serve proceedings on the defendant out of the jurisdiction" in *B.P. Exploration Co Ltd.* v. *Hunt.*

[98] Section 1(1) of the Law Reform (Frustrated Contracts) Act 1943.

rule upon the effectiveness of a contract, owing to it having been made in England, it being governed by English law or it containing an English jurisdiction clause, surely it should also have jurisdiction to hear the consequential restitutionary claim? Moreover, it might be considered inappropriate that the English court have jurisdiction to rule on the nullity of a contract and not have jurisdiction to hear the consequential restitutionary claim.

A further issue which must be addressed is whether Rule 6.20 (5) presupposes the actual existence of a contract. Does it cover situations where it is claimed that there was no contract, or that a contract was void *ab initio*? If it does not, the availability of this provision to consequential restitutionary claims may be significantly limited. There was a view, in relation to RSC Order 11, rule 1(1)(d), that it was limited to situations where there was "a contract".[99] It was noted in *Finnish Marine Co Ltd.* v. *Protective National Insurance Co*, in relation to sub-rule (d):

> There is a clearly recognised distinction between the case where there has been a contract, which has later been discharged by an accepted repudiation, frustration or rescission, and a "contract" which has never been entered into at all.[100]

Accordingly, it was held that the latter situation, namely that there was no contract, could not be brought within sub-rule (d). However, more recent authorities considered that sub-rule (d) extended to claims seeking a declaration that a contract is void or non-existent.[101] In *DR Insurance Co.* v. *Protective National Insurance Co.*[102] a claim that a contract was void for illegality was held to fall within sub-rule (d). It was stated by Mr. Moore-Bick Q.C. that:

> the policy which underlies O.11, r. 1(1)(d) is to enable all disputes about the existence or effect of contractual rights and liabilities falling within the scope of sub-paras. (d)(i)–(iii) to be brought before the English Courts. In my view an unduly technical approach to the construction of the rule is liable to frustrate its purpose. . . . Lawyers commonly speak of a "contract" being rendered void by reason of illegality or other matters and I see no reason why the language of O.11, r. 1(1)(d) should be construed with any greater technicality so as to exclude cases such as the present.[103]

If one were to apply such an analysis to Rule 6.20 (5), it would follow that the expression "a contract" does not presuppose the actual existence of a contract. The provision would extend to a situation where a contract was null and void. Part of this problem has now been solved by Rule 6.20 (7). It provides jurisdiction for claims seeking "a declaration that no contract exists where, if the con-

[99] *Hemelryck* v. *William Lyall Shipbuilding Co.* [1921] 1 A.C. 698, 701; *Cromie* v. *Moore* [1936] 2 All E.R. 177; *Finnish Marine Insurance Co. Ltd.* v. *Protective National Insurance Co.* [1990] 1 Q.B. 1078.

[100] [1990] 1 Q.B. 1084, *per* Adrian Hamilton Q.C.

[101] *The Olib* [1991] 2 Lloyd's Rep. 108, 118–19 *per* Webster J; *Gulf Bank K.S.C.* v. *Mitsubishi Heavy Industries Co* [1994] 1 Lloyd's Rep. 323, 327, *per* Hobhouse J.; *DR Insurance Co.* v. *Central National Insurance Co.* [1996] 1 Lloyd's Rep. 74. See also Briggs and Rees, p.226.

[102] [1996] 1 Lloyd's Rep. 74.

[103] *Id.*, 80.

tract was found to exist, it would comply with the conditions set out in paragraph (5)". As such, there is now no longer any doubt as to whether there is jurisdiction for negative contractual declarations. However, given that this is specifically dealt with under a separate sub-rule, it may be argued that the claims which may be brought under sub-rule (5) presuppose the existence of an actual contract. In support of such an argument is the fact that sub-rule (7) only allows for claims seeking a declaration that no contract exists and does not extend to any consequential claims. On such an analysis, the only restitutionary claims which might be brought under sub-rule (5) would be ones brought upon the termination of a contract, the frustration of a contract,[104] and also possibly claims for rescission.[105]

Nevertheless, there are compelling arguments against allowing consequential restitutionary claims to be brought under the contractual provisions. First of all, as already discussed above, the contractual provisions are not designed to accommodate consequential restitutionary claims. Jurisdiction may be justified in a case where parties enter into a contract within the jurisdiction, or where a breach, or the intended performance which was breached, occurred within the jurisdiction, on the basis that the parties voluntarily entered such an agreement. As such, they have impliedly consented to the jurisdiction. Such a justification does not apply so readily to a claim that arises independently by operation of law. Secondly, in many cases involving ineffective contracts, the factor which renders the contract ineffective is often a good argument for not adopting a contractual connecting factor as a jurisdictional basis for subsequent restitutionary claims. Thus, where a contract is void for mistake, the justification for jurisdiction, on the basis that the parties voluntarily entered the particular agreement and thus chose the particular connecting factor (e.g. the law applicable to the contract), is less obvious, if not absent altogether. *A fortiori*, where a claim is, for example, void for duress, it might seem spurious to justify jurisdiction for the claim for restitution on the footing that the void contract was "made" within the jurisdiction. Thirdly, and most significantly, it flies in the face of reason to entitle a plaintiff, who has just established the nullity or non-existence of a "contract", to resort to the purported creation, *lex causae* or choice of court agreement, of the previously denied contract, as a jurisdictional basis for a claim which does not arise under the contract. As a result of sub-rule (15), consequential restitutionary claims do have a jurisdictional basis, which applies a connecting factor more geared to their nature. Where a restitutionary claim does not fall within sub-rule (15), namely because

[104] Where a consequential claim is brought upon a contract being frustrated, it is, strictly speaking, not a claim in unjust enrichment but a claim under the Law Reform (Frustrated Contracts) Act 1943, where such a contract was governed by English law.

[105] Given that rescission has the effect of a wiping away a contract *ab initio*, it might be viewed that there never was "a contract". As such, it could be argued that such a claim may not be brought under CPR 6.20 (5). Nevertheless, despite the effect of rescission, the contract is valid until rescinded and, as such, there exists "a contract" at the time of bringing a claim for rescission. Moreover, a claim for rescission was available under RSC, Order 11, rule 1(1)(d).

there were no substantial acts committed within the jurisdiction, there is a strong basis for denying jurisdiction. Service *ex juris* in relation to a particular claim should be based on the existence of a significant connection with the jurisdiction and not on questions of expediency, namely that related claims may be heard within the jurisdiction.

It is therefore submitted that the only restitutionary claims which fall within the contractual provisions are those brought in connection with an actual contract. This will cover restitutionary claims brought consequent upon termination of a contract, the frustration of a contract and also claims for rescission. It would therefore follow that a restitutionary claim arising under a void contract, such as that in *Kleinwort Benson* v. *Glasgow City Council*,[106] could not be brought under the contractual provisions in CPR 6.20. As already noted, such a result makes a great deal of sense, as such a claim does not arise under the alleged contract but under the law of unjust enrichment. It is also consistent with the House of Lords' interpretation of Article 5(1) of the Brussels Convention in *Kleinwort Benson* v. *Glasgow City Council*. Indeed, this decision may be further support for the analysis put forward above, as the likely path in relation to CPR 6.20(5), (6) and (7).

2.3 Sub-rule (8): claims in tort

The law may allow restitution in relation to a tort.[107] The preferred view is that such matters do not, as a matter of English domestic law, form part of the law of unjust enrichment but instead they belong to the law of wrongs. It has been submitted in the context of characterisation for choice of law purposes and in the context of the Brussels Convention, that restitution for wrongs should be classified as wrongs; and thus restitution for torts should be characterised as issues of tort.[108] It is submitted that the same approach should be adopted in relation to the common law jurisdiction rules. A claim may be brought in tort, where the plaintiff seeks restitution, or disgorgement, as opposed to compensation. In such an event the plaintiff may base his claim on CPR 6.20 (8) in relation to service out of the jurisdiction, as he would for any other claim in tort. There are however several issues which should be dealt with here in relation to the bringing of such claims.

2.3.1 Meaning of "tort"

The predecessor to this provision, namely RSC Order 11, rule 1(1)(f), required that "the claim is founded on a tort". It would seem that the change, from

[106] [1999] 1 A.C. 153. See the discussion of the case above, pp.207–14.

[107] See ch. 1.4.1. This covers, *inter alia*, those cases which were traditionally referred to as "waiver of tort" cases.

[108] See generally ch. 4.4.1; ch. 9.4.4.3.

requiring that a claim be "founded on a tort" and the present requirement that a claim is made "in tort", is a semantic one which is unlikely to be of any significance. The question here is whether the word "tort" is restricted to a strict domestic definition of tort or, whether it extends to, for example, torts which are uknown to English law or equitable wrongs such as "knowing assistance". In *Metall und Rohstoff A.G.* v. *Donaldson Lufkin & Jenrette Inc*, RSC Order 11, rule 1(1)(f) was held to require a tort according to English law.[109] As a result, claims for knowing assistance, or procuring a breach of trust, were not claims founded on a tort.[110] The analysis laid down in *Metall und Rohstoff* may have been based on the wording of the old provision.[111] By requiring that there be "a tort", this was taken to mean that there is an actual broken obligation giving rise to a cause of action. Such an answer could only be given by reference to the rules of private international law.[112] Traditionally, this meant applying the double actionability rule in circumstances where the tort had in substance occurred overseas[113] and, in so doing, it would have to be shown that the alleged conduct would have been actionable as a tort as a matter of English domestic law. Alternatively, if in substance the tort had been committed within the jurisdiction, it would also be necessary to show that the conduct complained of amounted to a tort as a matter of English domestic law. Therefore, in requiring that there be "a tort" under the old jurisdictional provision, one necessarily had to establish that the alleged conduct constituted a tort as a matter of English law.

It is submitted that sub-rule (8), which requires there to be a claim that is "in tort", will be subject to a similar analysis. The requirement is that a claim is made "in tort" and not otherwise. The question of whether the particular claim is "in tort", will still be answered according to English law, including its rules of private international law. It will not therefore be necessary to show there is actual liability, but it will be necessary to show that the complaint raised, in relation to the particular conduct, constitutes a claim "in tort". Owing, however, to certain other developments, the question of what constitutes a claim in tort will receive a more liberal definition. As a result of the Private International Law (Miscellaneous Provisions) Act 1995 (the "Act") the double actionability rule has been abolished in relation to almost all torts[114] and has been replaced

[109] *Metall und Rohstoff A.G.* v. *Donaldson Lufkin & Jenrette Inc.* [1990] 1 Q.B. 391, 437, 441 (C.A.).

[110] *Id.*, 473–4, 480–1. *Cf. Arab Monetary Fund* v. *Hashim* (*No.9*) *The Times*, 11 October 1994.

[111] See also Briggs and Rees, p.231.

[112] See also above §2.1.1.

[113] Under the double actionability rule, it would have had to be shown that the alleged conduct would have been actionable as a tort under English domestic law and that it gave rise to civil liability under the law of the place where the alleged tort occurred: see *Boys* v. *Chaplin* [1971] A.C. 356. This was subject to a flexible exception to the rule: see *Red Sea Insurance Co. Ltd.* v. *Bouygues S.A.* [1995] 1 A.C. 190.

[114] Section 10. The Act does not apply in relation to acts or omissions giving rise to a claim which occurred before 1 May 1996: s.14(1). Furthermore, the Act does not apply to claims for defamation: ss.9(3), 13.

by a rule that claims in tort are governed by the law of the place where the most significant elements occurred.[115] This choice of law rule applies irrespective of whether the tort occurred in England or elsewhere.[116] The question of whether a claim is "made in tort" is to be answered by applying the new choice of law rule.[117] This may have the result of allowing claims which are technically not "torts" as a matter of English domestic law. Under the Act, the relevant choice of law rules apply to issues relating to tort.[118] What constitutes issues relating to a tort is matter of characterisation for the courts of the forum.[119] An issue may be characterised as relating to a tort, even though it may not amount to a tort for the purposes of domestic law.[120] Therefore, there is a strong argument for saying that certain equitable wrongs are now to be characterised as torts for the purposes of private international law. Moreover, although it is said that s. 14(2), when read together with s. 10, limits the operation of the Act to those matters which were previously governed by the rule in *Boys* v. *Chaplin*,[121] equitable wrongs such as knowing assistance were already governed by this rule as a result of Chadwick J.'s judgment in *Arab Monetary Fund* v. *Hashim (No.9)*.[122]

The way equitable wrongs should be characterised has already been examined in the context of characterisation.[123] It has been submitted those equitable wrongs which do not involve a breach of a fiduciary relationship should be characterised as wrongs[124] and that they therefore will raise issues of "tort", for the purposes of the Act. Cases of knowing assistance[125] are an example falling

[115] Section 11. There are certain presumptions in s.11(2) in cases of personal injury or death and in cases of damage to property. Furthermore, there is a general exception in s.12 where in all the circumstances, it is "substantially more appropriate for the applicable law" to be the law of another country.

[116] Section 9(6). See also Cheshire and North, pp.625–6; *Cf.* A. Briggs, "Choice of law in tort and delict" [1995] L.M.C.L.Q. 519, 520, n. 18.

[117] Briggs and Rees raise this argument in relation the question of whether a claim is "founded on a tort": p.232. Such an argument applies *mutatis mutandis* to the question of whether a claim is "made in tort".

[118] Section 9(1).

[119] Section 9(2).

[120] See Dicey and Morris, pp.1517–18; Cheshire and North, pp.618–19; C. Morse, "Torts in Private International Law: A New Statutory Framework" (1996) 45 I.C.L.Q. 888, 893–4; A. Briggs, "Choice of law in tort and delict" [1995] L.M.C.L.Q. 519, 521–2; Fawcett and Torremans, p.150. Fawcett and Torremans consider that the infringement of intellectual property, should be regarded as raising issues of tort under the Act: pp.615, 620–33. *Cf.* however P. Carter (1996) 112 L.Q.R. 190, 193.

[121] See A. Briggs, "Choice of law in tort and delict" [1995] L.M.C.L.Q. 519, 521–2.

[122] *The Times*, 11 October, 1994.

[123] See ch. 4.4.3 *seq.*

[124] Those equitable wrongs which amount to a breach of a trust should be characterised as issues of breach of trust, while others which are breaches of a fiduciary relationship should be characterised as issues of contract.

[125] See *Barnes* v. *Addy* (1874) 9 Ch. App. 244, 251–2; *Selangor United Rubber Estates Ltd.* v. *Craddock (No.3)* [1968] 1 W.L.R. 1555; *Belmont Finance Corporation Ltd.* v. *Williams Furniture Ltd.* [1979] Ch. 250 (C.A.); *Consul Development Pty Ltd.* v. *D.P.C. Estates Pty Ltd.* (1975) 132 C.L.R. 373 (H.C.A.); *Royal Brunei Airlines* v. *Tan* [1995] 2 A.C. 378 (P.C.).

within this category.[126] Third parties may become liable if they knowingly assist a fiduciary breach his fiduciary relationship. Such an action is equity's version of the tort of inducing contractual breaches.[127] This analysis should follow in the context of jurisdiction. A claim for knowing assistance should constitute a claim "in tort" for jurisdictional purposes.[128] On the other hand, as in the context of characterisation,[129] a claim for knowing receipt should not be characterised as one in tort, but as restitutionary. In *Metall und Rohstoff*,[130] a claim for knowing assistance was held not to constitute a "tort" for the purposes of RSC Order 11, rule 1(1)(f). However, it is submitted that, as a result of the Act, which allows for a more liberal definition of tort, the limitations placed by *Metall und Rohstoff* have now been overcome. As such, CPR 6.20 (8) may now constitute a jurisdictional basis for certain restitutionary claims for equitable wrongdoing, which can now be characterised as "torts" under the Act.

2.3.2 Damage Sustained within the Jurisdiction

One of the two jurisdictional bases for torts under CPR 6.20 (8) is that "damage was sustained within the jurisdiction". It is not necessary for all the damage to have been sustained within the jurisdiction but only that "some significant damage has been sustained in England".[131] In many restitution for torts cases there may not necessarily have occurred damage or loss. Unlike in compensation claims, or claims for damages, the plaintiff sues in relation to the defendant's gain and not in relation to his loss. It may therefore be that this jurisdictional basis is unavailable in restitution for torts cases, unless the plaintiff can also show that he suffered some physical damage within the jurisdiction. Nevertheless, in restitution for wrongs cases the defendant has usually made his gain by infringing a right or commiting some sort of wrong against the plainitiff. For example, where a defendant trespasses on the plaintiff's property[132] or, where intellectual property rights are infringed,[133] the particular trespass or infringement may be viewed as "damage" for jurisdictional purposes. In a case where the particular infringement or trespass has been "sustained within the

[126] Another possible example is what is called *executor* or *trustee de son tort*. See C. Harpum, "The Basis of Equitable Liability" in P. Birks (ed.), *Frontiers of Liability* (Oxford, 1994), p.9; P.H. Pettit, *Equity and the Law of Trusts*, 8th ed. (London, 1993), p.140.

[127] See *Royal Brunei Airlines Shn. Bhd.* v. *Tan* [1995] 2 A.C. 378, 387B–C; *Polly Peck International plc* v. *Nadir* (unreported), 17 March 1993, transcript, 13, *per* Hoffmann L.J. See also Smith, "Constructive Fiduciaries", pp.258–61. Meagher, Gummow and Lehane, p.881.

[128] A claim for knowing assistance may alternatively fall within CPR 6.20 (14).

[129] See above, ch. 4, §4.3.1.

[130] *Metall und Rohstoff A.G.* v. *Donaldson Lufkin & Jenrette Inc.* [1990] 1 Q.B. 391.

[131] *Metall und Rohstoff A.G.* v. *Donaldson Lufkin & Jenrette Inc.* [1990] 1 Q.B. 437.

[132] See *Penarth Dock Engineering Co. Ltd.* v. *Pound* [1963] 1 Lloyd's Rep. 359. See also *Strand Electric & Engineering Co. Ltd.* v. *Brisford Entertainments Ltd.* [1952] 2 Q.B. 246.

[133] The infringement of intellectual property is characterised as tortious: see *House of Spring Gardens Ltd.* v. *Waite* [1991] 1 Q.B. 241, 253 (copyrights); *Mölnlycke AB* v. *Proctor & Gamble Ltd.* [1992] 1 W.L.R. 1112, 1117 (patents). See also Fawcett and Torremans, p.150.

jurisdiction", there is a sufficiently close jurisdictional connection to warrant a claim falling within sub-rule (8).

It could not seriously be argued that "damage" is capable of covering the defendant's gain. In the context of the Brussels Convention, it has been argued that the phrase "place of the harmful event" in relation to torts, should also cover the place of the plaintiff's impoverishment.[134] Although such an argument may be respectable in relation to the plaintiff's impoverishment or loss, it could not seriously be run in relation to the defendant's gain. In a claim for restitution for wrongdoing, the defendant's gain is not damage or necessarily harmful. It represents benefits the defendant has acquired through the commission of, in this case, a tort. Any gain the defendant has made will not necessarily correlate with any corresponding loss on the plaintiff's side and in some situations, the plaintiff may have not suffered any loss whatsoever.[135]

2.3.3 Act Committed within the Jurisdiction

More commonly, restitution for torts cases would presumably be covered by this basis of jurisdiction. The relevant claim must be based on an act committed within the jurisdiction. It is not necessary that the entire act be committed within the jurisdiction, but only that it "resulted from substantial and efficacious acts committed within the jurisdiction".[136] There is however one significant drawback which may prevent the bringing of a restitution for tort claim under this jurisdictional basis. The sub-paragraph requires that "damage . . . resulted from an act committed, within the jurisdiction". It may therefore be argued that the acts must be causally connected to damage and that where no such damage has occurred, a plaintiff will not be able to bring a claim for restitution in relation to a tort, even if the relevant acts constituting the tort have occurred within the jurisdiction. It is submitted that such an interpretation would be unfortunate. Instead, the term "damage" should not be interpreted restrictively so as to only cover physical damage. It should be interpreted so as to include the infringement of a duty or right, to which the relevant acts relate, which forms the basis of the plaintiff's claim to restitution. Thus, where a defendant infringes the plaintiff's copyright[137] in music, by copying it in recording music in England, the relevant infringement of the copyright will have occurred in England.[138] The defendant may have made profits, in relation to which the plaintiff seeks an account, by selling the recording in the United States. The plaintiff may not be able to show that he actually suffered a loss. If damage were

[134] Peel, pp.23–31. See above, pp. 201–2.

[135] See *Strand Electric and Engineering Co. Ltd.* v. *Brisford Entertainments* [1952] 2 Q.B. 246; *Penarth Dock Engineering Co. Properties Ltd.* v. *Pound* [1963] 1 Lloyd's Rep. 359. See also *Colbeam Palmer Ltd.* v. *Stock Affiliates Property Ltd.* (1968) 122 C.L.R. 25, 32, *per* Windeyer J.

[136] *Metall und Rohstoff A.G.* v. *Donaldson Lufkin & Jenrette Inc.* [1990] 1 Q.B. 391, 437.

[137] See n. 134 above.

[138] On the issue of where an infringement of intellectual property occurs, see generally Fawcett and Torremans, pp.156–61, 244–9.

to be limited to loss, then the plaintiff would be denied jurisdiction in relation to an infringement of copyright which occurred within the jurisdiction. Yet, a significant act had occurred within the jurisdiction. If however damage were said to cover the actual infringement of the copyright, jurisdiction would be available.

2.4 Sub-rule (10): property within the jurisdiction

Sub-rule (10) will apply in relation to claims of proprietary restitution over property[139] located within the jurisdiction. The only qualification is that the "whole subject matter" of the claim must relate to the property within the jurisdiction. This provision is essentially a merger of the previous RSC Order 11, rule 1(1)(g) and (i). These provisions applied to claims relating to immovable property and moveable property respectively. By referring generally to "property" located within the jurisdiction, sub-rule (10) does not seek to distinguish between types of property and thus should apply to all forms of property. There is no reason why, in principle, such a provision might not apply to moveable intangibles, which are also capable of having a *situs*.[140]

This head of jurisdiction is quite broad and would conceivably cover all possible claims where a proprietary remedy is sought over property located in England. It is unlikely that a provision of this nature would be interpreted in anything other than a liberal manner. It would be highly undesirable to deny jurisdiction in a claim concerning land situated in England, even where it might be argued that the immovable nature of the property which forms the subject-matter of the action and its location are irrelevant to the issues to be determined.[141] Similarly, where the subject matter of a claim amounts to a moveable, the location of the propery in England is a convincing connecting factor. Thus, where a plaintiff asserts an equitable interest in a car located in England, on the basis that the car represents the traceable value of his money which was fraudulently acquired by the defendant outside England, the plaintiff's claim will fall within this head of jurisdiction. Jurisdiction would be justified on the basis that the relevant property is within England and, as such, the claim will necessarily be connected with the jurisdiction. Consequently, any order made will be readily enforceable.

139 On proprietary restitution see ch. I.3.
140 As to the *situs* of moveable intangibles, see Dicey and Morris pp.924–35.
141 *Cf. Webb* v. *Webb* (294/92) [1994] E.C.R. I-1717; [1994] Q.B. 696.

Conclusion

THIS WORK HAS explored how restitution and the various related topics, function within the framework of private international law. The law of restitution, based on the principle of unjust enrichment, has only recently received official recognition as a matter of domestic law. Nevertheless, it has its own, distinct position in private international law, as do other, more established, areas of law. This position extends to both matters of choice of law and jurisdiction.

It has been concluded that characterisation is to be conducted in accordance with the liberal *lex fori*. Although the courts are not bound by the particular domestic rules, they nevertheless are to pay attention to the essential and fundamental elements of the domestic law of restitution. Thus, the fact that the law of restitution is not based on the theory of implied contract but rather on the unifying principle of unjust enrichment, should be reflected in private international law. The few previous decisions which are based on the theory of implied contract, whether relating to jurisdiction or choice of law, must be reconsidered, while any new principles developed must be done so in accordance with a correct understanding of the law of restitution. Characterisation is directed to particular issues that warrant the application of a particular legal system and thus fit within a recognised choice of law rule or justify the creation of a new choice of law rule. Restitution evinces a theoretical unity that warrants the application of a single legal system to determine such an issue and, therefore, a separate choice of law rule. Thus, there is essentially one restitutionary issue for the purposes of characterisation and not several component issues. At the same time, restitutionary claims may involve other ancillary issues, for the purposes of characterisation, which attract their own choice of law rule. Thus, the ineffectiveness of a related contract is a contractual issue, to be determined by the *lex contractus*, yet the consequential restitutionary claim raises a restitutionary issue. Likewise, a claim for proprietary restitution may be met by a defence of *bona fide* purchase, which attracts a proprietary characterisation.

Characterising in accordance with the liberal *lex fori* also means that essential divisions within domestic law should be observed. Thus, the fact that restitutionary claims connected with a contract are independent of the contract is particularly significant. The consequential restitutionary claim is not to be characterised as a contractual issue but as a separate restitutionary issue, governed by its own choice of law rule. Likewise, restitution for wrongs should generally be characterised as wrongs and not as matters of unjust enrichment, as such claims do not form part of the law of unjust enrichment. Yet, the liberal *lex fori* is able to go beyond the form and look at the substance, thereby recognising that certain equitable wrongs are essentially contractual issues, others breaches of trust, while others are actual wrongs or issues of unjust enrichment.

A significant part of the law of restitution consists of various equitable claims. It has been concluded that the theoretical unity of the law of restitution extends to those restitutionary claims which are in equity. In fact, it has been argued that matters of equity should be characterised in the same way as are their legal counterparts; that is, by reference to the causative event giving rise to the equitable response. Recent authorities as well as academic opinion confirm the view that equitable matters should not be given a different treatment in private international law.

The same theoretical unity extends to matters of proprietary restitution, where it has been concluded that such issues attract an initial restitutionary characterisation. Such a characterisation accepts that the proprietary result is a remedy and that the remedy is an essential part of the substance of the claim. By characterising proprietary restitution as issues of property, we divorce ourselves from the restitutionary issue and apply a law which is not necessarily connected with the right of restitution. Moreover, claims of proprietary restitution are invariably in equity and there is significant authority in favour of characterising equitable proprietary claims, which arise by operation of law, by reference to the causative event and not the proprietary interest. The significant policy arguments in favour of a proprietary characterisation are not so persuasive insofar as the initial characterisation is concerned. Yet they are accommodated where ancillary proprietary issues, such as a subsequent purchase, arise.

Where a restitutionary claim involves an element of tracing, the theoretical unity of the subject extends to the issue of tracing. An issue of tracing is not a procedural issue to be governed by the *lex fori*, nor is it an issue of the sort which attracts a separate choice of law rule. Tracing is an extension of rights with an independent source and, thus, the choice of law rule governing the issue arising out of such rights must also govern any related tracing issues. Thus, where a restitutionary claim contingent on tracing is brought, the issue of the availability of tracing, as well as the question of whether the plaintiff can trace into a particular asset, is to be determined by the law applicable to the restitutionary issue.

Although various choice of law rules for matters of restitution have been proposed, none are binding. Moreover, there are significant criticisms against the various proposed choice of law rules. The place of enrichment rule finds its origins in the implied contract theory. It is an arbitrary connecting factor, not necessarily pointing to a legal system which is closely connected to the restitutionary issue, while it does not provide anywhere near the degree of certainty presumed. A choice of law rule of the proper law of the obligation is circular and vague. Although it may seem to allow for flexibility, this is at the expense of providing any real direction as to what the applicable law might be.

Applying the law of a related contract to restitutionary claims connected with a contract, undermines the independence of the consequential restitutionary issue. The restitutionary liability is imposed by operation of law, independently of any contract. In most cases involving ineffective contracts, the factor which renders the contract ineffective is often a compelling reason for not applying the law expressly or impliedly chosen by the parties to determine the consequential restitutionary issue. Moreover, a contract may be rendered ineffective by a law other than its proper law. By applying the law of the contract to consequential restitutionary claims we would not necessarily be applying the law most closely connected to the issue of restitutionary liability. Furthermore, a different choice of law rule would apply to what are essentially identical claims, namely restitution claims on the basis of failure of consideration, depending on whether they arose in or outside of a contractual context.

The *lex situs* as a choice of law rule for restitutionary claims arising in connection with an immovable must also be rejected. Such a choice of law rule is not in fact supported by authority. Where the relevant issue has been characterised as restitutionary, it is proper to apply the choice of law rule for restitutionary issues; the immovable nature of the property and its location is, in such circumstances, irrelevant to the issues to be determined.

The preferred choice of law rule for restitutionary issues is the proper law of the alleged unjust factor. Such a choice of law rule identifies the legal system which is most closely connected with the reason for restitution and follows the logic of the choice of law rule for tort. Certain unjust factors are better at identifying a place whereas others may be more suited at identifying a legal system. There are those unjust factors which are event-based and therefore identify the law of the place with which the alleged unjust factor has its closest and most real connection, while secondly, there are law-based unjust factors, where the choice of law rule identifies the law with which the alleged unjust factor has its closest and most real connection. The "unjust factor" choice of law rule accommodates the different circumstances in which restitution is claimed and allows for a degree of flexibility, by focusing on the particular circumstances and events surrounding a claim for restitution. Such flexibility is not however created at the expense of certainty, as this choice of law rule provides a clear direction towards the *lex causae*. Although there is essentially one choice of law rule, it will vary depending on the particular unjust factor in issue. As such, its application is specific to particular types of cases and at the same time, sensitive to the complexities of such claims.

Insofar as jurisdiction is concerned, the Brussels Convention does not specifically provide for special jurisdiction in cases of unjust enrichment. It has been concluded that matters of unjust enrichment do not fall within Articles 5(1) or (3) and thus Article 2, namely the courts of the defendant's domicile, generally provides for jurisdiction in such cases. It is therefore clear that a new provision is required if one wanted to create special jurisdiction for all matters of unjust enrichment. Nevertheless, specific restitutionary claims may be caught by other provisions in the Convention. Restitutionary claims brought consequent to an ineffective contract will generally not fall within Article 5(1) unless the plaintiff's action is based on a "contractual obligation" for the purposes of the Convention. This may cover situations where a plaintiff seeks to recover, on the basis of failure of consideration, moneys paid under a contract which is discharged. Article 16(1) will generally not catch proprietary restitutionary claims brought in relation to land in a Contracting State. Alternative jurisdiction may be available in certain specific cases; where, for example, there exists a choice of court agreement pursuant to Article 17, this may extend to a restitutionary claim. The Convention does not distinguish restitutionary claims in equity, or proprietary restitutionary claims. Such claims are to be treated in the same way as their thematic counterparts.

In contrast, under the traditional rules we do find a jurisdictional provision for restitutionary claims: CPR 6.20(15). This provision catches almost all restitutionary claims. There are authorities suggesting that restitutionary claims fall within the jurisdictional provisions for contracts. These are of course based on the implied contract theory and must be taken as having been implicitly overruled with the acceptance of the principle of unjust enrichment. Furthermore, there is no longer any need to rely on the fiction of a "quasi-contract", for the purposes of service out of the jurisdiction, in light of the specific restitutionary provision. Nevertheless, restitutionary claims do arise in connection with ineffective contracts, and some of these claims may be brought within the contractual provisions. This will be the case for restitutionary claims brought consequent upon termination of a contract, the frustration of a contract and also claims for rescission. There is therefore a degree of consistency between the traditional rules and the Brussels Convention in relation to restitutionary claims brought in connection with a contract.

Besides responding to the practical need of dealing with the choice of law and jurisdictional issues relating to restitutionary claims, this work has been able to illustrate two other important matters. First, this work is part of the process of coming to a further understanding of the law of restitution. Being an area of law which until recently struggled for its recognition, the law of restitution's place in private international law forms an integral part of its overall identity and self-esteem. Moreover, unless we have a better understanding of restitution in private international law, courts are less likely to tackle the international restitutionary issues which are appearing before the courts with increasing frequency. The other important matter to arise from this work, is to provide a practical analysis of private international law. By examining a relatively new topic such as the law of restitution, this work has also been an exercise in illustrating how private international law can deal with new topics and problems. It has been shown that despite certain difficulties, the current framework of private international law is able to both deal with and accommodate claims of unjust enrichment.

Appendix

The following examples are given as illustrations of the analysis in this work

1. A New York bank mistakenly pays a sum into the defendant's account with another New York bank. The defendant carries on business in England. The defendant becomes insolvent and liquidation proceedings arise. The first New York bank claims that the defendant holds the proceeds of the payment on constructive trust and is therefore entitled to a priority in the liquidation.
   No question of jurisdiction arises as the defendant carries on business and is domiciled in England.

   The plaintiff's claim is to be characterised as raising a restitutionary issue. This is despite the fact that the plaintiff's claim is: (a) in equity; and (b) is a claim for proprietary restitution. The restitutionary issue extends to the related issue of whether the plaintiff can trace into the proceeds of the payment, as currently held by the defendant.

   The alleged unjust factor, or reason for restitution, is mistake. This has its closest and most real connection with New York, as the place where the mistake, as well as the corresponding shift of wealth, occurred. Thus, the law of New York governs the issue of whether the plaintiff is able to trace into the moneys held by the defendant, in addition to whether there exists a right of restitution in the form of a proprietary remedy.

   The law of New York would still have applied if the payment had been received in England, i.e. to the defendant's account held with a bank in England. The mistake would still have had its closest and most real connection with New York as the place where the mistake, as well as where the relevant act giving rise to the shift of wealth, occurred.
   (See *Chase Manhattan Bank N.A.* v. *Israel-British Bank (London) Ltd.* [1981] 1 Ch. 105).

2. A induces B, through threats of criminal prosecution, to enter into a contract for the lease of premises in Ruritania for 5 years. The contract is executed in England and is expressed to be governed by the law of Ruritania.

   B brings proceedings in England seeking a declaration that the contract was void and restitution of moneys paid.

   The court will have jurisdiction to hear that contractual claim under the traditional rules, as it amounts to a claim to annul a contract which was made within the jurisdiction. The court will also have jurisdiction to hear the consequential restitutionary claim by virtue of the fact that the claim is brought for money had and received/

restitution and the executing of the connected contract amounts to substantial acts committed within the jurisdiction.

The issue of whether the contract is void is a contractual issue, *prima facie* to be determined by the law of the contract. However, the particular coercion in this case is likely to be considered so severe, or manifestly incompatible with the public policy of the forum, that the contract will not be enforced, irrespective of whether it is valid under Ruritanian law.
(See *Kaufman* v. *Gerson* [1904] 1 K.B. 591; *Dimskal Shipping Co. S.A.* v. *I.T.W.F.* (*The Evia Luck* (*No.2*)) [1992] 2 A.C. 152; *Royal Boskalis Westminster NV* v. *Mountain* [1999] Q.B. 674 (C.A.))

The issue of whether B can have restitution of the payments made is a restitutionary issue. The alleged unjust factor will be illegitimate pressure. Such illegitimate pressure has its closest and most real connection with England, where B was coerced to enter into the relevant contract, while the threatened criminal proceedings were to occur in England.
The restitutionary issue will extend to the question of whether the B must make counter-restitution in respect of the benefit received through the use of the particular premises.

3. The plaintiff seeks to claim moneys in the defendant's account as the traceable proceeds of his initial property. The restitutionary issue is governed by the law of X. Under the law of Y, the *lex fori*, tracing is only recognised in the form of "clean substitutions" such that the tracing process is frustrated if the moneys have become mixed with other moneys in a bank account. Under the law of X, a claimant may trace through mixtures.
The law of X, as the *lex causae* of the restitutionary issue, will determine the tracing issue.

4. E an employee in England forges his employer's cheques and pays them to his account in England. He subsequently withdraws cheques made payable to his mistress in Hungary, D. She pays them into her account.
Alternative claims are brought for money had and received and that D holds such moneys on trust.

Assuming that D is neither domiciled nor present in England, the court will have jurisdiction to hear E's claim against D. The defendant's alleged liability arises out of substantial acts committed, even though not necessarily by D, within the jurisdiction.

Both the common law action for money had and received and the equitable claim for a constructive trust are to be characterised as a restitutionary issue.
The proper law of the restitutionary issue is the law of England, being the law of the place with which the relevant unjust factor, namely the unauthorised transfer or interference, had its closest and most real connection. It is not the law of France as the law of the place of ultimate enrichment.

The issue of whether the plaintiff can trace into D's account is also governed by the law of the restitutionary issue. Assuming the *lex causae* is English, the plaintiff will

be entitled to trace into D's account for the purposes of bringing a claim for proprietary restitution.
No ancillary proprietary issue arises as D is not a "purchaser".
(Example based on *Banque Belge pour l'Etranger* v. *Hambrouk* [1921] 1 K.B. 321).

5. An employee in England fraudulently obtains his employer's moneys. With their proceeds he purchases as car. The car is subsequently sold to D in Germany.

   D is an English domiciliary and thus the English court has jurisdiction.
   The plaintiff's claim that D holds the car as trustee is to be characterised as restitutionary. The relevant unjust factor is unauthorised appropriation. This has its closest and most real connection with England, as the place where the employee obtained his employer's moneys.

   D's defence that he purchased the car raises an ancillary proprietary question. Whether D was a good faith purchaser will be determined by German law, as the *lex situs* of the car at the time of purchase.

6. In breach of trust, a trustee transfers shares in a company incorporated in New York to an overseas company in which he has an interest. The beneficiaries bring an action claiming that the recipient company holds such shares as constructive trustee.
   The English court will have jurisdiction as the claim is one for relief against the defendant as a constructive trustee and the breach of fiduciary duty has occurred as a result of substantial acts committed within the jurisdiction.
   (See *ISC* v. *Guerin* [1992] 2 Lloyd's Rep. 430; *Ghana Commercial Bank* v. *C. & ors* (*The Times*, 3 March 1997); *Polly Peck International plc.* v. *Nadir* unreported, 17 March 1993.)

   The claim raises a proprietary issue, as the beneficiaries are seeking to assert a pre-existing equitable title in the shares that is not generated by unjust enrichment. They are not claiming that the shares represent the traceable proceeds of their property.

   The question of who has title to shares is to be decided by the *lex situs* of the shares, namely the law of the place where the company was incorporated.
   (See *Macmillan Inc.* v. *Bishopsgate Investment Trust Plc (No.3)* [1996] 1 W.L.R. 387.)

7. In breach of trust, a trustee this time sells trust property and with the money purchases shares. These shares are registered in the name of D. The beneficiaries bring a claim that D holds such shares on constructive trust.
   The claim ought to be characterised as raising a restitutionary issue, as the beneficiaries are seeking to assert a title, which is generated by unjust enrichment, in the traceable proceeds of their original property.

   The relevant unjust factor here is unauthorised transfer or appropriation. The restitutionary issue therefore ought to be governed by the law of the place where the unauthorised appropriation occurred, namely, where the trust property was sold. Such law should also determine the question of whether beneficiaries can trace into the shares.

D's claim that he was a *bona fide* purchaser of the shares is an ancillary proprietary issue, to be determined by the *lex situs* of the shares, namely the law of the place where the company was incorporated.
(See *Macmillan Inc.* v. *Bishopsgate Investment Trust Plc* (*No.3*) [1996] 1 W.L.R. 387.)

An alternative claim by the beneficiaries against the trustee, seeking to make him liable for breach of trust, is an issue concerning the relationship between the trustee and the beneficiaries, pursuant to Article 8(g) of the Hague Convention on Trusts, to be determined by the law governing the trust.

8. A bank in France enters into an interest rate swap with a local council in England. The swap agreement was *ultra vires* the local council. It now seeks to recover the overpayments made to the bank in France.

   The English courts will have jurisdiction to hear a claim by the local council for a declaration that the contract is void. This is regardless of the fact that the council will be denying the existence of the contract. It is sufficient that the bank seeks to affirm the contract. The obligation in question here is the bank's obligation to make the relevant payments under the swap agreement and its place of performance is England.
   (See *Effer* v. *Kanter* (*38/81*) [1982] E.C.R. 825; *Boss Group Ltd.* v. *Boss France SA* [1996] 4 All E.R. 970; *Kleinwort Benson Ltd.* v. *Glasgow City Council* [1999] 1 A.C. 153.)

   The English court would not have jurisdiction to hear the consequential restitutionary claim, as the claim is not founded on a contractual obligation. The council will have to bring proceedings in France, being the domicile of the bank.
   (See *Kleinwort Benson Ltd.* v. *Glasgow City Council* [1999] 1 A.C. 153.)

9. H is employed as the director of a public company in Abu Dhabi. His employment contract is expressly governed by the law of Abu Dhabi. During the course of his employment he accepts large bribes.
   The company brings proceedings to recover the bribes received by H.
   Assuming that the English courts do have jurisdiction, the issue is H's breach of his fiduciary duty; namely, of his consensual relationship with the company. This is to be characterised as a contractual issue and thus H's liability to disgorge the bribes is governed by the law of Abu Dhabi.
   (See *Arab Monetary Fund* v. *Hashim* [1996] 1 Lloyd's Rep. 589.)

10. B, in London, enters into a sale of goods contract with an exporter, S, in Athens. The contract stipulates that "time is of the essence". The contract is expressed to be governed by Greek law and contains an English choice of court agreement, stating that the "courts of England shall have exclusive jurisdiction to hear any disputes which may arise under this contract, including any related claims".

    B has made certain pre-payments under this contract to S in Athens. S has significantly delayed in delivering the goods. B treats this breach as a repudiation and terminates the contract.

    B brings proceedings in England seeking a declaration that the contract has been terminated and that he is accordingly entitled to restitution of the moneys paid.

The question of whether under Article 17 of the Brussels Convention, the choice of court agreement covers the consequential restitutionary claim will be determined by the English court in accordance with its rules of private international law. It therefore must apply Greek law to determine whether the choice of court agreement confers such jurisdiction on the English courts.
(See *Powell Duffryn plc* v. *Petereit* (*214/89*)[1992] E.C.R. I-1745; *Benincasa* v. *Dentalkit Srl* (*269/95*) [1997] E.C.R. I 3767.)

Pursuant to Article 5(1), the English court will have jurisdiction to hear the consequential restitutionary claim as a result of the breach of contract. Such a claim is founded on a contractual obligation for the purposes of the Convention. The place of performance of the obligation in question is England, being the place where the seller was due to deliver.
(See *De Bloos* v. *Bouyer* (*14/76*) [1976] E.C.R. 1497; *Peters Bauunternehmung GmbH* v. *Zuid Nederlandse Aannmers Vereneging* (*Case 34/82*) [1983] E.C.R. 987; *Agnew* v. *Lansförsäkringsbølagens AB* [2000] 2 W.L.R. 497; *Kleinwort Benson Ltd.* v. *Glasgow City Council* [1999] 1 A.C. 153.)

The question of whether B is entitled to restitution of the moneys paid is a restitutionary and not a contractual issue. The unjust factor, is failure of consideration, namely the failure on the part of S to deliver the goods in England. English law governs the consequential restitutionary claim.

11. D allegedly infringes the P's intellectual property right in England by copying a particular product and selling it in the United States. P brings an action in England seeking an account of profits, or restitution. D is an English domicile.

The English courts will have jurisdiction as the claim is founded on a tort, whilst the damage, namely the infringement, resulted from substantial and efficacious acts committed within the jurisdiction.

The issue is to be characterised as a tort and not as an issue of unjust enrichment. Thus, the applicable law will be determined under ss. 11 and 12 of the Private International Law (Miscellaneous Provisions) Act 1995.
(See *House of Spring Gardens Ltd.* v. *Waite* [1991] 1 Q.B. 241 (copyrights); *Mölnlycke AB* v. *Proctor & Gamble Ltd.* [1992] 1 W.L.R. 1112 (patents).)

12. A, a partner in a law firm was addicted to gambling. A took moneys from the partnership account and gambled them away at the Crown Casino in Melbourne, Australia. The firm seeks restitution of the moneys from the casino by bringing an action for money had and received.

The English courts will have jurisdiction to hear the matter as the restitutionary liability of the defendant arises as a result of substantial acts committed within the jurisdiction, namely the appropriation of the moneys by A.
(See *ISC* v. *Guerin* [1992] 2 Lloyd's Rep. 430; *Polly Peck International plc.* v. *Nadir* unreported, 17 March 1993.)

The firm's claim for restitution will be governed by English law. The relevant unjust factor is an unauthorised transfer. This has its closest and most real connection with England as the place where the unauthorised appropriation occurred.

The availability and the effect of the casino's defence of *bona fide* purchaser is an ancillary proprietary issue which is to be governed by the law of Victoria.

13. P and D are joint-owners of a property in France. They are jointly and severally liable for certain local rates. P discharges the entire amount due. He brings proceedings against D, an English domiciliary, in respect of the amounts which were due by D.

    The claim raises a restitutionary issue. This is a case of compulsory discharge of another's liability. The relevant unjust factor was the fact that P was legally compelled to make the relevant payment. The unjust factor has its closest and most real connection with France, as it was the law of France which compelled P to make the payment.

Index

www.ingramcontent.com/pod-product-compliance
Ingram Content Group UK Ltd.
Pitfield, Milton Keynes, MK11 3LW, UK
UKHW020832290926
15470UKWH00009B/1851/J

9 781841 131429